Understanding and Using

Microsoft® Access 2.0

Bruce J. McLaren
School of Business
Indiana State University

WEST PUBLISHING COMPANY
Minneapolis/St. Paul • New York
Los Angeles • San Francisco

WEST'S COMMITMENT TO THE ENVIRONMENT

In 1906, West Publishing Company began recycling materials left over from the production of books. This began a tradition of efficient and responsible use of resources. Today, 95 percent of our legal books and 70 percent of our college texts are printed on recycled, acid-free stock. West also recycles nearly 22 million pounds of scrap paper annually—the equivalent of 181,717 trees. Since the 1960s, West has devised ways to capture and recycle waste inks, solvents, oils, and vapors created in the printing process. We also recycle plastics of all kinds, wood, glass, corrugated cardboard, and batteries, and have eliminated the use of styrofoam book packaging. We at West are proud of the longevity and the scope of our commitment to the environment.

Production, Prepress, Printing and Binding by West Publishing Company

Project Management by Labrecque Publishing Services

 Printed on 10% Post Consumer Recycled Paper

Copyright ©1995 by West Publishing Company
             610 Opperman Drive
             P.O. Box 64526
             St. Paul, MN 55164-0526

Printed in the United States of America
02 01 00 99 98 97 96   8 7 6 5 4 3

Library of Congress Cataloging-in-Publication Data:

McLaren, Bruce J.
    Understanding and using Microsoft Access 2.0 / Bruce J. McLaren.
         p.   cm. – (The Microcomputing series)
    Includes index.
    ISBN 0-314-04653-4 (alk. paper)
    1. Database management. 2. Microsoft Access. I. Title.
II. Series.
QA76.9.D3M395396 1995
005.75'65–dc20   *93-31178*
                                                              CIP

British Library Cataloguing-in-Publication Data. A catalogue record for this book is available from the British Library.

Contents

Intermediate Database Management with Access   *163*

Advanced Database Management with Access   *289*

Preface

Understanding and Using Microsoft Access 2.0 is about managing data with a personal computer. Even more, it will help you design forms and reports for retrieving and viewing the information necessary to run an organization. Because it is based on Microsoft Windows, Access is easy to use and a very powerful way to organize data. The built-in Wizard templates enable you to build attractive and useful database objects with no programming.

Why This Book?

It is our intention to offer a book that not only teaches how to use Microsoft Access, but also examines the design of databases in an understandable manner. Students are first drawn through the process of creating a database with just enough attention to detail to make them aware of optional features that can facilitate their work. Then more advanced concepts are presented in realistic scenarios with an emphasis on *why* rather than simply *how*.

This book serves a different role than the documentation packaged with Microsoft Access. While those manuals are comprehensive, they tend to be "cookbook" oriented. That is, they focus on how to accomplish a specific task with a precise recipe and require some prior knowledge on the part of the user to locate the proper section of the manuals. By contrast, this book will lead you through Access tutorials in a step-wise fashion.

Finally, *Understanding and Using Microsoft Access 2.0* serves as a member of THE MICROCOMPUTING SERIES published by West Publishing Company. It can be used alone, in combination with other books in the series (listed in the Publisher's Note on pages xv–xx), or to supplement any other book in a course where a knowledge of Access is desired.

Content Highlights

Understanding and Using Microsoft Access 2.0 is divided into three parts. Part One offers a general overview of database management concepts and an introduction to Access for new users. It covers the use of Access for simple data files, using the built-in templates called Wizards. You will learn how to get started in Microsoft Windows, build a data table, examine its contents through queries and forms, and print reports.

Part Two of this book builds on the concepts learned in Part One. Here you will learn how to prepare customized queries, forms, and reports. The relational database concept is introduced. A unit on Access controls forms the basis for making changes to Access objects that were prepared with the Wizards, or for creating new objects without the Wizards.

The last part of this book, Part Three, is aimed at those who want to know how to develop application systems using Access. Advanced concepts such as graphs and embedded pictures are covered in this part. It also covers use of Access programs called macros and modules that provide linked menus, forms, queries, and reports. This section also covers importing and exporting data files with Access. The book includes the development of a medium-sized custom application using Access. The final unit describes security methods for protecting Access databases and introduces multiuser concepts when Access is used in a network.

How to Use This Book

The Introduction unit contains an overview of Microsoft Windows for new Windows users. You should complete the first six units (chapters) of Part One to gain a basic understanding of Access database features. After that background, you can cover the material in Parts Two and Three in the desired order. Unit 9 contains important concepts about controls that can be used in building custom forms and reports. Although nearly all of the units are intended to be studied while sitting at the computer, you will benefit by first reading the unit, before trying the hands-on work. We strongly recommend that you work through *all* of the Guided Activity examples, Exercises, and Applications. As with other skills, with more practice your Access understanding will increase. Use this knowledge to solve problems from other courses, your job, or your personal life while you are learning Access.

Each unit contains the following features:

LEARNING OBJECTIVES the knowledge and skills covered in the unit.

IMPORTANT COMMANDS the keyboard and mouse commands covered in the unit.

COMPUTER SCREENS accurate copies of the screens you will see as you use Access.

GUIDED ACTIVITIES step-by-step, hands-on illustrations of the database activities described in the text. The activities contain **Checkpoints**, which ask questions to increase your knowledge and understanding while you work. Answers to the Checkpoints are found in Appendix B.

COMMAND REVIEW a summary of important commands presented in the unit.

EXERCISES additional assignments to give you practice. Some exercises have specific instructions, while others are less structured. Most exercises will use the computer.

REVIEW QUESTIONS discussion questions that test your knowledge of the material in the unit. Answers to the odd-numbered questions appear in Appendix B.

KEY TERMS a list of important terms and concepts introduced in the unit. This list is intended for self-review.

DOCUMENTATION RESEARCH exercises that require you to search through the Access printed documentation or to use the on-line Help system within Access.

Other features of *Understanding and Using Microsoft Access 2.0* include:

APPLICATIONS comprehensive, hands-on minicases that summarize the activities of several units. Applications tend to be more challenging than Exercises and test your ability to use Microsoft Access in a realistic fashion. These applications require the student to structure the work.

APPENDIX A—GLOSSARY OF MICROSOFT ACCESS DATABASE TERMS a list of important database terms with definitions.

APPENDIX B—ANSWERS TO ODD-NUMBERED REVIEW QUESTIONS AND CHECKPOINTS this appendix contains answers to odd-numbered Review Questions and to all Checkpoints.

APPENDIX C—QUICK REFERENCE TO ACCESS COMMANDS AND TOOLBARS this section contains a summary of the keyboard commands as well as Access tool icons and symbols used in this textbook. It is designed to be used at the computer.

STUDENT DATA DISK a set of database files used with Guided Activities, Exercises, and Applications, available for instructors who adopt this book. Instructors may make disk copies available for students or place the database files on a local area network where students may copy them. Specific instructions for using the data disk appear in a README file included on the disk.

INSTRUCTOR'S MANUAL a comprehensive Instructor's Manual is available for adopters of this textbook. It contains teaching suggestions with sample syllabi; solutions to Guided Activities, Exercises, and Applications; test questions; and transparency masters. A disk with sample data files and solution files accompanies the Instructor's Manual.

A Note of Thanks

- To Connie, my wife and colleague, for her steady encouragement and careful reading of everything associated with this manuscript. Without her support this book would not exist.

- To my children, Anne and Cathy, who have unlimited patience with my writing habit, even on family camping trips.

- To Dean Herb Ross and my colleagues in the School of Business at Indiana State University for their support.

- To Nancy Hill-Whilton of West Publishing for initiating the project and keeping the book on track.

- To Lisa Auer, Mark Woodworth, Gail Carrigan, Curtis Philips, Mark Rhynsburger, and others involved in the production of this book. Their professionalism and careful attention to details have made this an enjoyable task and a learning experience for me.

- To the reviewers of this and previous versions of the manuscript—Henry Bojack, SUNY at Farmingdale; Susan Boleware, Mississippi State University; Lister W. Horn, Pensacola Junior College; and G. W. Willis, Baylor University—for their helpful comments and assistance in development of an accurate and appropriate textbook.

- To my students, who inspire me to write in a way that they can understand.

B.J.M.
Terre Haute, Indiana
July 1994

This book is part of THE MICROCOMPUTING SERIES. This popular series provides the most comprehensive list of books dealing with microcomputer applications software. We have expanded the number of software topics and provided a flexible set of instructional materials for all courses. This unique series includes five different types of books.

1. *West's Microcomputing Custom Editions* give instructors the power to create a spiral-bound microcomputer applications book especially for their course. Instructors can select the applications they want to teach and the amount of material they want to cover for each application—essentials or intermediate length. The following titles are available for the 1995 Microcomputing Series custom editions program:

Understanding Information Systems	*Lotus 1-2-3 Release 2.2*
Management, Information, and Systems: An Introduction to Information Systems	*Lotus 1-2-3 Release 2.3*
	Lotus 1-2-3 Release 2.4
Understanding Networks	*Lotus 1-2-3 Release 3*
DOS (3.x) and System	*Lotus 1-2-3 for Windows Release 4*
DOS 5 and System	*Lotus 1-2-3 for Windows Release 5*
DOS 6 and System	*Microsoft Excel 3*
Microsoft Windows 3.0	*Microsoft Excel 4*
Microsoft Windows 3.1	*Microsoft Excel 5.0*
Microsoft Windows 95	*Quattro Pro 4*
WordPerfect 5.0	*Quattro Pro 5.0 for Windows*
WordPerfect 5.1	*Quattro Pro 6.0 for Windows*
WordPerfect 6.0	*dBASE III Plus*
WordPerfect for Windows (Release 5.1 and 5.2)	*dBASE IV Version 1.0/1.1/1.5*
	dBASE IV Version 2.0
WordPerfect 6.0 for Windows	*Paradox 3.5*
Microsoft Powerpoint 4.0	*Paradox 4.5 for Windows*
Microsoft Word for Windows Version 1.1	*QBasic*
Microsoft Word for Windows Version 2.0	*Microsoft Visual Basic*
Microsoft Word for Windows Version 6.0	*Microsoft Access 1.1*
PageMaker 4	*Microsoft Access 2.0*
PageMaker 5.0	
Lotus 1-2-3 Release 2.01	

For more information about *West's Microcomputing Custom Editions*, please contact your local West Representative, or call West Publishing Company at 512-327-3175.

2.   General concepts books for teaching basic hardware and software philosophy and applications are available separately or in combination with hands-on applications. These books provide students with a general overview of computer fundamentals including history, social issues, and a synopsis of software and hardware applications. These books include *Understanding Information Systems*, by Steven C. Ross, and *Management, Information, and Systems: An Introduction to Information Systems*, by William Davis.

3.   A series of hands-on laboratory tutorials (*Understanding and Using*) are software specific and cover a wide range of individual packages. These tutorials, written at an introductory level, combine tutorials with complete reference guides. A complete list of series titles can be found on the following pages.

4.   Several larger volumes combining DOS with three application software packages are available in different combinations. These texts are titled *Understanding and Using Application Software*. They condense components of the individual lab manuals and add conceptual coverage for courses that require both software tutorials and microcomputer concepts in a single volume.

5.   A series of advanced-level, hands-on lab manuals provide students with a strong project/systems orientation. These include *Understanding and Using Lotus 1-2-3: Advanced Techniques Releases 2.2 and 2.3*, by Judith C. Simon.

THE MICROCOMPUTING SERIES has been successful in providing you with a full range of applications books to suit your individual needs. We remain committed to excellence in offering the widest variety of current software packages. In addition, we are committed to producing microcomputing texts that provide you both the coverage you desire and also the level and format most appropriate for your students. The Executive Editor of the series is Rick Leyh of West Educational Publishing; the Consulting Editor is Steve Ross of Western Washington University. We are always planning for the future in this series. Please send us your comments and suggestions:

Rick Leyh
West Educational Publishing
1515 Capital of Texas Highway South
Suite 402
Austin, TX 78746
Internet: RLEYH@RESEARCH.WESTLAW.COM

Steve Ross
Associate Professor/MIS
College of Business and Economics
Western Washington University
Bellingham, Washington 98225-9077
Internet: STEVEROSS@WWU.EDU

We now offer these books in THE MICROCOMPUTING SERIES:

General Concepts

Management, Information, and Systems: An Introduction to Information Systems
by William Davis

Understanding Information Systems
by Steven C. Ross

Understanding Computer Information Systems
by Paul W. Ross, H. Paul Haiduk, H. Willis Means, and Robert B. Sloger

Understanding and Using the Macintosh
by Barbara Zukin Heiman and Nancy E. McGauley

Operating Systems/Environments

Understanding and Using Microsoft Windows 95
by Steven C. Ross and Ronald W. Maestas

Understanding and Using Microsoft Windows 3.1
by Steven C. Ross and Ronald W. Maestas

Understanding and Using Microsoft Windows 3.0
by Steven C. Ross and Ronald W. Maestas

Understanding and Using MS-DOS 6.0
by Jonathan P. Bacon

Understanding and Using MS-DOS/PC DOS 5.0
by Jonathan P. Bacon

Understanding and Using MS-DOS/PC DOS 4.0
by Jonathan P. Bacon

Networks

Understanding Networks
by E. Joseph Guay

Programming

Understanding and Using Visual Basic
by Jonathan Barron

Understanding and Using QBasic
by Jonathan Barron

Word Processors

Understanding and Using WordPerfect 6.0 for Windows
by Jonathan P. Bacon

Understanding and Using WordPerfect for Windows
by Jonathan P. Bacon

Understanding and Using Microsoft Word for Windows 6.0
Emily M. Ketcham

Understanding and Using Microsoft Word for Windows 2.0
by Larry Lozuk and Emily M. Ketcham

Understanding and Using Microsoft Word for Windows (1.1)
by Larry Lozuk

Understanding and Using WordPerfect 6.0
by Jonathan P. Bacon and Robert G. Sindt

Understanding and Using WordPerfect 5.1
by Jonathan P. Bacon and Cody T. Copeland

Understanding and Using WordPerfect 5.0
by Patsy H. Lund

Desktop Publishing

Understanding and Using PageMaker 5.0
by John R. Nicholson

Understanding and Using PageMaker 4
by John R. Nicholson

Spreadsheet Software

Understanding and Using Microsoft Excel 5.0
by Steven C. Ross and Stephen V. Hutson

Understanding and Using Microsoft Excel 4
by Steven C. Ross and Stephen V. Hutson

Understanding and Using Microsoft Excel 3
by Steven C. Ross and Stephen V. Hutson

Understanding and Using Quattro Pro 6.0 for Windows
by Lisa Friedrichsen

Understanding and Using Quattro Pro 5.0 for Windows
by Larry D. Smith

Understanding and Using Quattro Pro 4
by Steven C. Ross and Stephen V. Hutson

Understanding and Using Lotus 1-2-3 Release 5
by Steven C. Ross and Dolores Pusins

Understanding and Using Lotus 1-2-3 for Windows Release 4
by Steven C. Ross and Dolores Pusins

Understanding and Using Lotus 1-2-3 Release 3
by Steven C. Ross

Understanding and Using Lotus 1-2-3 Release 2.3 and Release 2.4
by Steven C. Ross

*Understanding and Using Lotus 1-2-3: Advanced Techniques
Releases 2.2 and 2.3*
by Judith C. Simon

Understanding and Using Lotus 1-2-3 Release 2.2
by Steven C. Ross

Understanding and Using Lotus 1-2-3 Release 2.01
by Steven C. Ross

Database Management Software

Understanding and Using Microsoft Access 2.0
by Bruce J. McLaren

Understanding and Using Microsoft Access 1.1
by Bruce J. McLaren

Understanding and Using Paradox 4.5 for Windows
by Larry D. Smith

Understanding and Using Paradox 3.5
by Larry D. Smith

Understanding and Using dBASE IV Version 2.0
by Steven C. Ross

Understanding and Using dBASE IV
by Steven C. Ross

Understanding and Using dBASE III Plus, 2nd Edition
by Steven C. Ross

Integrated Software

Understanding and Using Microsoft Works for Windows 3.0
by Gary Bitter

Understanding and Using Microsoft Works 3.0 for the PC
by Gary Bitter

Understanding and Using Microsoft Works 3.0 for the Macintosh
by Gary Bitter

Understanding and Using Microsoft Works 2.0 on the Macintosh
by Gary Bitter

Understanding and Using Microsoft Works 2.0 on the IBM PC
by Gary Bitter

Understanding and Using ClarisWorks
by Gary Bitter

Presentation Software

Understanding and Using Microsoft Powerpoint 4.0
by Karen Young

Combined Books

*Essentials of Application Software, Volume 1: DOS, WordPerfect 5.0/5.1,
Lotus 1-2-3 Release 2.2, dBASE III Plus*
by Steven C. Ross, Jonathan P. Bacon, and Cody T. Copeland

*Understanding and Using Application Software, Volume 4: DOS,
WordPerfect 5.0, Lotus 1-2-3 Release 2, dBASE IV*
by Patsy H. Lund, Jonathan P. Bacon, and Steven C. Ross

*Understanding and Using Application Software, Volume 5: DOS,
WordPerfect 5.0/5.1, Lotus 1-2-3 Release 2.2, dBASE III Plus*
by Steven C. Ross, Jonathan P. Bacon, and Cody T. Copeland

Advanced Books

*Understanding and Using Lotus 1-2-3: Advanced Techniques
Releases 2.2 and 2.3*
by Judith C. Simon

About the Author

Bruce J. McLaren is Professor of Systems and Decision Sciences at Indiana State University. He holds a B.S. degree in Aeronautical Engineering and a Ph.D. in Operations Management from Purdue University. He has been a consultant to many organizations in the integration of management information systems, and serves on numerous university computing committees at ISU. He formerly taught at the University of Virginia.

He currently teaches courses in database management, distributed data processing, advanced microcomputer applications, business information processing systems, and operations management. He has been recognized for outstanding teaching at Indiana State University.

McLaren has authored or coauthored ten textbooks in the computer and business areas. He would like to hear from users of this book, and can be contacted on Internet at MFBJM@BEFAC.INDSTATE.EDU.

Essentials of Microsoft Access

■ **PART ONE** introduces the Microsoft Windows graphical user interface as well as general database management and database design concepts. An overview of Microsoft Access demonstrates the use of database objects such as tables, queries, forms, and reports. Each type of data object is given its own introductory unit. Focus is placed on the use of Access Wizards to create attractive, functional data objects without the need to know database procedures in detail.

Introduction: Working in the Windows Environment

This unit serves as an introduction to the Microsoft Windows environment for IBM-compatible personal computers. The unit presents the basic Windows components and gives essential keyboard and mouse commands. A section is devoted to working with Windows boxes and the use of Windows Help. Instructions on starting applications from the Program Manager are given. *Those who are not experienced with Windows should study this unit; others with Windows knowledge can proceed directly to Unit 1.*

Learning Objectives

At the completion of this unit you should know

1. the advantages of using Windows on a personal computer,

2. the basic Windows components such as desktop, icons, dialog boxes, and application windows,

3. the accessory applications included with Windows.

At the completion of this unit you should be able to

1. use the mouse to manipulate windows,

2. access Windows menus with the keyboard and a mouse,

3. transfer information using the Clipboard,

4. start a Windows application from the Program Manager,

5. use Windows Help screens,

6. close a Windows application.

Important Commands

Alt Spacebar

Alt Tab

Ctrl Esc

Click, double-click

Close (Alt F4, Ctrl F4)

Drag

Help (F1)

Maximize

Minimize

Move

Restore

Size

Understanding the Windows Interface

Microsoft Windows is a *graphical user interface* (*GUI*, pronounced *goo-ee)* for operating application programs on a personal computer. It is graphical in that users make choices from menus of icons (pictures) presented on the screen, instead of typing often-inscrutable DOS commands in at the DOS prompt. Windows presents the user with a consistent environment across Windows applications. That means you can learn one set of commands and expect to make use of similar commands in other Windows programs. Applications run in windows, and manipulating windows is standardized within the Windows GUI. Although not strictly necessary, using a mouse pointing device to select commands and move objects greatly increases your speed when you work in Windows.

Another advantage of Windows comes when you install new hardware or software in your computer. Because programs work within the Windows setup configuration, you need to configure new hardware only one time—within Windows itself. Once properly configured there, all other Windows programs should be able to communicate correctly with the new item. For example, suppose you have just purchased a new inkjet printer. It needs to be configured only in Windows; all of the Windows applications can print to that new printer. By contrast, DOS applications require that you configure each application for the new hardware. The same thing is true when you upgrade to a new video display, or purchase a CD-ROM drive, or buy a better mouse.

Although Windows offers increased productivity, this new speed comes only when you have learned the basic Windows interface and have mastered use of the mouse to select commands. You should note that most of the commands and techniques learned in this unit are applicable both to Microsoft Access and to other Windows applications as well, and therefore time spent here will reduce the time you need to learn a new Windows program.

Components of the Windows Environment

This section contains explanations of the most common components that appear on the screen in Windows. Note that this book uses 800×600 Super VGA resolution for all Windows screen reproductions. If your computer uses 640×480 VGA resolution, you may not see quite as much information on your screen at one time, although the material is essentially equivalent.

The Windows Desktop

The *desktop* is the area on the screen where all of the Windows components appear. The desktop is similar to your own desk, with information appearing in rectangular boxes called *windows*. Figure 0.1 shows the desktop with various items highlighted. *Application programs*, sometimes called *apps*, appear in windows, along with the objects you are creating, called *documents*.

Also appearing on the desktop are various *icons*, or pictures representing applications or commands. For example, a picture of a calculator represents the Calculator application. When you install Windows on your computer, it represents each application program with a different icon. You can *minimize* an application's window to

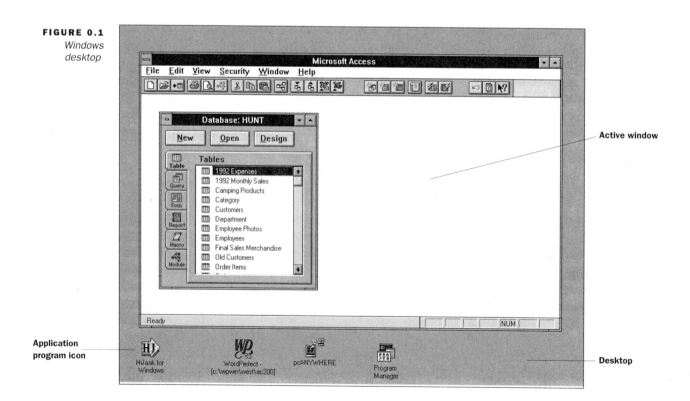

FIGURE 0.1
Windows desktop

Active window

Application program icon

Desktop

FIGURE 0.2
Windows Program Manager

Applications program group

One application

Minimized program groups

Accessories program group

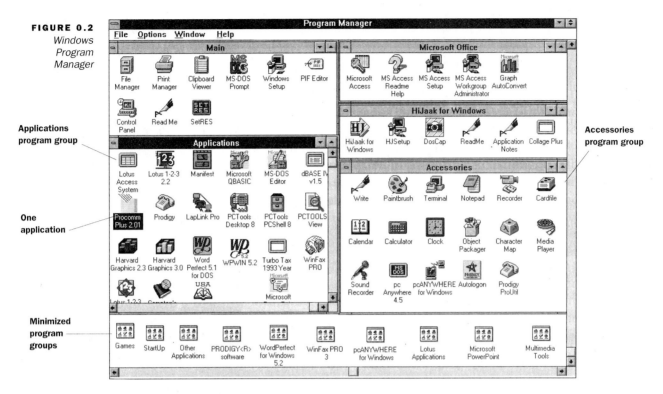

appear as an icon at the lower edge of the screen. It continues to run, even while minimized. It can be restored, or *maximized*, to a full *application window*.

Windows is designed for use with a pointing device, usually a *mouse*. The mouse pointer gives the location of the mouse. You can choose actions from menus with the mouse, or mark text or other items in a document. Use of the mouse with Windows is covered in a later section of this unit.

The *Program Manager* is the main window used to launch applications, and is shown in Figure 0.2. Your Program Manager will not necessarily look the same. It contains windows called *program groups* with multiple applications. Program groups are useful in holding related application programs. The standard Windows installation will produce at least three or four program groups:

- The *Main* program group contains frequently used Windows tools such as Windows Setup, Control Panel, File Manager, Print Manager, and MS-DOS Prompt.

- *Accessories* are useful programs packaged with Windows. Sometimes called *miniapps*, these tools help you do essential tasks. Accessories include Notepad, Write, Terminal, Paintbrush, Cardfile, Calculator, Clock, and other helpful tools.

- The *Applications* program group contains DOS and Windows programs that the Windows setup program found on your hard disk when it was installed. Some users will prefer to create separate program groups and move applications to specific groups.

- Windows version 3.1 and later creates a *StartUp* program group for those applications that you wish to begin automatically each time you start up Windows.

- The *Games* program group includes Solitaire and Minesweeper games. Many users will remove this program group to save space.

When you install a new Windows application within the Program Manager, it can be added to an existing program group, or placed in a new program group. For instance, the Access installation program first creates a new program group called Microsoft Access, then places the Access program in it along with several help files.

Components of a Window

Figure 0.3 shows a typical window for the Write word processing application. Running at the top of the window is the *window title*, which describes the window. The *title bar* appears within the window title and gives the name of the application in that window and the document name, if applicable. In Access the document name refers to the database in use or the database object being viewed. Unit 2 of this book gives numerous examples of Access windows. Surrounding the window is the *window border*, a thin bar that can be shortened or lengthened when you change the size of the window. The *window corner* is used to change the length of two adjacent borders of the window at the same time.

A *menu bar* appears just beneath the title bar in most application windows. You can select commands from the menu bar by using the keyboard or with a mouse or

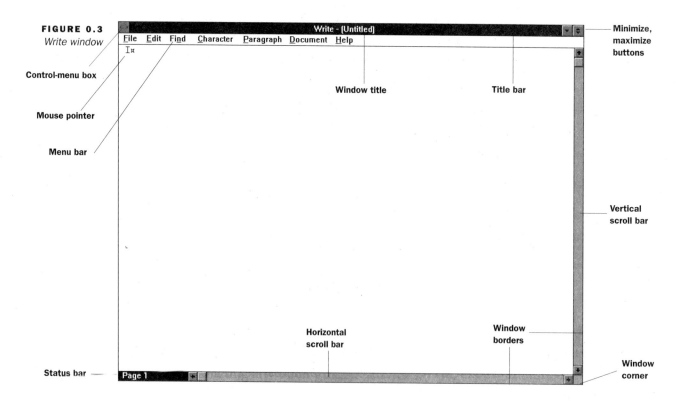

FIGURE 0.3
Write window

Control-menu box

Mouse pointer

Menu bar

Minimize, maximize buttons

Window title   Title bar

Vertical scroll bar

Horizontal scroll bar

Window borders

Status bar

Window corner

other pointing device. When a menu item is selected, a *pull-down menu* appears with additional command choices. Most Windows applications have similar File, Edit, and Help menus, so it is easy to find commands in different programs.

The majority of windows have *horizontal* and *vertical scroll bars* at the bottom and right sides, respectively. The scroll bar is a tool that allows you to move different parts of the document into view within the window. The square block (or scroll box) between the arrows in each scroll bar gives the current relative location of the view area within the document; if the square block is at the top, you are looking at the beginning of the document. Click the scroll arrow to move the view area.

The *Control-menu box* is in the upper-left corner of each window. It allows you to resize, move, maximize, minimize, and close a window, or to switch to another window. The Control-menu box is particularly useful for those who use a keyboard instead of a mouse for making these changes.

The *maximize* button appears in the upper-right corner. It is used to enlarge the active application so that it fills the entire desktop. The *minimize* button is used to shrink the window to an icon at the lower part of the desktop.

The *mouse pointer* appears if you have a mouse installed. It indicates the current location and takes on different appearances, depending on its use. While in the document portion of the window, the pointer looks like an *I-beam*. When the left mouse button is clicked, it marks the *insertion point* at which information can be inserted. When used to select choices from a menu, the pointer shape changes to an arrow that points to the upper left. Microsoft Access uses more than a dozen different pointer shapes to indicate different uses; these are discussed later in the book. Use of the mouse in Windows is covered in a later section of this unit.

Types of Boxes in Windows

There are four kinds of boxes in Windows. *Dialog boxes* request information from the user. They resemble small document windows. Dialog boxes may also provide warning information to the user. *List boxes* show a column of available choices for a particular menu item. *Drop-down list boxes* are used in dialog boxes that are too small to contain the entire list. You can click the mouse on a drop-down box to display the remaining list. *Check boxes* and *option buttons ("radio buttons")* represent options that can be turned on or off; you can *toggle* (reverse) the value by a mouse click or by pressing the spacebar. Dialog boxes frequently contain one or more of the other types of boxes.

Starting Windows

This section will show you how to start Windows and perform some basic operations. It is necessary to have a hard drive or a local area network connection to use Windows and Access. The manner in which you start Windows may depend on your system configuration. We will present a general method for starting Windows from drive C: on your own computer. Your instructor or lab assistant will have specific instructions for your own situation.

It is assumed that you are using Windows 3.1 or Windows for Workgroups 3.11 with your computer. Windows 3.0 users will see few differences in most Windows operations. Where there are differences between versions, this book will point them out. Windows 3.1 (or Windows for Workgroups 3.11) is a more stable environment and is recommended for all Windows 3.0 users.

GUIDED ACTIVITY 0.1

Starting Windows

This Guided Activity will demonstrate how to start up the computer and begin Windows.

1.   Turn on your computer and its monitor. After a few moments, it will boot up (load the operating system) and go through the initialization sequence. If it asks, enter the correct date and time.

2.   The monitor will display the DOS prompt C>, or perhaps F> if you're on a local area network. Some computers may boot into a shell program rather than the DOS prompt.

3.   At the DOS prompt, type WIN and press [Enter] to start Windows.

4.   After a few seconds you will see the Windows logo, then the desktop will appear. You will probably see the Program Manager in the center of the desktop, as well as some icons at the lower edge of the desktop. Because each individual is likely to arrange the desktop differently, no two screens will be exactly alike at this point.

5.   Go on to the next section. We will return to Windows shortly to try out some Windows features.

Using the Mouse

Although it is possible to use Windows without a mouse, we don't recommend it. Access requires use of the mouse for certain operations, and the mouse enables you to quickly select commands, move and resize windows, and activate certain features of Windows applications. This section discusses how to use the mouse in Windows.

Types of Mouse Devices

The term *mouse* in this book refers to the class of ***pointing devices*** that allow you to move the pointer (also called the ***cursor***) on the desktop by moving the device with your hand or finger. Most pointing devices are ***mechanical mice*** with two or three buttons. They are called mice because of their mouse-like shape and their cord, which resembles a mouse tail. The mechanical mouse has a rubber ball underneath that picks up your hand movements as you roll it across the table top. A mouse pad provides a tactile surface that results in smooth pointer movement as you roll the mouse across the pad.

Another popular pointing device is the *optical mouse*. The optical mouse does not have a rubber ball; rather, it uses a reflective mouse pad with a grid of horizontal and vertical lines. The mouse detects the presence of these gridlines as you slide the mouse over a line, and this movement is transferred to the screen.

A new pointing device is becoming popular for notebook computer users. The *trackball* uses a plastic ball that you slide with your thumb to represent movement of the pointer. Because the trackball stays in one place while you manipulate its ball, you don't need extra room for a mouse pad. This is particularly useful for those working on laptop computers or in tight spaces such as in an airplane. It takes some dexterity and experience to reproduce the same smooth mouse movement with a trackball.

Mouse Actions

There are four standard operations performed with a mouse or pointing device in Windows. They begin with the user's moving the mouse to the desired area on the desktop. The tip of the mouse arrow pointer is the active location for mouse operations.

CLICK OR SELECT

The *select* action involves moving the mouse to a particular menu or box and clicking the left mouse button one time. This will activate the command or toggle the button that was selected. For instance, you could move the mouse pointer to the File choice in the Program Manager menu bar and *click* the left button anywhere on the word File. If you were in a dialog box and were finished with all selections, you could click once on the OK button.

DOUBLE-CLICK OR CHOOSE

Some menu choices require that you select an item from a list, then press [Enter] or click on OK to choose that selection. Most dialog boxes permit you to *choose* an item and leave the dialog box by *double-clicking* on that item, without the need to click OK as well. The double-click of the left mouse button must be entered quickly; the timing of the two clicks is adjustable in the Control Panel of the Main program group. Be careful not to move the mouse itself while you double-click an icon or item. Some Windows applications like Access have other uses for a double-click. Figure 0.4 shows the Mouse dialog box in the Control Panel window.

HIGHLIGHT OR DRAG

The *highlight* technique requires that you move the pointer to the beginning of the text or object to be highlighted, then depress the left mouse button and drag the pointer across the entire object to be highlighted. Windows will usually display the

FIGURE 0.4
*The Mouse
dialog box in the
Control Panel*

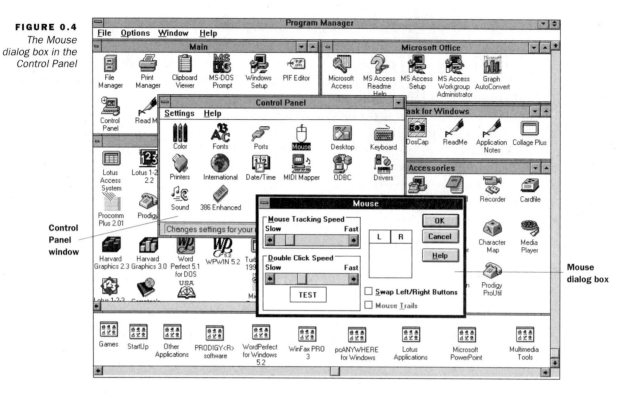

highlighted area in reverse on the screen—white letters on a black background in the case of text. You must highlight an object before it can be chosen, copied, or moved.

DRAG-AND-DROP

The *drag-and-drop* technique allows you to highlight an object, then drag or move it to another location in the document. For instance, move the pointer to a specific location, then depress the left mouse button. While holding down the button, drag the highlighted object to another location. When you release the mouse button, the object will remain in its new location. Some drag-and-drop activities move the object, while others place a copy of the object in the new location. This is the technique used to move a window to another location, as well as to move a database field to a query, form, or report.

Using a Windows Menu

Many Windows applications use a standardized menu and keyboard system referred to as *Common User Access (CUA)*. Windows commands can be selected from menus. The menu bar listing the principal categories of commands appears at the top of an application window and can be activated by either mouse or keyboard. In addition, the Control-menu box appears in the upper-left corner of each window. This section describes how to use these Windows menus.

FIGURE 0.5

The Access File menu

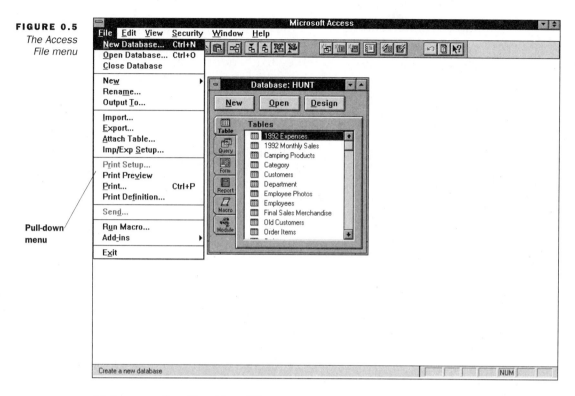

Pull-down menu

Using an Application Menu

The preferred way to open a menu is to move the tip of the mouse pointer to the name of the menu in the menu bar and click the left mouse button. Another way is to press and hold down the [Alt] key, then press the underlined letter of the desired menu name. For example, to open the File menu you would press [Alt][F]. The Access File menu is shown in Figure 0.5. If there is no underlined letter, you can press the [Alt] key to highlight the first menu, then use the right or left arrow keys ([→] and [←]) to move the highlight to the desired menu, and finally press [Enter] to open that menu.

In either case, the menu will open or "pull down" and you will see the choices in that menu. To select a command with the mouse, move the pointer to the desired command and click once on its name. If you are using the keyboard, you can use the up or down arrow keys ([↑] and [↓]) to highlight the desired choice, then press [Enter] to carry out that command. Or you could hold down the [Alt] key and press the underlined letter in the desired choice.

NOTE *If you accidentally press the [Alt] key, the first menu choice may be highlighted. Press [Alt] or [Esc] to clear the highlight.*

In some instances, one or more of the choices in the menu will appear in gray instead of black. A grayed (or "dimmed") choice means that the command is not available at the current time. For example, the Edit menu has choices for Copy and Cut; these are not available unless you have selected (highlighted) something to be copied or cut from the current document.

If you don't want to choose any of the commands in the menu, simply click anywhere else on the desktop outside of the menu and the menu will disappear. If you are using the keyboard, press the `Esc` key to abandon a menu choice.

Using the Control Menu

FIGURE 0.6
The Control menu

In the upper-left corner of each window is the Control-menu box; it appears as a horizontal line. The horizontal line icon in application windows is wider than that in document or group windows. This menu is used to resize, move, or close a window by using the keyboard. To open the Control-menu box, click on it with the mouse. Using the keyboard, press `Alt` `Spacebar` for an application window or press `Alt` `-` (hyphen) for a document or *group window*. Figure 0.6 shows the Control menu. Table 0.1 describes the choices available in this Control menu.

TABLE 0.1
Control menu options

COMMAND	FUNCTION
Restore	Restores a window to its previous size following a Minimize or Maximize operation
Move	Lets you move the window with the arrow keys
Size	Lets you change the size of the window with the arrow keys
Minimize	Reduces the window to an icon at the bottom of the desktop
Maximize	Expands the window to full size
Close	Closes the window
Switch To	Opens the Task List dialog box and allows you to switch to another application that is currently running
Next	Switches to the next document window within this application

GUIDED ACTIVITY 0.2

Selecting Menu Items with the Mouse

This Guided Activity will demonstrate how to select Windows menu items with the mouse.

1. We assume that you are already in Windows with the Program Manager on the screen. If not, return to Guided Activity 0.1 and start Windows.

2. Notice what appears on the Windows desktop. You should see the Program Manager window in its maximized form. If it appears as an icon, move the mouse

FIGURE 0.7
*About Program
Manager window*

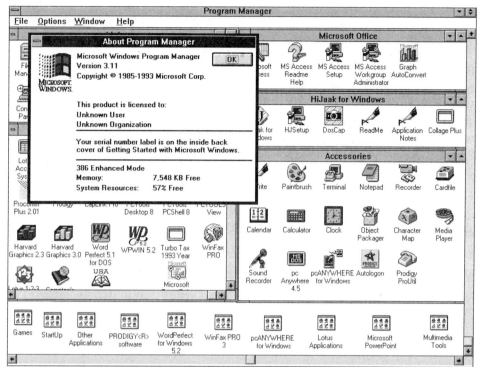

pointer to that icon and double-click on the icon to maximize the Program Manager.

3. Move the mouse pointer to the Help command in the menu bar and click on it. You should see the Help menu drop down and appear beneath the Help command. If you inadvertently clicked on another menu, move the mouse pointer to Help and click again to open that menu.

4. Click once on the About Program Manager line. You will see a dialog box like that shown in Figure 0.7 with information about the Program Manager, including the Windows version, the person to whom Windows is licensed, the Windows operating mode, and the amount of memory and system resources available.

5. Notice the shaded button titled OK in this dialog box. You can select this button to indicate that you have read the message and wish to return to the previous menu. It is the *default* (or preset) selection for this dialog box, so denoted by the dotted lines surrounding the OK message. Press the ⌷Enter⌷ key to select OK, or click on it with the mouse pointer.

6. Next, click on the Control-menu box in the upper-left corner of the Program Manager window, next to the title bar. The Control menu will appear. Click next on the minimize line. The Program Manager should shrink to an icon in the lower portion of the desktop.

7. Click once on the Program Manager icon. The Control menu will reappear just above the Program Manager icon. Click on the Restore line and the Program

Manager window will expand to its full size. Leave the Program Manager now while you learn how to open an application.

Opening an Application

In this section we will learn how to open a Windows application from the Program Manager. Clicking on the application icon will select the application. To choose it, press [Enter] or double-click on its icon. The application will load from the hard disk, taking anywhere from a few seconds to nearly one minute, then open its application window and display its menu bar.

At this time you can begin using the application. Most Windows applications will create one or more *document windows* as you create or edit documents. Access uses a Database document window to keep track of the tables, forms, queries, and reports associated with a database, and it opens more windows as you build new database objects.

If you have more than one application running on the desktop, you can switch between them by clicking on the window you want to move to, if it is visible. Or you can press [Ctrl][Esc] to bring up the Windows *Task List*. This dialog box lets you select the Switch To button even if the other window is not visible on the desktop.

GUIDED ACTIVITY 0.3

Opening an Application

In this Guided Activity you will open one of the applications packaged with Windows. It will also be used in the next section. We assume that you have started Windows and see the Program Manager group on your desktop. If it is not already maximized, be sure to do so now. Because each computer may have a different desktop, you may have to consult with your lab assistant if the application described below cannot be found.

1. Examine the program groups that appear on the Windows desktop. You should see one called Accessories. If it is an icon, double-click on it to restore it to a group window.

2. The Windows Setup program created this program group when Windows was installed on your computer. In it you will find a dozen or more applications that come with Windows. The one we will work with for now is the word processor called Write. Its icon is a fountain pen and the letter A. Double-click on the Write icon to choose it.

3. You will see the Write application window appear after a few seconds. You saw this window in Figure 0.3 earlier in this unit. In the title bar appears Write - (Untitled). This means that the current Write document does not yet have a name. You will give it a name when you save it to your hard disk.

NOTE *If the Write window opens in maximized mode, click on the double-headed arrow in the upper-right corner so that you see a portion of the Program Manager.*

4. Experiment by opening some of the Write menus in the menu bar. Use both the mouse and the keyboard ([Alt] + the underlined letter of the command) to activate these menus.

CHECKPOINT 0.A What commands do you use to use to open a menu?
The answers to checkpoint questions are contained in Appendix B.

5. Make the Program Manager the active window by clicking anywhere on its surface with the mouse. Notice that the title bar of the active window is highlighted and that the title bar of the inactive window becomes white. If you have chosen to run the Program Manager in full screen, the Write window will disappear.

6. Let's make Write the active window. If you can see a portion of the Write window, click on it. If none of the Write window is visible, press [Ctrl][Esc] to open the Task List. Click on Write and select the Switch To button; Write will become the active window.

7. We will use this application for several Guided Activities in this unit, so don't close its window at this time.

Resizing and Moving a Window

Most windows are displayed in the proper size and in the proper place, but you may want to change the size or location to better fit your desktop. Resizing and moving can be accomplished with the mouse or with the keyboard, but the mouse is much preferred. Some activities in Access cannot be done without a mouse or other pointing device.

Resizing a Window

Recall that the window's borders can be used to change the size of a window. The *mouse* can be used to enlarge a side of the window by dragging the border adjacent to that side. For instance, to make the box wider, move the cursor slowly over the left or right border of the window until the pointer changes into a double-headed arrow. Then hold down the left mouse button and drag the border out or in until the box is sized correctly. The opposite side of the window will remain in place while the window expands or contracts.

You can change two sides at the same time by dragging the corner border of the window. In this case, slowly move the mouse over the corner border until the shape changes into a double-headed arrow pointing to the diagonals. Then press the left mouse key and drag the corner to the desired location. The opposite side of the window will remain fixed while that corner expands or contracts.

To resize the window with the *keyboard*, use the Control-menu box and select Size. The pointer turns into a four-headed arrow. Press one of the four arrow keys ([↑][↓][→][←]) to move the pointer to the edge of the window, then press the arrow keys until that side is in the proper location. Press [Enter] to complete the size command.

Moving a Window

To move the window with the *mouse*, move the pointer until it is within the title bar of the window to be moved. Then press the left mouse button and drag the window to the new location. You will see a dotted outline of the window as you move the mouse. When you drop the box by removing your finger from the left button, the entire window and its contents will jump to the new location. This is a frequent command in Microsoft Access.

To move the window with the *keyboard*, use the Control-menu box and select Move. The pointer turns into a four-headed arrow. Use the arrow keys (↑↓→←) to move the window to the desired location, and press Enter to complete the move command.

GUIDED ACTIVITY 0.4

Resizing and Moving a Window

In this Guided Activity you will work with the Windows Write application that was opened in the previous Guided Activity. If you have not yet done that activity, you should do so now.

1. Examine your desktop. You should still have the Write application window in view from the previous Guided Activity. The application window should not be an icon nor running in full screen. In other words, you should be able to see the desktop behind the Write window on all four sides.

2. We will use the mouse to resize the window. Slowly move the mouse over the bottom border until the pointer becomes a two-headed vertical arrow. See Figure 0.8. While you press the left mouse button, drag the bottom border up about an

FIGURE 0.8
Resize window mouse pointer

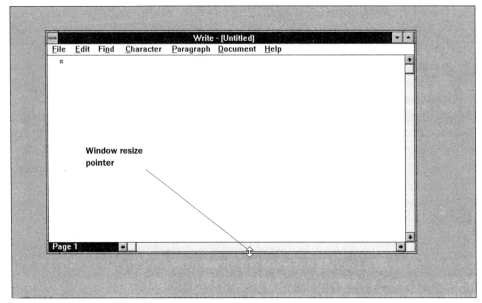

inch on your screen. When you let go of the mouse button, the window will be resized to your new specification.

3. Next, try the same operation with the left border, this time making the box narrower by about an inch.

CHECKPOINT 0.B What shape will the mouse pointer take when you move it over the left border of the window?

4. Now we'll learn to change two sides of the box at one time. Slowly move the mouse pointer over the lower-left corner border of the box until it changes into a two-headed arrow pointing northeast and southwest. Then press the left button and drag the corner of the box down and to the left until the window is approximately the starting size. Figure 0.9 shows the window after it is resized.

FIGURE 0.9
Window after resizing

Window resize pointer

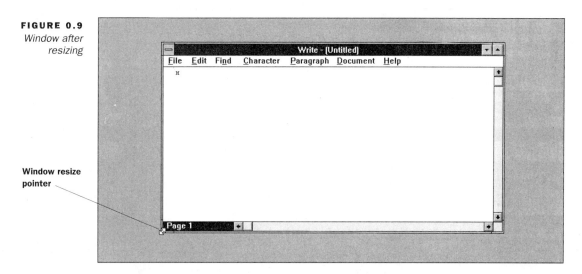

5. Next we will move the box. Move the mouse pointer into the Write title bar. While holding down the left mouse button, drag the window to a new location on the desktop. If you are not happy with the new location, drag it again to a better place.

CHECKPOINT 0.C What happens if you drag the window so that part or all of it is off the desktop?

Using Help in Windows

Most Windows applications have an extensive Help system. This section will show you how to use the general help menus and how to use the context-specific help screens that pertain to your current problem. We will also introduce the Cue Cards feature of Microsoft Access.

Using an Application's Help Menu

In all Windows applications, including the Program Manager and Windows Accessories, the right-most command is the *Help menu*. Click on Help, or press [Alt][H] with the keyboard, to activate the Help system. Most applications use a similar structure for the Help menu. The first choice is Contents, which gives an overall table of contents for help topics. The next choice is Search for Help on, which gives you a dialog box in which you can enter topics you would like help with. Next, How to Use Help gives basic instructions on using the help facility. The final choice, About, gives an information screen about the version of the application and other details. Applications may have additional choices that are specific to that application. Figure 0.10 shows the Help menu for the Write accessory.

FIGURE 0.10
The Write Help menu

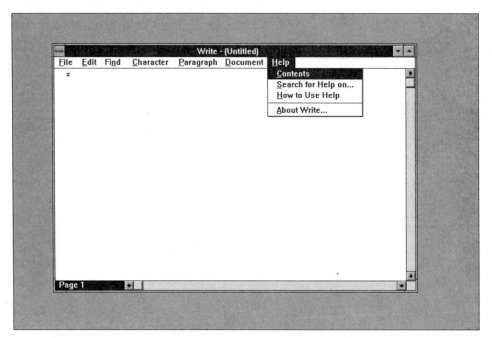

To see help, select one of the topics listed. After choosing the help topic, a Help window will open on top of the application window, and the opening help screen will appear for that topic. For instance, if you click on the Contents line of the Write Help menu, you will see an alphabetical list of topics. Use the pointer to select the topic of interest. If there are more topics than will fit on a single screen, Windows shows a vertical scroll bar at the right edge of the help window that can be used to show more topics.

Help topics are underlined and usually appear in green on a color screen. When you move the mouse pointer to a topic, the arrow turns into a hand with an index finger pointing to that topic. Click on the topic and the relevant help screen will appear. Help also offers definitions of key terms in some screens; if the term's underline is dotted, clicking on the term will bring up the definition of that term. After reading the definition, press any key or click the left mouse button to close the definition box.

Obtaining Help in a Specific Instance

To display help at a specific point in your application, press the [F1] function key. Windows will display the help screen that is appropriate for your situation in the application. For instance, suppose you have opened a menu and are not sure about the choices in that menu. Press the [F1] key and you will see the help screen that pertains to the highlighted choice. Although not all applications offer this feature, Microsoft Access does. It also has a question mark icon in the toolbar just below the menu bar that serves the same purpose.

Some dialog boxes have their own Help button. Click on that button to receive help that is customized for that particular box. See Figure 0.11 for an example of the Help available for the Select Printer Options menu.

FIGURE 0.11
Print Setup window with Help button

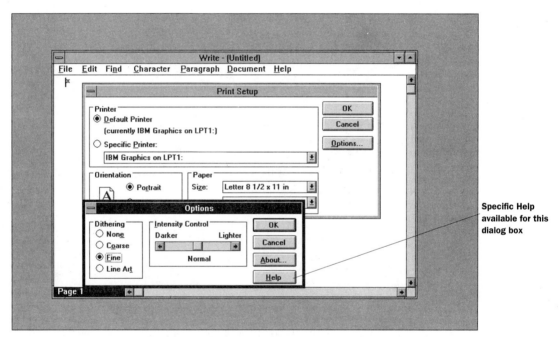

Specific Help available for this dialog box

Working with the Help Window Menu and Commands

When you activate the Help system for your application, it appears in a Help application window with its own menu system, shown in Figure 0.12. Most applications share the same Help menu structure. The File choice lets you print the help topic or exit from the Help system. The Edit menu lets you copy the help information to the Clipboard where it can be pasted into another application. The Bookmark menu lets you place a bookmark in the help file so that you can quickly return to that topic. The Help menu gives you information about how to use the Help system.

There are five *command buttons* located just below the menu bar in help windows. These are shortcut commands to assist you in working with Help. They are shown in Table 0.2.

FIGURE 0.12
Write Help
window

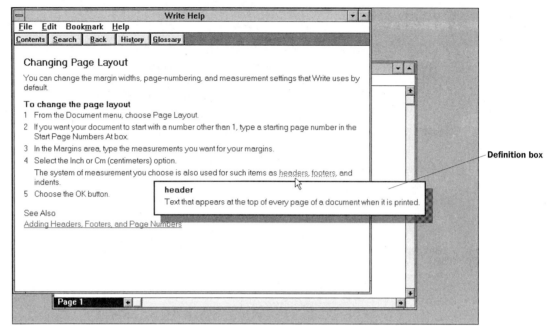

Definition box

Leaving the Help System

Because the Help system runs in an application window, you leave it like any other application. You can switch to another application, or close the window. Press `Ctrl` `Esc` to bring up the Task List and switch to another application, or select the File menu and choose the Exit command to close Help. If you don't anticipate coming right back to help, it is preferable to close the Help window and return to the application (to conserve memory).

TABLE 0.2
Help command
buttons

COMMAND	FUNCTION
Contents	Brings up the table of contents screen
Search	Lets you search for specific help topics by name
Back	Returns to the last help screen you viewed—you can use this command repeatedly if you have followed several help references (when you get back to the first help screen, the Back choice is dimmed, indicating that it can no longer be used)
History	Opens a box that displays the last 40 help screens in the order that you viewed them; you can jump directly to a specific help screen by choosing it from the list
Glossary	Opens a box that shows an alphabetical list of terms and their definitions (not all applications have a Glossary button in the Help system; for instance, in Access you should search for the Glossary term)

Using the Access Cue Cards

Microsoft Access has included a new kind of help system called *Cue Cards*. This facility is different from regular help in that the Cue Cards help screens remain visible on the screen while you work with Access. Regular help appears in a separate window and requires that you switch back and forth between the application and its help. Cue Cards contain "how-to" tips in numbered sequence to remind you how to perform specific tasks. We will illustrate Cue Cards in later units of this book.

GUIDED ACTIVITY 0.5

Using Help in Windows

This Guided Activity will use the Help system in Windows Write. If you have not completed the earlier activities of this unit, you should do so now to activate the Write accessory. In this Guided Activity you will access the Help system, search for topics, and print a help topic if your printer is functional in Windows.

1. Examine your desktop to be sure that the Write window is present. Notice that the Help menu is the last choice at the right of the menu bar.

2. Click on Help to display the Help menu. From this menu select the Contents command.

3. From the alphabetical topic list choose the Change Page Layout topic. You will see instructions on how to change margins and the starting page number.

4. Click on the word `headers` that is underlined with dots. Windows will display the definition of that term. Most Windows applications contain such definitions of key terms. See Figure 0.12 for an example of this definition. Click on the left mouse button again to remove the header definition box.

CHECKPOINT 0.D   How would you go about getting more help about the Header topic?

5. At the bottom of the screen is a See Also section with another underlined topic. If you click on this topic, you will see related information.

6. Click on the Back button to return to the previously viewed help screen.

7. If a printer is attached to your computer and operational within Windows, select the File menu in the Help screen and click on the Print Topic choice. After a few seconds, the contents of this help topic will be printed on the default printer. Ask your instructor or lab assistant for specific instructions about printing in your lab. Figure 0.13 shows the printed output from the File I Print Topic command.

8. Finally, choose File I Exit from the menu bar to close the Help menu. You will return to the Write application.

Closing a Window

There are several ways to close a window. Most dialog boxes have an OK button that can be clicked to finish. If you have a dialog box in which you have made responses that you don't wish to keep, click on the Cancel button. If the window has a Control-menu box, you can click on it and choose the Close command. Finally, you can select the File menu in an application window and choose the Exit command.

There is a shortcut for closing an application window. Press [Alt][F4] in most applications and the applications window will close. *Windows is very careful in treating your documents that have not been saved if you use this shortcut:* you will be asked whether you wish to save any documents before the window is closed. To close a document window, press [Ctrl][F4] as a shortcut command.

FIGURE 0.13
Sample printed output from Print Topic command

Changing Page Layout

You can change the margin widths, page-numbering, and measurement settings that Write uses by default.

To change the page layout

1 From the Document menu, choose Page Layout.
2 If you want your document to start with a number other than 1, type a starting page number in the Start Page Numbers At box.
3 In the Margins area, type the measurements you want for your margins.
4 Select the Inch or Cm (centimeters) option.
   The system of measurement you choose is also used for such items as headers, footers, and indents.
5 Choose the OK button.

See Also
Adding Headers, Footers, and Page Numbers

HINT *One way to tell if you have selected a document window is to look at its Control-menu box—the document window horizontal line icon is short, less than half the width of the box. In applications windows, the horizontal line icon extends nearly all the way across the box.*

GUIDED ACTIVITY 0.6

Closing an Application Window

This Guided Activity will demonstrate how to close the Write application window.

1. Examine the desktop for the Write window. Note that it is in an application window because it has a menu bar and its Control-menu box has a long horizontal line icon.

2. Close this application by using the File | Exit command. You should return to the Program Manager.

3. For practice, we will start Write and close it in another way. Find the Write icon in the Accessories group and double-click on it. Be careful not to move the mouse when you double-click, or you will have to repeat the double-click.

4. After Write opens, type your name into the word processor. It doesn't matter about spelling here—we're not going to save this file.

5. Next, click on the Control-menu box and choose Close. Notice that Windows displays a warning box that informs you that your changes have not been saved and asks you to choose whether to save them. Click on No and Write will close, discarding the changes to the document. If you had selected Cancel, Windows would cancel your Close command and leave you in Write. The warning box is shown in Figure 0.14.

 CHECKPOINT 0.E What happens if you press the [Enter] key with the Yes button highlighted in the warning box?

FIGURE 0.14
Windows
warning box

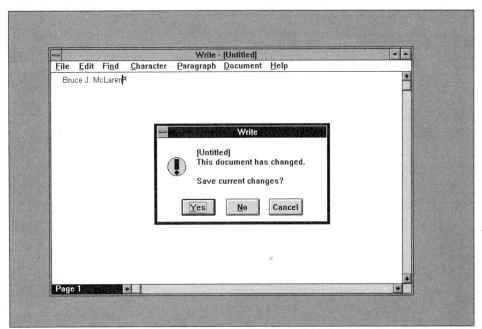

Windows Accessory Applications

As mentioned previously, Windows comes with several built-in accessories or miniapplications. You may wish to learn more about these programs, particularly if you are a new Windows user. Each program has significant capabilities, yet lacks one or more important features that come with third-party applications (those from other software publishers). You can use the Paintbrush application with Microsoft Access when importing pictures or graphic images into a database. You will find the Windows accessories in the Accessories program group in the Program Manager.

Write

Although we visited Write in the Guided Activities of this unit, we did not discuss its features. Write is a word processor, useful when you want to create and edit a document electronically. It has the ability to use multiple fonts and can accomplish a moderate amount of page formatting such as headers, footers, and page numbers. Print features such as subscript, superscript, bold, underline, and italic are also available in Write. It has the ability to import text and pictures from the Windows Clipboard. Write can handle line justification (left, center, right, full alignment) and line spacing.

Paintbrush

This accessory is used for drawing pictures. You can place text, lines, and boxes on the screen in many colors. You can draw freehand, or fill in areas with colors or patterns. Some users will capture the contents of the screen to the Windows Clipboard, then copy the Clipboard contents into Paintbrush where the image can be edited or cropped. Microsoft Access has the ability to use pictures and graphics in its databases. To do this, you have to bring the image into Paintbrush (or another graphics editor) first. In Unit 12, further instructions are given for using Paintbrush to insert pictures into a database.

Terminal

Windows comes with a terminal emulation accessory called Terminal. This program enables you to communicate in Windows with other computers over a telephone line using a modem. The Terminal accessory emulates a DEC VT-100 terminal or a generic TTY terminal. This program offers print logging and file capture to disk. You can copy selected text to the Clipboard and paste it into other documents.

Notepad

While Write is used for creating documents, Notepad is used for creating short notes of text. It does not have word wrap, so each line must end with the ⏎Enter key. Notepad is frequently used to view and edit text files that end with the .TXT file extension. While we do not need to use the Notepad accessory with Windows, it can be very handy for making quick changes to text files such as the Windows INI initialization files and the DOS CONFIG.SYS and AUTOEXEC.BAT files, which must have no formatting codes.

Recorder

This accessory is used to record keystrokes and mouse commands for later use. These commands are stored in something called a macro. We will create macros in Access in a different manner.

Calendar, Calculator, and Clock

These accessories may be helpful for you. The Calendar keeps track of appointments and functions like an appointment calendar that people keep by hand. It comes with an alarm that will sound when you have an appointment.

The Calculator accessory provides a four-function calculator with memory, square root, and percent keys. You can also select a sophisticated scientific calculator with trigonometric and math functions. The calculator will also convert between decimal and hexadecimal numbers. Contents of the calculator can be copied to the Clipboard.

The Clock accessory provides for display of an analog or digital clock on the screen. The Clock displays the date and time according to the computer's system clock.

Other Accessories

Several other accessories ship with Windows, some of which only come with version 3.1 or later. For more information about all the accessory applications, see the Windows documentation from Microsoft or the *Windows* books in the West Publishing *Understanding and Using Microcomputers* series.

Main Program Group Tools

The Windows Setup program creates a Main program group and places in it several utility programs or tools. Many users will access one or more of these tools during Windows sessions.

File Manager

The *File Manager* tool is used to display the directories and files on your disk drives, and can be used to manipulate files. You may also start programs from the File Manager window. The Windows 3.1 File Manager is much improved over that included with Windows 3.0.

Print Manager

The *Print Manager* utility controls the printers attached to your computer and manages the printing process for applications. It allows your application to create a print spool file (a special area of memory) on the disk, then the application returns to your command while Print Manager prints the document. The Print Manager also allows several applications to use the same printer without interfering with one another. It is not necessary to use the Print Manager to print in Windows.

Clipboard Viewer

When you *copy* or *cut* material from a window, it is placed on the *Clipboard*. Cutting material from a document removes it from the document. When you copy material from the document, it also remains in the original document. The Clipboard Viewer lets you view the contents of the Clipboard and optionally save it to disk. Most Windows applications allow you to *paste* information from the Clipboard into that application's document. We will demonstrate use of the Clipboard with Access in later units.

MS-DOS Prompt

Windows includes a facility to work with DOS commands without leaving Windows. If you choose the *MS-DOS Prompt* (DOS Prompt in Windows 3.0) icon, Windows will open a full DOS session complete with DOS prompt. You can issue DOS commands and run DOS programs in this window. It is possible in some situations to copy text to and from the Clipboard while in a DOS window.

CAUTION   *Do not use the CHKDSK/F command or other commands such as disk compaction or optimization programs from the Windows MS-DOS prompt.*

To close the DOS window and return to Windows, type Exit at the DOS prompt and press Enter.

Windows Setup

The *Setup* utility enables you to make changes to the hardware configuration of Windows on your computer. For instance, you can use this utility to change to a new video driver, or add a new printer or mouse to your system. It can also be used to add new Windows applications to the Program Manager.

PIF Editor

The *PIF Editor* is used to create or change Windows *program information files (PIFs)*. PIF files contain the settings for running a DOS application under Windows. PIF files are usually packaged with the application and can be copied to the Windows directory on the disk drive. Most users will not work with this utility.

Control Panel

The *Control Panel* is used to make changes to the Windows desktop. Here you can make adjustments to the system colors, mouse response, fonts, time convention (USA or international), printers, and desktop look, as well as make other custom changes. Although most users will not need to make changes to the desktop, you might want to explore this Windows feature.

GUIDED ACTIVITY 0.7

Exiting from Windows

In this Guided Activity you will learn how to exit from Windows and return to DOS.

1. If you are finished with Windows for this session, you can close Windows by exiting from the Program Manager. You may choose File | Exit, or click on the Control-menu box and select Close, or press [Alt][F4].

2. The screen will display a dialog box with the message `This will end your Windows session`. To remain in Windows, click on the Cancel button. To leave Windows, click on the OK button. (If you are using Windows 3.0, you will see a Save Changes check box below the prompt. Be sure it is not selected—that is, no X in the check box—and click OK.)

3. To leave Windows, click on OK. Windows will close any open applications. If there are any unsaved documents, Windows will ask if you wish to save them. You will return to the DOS prompt (or the DOS shell if that is how you started Windows).

4. This completes the Guided Activities for this unit. If you are finished with the computer, follow the directions for your computer lab.

Command Review

In this unit you have read about several Windows commands. The following forms of this unit's commands are commonly used and should be reviewed carefully:

[Alt][Spacebar]	Activate the Control-menu box from the keyboard.
[Ctrl][Esc]	Open the Task List dialog box.
Close ([Ctrl][F4] or [Alt][F4])	[Ctrl][F4] closes a document window; [Alt][F4] closes an application window.
Help ([F1])	Open help for the current window.
Maximize	Enlarge a window to fill the screen.
Minimize	Reduce a window to an icon.

Move	Move a window.
Restore	Change a window to its normal size.
Size	Change the size of a window.
Click	Select an object by pressing the left mouse button.
Double-click	Choose an object when you quickly press the left mouse button two times.
Drag	While you hold down the left mouse button, moves an object when you slide the mouse to the desired location.

Review Questions

The answers to odd-numbered questions are contained in Appendix B.

1. What is meant by a graphical user interface?
2. What is the desktop in Windows?
3. What is the cursor called in Windows?
4. What is an icon, and why are icons used in Windows?
5. What is a minimized application window?
6. How do you scroll the screen up or down in a Windows application?
7. Why does Windows use program groups?
8. What is a check box?
9. What are the differences between selecting and choosing an object?
10. How do you drag an object with the mouse?
11. Which mouse button do you push to select an object?
12. How do you change the size of a window?
13. How do you obtain help about a menu choice?
14. What functions are available through the Control-menu box?
15. How do you close an application if you do not have a mouse attached?
16. How do you move a window to a new location on the desktop?

Key Terms

The following terms are introduced in this unit. Be sure you know what each of them means.

Accessory (miniapp)	Drag-and-drop	Option button (radio
Application program	Drop-down list box	button)
(app)	File Manager	Paste
Application window	Games	PIF Editor
Check box	Graphical user interface	Pointing device
Choose	(GUI)	Print Manager
Click	Group window	Program group
Clipboard	Help menu	Program information file
Command button	Highlight	(PIF)
Common User Access	Horizontal scroll bar	Program Manager
(CUA)	I-beam	Pull-down menu
Control-menu box	Icon	Select
Control Panel	Insertion point	Setup
Copy	List box	StartUp
Cue Card	Main program group	Task List
Cursor	Maximize button	Title bar
Cut	Mechanical mouse	Toggle
Default	Menu bar	Trackball
Desktop	Minimize button	Vertical scroll bar
Dialog box	Mouse	Window
Document	Mouse pointer	Window border
Document window	MS-DOS Prompt	Window corner
Double-click	Optical mouse	Window title

Documentation Research

Using the Windows and Access documentation and on-line Help, find the answers to these questions. Record the page number of the manuals if you use them as your source.

1. Explain the differences between the Windows | Cascade and Windows | Tile commands in the Program Manager menu bar.

2. What is the Windows Tutorial command, found in the Help menu of the Windows 3.1 Program Manager? (*Note*: Windows 3.0 users may not have this command.)

3. Use the *Getting Started with Microsoft Windows 3.1* manual to note the new features of Windows 3.1 that are not in Windows 3.0.

4. What is the purpose of the Windows Control Panel program found in the Main program group? How can you use it to change the response of the mouse?

5. Use the Control Panel to view the fonts that have been installed on your copy of Windows. Do not make any changes to the set of fonts.

Introduction to Database Management Concepts

This unit serves as an introduction to database concepts. You do not need a computer to complete it. In this unit we discuss the basic terminology of database management and present some important factors to consider before you sit down at the computer to create a database system.

Learning Objectives

At the completion of this unit you should know

1. the definition of database management terms,

2. important considerations before you begin to create a database system.

At the completion of this unit you should be able to

1. design a simple database system on paper.

Database System Terminology

This section contains brief definitions of some terms that are illustrated in the following section.

Basic Terminology

A *database management system (DBMS)* is a package of computer programs and documentation that lets you establish and use a database. The Access package is a new personal computer DBMS designed for use with Microsoft Windows. A DBMS allows you to store data and retrieve it according to your criteria.

A *database* is a collection of related data in tables, queries, reports, forms, macro programs, and so forth. A database contains data about a particular topic or purpose; it is not itself the programs that manage the data. The database is organized for easy user access. The Access database is stored in a single, large file that contains all of the database objects for a particular application.

A *table* is the part of the database that holds the data. A table is similar to a two-dimensional table in which the horizontal rows are records and the vertical columns are fields. In Access, the table is also known as the *datasheet*. In other DBMS packages, the table is known as a *file*.

A *record* is a group of related fields of information about one object or event in the database. A *row* of a table is analogous to a record.

The *fields* of a record contain the data items. Fields correspond to *columns* in tables. A field represents an attribute or measurement of some object or event. A field has certain characteristics such as data type and length. (Access contains text, number, currency, yes/no, counter, date/time, and graphic picture field types. We will discuss field types later in this unit, and in much more detail in Units 2 and 3.)

An *index* contains a table of record numbers, called *pointers*, arranged in some order (for example, alphabetical, numerical, chronological) to permit the rapid location of a particular record.

A *key* is an identifier for each record. It can be a single field like a catalog number, or a combination of several fields such as last name and first name. All Access tables must have a *primary key* that uniquely identifies each record. Other keys for a table are known as *secondary keys*.

Additional Access Data Objects

A *query* is a set of conditions that provide for retrieval of certain records from a table. You can add more than one table to a query and relate tables by matching common fields. Unit 4 contains an introduction to Access queries.

A *form* represents a customized manner of inputting data in a database or presenting data on the screen. A form usually presents a single record at a time, or a single record from one table together with records from another table that match it. Unit 5 contains an introduction to Access forms.

A *report* provides the specifications for output of data in a tabular format. In Access you may display a report on the screen or send it to the printer. A report usually has multiple records, organized in a particular order. Unit 6 contains an introduction to Access reports.

A *graph* is a way to present numeric data from multiple records in a graphic fashion. Access provides bar charts, line graphs, and other graph types that may be added to forms and reports. Unit 13 contains an introduction to graphing with Access.

A *macro* is a set of Access commands that cause an action. These commands are stored as a miniature program. A macro can be replayed when necessary without reentering those commands from the keyboard or with the mouse. Unit 14 contains an introduction to Access macros.

A *module* is a collection of Access Basic statements grouped together as a program. Modules are used to provide specialized processing calculations that cannot be accomplished with ordinary Access methods. Modules are an advanced topic and hence are beyond the scope of this book.

Database System Example

With the preceding definitions as a basis, let us consider an example of a database. Assume that you are the operator of a sporting goods store, Hunter River Sporting Goods Inc. In your store, you stock recreational items from many suppliers for resale to retail customers.

Like many managers, you are concerned about your inventory. You want to minimize the amount of materials on hand because keeping inventory is costly. You also worry about obsolescence, particularly with clothing and other seasonal fashion items. Yet without your having ample inventory on hand, a customer may be unable to make a purchase. Before you started using a computer, you kept your inventory on index cards that looked like Figure 1.1.

As a first step in database development, you transferred a portion of your inventory records from index cards to a sheet of paper with a result

FIGURE 1.1
Inventory card

Stock Number: 20235

Description: Outdoor 285 Basketball

Unit Cost: 24.95

Quantity on Hand: 30

Date of Last Order: 10/4/93

that looked like Table 1.1. Many of the key database concepts can be illustrated by considering this example.

Each entry on the card and each column in the table is a *field*. Notice that the type of data is consistent as you read down the column: either numbers, text, or date data. Fields are identified by *field names* such as Stock Number, Description, Unit Cost, Quantity on Hand, and Date of Last Order. (Some DBMS packages require us to use shorter names than these illustrations; Access permits field names of up to 64 characters long.) As you design a database, consider the types of information you want to keep, as a start toward field definition.

The Stock Number field is a *key* field—a number or text string that is unique for each record. The DBMS will allow us to locate a record rapidly, once we know its key number. As you become more familiar with the arrangement of your data, consider how you want to search for items (such as by stock number or perhaps by description). You will use key fields to sort data in tables. Access requires that each table have a primary key.

Each card represents a separate *record*. Reading across the rows of the table, we also see what a record is: a group of related fields of information treated as a unit. Read across the top row and note how the five fields are all related to each other: we

	STOCK NUMBER	DESCRIPTION	UNIT COST	QUANTITY ON HAND	DATE OF LAST ORDER
TABLE 1.1 *A partial inventory list in table format*	20235	Outdoor 285 Basketball	24.95	30	10/04/93
	20237	Michael Jordan 285 Basketball	15.95	12	10/04/93
	20238	Larry Bird 33 Basketball	19.95	5	08/02/93
	20239	Girls League Basketball	29.95	3	08/02/93
	20241	NCAA Tourney Basketball	24.95	10	10/04/93
	20254	Joe Montana Football	21.95	6	06/24/93
	20255	Official NFL Football	64.95	2	06/24/93
	31204	Par 72 Men's Stainless 8 Club Set - Rt	199.95	4	11/29/92
	31205	Par 72 Men's Stainless 8 Club Set - Lt	199.95	0	03/30/93
	31211	John Boyd Driver	129.95	5	03/30/93
	31215	PowerHit 11-pc Golf Club Set	229.95	10	11/29/92
	31233	Professional Golf Balls 6-pack	8.95	24	11/29/92
	31234	Professional Golf Balls 15-pack	17.95	13	03/30/93

have on hand 30 Outdoor 285 basketballs that sell for $24.95 each and were last ordered on October 4, 1993. We need one record for each unique unit, and we must make sure that the database system has sufficient capacity to hold records for all of our products.

The computer stores this information in a *data table*. Without a computer, a data table might be simply a box of index cards or a manila folder in a file cabinet. At this point, we might want to start thinking of appropriate names for our data tables. Typically, we choose names that represent the kinds of objects that are stored in the table. Information about products, customers, vendors, and employees might be stored in tables of the same names.

Collectively, these tables constitute the *database* of the business. Recall that the database is a collection of interrelated data. An Access database contains not just the data tables, but also the queries, forms, reports, and programs that manipulate the tables. As you will see in the next unit, Access stores all of the database objects in a single database file.

Finally, the *database management system* is the method by which we manage all this data. Before computers, people used an amazing variety of colored index cards, and often inscrutable notes to themselves, to keep track of their information. A DBMS such as Access can enhance your ability to manage large amounts of data efficiently. The remainder of this book will explain how to do that.

Database System Design

When designing a database system, you must keep in mind the *purpose* of the database. You must decide *which facts* are needed by the users, and in *what format*. Sometimes the desired information is a list, such as a set of mailing labels or a sales report. Sometimes the desired information is a single item, such as the product with the largest sales in the last month. For instance, if you wish to have a database that will provide you with a list of products that must be reordered from the vendor, then you will need both data that define reorder status (for example, quantity on hand, current sales rate, last purchase date, minimum order quantity) and data that enable you to contact the vendor (such as name, address, telephone number). Also, you must consider whether you want to view the answers on the screen, or get a printed report.

Design Components

Timing is important. *When* do we need the output, and when will we update the data? If you need daily lists, then you need to update the data daily. You might have a system that can collect data continuously, such as a computerized cash register, or alternatively your input might be based on periodic reports from others, such as monthly sales reports. A good rule of thumb is to update as often as possible, and at least as often as you expect to extract useful data.

Now is a good time to ask *where* the data comes from. Do you have or can you collect the necessary data using current organizational resources, or must you buy the data from elsewhere? Suppose that a salesperson wants to know names of good customer prospects. The salesperson might have a record of previous purchases and addresses but might not know the customers' incomes or ages.

Now you are ready to address *how* the computer provides the output, given the available data. Do we need to make calculations? Must we make decisions? Are there criteria for selection? Must we sort the output in a particular order? Should we summarize the data? Our salesperson might want mailing labels, sorted in zip code order, of all persons who have made purchases in the past two years and whose household income is more than $20,000. He or she does not want to send more than one copy to a household, so duplicate addresses must be avoided.

Finally, you must decide *who* will design the system, who will build the tables and other database objects, and who will input the data. After you establish the database, who will be responsible for maintaining it: adding, deleting, or changing data and ensuring that the programs continue to function as required? Who will be authorized to have access to the database? Who will maintain accounts for authorized users and see that unauthorized users cannot access the database? Who will be charged with backing up the data so that a safe copy is available in case of fire or a system failure causing loss of data?

Systems Analysis

Where would you find out the answers to these and other important design questions? A *systems analyst* is an individual who analyzes the organization and arrives at a design for a system that would solve the organization's problems. The analyst interviews workers and managers of the organization to learn about its operations. The analyst would observe work being done within the organization and draw conclusions about improvements that could be made. The analyst would also want to talk with customers and suppliers to understand other viewpoints about the organization and its products.

The systems analysis procedure may be likened to peeling away layers. The layers represent levels of detail about the organization being modeled. As you learn more about the organization, you "peel" back a layer to build a better understanding of what information is needed for a particular department and how that information may be best delivered. Remember that first glances may not provide the most realistic understanding about the system being studied. In fact, because of familiarity with an existing system, the workers may make suggestions regarding the *old* system and not see the benefits of taking a new approach. As the systems analyst, your role is to remain objective and draw conclusions only when the facts are well understood.

The process of designing a new system can be time-consuming, particularly when the organization is complex. It may be tempting to stop the investigation early and get to work on the computer, building database tables and the like. Most information system managers recommend that the analyst spend more time in the design stage before actually creating parts of the database. The extra planning time spent will result in a database system that better reflects the needs of the organization and will need less rework in the future.

However, it is also clear that organizations evolve over time. Customer needs change, products are modified, more locations are used, personnel come and go, suppliers have different interfacing needs, government regulations mount up. The end result is that a database with a good design can be modified to accommodate these changes. A poorly designed database will become increasingly difficult to change to fit new needs.

We will continue to address database design issues in later units of this book. For example, Unit 3 on building tables contains information about how to choose a particular field type for a table. Other introductory units on queries, forms, and reports will help you design those objects.

DBMS Capacity Considerations

Several aspects of *database capacity* are important to understand. First, the DBMS must allow enough fields to accommodate our needs (see Table 1.2 for a summary of Access capacity constraints). Second, the DBMS imposes a certain maximum number of characters per record. Third, the DBMS must be capable of maintaining the required number of records. Finally, the DBMS imposes a limit on how many tables can be in use at one time.

TABLE 1.2	ITEM	CAPACITY
Access capacity constraints	Maximum size of a database	1 gigabyte* (GB) in Access v1.1, v2.0 128 megabytes[†] (MB) in v1.0
	Tables per database	32,768
	Fields per table	255
	Characters in object names	64 *(doesn't like periods)*
	Characters per text field	255
	Open tables	254
	Maximum report size	22 inches wide; 22 inches high/section

*Roughly, 1 billion bytes, or 1,000 megabytes
[†]Roughly, 1 million bytes, or 1,000 kilobytes

Your specific computer system might also impose capacity limitations. The hard disk of most PCs would permit storage of many thousands of records. Floppy disks have much less capacity and are generally not used by organizations as the location for databases. Floppy disks provide a means of backing up and transferring data between computers. You may use a floppy disk as a student while you learn Access.

The Hunter River Sample Database

For the remainder of this book we will use Hunter River Sporting Goods Inc. as the sample database for Guided Activities and Exercises. We introduced this fictional company earlier in this unit. Hunter River is a retail sporting goods company with a full line of sports, camping, hunting/fishing, fitness, and other merchandise. A different organization will be used for Applications that appear at the end of some of the units.

The database for this company will contain information about products, customers, employees, departments, vendors, customer orders, purchase orders, and sales. We will use separate tables for each of these items. We will create other tables for reasons that are explained as you work your way through this book. The Hunter River database file is found on the West Student Data Disk that accompanies this book. Your instructor or lab assistant can provide more information about how to access the information from this database on your own computer and transfer needed files to your personal student data disk.

Exercises

1. What tables would be appropriate for use by your school for keeping track of student academic information, including permanent information and classes taken? Describe the fields within the tables.

2. Suppose you have just been hired by the manager of a local video rental store to help her design a database for the store. Describe the data tables that would be used with the database. What kind of reports would this system need?

3. The telephone company is putting together a 911 emergency information system for the local community. Describe how this system will be used. What tables would be used with this system? What fields would be appropriate within these tables?

4. The local automobile dealer is interested in preparing a customer database. Describe the kinds of information that such a system would contain, and tell how it would be used. What tables and fields would be needed?

5. The Solutions With Computers store has asked you to assist them in preparing a database for their inventory. Describe the kinds of information that such a system would contain, including the tables and fields needed.

Review Questions

The answers to odd-numbered questions are contained in Appendix B.

1. Define the following terms:

   a. Database management system

   b. Database

   c. Field

   d. Key

   e. Record

   f. Table

   g. Form

2. What are the differences between a database and a table?

3. What are the differences between a field and a record?

4. If each field were 10 characters wide, what would be the width of a single Access record if it contained the maximum number of fields for a table?

5. Consider the example in Table 1.1. What is the minimum width in characters necessary for each of the following fields?

   a. Stock Number

   b. Description

   c. Unit Cost

   d. Quantity on Hand

   e. Date of Last Order

6. Put yourself in the position of the owner of the sporting goods store discussed in this unit. Describe a useful database system for this store. Be creative.

Key Terms

The following terms are introduced in this unit. Be sure you know what each of them means.

Column	Form	Query
Database	Graph	Record
Database capacity	Index	Report
Database management system (DBMS)	Key	Row
	Macro	Secondary key
Datasheet	Module	Systems analyst
Field	Pointer	Table
File	Primary key	

Physicians' Medical Clinic (I): Designing the Database

In this application you will create on paper the preliminary design for a medical clinic database. In later applications you will have an opportunity to use Microsoft Access and implement a portion of the database on the computer.

You have been hired by Dr. Thomas Greenway, chief administrator of the Physicians' Medical Clinic (PMC), to assist in the development of a working database system to handle patient visits, insurance, billing, and other pertinent transactions of a large medical office. There are nearly 50 physicians on the PMC staff, along with about 100 medical technicians, nurses, and business staffers. Although PMC operates a leased minicomputer-based information system, the administrator believes it is time to develop alternative database approaches that would make use of personal computers and a local area network (LAN).

Goals for the PMC database would include storage of permanent patient information, information about patient visits to the clinic, cost of individual medical procedures and tests, insurance billings, employee information, supply inventory data, and information about supply vendors.

To help guide your thinking in the development of the PMC database, consider the following questions:

1. What tables would be useful for the PMC database? Remember that each kind of object in the database is usually represented by a separate table.

2. What kinds of reports would PMC want from the database? Arrange them in groups according to type of information. For example, you would have several reports dealing with individual patient visits to the clinic. Would these reports be printed *on demand*, or be based on a *fixed-time interval*? If the latter, how frequently would they be printed?

3. Describe the fields found in the permanent patient information table. That table describes information about the patient that doesn't change with each visit made to the clinic. What characteristics should you consider for each field?

4. Next, describe the fields found in the supplies table. Give the name of the field, the type of data found in that field, and the approximate size of the field necessary to hold the largest value (or longest text phrase) in that field.

Overview of Microsoft Access

This unit serves to introduce you to database management with Microsoft Access. It presents the basic database organization and describes the five main Access objects. Important Access tools and icons are introduced. The unit includes a discussion of the documentation and Help systems that come with Access. The Guided Activities demonstrate how to start Access and open a database.

Learning Objectives

At the completion of this unit you should know

1. the basic database structures of Access,

2. what the toolbar icons represent,

3. the various documentation and Help systems packaged with Access.

At the completion of this unit you should be able to

1. start Access and open a database,

2. use the Access database window,

3. use Access Cue Cards to open and use a database,

4. close databases and exit from Access.

Important Commands

[F1], [Shift][F1] (Help)

File | Close Database

File | Open Database

File | Exit

Help | Cue Cards

Getting Started in Access

This section will describe the procedure for starting Access and using an Access database. It will delineate the hardware and software requirements for running Access under Windows.

Software and Hardware Requirements for Access

Before you can use Access, it must be installed from the distribution disks on your computer or local area network. For most schools, this will be done for you. In case you have your own copy of Access or wish to reinstall the software, this section will explain the software and hardware requirements. Access must be installed under Microsoft Windows, explained in the next section.

WINDOWS 3.0 OR WINDOWS 3.1

Although Windows 3.0 is acceptable, most users will benefit from an upgrade to Windows 3.1. Windows 3.1 includes TrueType fonts, which print well on nearly any kind of printer and reproduce accurately on the screen. Windows 3.1 is more robust in detecting and preventing software crashes that require a reboot. According to software vendor technical support staff, 95 percent of users calling for support are running DOS 5.0 or 6.0 and Windows 3.1. Windows 3.1 is necessary if you are using the OLE 2.0 features of Access 2.0. This textbook assumes that you are using Windows 3.1 or Windows for Workgroups 3.11.

SYSTEM REQUIREMENTS

Like many applications that run under Windows, Access uses a significant amount of system resources. System requirements to run Access are detailed in the following list. If your system does not meet these requirements, you will have difficulties when running Access under Windows.

- Windows 3.0 or later (3.1 required to use OLE 2.0)

- DOS 3.1 or later *(Dos 6.22)*

- IBM-compatible personal computer with 386SX or higher microprocessor *486 100 or*

- 6MB RAM (8+MB is recommended) *(16 meg) (Big stuff 24 or 36)*

- 23MB available hard disk space for full Access installation (5.5MB minimum needed) *1 gig or 2*

- Mouse or other pointing device

- EGA or higher display (VGA or Super VGA are recommended)

- Windows-compatible printer is recommended

Access can be run from a local area network server if insufficient local hard disk space is available. Instructions for installing Access on a network are found in the Microsoft Access *User's Guide.*

Installing Microsoft Access

We will assume that Access has already been installed in your computer lab. Like other Windows applications, Access has a setup program that automates the installation process. If the setup program detects that your system does not have sufficient resources, a warning message is issued and the installation stops. The standard installation places three sample databases on the disk drive containing Access. These databases are used extensively in the Access documentation to describe various features and database techniques. If they are not present, consult with your lab assistant or instructor.

NOTE *We are using version 2.0 of Microsoft Access for the remainder of this textbook. Upgrades from version 1.1 are available.*

The Access Program Group

The Access setup program will create an *Access program group* within the Windows Program Manager. We assume that your computer lab uses this convention.

FIGURE 2.1
Microsoft Office Program Group (v2.0)

Check with your lab assistant or instructor for any other special configuration information. Figure 2.1 shows the Microsoft Office program group created through the installation procedure.

In the Office program group are several icons. The *Access icon* looks like a key superimposed on a spreadsheet background and represents the Access program. The question mark icon labeled "Microsoft Access Readme Help" represents the Access Help system and can be used to answer questions about Access before you actually load the program. The README file contains late-breaking information arriving too late to be placed in the Access manuals. The third icon from the left in Figure 2.1 represents the setup program for making further changes to the Access workgroup configuration. The last icon is used to turn on the Graph autoconvert feature so that graphs created by previous Microsoft Graph versions are converted to the current format when retrieved. Your system may not contain all of these icons.

Starting Microsoft Access

As with other Windows applications, the preferred way to start Access is to choose its icon. Locate the Access icon in the Access program group or elsewhere on your desktop and choose it by double-clicking.

TIP *If you are not familiar with Windows terminology, go back to the Introduction and read the discussion on Windows.*

After a few seconds, a screen will appear with license and system configuration information. After that, you will see either a temporary Welcome to Microsoft Access box or the Access *startup menu*. The Welcome box, shown in Figure 2.2, is installed by the setup program but it can be removed from future sessions by clicking on the check box. Because many labs will not show this welcome box, we will not use it as part of the presentation in this book. Double-click the Control-menu box to close this window.

FIGURE 2.2
*Access
welcome screen*

Control-menu
box

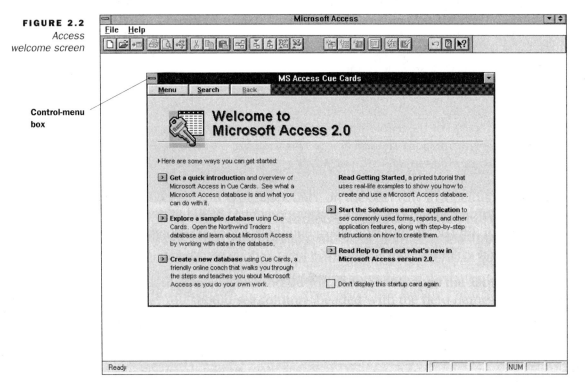

The Access Display

The opening Access display is quite plain, as shown in Figure 2.3. The title bar shows the name of the application, Microsoft Access. At this point there are only two commands in the menu bar, File and Help. The first two buttons in the toolbar let you create a new database or open an existing database. The large question mark icon toward the right side of the toolbar, beneath the menu bar, is used for context-specific help. In other words, you can click on the *help icon*, then click on a menu item or button, if you are having trouble with that menu or choice. Of course, the regular Help command in the menu bar is also used for help, but you have to search for the specific topic if you use that help method.

FIGURE 2.3
*The Access
startup menu*

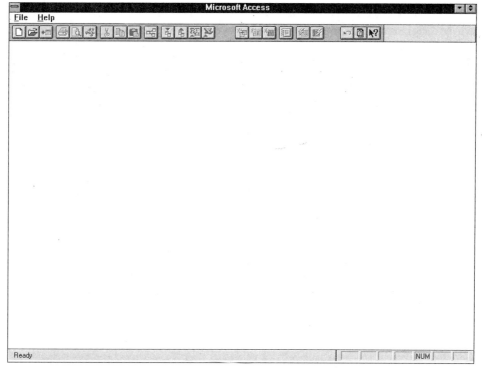

The File Menu

The *File menu* is used to Open an existing database, to create a New database, to perform file maintenance on existing databases (Compacting or Repairing a damaged file), and to Exit from Access. As with most Windows applications, Access will present a dialog box in which you can specify the disk drive, subdirectory, and file name for database files to be opened when you select that command. We will demonstrate the startup procedure in the first activity.

GUIDED ACTIVITY 2.1

Starting Microsoft Access and Opening a Database

In this Guided Activity you will locate the Access icon and start the Access program. You will open the NWIND sample database packaged with Access.

1. If you have not already started Windows, do so at this time.

2. Examine the desktop and locate the Access program group. If it is an icon at the lower edge of the screen, maximize or restore it at this time. If this program group does not exist on your computer, search for the Microsoft Access key icon, shown in Figure 2.1, among other program groups on the desktop.

3. Once you have located the Access icon, choose Access by double-clicking the icon.

4. After a few seconds, the initial Welcome to Microsoft Access window may appear. Choose the Close button to clear this window.

5. The screen will clear and you should see the startup Access display with File and Help in the menu bar. Compare your display with Figure 2.3.

6. Use the mouse to select the File menu, then choose the Open Database command.

7. In the File Name list box, select NWIND.MDB. You may have to change to the SAMPAPPS subdirectory to find the NWIND database. This is the large sample application that comes with Access. If this database is not listed, consult with your instructor or lab assistant.

8. Choose the OK button to open this database.

   We will continue at this point in the next Guided Activity.

The Access Database Window

Access will display the Database window when you create a new database file or open an existing database file. The *Database window* contains all of the database objects associated with that database, organized by type of object. From here you can use one of these objects, or create a new one of your own. Figure 2.4 shows the NWIND Database window.

.MDB Database File

Access stores all of the objects in the database in a single file with the *.MDB file* extension (for "Microsoft database"). Unlike other database management packages

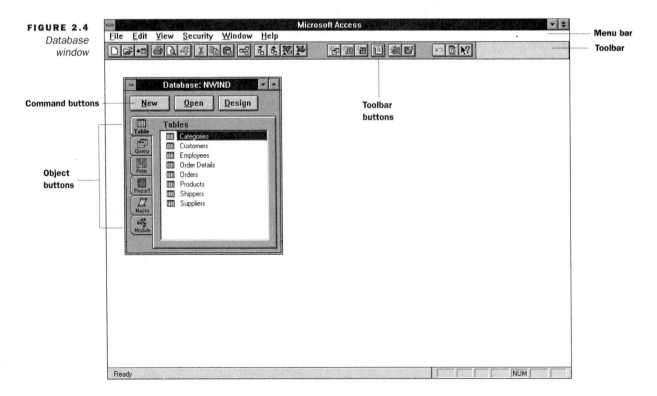

FIGURE 2.4
Database
window

like dBASE or Paradox, you can copy a *single file* and transfer *all* of the objects associated with that database. This also means that the DOS file name restriction of 8 characters can be relaxed for objects stored within the database file. In Access, names of tables and other database objects can be up to 64 characters long, with embedded spaces. This makes it possible to accurately name your objects without ambiguity. Which is more meaningful, "1993 Sales Report by Region" or "SALES93R"?

Object Buttons

The *object buttons* are shown ranging vertically down the left side of the window. Notice that one of the buttons is selected. In this window the Table button is selected. A list of objects in that category, in this case the tables, appears in the middle of the box. If you were to push another object button with the mouse, only the objects in that category will appear. Thus, you can examine all of the objects in your database by repeatedly cycling through the Table, Query, Form, Report, Macro, and Module buttons. We will discuss each of the objects later in this unit.

Command Buttons

The Database window's *command buttons* appear in the toolbar just beneath the title bar. The *New button* is used to create a new object of the type whose object button is selected. The other two buttons work with the selected object, so be sure to select the correct object before using the command button. The *Open button* will open the existing object whose name is selected and display the object's contents. The *Design button* is used to make a change in the design or structure of the highlighted object.

Menu Bar Commands

Notice that in addition to File and Help, Access displays several new menu bar commands when the Database window is open. The new choices are Edit, View, Security, and Window and are described below.

EDIT

The *Edit menu* is used with the Windows Clipboard with the cut, copy, and paste commands. It is also used to undo changes just made to the database object, and to create relationships between tables. We will talk more about relationships in Unit 8.

VIEW

The *View menu* allows you to choose which type of database object appears in the Database window. The default choice is to view Tables, but you can select Queries, Forms, Reports, Macros, and Modules. The Toolbars command is used to select or customize toolbars used in Access 2.0. You can use the Options command from this menu to view and change system option settings. We will not work with the

Toolbars or Options choices in this unit. You can use the Help command to learn more about these settings.

SECURITY

The *Security menu* is used to establish passwords and permissions for one or more users. You can also create or change user groups. Security issues are discussed in Unit 18.

WINDOW

Nearly all Windows applications share the *Window menu*. This menu allows you to arrange windows on the screen, or to switch to a different active window. Most users will not need to use this command because Access windows are not maximized and always remain visible on the desktop. It is easier to switch to another visible window by clicking on it with the mouse pointer.

Access Database Objects

This section will describe the six main objects that compose a database. It gives a short example of each type of object, taken from the Northwind Traders sample database packaged with Access. This book contains separate units for most of these Access database objects.

Tables

Recall from Unit 1 that a database *table* is the basic structure that holds the data values for the database. It is called a table because its rows represent records and its columns are data fields. In Access you can have up to 32,768 tables per database. Most databases will have from 5 to 15 tables, depending on the complexity of the system modeled in the database. When you create a new table, you will give the field name and data type for each column, along with the width of that column and any special rules for field values. When we examine the table's field definitions, Access displays it in *Design view*. We will build a new table in the next unit.

When we see the table and its field values, Access displays it in *Datasheet view*. This view resembles a spreadsheet. The icon for a table has the Datasheet view in its background. Figure 2.5 shows a table in Datasheet view.

Query

In Access you can use a *query* to display only the data that meets certain criteria. A query takes fields from one or more tables and allows you to enter criteria expressions to qualify records. In Access this facility is also referred to as *Query-by-Example (QBE)* because you provide an example of the kind of data that will qualify according to your criteria. You can also use the Query facility to link two

FIGURE 2.5
*Table in
Datasheet view*

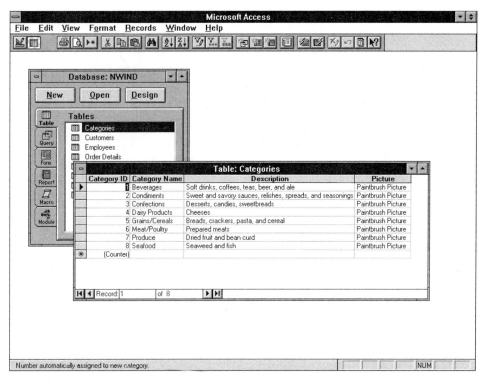

tables so that records with matching field values appear together. For example, suppose you were working with an Order table that contained a customer number in a recent order. You could match that table to a Customer table that contained the customer's name, and thus supply the name with the order. Figure 2.6 contains a query example in Design view that shows the link between two tables.

Form

A *form* is used to display records and allow the user to make changes to the field values in a record. Although the default Datasheet view can be used to examine data, the *Form view* allows customized designs that display field values, using Windows techniques such as list boxes and check boxes. You can also build forms that display the contents of more than one table at a time. Forms are designed primarily for screen output of a record at a time, although forms may also be sent to the printer. Figure 2.7 shows an Access form.

Report

A *report* is used primarily for printed output, although reports can also be viewed on the screen. You can design tabular reports that look like spreadsheets, or columnar reports with fields in different columns. Access has a facility for creating mailing label reports, and also allows you to design your own report formats. Figure 2.8 shows an example of an Access report. You cannot alter data in a report.

FIGURE 2.6
*Linked query in
Design view*

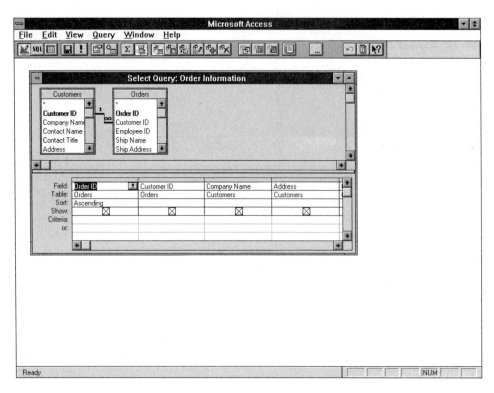

FIGURE 2.7
*Categories form
with products
subform*

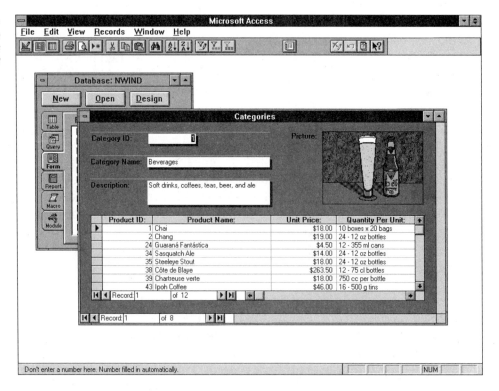

FIGURE 2.8
*Print Preview of
alphabetical
products report*

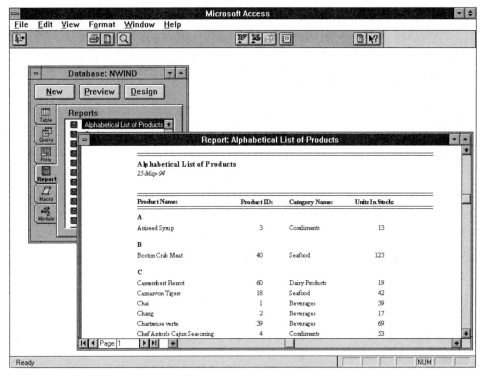

Macro

An Access *macro* is a list of actions that you use to automate repetitive tasks. Macros are stored by name, and can be attached to an on-screen toolbar button in such a manner that the macro executes when you press the button. Other macros can be called upon to do something automatically when you open a particular database. Although some would consider this "programming," it is fairly easy for end users to create Access macros. Other applications like spreadsheets and word processors use similar macros. Macros are covered in Units 14 and 15.

Module

Access contains a full programming language called *Access Basic*, derived from the language used in Microsoft Visual Basic. Although most applications can be built without programming, this language is used for customized situations that cannot be handled otherwise. You can write custom *modules* in this language that perform automatic updates to your data. We will not cover modules formally in this textbook.

Important Access Toolbar Buttons

Many Windows applications use tool buttons to represent frequently used commands. In Access these tool button icons appear in the toolbar, just beneath the menu bar. There are more than 30 *toolbar buttons* that are used in various circumstances. They do not all appear at the same time, but depend on the mode in use. The most important are described below, and are summarized in the Quick Reference section at the end of the book. Individual toolbars for each Access object are also described in the appropriate unit of this book.

	Datasheet View	Display the table's values in Datasheet view
	Design View	Display the Design view of the specified object (table, query, form, report) so that it can be modified
	Form View	Display the Form view of the data
	Open	Open a new database file
	Save	Save database object
	Find | Replace Data	Find and/or replace specific data
	Print Preview	Display preview of print on screen
	Print	Print database object
	Build	Activate Access Builder
	Cue Cards	Activate Cue Cards
	Help	Activate Access context-specific help
	Undo	Cancel (erase) the last change made to the object

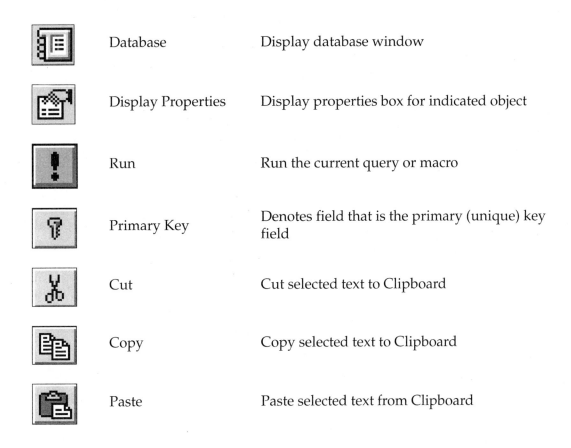

	Database	Display database window
	Display Properties	Display properties box for indicated object
	Run	Run the current query or macro
	Primary Key	Denotes field that is the primary (unique) key field
	Cut	Cut selected text to Clipboard
	Copy	Copy selected text to Clipboard
	Paste	Paste selected text from Clipboard

Access Documentation

Knowing what kind of documentation accompanies a package can often help you solve a problem more quickly, without having to go to other sources for help. The three manuals packaged with Microsoft Access provide an important knowledge base.

Getting Started

This manual is an excellent tutorial on Microsoft Access. Its 168 pages offer examples of nearly everything contained in Access. It is organized with "how-to" section headings, making it easy to find help on a particular operation. We recommend that users spend time with this manual if it is available in your computer lab.

Access User's Guide

This 800-plus-page manual is an exhaustive reference to Microsoft Access. It is organized in parts by type of data object, with a total of 26 chapters. It contains more than 100 examples that are cross-referenced for easy access. This manual is primarily for experienced users who already have a basic knowledge of Access.

Building Applications

This 428-page manual shows how to link Access objects into applications and serves as an introduction to the Acess Basic programming language. Although we don't cover Access Basic in this textbook, you should plan to read through this manual and work its examples prior to creating your own applications.

Access Language Reference (not included but available separately for $9.95)

This large book serves as a detailed reference manual for those who wish to write Access Basic program modules. It is organized alphabetically by programming statement. Only an experienced programmer will find this manual useful with Access.

Access Help Methods

This section will present the kinds of on-line Help available in Access. A general discussion of Windows help appears in the Introduction to this book.

ToolTips

This feature is new to Access 2.0. Place the tip of the mouse pointer on a toolbar button and Access will display its name below the button and a sentence about its use at the bottom of the desktop. Use *ToolTips* to learn about new buttons.

Help Menu

The usual kind of Windows help is available in the Access menu bar. You can display the contents of the help files, or search for specific help topics. This Help system is not context-specific. That is, you will not automatically see help for the particular choices on the screen unless you search for them.

Help Button

Some dialog boxes have their own *Help button*. Press this button to receive customized help for the particular box.

🄵🄰 Function Key

You can press the 🄵🄰 *function key* and context-specific help about the highlighted object will appear. We suggest that you choose this method when you have a question about a particular entry or command.

[Shift] [F1] *Help*

If you press [Shift] [F1] for help (or click on the Help button), the pointer changes to an arrow-question mark. You can then move the pointer to any object on the Access desktop and click the left mouse button to receive specific help about that object. This help is particularly useful for information about toolbar buttons and menu bar commands.

Cue Cards

This innovative feature is an on-screen tutorial for doing basic Access database functions. You can use the tips in the *Cue Cards* while you learn how to create database objects like tables, forms, and queries. There are six main topics covered in the Cue Cards plus a general topic that describes Access database concepts. To activate the Cue Cards feature, select the Help menu and choose the Cue Cards command or click the Cue Cards button in the toolbar. The following Guided Activity shows you how to use Cue Cards.

GUIDED ACTIVITY 2.2

Using Access Cue Cards

This Guided Activity illustrates how to use the Cue Cards help facility in Microsoft Access.

1. We assume that you have started Access and loaded the NWIND.MDB database as shown in the previous Guided Activity. If you have not completed these tasks, go back to the prior activity now.

2. To activate the Cue Cards feature, select the Help menu and choose Cue Cards.

3. In the Cue Cards help screen shown in Figure 2.9, select the first entry, See a quick overview. This choice will present a brief overview of Access database objects and terminology.

4. In a few seconds you will see the Quick Overview box that lists several topics you can select. See Figure 2.10 for this window. You may select any of these topics and Cue Cards will display information about that type of database object.

5. In this case select the first topic about Databases. You will see a box with examples of databases. When you have finished reading that box, click on the Next button to see the next box.

6. After reading the second Cue Cards box about databases, click the Next button and you will return to the Quick Overview box.

7. Click on the Menu button to return to the main Cue Cards menu.

8. At this point you could select a Cue Cards topic and build a database object. We will pursue this in the next unit when we build database tables.

9. Close the Help window and return to Access.

FIGURE 2.9
*The main
Cue Cards menu*

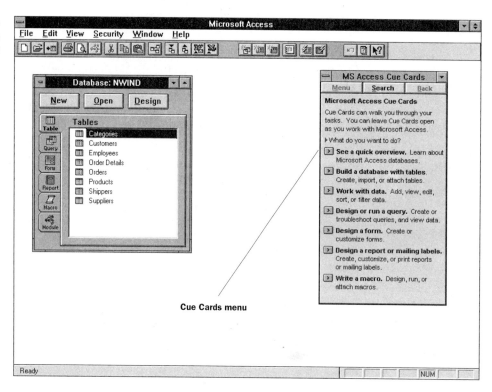

Cue Cards menu

FIGURE 2.10
*Cue Cards
Quick Overview
box*

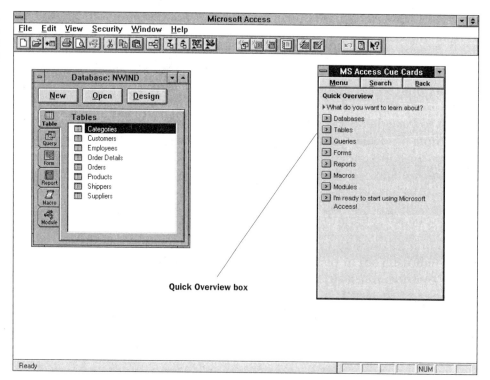

Quick Overview box

Leaving Access

Ordinarily, you would close the current database before you exit from Access. But nearly all Windows applications share a special feature: you can exit from the application and Windows will automatically close all files that are open. If you have made changes to any database object, you will be prompted to decide whether you want those changes to be made permanent. After you reply, Access will close and you will return to the Program Manager.

GUIDED ACTIVITY 2.3

Leaving Access

In this Guided Activity you will close the database and exit from Access.

1. Select File | Close Database from the menu bar. The Database window will close and you will see the opening display.

2. Select File | Exit from the menu bar. Access will close and you will return to the Program Manager.

3. If you are finished with Windows at this time, you can also close the Program Manager with File | Exit. You will return to the DOS prompt or DOS Shell.

Command Review

F1, Shift F1 (Help)	Activate context-specific help.
File	Close Database	Close the database file and return to Startup menu.
File	Open Database	Open an existing database file.
File	Exit	Exit from Access and return to the Program Manager.
Help	Cue Cards	Activate the Cue Cards help system.

Exercises

In these exercises you will use the computer for additional practice with Access. Begin Windows and start Access as usual.

1. Use the File | Open Database command to determine what sample databases have been stored on your computer or local area network. The standard Microsoft Access setup program will create three databases. List the names of all the databases on the default drive here. You may have to switch directories to locate the sample databases.

2. Use the File | Open Database command to open the NWIND database. List the names of the tables stored in this database. How many forms and reports are defined with this database?

3. Use Help | Cue Cards and choose the first command, See a quick overview. Cue Cards will display a Quick Overview box that describes the Access data objects. You worked through part of this in a Guided Activity in this unit. Complete the work by clicking through all of the choices in this menu. Describe the examples used to illustrate the database, tables, queries, forms, reports, macros, and modules.

Review Questions

1. Describe the minimum hardware required to run Microsoft Access.

2. Give the purposes for having the Access program group on your Windows desktop.

3. Describe the components of the Database window in Access.

4. Why would a user want to use a toolbar button instead of the corresponding pull-down menu?

5. Discuss the various ways to receive on-line Help about Microsoft Access. Which is preferred, and why?

6. What are the advantages of using an Access form to add and view data, instead of using the datasheet alone?

7. Describe the differences between Access forms and reports. When would each be preferred, and why?

8. Give the purpose for each of the following toolbar buttons:

a.   e.

b.   f.

c.   g.

d.   h.

9. Suppose your company has just purchased Access and wants to teach managers how to use it. What documentation is available for this purpose?

10. How do the Access Cue Cards differ from the regular Access Help system?

Key Terms

[F1] Function key	Design view	Open button
[Shift][F1] Help	Edit menu	Query
.MDB file	File menu	Query-by-Example (QBE)
Access Basic	Form	Report
Access icon	Form view	Security menu
Access program group	Help button	Startup menu
Command button	Help icon	Table
Cue Cards	Macro	Toolbar button
Database window	Module	ToolTips
Datasheet view	New button	View menu
Design button	Object button	Window menu

Documentation Research

Use the printed documentation and the on-line Help available with Microsoft Access to answer the following questions. If you use one of the manuals, provide the page number for your reference in that manual.

1. What is the purpose of the File | Compact Database command in the main Access menu?

2. Using the Microsoft Access window help topic, list the seven mode and locking key status messages that appear in the status bar in the lower-right corner of the Access database window.

3. Start Cue Cards from the menu bar and select the Build a Database with Tables option, then select the first choice—See what databases and tables are. Describe the sample databases and tables illustrated in this Cue Cards selection.

4. Open the main Access Help menu and select Contents. What topics are available through this table of contents?

5. Suppose you open one database, then open a second database. What happens to the first database?

6. Use the [Shift][F1] Help command to learn about the buttons on the toolbar.

Building a Table

This unit will introduce you to building and working with database tables. It will demonstrate how to open an existing table and access it in Datasheet view, as well as how to create a new table and populate it with data values. It will describe the various data types available in Access and show how to make changes to the design of a table in Design view. The unit concludes with a discussion about printing the contents of the table.

Learning Objectives

At the completion of this unit you should know

1. the eight data types used in Access,
2. the features of Datasheet view and Design view,
3. the function of the various components of the table window.

At the completion of this unit you should be able to

1. open an existing database and create a new database,
2. create a new table and define fields for the table,
3. make changes to the table definition,
4. add data to a table and make changes to the contents of the table,
5. resize the columns and rows in a datasheet,
6. print the contents of a datasheet,
7. use the Table Wizards to create a new table.

Important Commands

 Esc

F6

 Ins

Shift F2

Shift Tab

 Tab

Edit | Insert Row

File | New Database

File | Open Database

File | Print

File | Save Table

View | Table Properties

Creating a New Database

As discussed in the previous unit, Microsoft Access uses a single comprehensive database file to hold all of the database objects. To open an existing database, use the File menu and select Open Database. To create a new database, use the File | New Database command, then specify the name for your database. Remember that file names must be eight or fewer characters, with no embedded spaces. If you choose a different file extension than .MDB, Access may not be able to find your database when you open it again.

GUIDED ACTIVITY 3.1 ❋

Creating a New Database

In this Guided Activity you will create a new database and will store the .MDB file on the drive of your choice. We will use this database for the remainder of this unit.

1. If you have not already started Access in Windows, do so at this time by choosing its icon. If the Welcome to Access screen appears, double-click on the Control-menu box to reach the opening screen.

2. Use the File | New Database command to create a new database. You will see the New Database window, shown in Figure 3.1.

FIGURE 3.1
*New database
window*

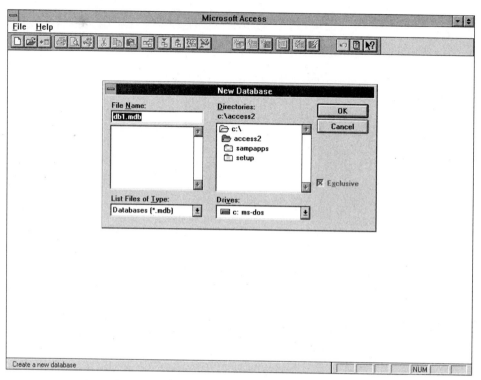

NOTE *Your machine may have Access installed in a different directory than shown in the figure.*

3. If you want to place the database file on the default disk drive, go on to the next step. If you want to place the file on a different disk drive, select the Drives list box and choose the proper drive.

NOTE *You can also type in the drive letter and path when you type in the name of the database file.*

4. Next, type First in the File Name box and press ⏎. Access will create a file called FIRST.MDB on the default disk drive, and display the FIRST Database window shown in Figure 3.2. Leave this window in place for now and we will create a table for it in the next Guided Activity.

CHECKPOINT 3A How many characters long can the database name be? Remember that Access must use regular DOS file name conventions for the database name.

The Database Window Toolbar

After you open a database window, Access will display the **toolbar** shown in Figure 3.3. The first two buttons allow you to make a new database or open an existing database. There is nothing to print now so the Print and Print Preview buttons are grayed out. The Cut, Copy, and Paste buttons let you work with the Windows Clipboard. You can create a new query, form, or report from this toolbar. Undo is grayed out, indicating we haven't done any operations that can be undone. The last two buttons represent Cue Cards and Help, respectively. The Help button will give you help about the *next* object you click on the Access desktop. We will cover the other buttons in later units.

FIGURE 3.2
First database window

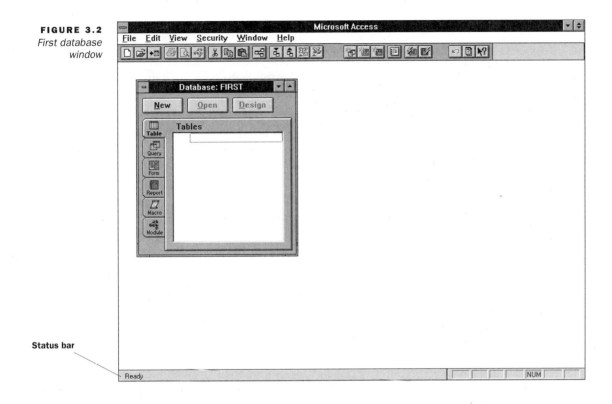

Status bar

Working with the Table Window

You work directly with Access tables in the Datasheet view, in which rows represent records and columns represent fields. This section also describes the process of creating a new table in Design view and the process of adding data to a table in Datasheet view.

Datasheet View

The Datasheet view is similar to a spreadsheet. Access displays the records in rows down the screen with fields in columns. You can scroll through the records one at a time or a screenful at a time. As with other Windows applications, Access lets you change the size of the rows and the columns to fit your data values. We will cover that procedure in a later section of this unit.

FIGURE 3.3
Database toolbar buttons

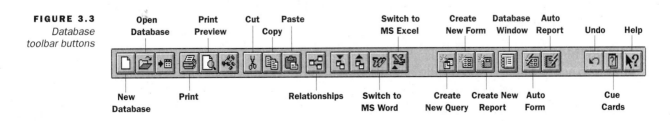

Design View

Before you can add data to a new table, you must first create the structure for the table in the Access Design view. In this mode you define each of the fields in the table. That is, you provide a name for the field, its field type, and an optional description of the field. There are numerous *field properties* for such things as field size, format, default values, validation rules, and index information. We will examine some of these properties in a Guided Activity.

Before you save the table definition, you must provide a primary key that uniquely identifies each record in the table. If you don't have a unique key in your field list, Access can create a counter field for this purpose.

Use the File | Save command to save the table definition. Access will ask you to enter a *table name*. As with most other Access objects, table names may have up to 64 characters, including spaces and punctuation. The table name should be explicit; that is, it should describe the contents of the table without ambiguity. Within a single database, the table names must be unique. You may, however, use the same table name in *different* databases.

The Table Window Toolbar

Access provides shortcut buttons in the toolbar for Datasheet and Design views, as illustrated in Unit 2. They are located just below the File menu. The triangle with ruler and pencil represents Design view, while the spreadsheet icon invokes the Datasheet view. If you have a table window open in either mode, you can immediately switch to the other view by clicking the corresponding button. If you have made changes to the design, Access will ask for your permission to save those changes before switching to Datasheet view. Figure 3.4 shows the buttons in the table window toolbar for Design view. For information about other commands in the toolbar, use the Help system entry for Toolbars.

FIGURE 3.4
Table toolbar buttons (Design view)

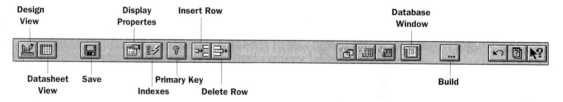

Design View   Display Properties   Insert Row   Database Window

Datasheet View   Save   Primary Key   Build
Indexes   Delete Row

The Status Bar

The lower portion of the desktop in Figure 3.2 contains the Access *status bar*. It will display unless you have elected not to display it.

NOTE *Although not covered here, this and other settings can be changed with the View/Options command.*

The left portion of the status bar shows messages such as field descriptions and menu explanations. The right portion shows specific modes and lock key status indicators. The modes and lock key messages are described in Table 3.1.

TABLE 3.1	MODE	MESSAGE MEANING
Modes and lock key messages	FLTR	A filter has been applied, limiting which records appear.
	MOV	The Move mode is on, in preparation for moving a column. Press [Esc] to release.
	EXT	The Extend mode is on, affecting selection of words, fields, and records. Press [Esc] to release.
	CAPS	Caps Lock is on.
	NUM	Num Lock is on.
	SCRL	Scroll Lock is on.
	OVR	The Overtype mode is on. Press [Ins] to release.

Types of Data Fields

Your database may include a wide range of objects. Access employs eight different *data types* to model your objects' attributes. Some data types represent numeric information while others represent text and dates. Each data type requires a different amount of storage space. These are described below along with examples and an explanation of the uses for each data type.

TEXT FIELDS represent attributes or short descriptions of objects. You would use text fields for such things as a name, address, state, color, size, manufacturer, course title, or telephone number. Remember that most database designers use text fields for number-like values that would not be used for arithmetic. Thus zip codes, Social Security numbers, and box numbers would be text fields. You can specify the size of the field in characters; Access will not allow you to exceed that length, so select a field size that would hold your largest data items. It is possible to lengthen a field after you start using the database, however. The maximum length is 255 characters.

MEMO FIELDS are used for long textual descriptions or comments. Memo fields expand to fit the length of the entry in each record, up to a maximum of 64,000 characters per field. You can scroll a memo field in an Access form to display its contents a few lines at a time. By contrast, text fields are fixed-length fields and take up space whether you store anything in the field or not; you might not want to use a text field where the contents of the field may be quite long or unpredictable in length.

NUMBER FIELDS are used to hold quantitative measurements about items in your database. The rule of thumb is to use a number field for an item when you might want to perform arithmetic operations on that field. Examples include number of shares, closing price, number of credit hours earned, grade point average, quantity on hand, and wholesale unit cost. Access provides a separate data type, called currency, for dollar and cents fields described below. It is possible to create custom number field formats. The field size for numeric fields can be chosen to allow integer numbers only, or to permit decimal places, as shown in Table 3.2. Generally, choose the shortest field size that will hold the largest number you will store in the database.

TABLE 3.2
Number field sizes

FIELD SIZE	EXPLANATION
Double	10 places, range −1.797*10^308 to 1.797*10^308
Single	6 places, range −3.4*10^38 to 3.4*10^38
Long Integer	no decimals, range −2,147,483,648 to 2,147,483,647
Integer	no decimals, range −32,768 to 32,767
Byte	no decimals, range 0 to 255

DATE/TIME FIELDS contain date and time information about events. Examples include date of birth, course drop date, inventory transaction time, and date and time of admission to a hospital. Dates can be shown in four different formats, and time can be shown in three formats. You can also create custom date and time formats. The Access help screen contains instructions for creating custom formats. Remember that Access will not accept a nonexistent date for a date/time field. Examples of date and time formats are shown in Table 3.3.

TABLE 3.3
Date and time formats

FORMAT	EXAMPLE
General Date (default)	3/1/95 04:14 PM
Long Date	Wednesday, March 1, 1995
Medium Date	01-Mar-95
Short Date	3/1/95
Long Time	4:16:33 PM
Medium Time	04:16 PM
Short Time	16:16 (military time)

CURRENCY FIELDS are used to store numeric money amounts. By default, these fields show a dollar sign (or other currency indicator as set up in Windows) in front of the value and show two decimal places, as in $99.95. Negative numbers are enclosed in parentheses. Numbers larger than 1,000 have a comma separator between hundreds and thousands place (although this too can be modified in Windows). Currency fields can contain up to 15 digits to the left of the decimal point and up to 4 digits to the right of the decimal point. It is also possible to design a custom format for number fields that makes them appear with dollar signs, commas, and fixed number of decimal places.

COUNTER FIELDS are special numeric fields that increment (increase) by one in each successive record. They count up as you add new records, usually starting with 1. You could use a counter field for a check number, purchase order number, or any other sequential value. Counter fields are frequently used as the primary key for a table. Counter field values *cannot* be changed once entered.

YES/NO FIELDS contain only the values yes (true) or no (false). They can be used to reflect a condition that is met or not met by the data item. Examples include in-state student, graduate student, local alumni, taxable item, and over 21. In each case the answer to a question can be stated as yes or no.

OLE OBJECT FIELDS are a special Windows feature in which another *Object* can be *Linked* to the originating application and *Embedded* in the Access database. The OLE object could be a spreadsheet, unformatted text, a graph, a picture, or a sound. A linked OLE object remains tied to the originating application; if there are subsequent changes to the OLE object in that application, the changes are automatically made to the Access database that contains the OLE object. OLE fields are discussed in Unit 12.

Creating a New Table

In this section we design a table for sale merchandise at the Hunter River Sporting Goods store. In the following Guided Activity you will actually input the table specifications. The sale merchandise table contains information about regular products that the store wants to promote. Preliminary fields for this table should consist of those listed in Table 3.4.

TABLE 3.4
Fields for sales promotion

FIELD NAME	DESCRIPTION
Stock Number	A unique five-character code that identifies an item (primary key)
Description	The item's description
Category	The store category selling this item; choices are Camping, Sports, Clothing, Hunting, Other
Unit Cost	The most current cost per unit of the item
Quantity on Hand	The current quantity in stock
Date of Last Order	The date the product was last ordered

Stock Number, Description, and Category are all text data type fields. Unit Cost is a currency data type field. Quantity on Hand is number data type. Date of Last Order is a date/time field.

There are three steps in creating a table:

- Give the name, data type, and field size for each field in the table. You may add an optional field description that will appear in the bottom of the table window whenever you select that field in a table or form.

- Name the field(s) you will use as the table's primary key.

- Save the table structure with the File | Save command.

GUIDED ACTIVITY 3.2 ✳

Creating a New Table

This Guided Activity will lead you through the process of creating the table definition for a new table. If you have not already completed Guided Activity 3.1, do so
at this time.

1. Your computer should be in Access with the FIRST Database window open.
    (Refer to Guided Activity 3.1.)

2. Click on the Table icon in the Database window to switch to Table mode, then
    click on the New button to create a new table. Click on the New Table button.

NOTE *We will take a look at the Table Wizards later in this unit.*

3. Access will open a Table window in Design view as shown in Figure 3.5. Note
    that there are blank rows for the field definitions.

4. In the first row, type in the first Field Name, Stock Number. Press ⟦Tab⟧ to finish
    the entry.

5. Access will automatically move the pointer to the next column, Data Type, and
    highlight the default value, Text. That is the correct data type for this field. Note
    that the lower pane of the Table window shows the highlighted default size of
    this field to be 50 characters. Press the ⟦F6⟧ function key to switch the pointer to
    the bottom pane and key in 5, replacing the 50. Press ⟦F6⟧ again to return the
    pointer to the Data Type column. Accept this choice by pressing ⟦Tab⟧.

FIGURE 3.5
*Empty table
design window*

**Field
Selector
button**

Bottom pane

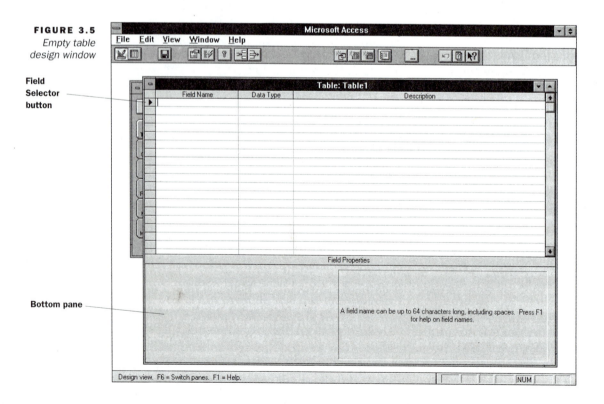

6. In the Description column, type `A unique five-character code that uniquely identifies an item (primary key).` and press `Enter`.

7. Repeat steps 4–6 with the second field, `Description`. It is also Text type with a field size of 25 characters. Its description is `The item's description.`

8. The pointer should be on the third row of the Table window. Key in the third field's name, `Category`, and press `Tab`. For this Text field type in `10` for the field size. The description for this field is `The store department selling this item; choices are Camping, Sports, Clothing, Hunting, Other`. Press `Enter` to complete this field's definition.

9. For the fourth field, input `Unit Cost` for the field name and press `Tab` to go on to the Data type column.

10. This field will be Currency type. To display all the data types, click on the arrow at the right of the Data Type drop-down list box.

11. From this list choose the Currency type with the mouse and press `Tab` to complete the entry.

CHECKPOINT 3B Can you type in the data type instead of choosing from the drop-down list box?

12. The description is `The most current cost per unit for this item.`

13. Next enter the `Quantity on Hand` field name. Its data type is Number. Press `F6` to move the pointer to the lower pane.

14. Press the arrow on the right of the Field Size box to display numeric subtypes. Select Integer and press `F6` to move the cursor back to the top pane and tab to the Description area. The description for this field is `The current quantity in stock.`

15. The final field is `Date of Last Order`. Its field type is Date/Time, and you should select Medium Date from the Format box in the lower pane. The description is `The date the product was last ordered.`

16. Access requires that every table have a unique primary key. We will declare that the Stock Number field is the primary key. Use the mouse to position the pointer at the first field. Then click on the key icon found in the toolbar of the desktop. Access will place a smaller version of the key to the left of this field.

17. Figure 3.6 shows the table definition at this point. Go back and review the entries to be sure that each is correct. You can use the mouse to move the pointer to any item that is not correct.

18. Finally, you are ready to save the table. Give the File | Save command. When prompted, key in `Sale Merchandise` as the table name and choose OK or press `Enter`. Access will save the table in the FIRST database file.

19. Double-click on the Control-menu box (or use the File | Close command) to close the Table window and redisplay the Database window. Figure 3.7 shows the First database window with your newly saved table.

FIGURE 3.6
Filled-in table design window

Primary Key

Field properties

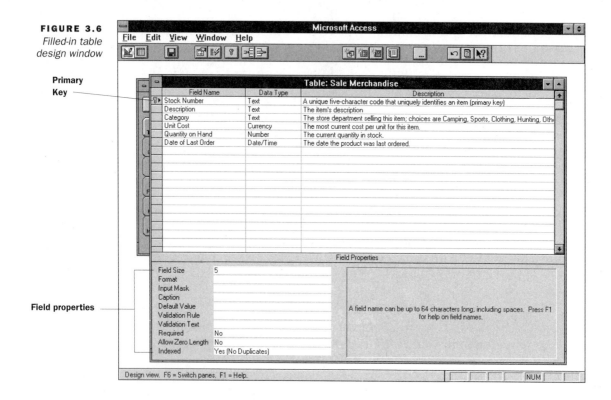

FIGURE 3.7
First database window after creating table

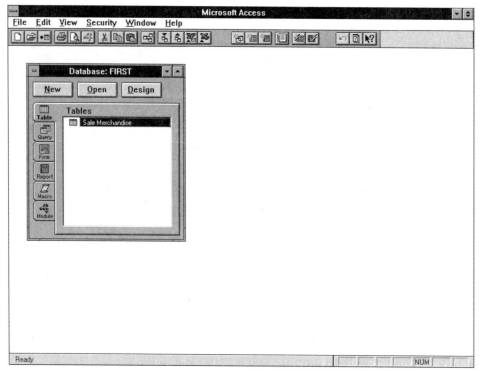

Table and Field Properties

You have seen that the Table window bottom pane contains property boxes for each of the fields. This pane will change slightly with different field types. The following list names the field properties and describes their meanings. For more information you can refer to Chapter 8 in the *Microsoft Access User's Guide.*

FIELD SIZE This is the length of the field in characters for text fields, or the subtype of field (integer, single, double) for number fields.

FORMAT This property enables you to customize the way the field will appear. You might use this property to format telephone numbers with parentheses around the area code or insert hyphens into Social Security numbers.

DECIMAL PLACES The number of decimal places to maintain for this number field.

INPUT MASK A pattern for all data to be entered into this field. An *input mask* is useful for fields such as telephone numbers and Social Security numbers. Only the variable information is stored in the field, not the mask.

CAPTION Ordinarily, Access displays the full field name as its caption. You can provide an alternate caption with this property.

DEFAULT VALUE This property lets you establish a default value for the field that will always appear when a new record is added. The user can override the value when the record is added or edited. Unless changed, the initial default value for text and date fields is blank, and for number and currency fields it is zero.

VALIDATION RULE This property allows you to specify a condition for valid values. If the field does not meet the validation rule, Access displays the validation text and will prompt the user to enter a valid value.

VALIDATION TEXT This is the message that you want to appear if the field does not meet the validation rule. The message should explain why the field does not meet the validation rule. If you give no validation text for a given rule, Access will warn `The value you entered is prohibited by the validation rule set for this field.`

REQUIRED Lets you determine whether the user must make an entry in this field. Values are yes or no.

ALLOW ZERO LENGTH Lets you determine whether to allow zero-length strings in this field. Values are yes or no.

INDEXED This is a yes/no property that indicates whether Access is to create an index for this field. Indexes are used to speed up access to frequently used fields. If you have a large file, you should establish indexes in the appropriate fields.

NOTE *You can view the primary key and other indexes for a table by clicking the Index button or using the View/Indexes command from the menu bar.*

The *table properties* are used to give a description of the table and a validation rule for the table. To see the Table Properties window use the View | Table Properties command. You can move the Table Properties window by dragging its title bar if it blocks a vital part of the desktop, or you can close the window altogether.

It is very important to complete the design of tables and fields, including proper-ties, *before* going on to create forms and reports. If you establish properties for the fields in Table Design view, Access will copy those properties into forms that you cre-ate. However, any changes made to table and field properties *after* a form is created will not be copied to the form. Particularly important are the Format, Input Mask, Caption, Default, Validation Rule, and Validation Text properties. Also important is the field's Description property, which becomes the Status Bar Text property for a form control containing that field.

Changing the Table Design: Design View

After saving the table you may find that you need to make changes to its design. You may need to add a field, change the size of a field, or remove a field. You can modify the field properties list, providing a caption or setting up validation rules for the field. In most cases Access will let you make the change without losing any data. If you change data type for a field, however, data may be lost, particularly if the new field size is shorter than the original one.

ADDING A NEW FIELD

To add a new field at the end of the table, move the pointer to the next available row and begin typing the field definition. To add a field in the middle of a table, click on the field selector button of the field that will *follow* the new field. Then issue the Edit | Insert Row command (or click the Insert Row button in the toolbar) and Access will open a blank row for you to fill with the new field's definition, moving the other fields down to make room.

MOVING A FIELD TO A DIFFERENT LOCATION IN THE TABLE

To move a field to a different position in the record, first change to Design view. Select the field by clicking on the field selector button to the immediate left of the field name. Access will highlight the entire row. Then click on the field selector but-ton and drag the field to a new location. Release the mouse button when you are sat-isfied with the new location. Access will rearrange the other fields to make room for this field.

DELETING A FIELD FROM THE TABLE

To delete a field definition from the table, click on the field selector button to highlight the field to be deleted. Then press the [Del] key (or click the Delete Row but-ton in the toolbar) and the field will be permanently removed from the table.

NOTE *You will be given a second chance to confirm the change(s) when you close the Design view window or save the table. If you do not save the design changes, Access will reverse all of the changes made since the table was last saved.*

GUIDED ACTIVITY 3.3

Changing the Table Design

In this Guided Activity you will make changes to the Sale Merchandise table's design created in the previous activity. We will add two new fields, and provide a validation rule for the Category field.

1. Make sure that you have the FIRST Database window open on your desktop, and click on the Table button to switch to Table mode.

2. Move the pointer to highlight the Sale Merchandise table.

3. Click the Design button to work with the table in Design view.

4. We will add a new field to the end of the table. Move the pointer to the row following Date of Last Order.

5. The field name is `Now On Order`. It is a Yes/No field and the description is `Is product now on order?`

6. We also need to insert a field into the table before the Category field. Move the pointer and click on the field selector button to the left of the Category row. The whole row will now be selected. Use the Edit|Insert Row command and Access will create a blank row, as shown in Figure 3.8.

7. The new field will be `Vendor`. It is a 15-character Text field whose description is `Name of the product vendor.`

FIGURE 3.8
Table design with inserted row

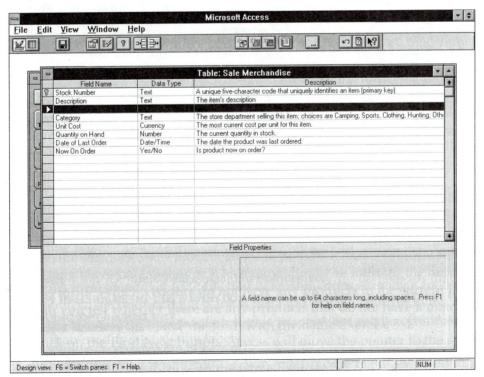

8. Next, we need to add a validation rule to the Category field. Click anywhere in the Category row and press `F6` to move to the bottom pane.

9. Click on the Validation Rule line and enter this expression: `In("Camping", "Sports", "Clothing", "Hunting", "Other")`. As you type the expression it will scroll across the small box. This validation rule will prevent you from entering any other category names not in the list. You can always add more departments to the list at a later time.

10. When you have finished typing the validation rule expression, use the `←` and `→` keys to check it. If you want to see the entire expression at once, click on the Build button at the end of the property line or in the toolbar, shown in Figure 3.9. You can make changes to the expression in this window. When finished with the ***Expression Builder*** window, click on OK to close it.

NOTE *Previous Access versions supported only the* `Shift``F2` *command to open a Zoom box window. Access 2.0 includes both the Expression Builder and zoom box.*

11. Use the File I Save As command to save this table with a new name. When prompted, give `Final Sales Merchandise` as the name. If you had chosen the File I Save command, Access would replace the original table with the revised table; with File I Save As you now have two tables under different names.

FIGURE 3.9
Expression Builder for Category Validation Rule

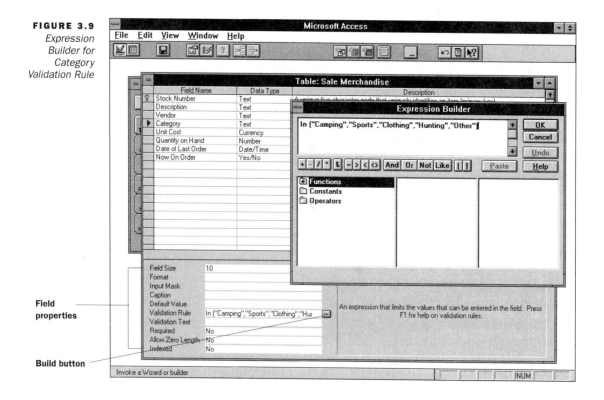

Field properties

Build button

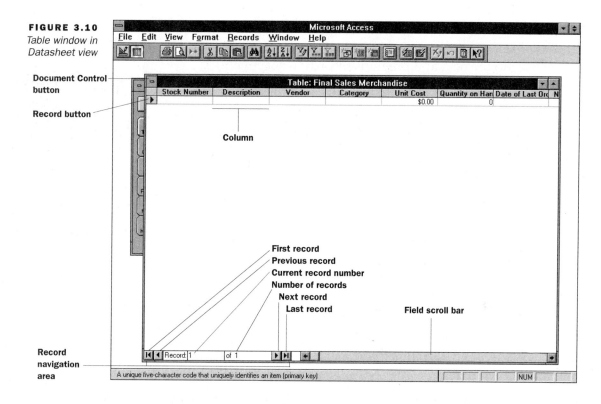

FIGURE 3.10
Table window in Datasheet view

Document Control button

Record button

Column

First record
Previous record
Current record number
Number of records
Next record
Last record

Field scroll bar

Record navigation area

Adding and Editing Data

Now that you have created the table, it is time to add data to the table. This section discusses the procedure for adding data and making changes to data in the table. Access uses the Datasheet view for this purpose.

The Table Window in Datasheet View

Access uses the *Table window* to display rows and columns in Datasheet view. Figure 3.10 shows the Table window. The components of this window and their purposes are explained below.

TITLE BAR shows the name of the table.

DOCUMENT CONTROL BUTTON controls the presentation of the document window.

COLUMN represents a field, with field name at the top of the column.

RECORD BUTTON The right-pointing triangle shows the location of the current record. This button changes shape as you work with a table. For instance, when it appears as a pencil, you have made changes that have not yet been saved in the database.

NAVIGATION BUTTONS move the record pointer. Individual buttons are explained below.

CURRENT RECORD SELECTION contains the current record number with record selection buttons that allow you to move the record pointer.

NUMBER OF RECORDS shows the total number of records in the table.

NEXT RECORD BUTTON The right- and left-pointing triangles will move the record pointer to the next and previous records, respectively.

LAST RECORD BUTTON The right-pointing triangle with vertical bar will move to the last record in the table.

FIRST RECORD BUTTON The left-pointing triangle with vertical bar will move to the first record in the table.

RECORD SCROLL BAR If there are more records than one screen can hold, Access will display a vertical record scroll bar at the right edge of the window. (Not seen in Figure 3.10.)

FIELD SCROLL BAR The table contains a horizontal field scroll bar if the table is wider than the screen can display at one time.

GUIDED ACTIVITY 3.4 ✳

Adding Data to the Table

In this Guided Activity you will add several records to the table created in the previous activity.

1. Open the FIRST Database window and select the Table button in that window.

2. If it is not already highlighted, move the pointer to the Final Sales Merchandise table.

3. Click the Open command button. Access will open the Table window for this table. You should see columns headed with the field names for this table, similar to Figure 3.10.

4. With the pointer positioned on the first row in the first column, type in the first Stock Number, 13021. If you make any mistakes, rekey the correct value.

5. Press ⌨Tab to move to the next column. Type in the Description, Cold 30 Cooler. If you notice an error in an earlier column, you can use the mouse to reposition the pointer, or use the ⌨Shift⌨Tab command to move to a previous column.

6. Press ⌨Tab and type in the Vendor, Icicle.

7. Press ⌨Tab and type in the Category name, Camp. You are deliberately misspelling this name.

CHECKPOINT 3C What does Access do with the category name you keyed in?

8. Click OK, then enter the correct category spelling, Camping. Press ⌨Tab, and type in the Wholesale Cost, 59.95.

9. Press ⌨Tab and type in the Quantity on Hand, 12.

10. Press ⌨Tab and type in the Date of Last Order, 5/4/93.

11. Press ⟦Tab⟧ and type in the Now On Order value, No. Or, just press ⟦Tab⟧ because No automatically displays here. This is the final field of the first record. Note that Access scrolled the columns over to display this field; the first column doesn't appear on the display.

12. Key in the remaining record values as shown below:

13034	Cold 36 Cooler	Icicle	Camping	129.95	7	5/4/93	No
13037	Ice Cold Lunch Tote	Icicle	Camping	14.95	3	5/4/93	No
13066	40-Qt. Cooler Kit	Slaw	Camping	29.95	0	4/15/93	Yes
20238	Larry Bird 33 Basketball	Johnson	Sports	19.95	5	8/2/93	No
20239	Girls League Basketball	Johnson	Sports	22.95	3	8/2/93	No
20241	NCAA Tourney Basketball	Johnson	Sports	24.95	10	10/4/93	No

13. Figure 3.11 shows the Datasheet view for this table after the data is entered. Note that your date entries appear in DD-Mon-YY medium date format as specified when you entered the table definition. We'll use this table in the next Guided Activity.

Moving the Record Pointer

Notice the value of the current record number at the bottom of the table window. It should agree with the location of the current record button in the left margin of the table. You can manipulate the record pointer in several ways.

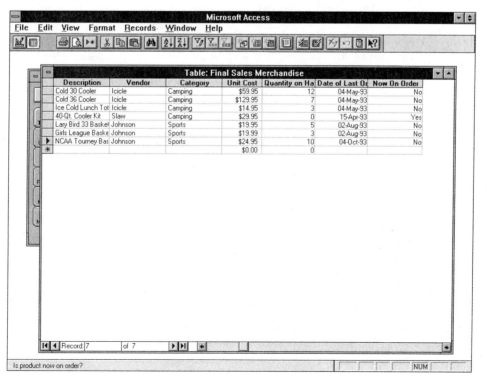

FIGURE 3.11
Table window with data added

USE ⎡Tab⎤ AND ⎡Shift⎤⎡Tab⎤ KEYS

The ⎡Tab⎤ key will move the pointer right to the next field in the current record, or down and left to the first field of the next record if you are in the last field when you press ⎡Tab⎤. ⎡Shift⎤⎡Tab⎤ has the opposite effect: it moves you left to the previous field.

USE THE MOUSE POINTER

You can simply move the mouse pointer to any field in the desired record and click the left button. The record pointer will automatically move to the field in that record.

USE THE ARROW KEYS

You can use the ⎡↑⎤ and ⎡↓⎤ keys to move the pointer to previous or next records. You can use the ⎡←⎤ and ⎡→⎤ keys to move to previous or next fields, as well. The default setup is for the ⎡→⎤ key to duplicate the effect of the ⎡Tab⎤ key.

NOTE *You can change the meaning of the right and left arrow keys so that they move from character to character in the same field instead of moving to adjacent fields. This and other custom settings can be accomplished with the View | Options command.*

USE THE NEXT/PREVIOUS RECORD BUTTONS

The next and previous record buttons are located on either side of the current record indicator in the table. Click either button to move a record at a time in either direction.

USE THE FIRST/LAST RECORD BUTTONS

The first and last record buttons are located next to the previous and next buttons at the bottom of the Table window. Clicking these buttons will take you to the table's first or last records, respectively.

USE THE SCROLL BARS

Like other Windows objects, Access uses scroll bars in the Datasheet view. The horizontal scroll bar at the bottom of the table appears when there are fields that do not appear in the table window. The vertical scroll bar at the right side of the table appears when there are records that do not appear in the window.

GUIDED ACTIVITY 3.5 ✳

Moving the Record Pointer

In this Guided Activity you will practice moving the record pointer.

1. Make sure the Final Sales Merchandise table window is open in Datasheet view on your desktop.

2. Position the record pointer at the first record by clicking on its record selector button with the mouse.

3. Press the ⬇ key 2 times to position the record pointer at record 3.

4. Use the mouse to click the last record button. Note the value that appears in the current record number.

5. Use the mouse pointer to click the minimize button in the upper-right corner.

CHECKPOINT 3D What happens to the table when it is minimized?

6. Click on the table icon in the lower part of the desktop. Select Restore from the Control-menu box.

7. Click on the first record button in the record navigation area in the lower part of the window.

Changing the Table's Appearance

You may want to make changes to the way the table appears in Datasheet view. It is easy to do so by dragging the table's row and column borders with the mouse. For example, in the last table (shown in Figure 3.11), some fields were quite wide while others were narrow.

GUIDED ACTIVITY 3.6

Changing the Table in Datasheet View

This Guided Activity will show you how to make changes to the physical appearance of rows and columns in the table's Datasheet view.

1. We will begin with the Final Sales Merchandise table in Datasheet view. Notice that each column is the same width in the Datasheet view, regardless of its contents.

2. Practice slowly moving the mouse pointer over the border between the Unit Cost and Quantity on Hand columns *in the field name area* of the table window. The pointer should change to a double-headed arrow pointing left and right. If your cursor does not change its shape, be sure that you are moving it in the area just above the first record.

3. Hold down the left mouse button and slowly drag the pointer to the left. Notice that the Unit Cost field will get smaller, and the following fields move over in its place. Adjust the column's width until you are satisfied that the header (field name) fits, but make it no wider than that. Release the mouse button when you are finished.

4. Next, move the pointer to the border between the Quantity on Hand and the Last Order Date fields. You may have to use the Field scroll bar to move to this area.

FIGURE 3.12
*Resized table
window in
Datasheet view*

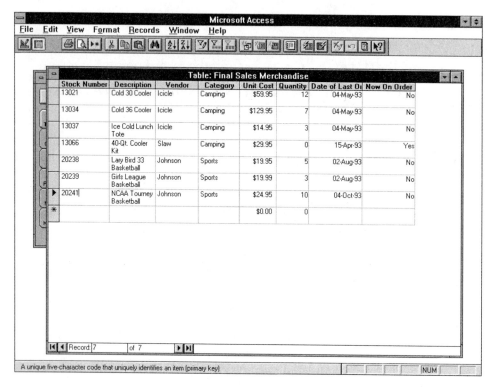

5. Following the same procedure as in step 3, drag the border to the left until just the word Quantity shows in the field name area, then release the mouse button.

6. Notice that the Description field seems to be chopped off. We can make this column wider, or adjust the row height and have the Description appear on two lines. We'll do the latter.

7. Move the pointer to the record button area between records 1 and 2. Notice that the pointer changes shape to a two-headed arrow pointing up and down. If your cursor does not change shape, make sure it is just to the left of the first column.

8. While holding down the left mouse button, drag the border down until there are approximately two lines for each record. Notice that longer descriptions will now spread over both lines. Release the mouse button when you are finished.

9. Use the File | Save Table command to save the changes to your worksheet. Access will remember layout changes made to a table or other database object. Figure 3.12 shows the table window after these appearance changes. Remember that nothing has changed with your data itself, just the way it appears in this view.

Editing Data in the Table

You may want to add more data to a table, or make changes to the contents of records already in the database. Access makes it easy to do so in Datasheet view. Simply use the mouse pointer to select the record and field you wish to change. Then type in the correction.

The last status box in the lower-right portion of the Access desktop shows the insert status. Access starts in *insert mode*; that is, if you position the cursor in a word and begin typing, characters to the right of the pointer are moved over to allow space for the new characters. If you press the [Ins] key, Access will display OVR in the insert status box, indicating that you are in *Overtype mode*. Any new characters typed in at the current insertion point will *replace* characters already in the word.

Changes to the table's field values are made permanent when you move the record pointer to a new record. If Access displays a *pencil icon* in the record selection button, it means that that record has changed but has not yet been saved to the database. You can issue the File | Save Table command at any time to save all of the changes.

GUIDED ACTIVITY 3.7 ✳

Editing Data in the Table

In this Guided Activity you will make some changes to the field values in the table, and work with the validation rule for the Category field.

1. Make sure that the Final Sales Merchandise table is open on your desktop.

2. Move the pointer to the Category field of the first record.

3. Replace the Camping category with Coolers and press [Enter]. What happens? Remember that you established a validation rule for category names.

4. Change the Coolers back to Camping.

HINT *You can do this quickly with the Edit/Undo Current Record command.*

5. Move the pointer to the record with Stock Number 20239. Change the Unit Cost from 22.95 to 19.99.

6. Move the pointer to the date field of the same record. Change the date to 8/32/93. What happens? Remember that Access automatically checks for invalid dates and prompts you when it finds one that is invalid. If you cannot fill in a valid date in a date/time field, it is best to leave it blank.

7. Change the date back to 8/2/93.

8. If a small pencil icon appears in the record button, Access has *not* yet committed your changes to the database. Your changes to the table are made permanent when you move the pointer to another record or save the table with the File | Save Table command.

Printing the Data from a Table

A simple print capability is built into the Datasheet view. You can print all the records in the table, or print certain records by clicking their record selection buttons. Activate print by clicking the Print Preview button in the toolbar. This button will format the datasheet and show a report preview on the screen. You have the option of scrolling through the print preview or zooming in on a portion of the report for careful scrutiny. You can send the output to the printer or cancel the print request and return to the datasheet.

Our sporting goods sales report will resemble a spreadsheet with boxes around each field. Although it is easy to invoke, this datasheet print facility lacks basic formatting capabilities that are found in the Report mode of the database, to be discussed in more detail in Unit 6.

GUIDED ACTIVITY 3.8

Printing the Datasheet

This Guided Activity will demonstrate how to print the table in Datasheet view.

1. Open the Final Sales Merchandise table window if it is not already open.

2. Use the mouse pointer to select the Print Preview tool button, or use the File | Print Preview command from the keyboard.

3. After a few seconds you will see the first page of the datasheet in the preview window. While in the datasheet preview, the pointer resembles a magnifying glass. You can move it to any part of the page and click the left mouse button to zoom in on that portion of the output. Figure 3.13 shows the initial Print Preview window, and Figure 3.14 shows a zoomed-in portion of that report.

FIGURE 3.13
Print Preview window

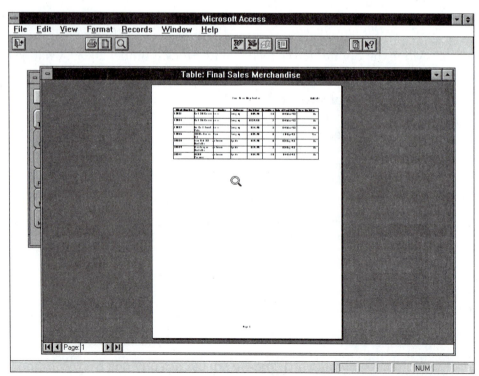

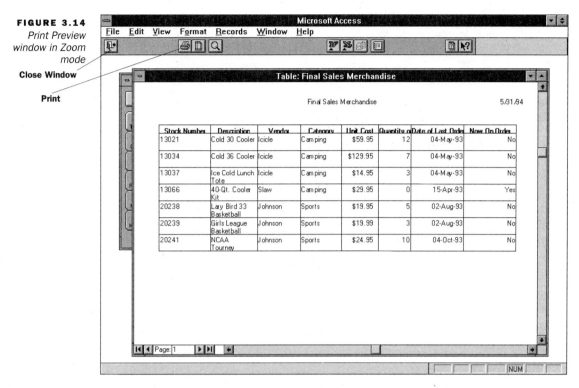

4. Notice that the status line at the bottom of the preview window contains a page number reference. If you had a larger table, you could scroll back and forth through multiple pages of the print preview output, using the page selection buttons in the status area.

5. If you have a printer attached to your computer that is set up for Windows output, click the Print button to send the output to the printer.

6. If you choose not to print this datasheet, click the Close button to return to Datasheet view.

7. Close the table and return to the Database window.

Using Table Wizards

Earlier in this unit we mentioned that Access 2.0 brings a new capability for designing tables. The Table Wizards provide dozens of sample tables, each with appropriate fields for that table. You must choose between Business and Personal categories, then select your table. Choose individual (or all) fields by clicking on the > or >> buttons. Access will quickly create the table and all the appropriate fields and properties. Figure 3.15 shows the opening Table Wizards window.

FIGURE 3.15
*Opening Table
Wizard screen*

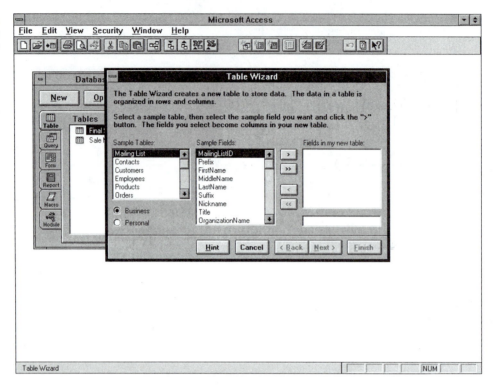

GUIDED ACTIVITY 3.9

Using Table Wizards to Create a Table

This Guided Activity will demonstrate how to use the Table Wizards to create a new table.

1. If you are not already there, return to the FIRST database window. Make sure you are in Table mode.

2. Click on the New button, then click on Table Wizards. You should see a window similar to Figure 3.15 with the Business category selected.

3. Click on the down arrow in the Sample Tables list box until you locate the Projects table.

4. Click on the >> button to select all of the fields in this table, then click Next to go on to the next step.

CHECKPOINT 3E   What would happen if you clicked the > button instead of >>?

5. In Figure 3.16, Access has displayed Projects as the name for this new table. Accept this suggestion and click Next to let Access choose a primary key for you.

6. Click Next in the following screen: the Projects table is not related to any existing table.

FIGURE 3.16
*Table Wizard
screen after
step 5*

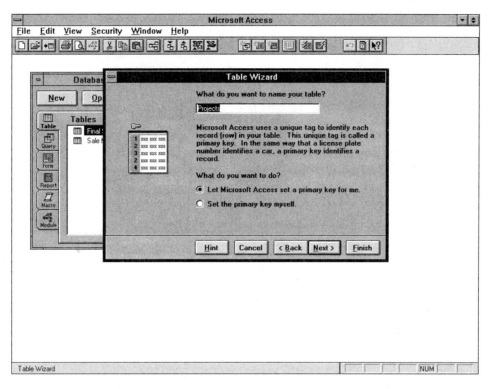

7. In Figure 3.17 you can choose to modify the table design or open the table in Datasheet view. Select modify design and click Finish. Figure 3.17 shows the new table in Design view.

FIGURE 3.17
*Design view for
Projects table*

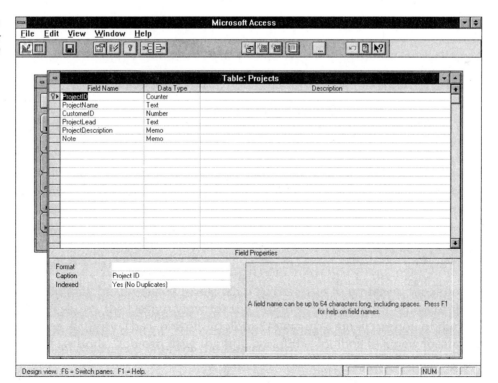

8. For now, close the table without making any changes.

Command Review

Esc	Undo change in current field or record.
F6	Move between upper and lower window panes in Design view.
Ins	Cycle between Overtype and Insert modes.
Shift F2	Open zoom box.
Shift Tab	Move to previous column or box.
Tab	Move to next column or box. Shift Tab moves to previous column.
Edit | Insert Row	Insert new row into table following selected row.
File | New Database	Create a new database file.
File | Open Database	Open an existing database file.
File | Save Table	Save layout changes made to table.
File | Print Preview	Enter Print Preview mode for selected table.
View | Table Properties	Examine and set table properties.

Exercises

1. Create a new table called Employees in the FIRST database. Fields are shown below, along with data type and size. The primary key is the Employee Number field. You should make up an appropriate description for each field.

Field Name	Data Type	Field Size
Employee Number	Text	11
First Name	Text	10
Last Name	Text	15
Department	Text	10
Date of Hire	Date/Time	
Current Salary	Currency	0 decimal places

2. Add the following data to the Employees table. You should place your own name as the last record in the table with suitable information. How would you handle Barbara Smith's middle initial? Print the datasheet after you save it to the database.

123-44-5678	Mark Cameron	Accounting	6/19/93	25,400
666-77-1111	Kelsey Palmer	Sales	1/29/93	21,200
001-42-0009	Elizabeth Crow	Sales	2/1/90	40,000
555-66-7890	William Prince	Shipping	11/30/92	16,955
987-65-4321	Barbara K. Smith	Sales	8/19/78	35,400
124-76-0000	John Roberts	Accounting	3/4/92	22,600
234-45-8237	Jean Sullivan	Sales	12/01/91	16,200

3. Add a new field to your Employee table definition. Called Part-Time, it is a Yes/No field that indicates whether an employee is considered part-time only. Palmer and Sullivan are considered part-time employees. Print the revised datasheet.

4. Open the FIRST database, then create a new table using the Table Wizards. From the Personal tables, select the Exercise Log table and copy all the fields over to a new table. List the field names in this new table and the data type for each field. (*Hint*: Choose the Design View button to see DataType.)

5. Open the FIRST database, then create a new table using the Table Wizards. From the Business tables, select the Customers table and copy all of the fields over to a new table called Current Customers. List the field names and the data type for each field. Show the input mask for the phone number fields.

6. Open the HUNT database found on the Student Data Disk. We will be using this database for the remaining activities and exercises in this book. It duplicates the work you did with the FIRST database in this unit and adds many new objects for the Hunter River store.

   a. List the tables in this database.

   b. Open the Employees table and print a copy of its contents.

   c. Open the Customers table and write out its structure.

Review Questions *

1. What data files does Microsoft Access use to store your database and its objects?
   tables in an mdb.
2. What are the purposes of the Access Datasheet view? to view all data, to update information
3. Why are the toolbar buttons useful? Are there alternatives to using them?
   Because they can be quickly accessed. Yes, keyboard strokes.

4. Explain the purpose of each of the following Access data types. Give an example field for each data type.

   a. Text — short description. (First Name for Ex.)

   b. Memo — long description or Comments. (Ms. Smith has blue hair)

   c. Number — quantitative measurements. (3+4) or ~~(●●●●●●)~~ (AIC of 8.2)

   d. Yes/No — logical Yes, No or True, false

   e. OLE Object — embedded objects (Excel Spreadsheet, Word document)

5. Explain the reasons for choosing each one of the following field sizes for a number field. Give an example of a field for each field size category.

   a. Double — large mathematical equations w/ decimals or large salary or price of a house

   b. Long Integer — large math equations w/o decimals

   c. Integer — math equations w/o decimals

   d. Byte — # times to be seen by a Dr. in one day, plain number

   e. Single — salary, price of item

6. What is meant by each of the following Date/Time formats? Give a sample for each format.

   a. General Date   3/1/95 04:14pm

   b. Long Date   Wednesday March 1, 1995

   c. Medium Date   01-Mar-95

   d. Short Date   3/1/95

   e. Long Time   4:16:33 Pm

7. Explain the use of each of the following field properties:

   a. Format — Customize the way the field will appear. (SS#)

   b. Caption — alternate name to field name

   c. Validation Rule — sets a condition for valid rules (Ex Sports, Company)

   d. Validation Text — error message when you go against a Validation rule.

   e. Indexed — yes/no property that says whether to create index.

8. Discuss the procedure for adding a new field to a table that already contains data. Will any data be lost? go to design view. Enter data name, & type, & descript. Save. No data will be lost.

9. Suppose that one of your columns is a long text field. When it displays in Datasheet view, other columns are pushed off the right side of the screen. What can you do to see more fields on the screen in Datasheet view? move the borders by clicking & dragging.

10. Explain at least three ways to move the record pointer in the Datasheet view.
    ~~(●●●●●●)~~ Click w/ mouse, Use arrow keys, Use next & previous record buttons

Key Terms

Counter field	Insert mode	Table property
Currency field	Memo field	Table window
Data type	Number field	Text field
Date/Time field	OLE Object field	Toolbar
Expression builder	Overtype mode	Validation Rule
Field property	Pencil icon	Validation Text
Field size	Status bar	Yes/No field
Input mask	Table name	

Documentation Research

Use the printed documentation and the on-line Help available with Microsoft Access to answer the following questions. If you use one of the manuals, provide the page number for your reference in that manual.

1. Suppose you created a table within the FIRST database, then decided you wanted to change its name. How would you go about *renaming* the table?

2. Use the Cue Cards facility to learn about changing the *appearance* of your datasheet. What kinds of changes are possible?

3. What are the restrictions on changing a field's *data type*?

4. What are the properties that apply *only* to tables and *not* to fields within the table?

5. Print the on-line Help windows for designing and creating a database.

6. Learn about the various input mask format characters. For example, what is the purpose of the ! format character?

Physicians' Medical Clinic (II): Building a Table

In this exercise you will create a table in the PMC (Physicians' Medical Clinic) database, using the material covered in previous units. You start an Access session, open a database, create the table definition, enter text and numeric values, save the results, and print the datasheet. Read the following instructions carefully—every word is important:

1. As presented in Application A, you were hired to assist with the development of a patient database for the clinic. Some database design planning has already been accomplished, and your next task is to create a table for permanent patient information. Tables for information about specific patient visits, doctors, standard procedures, insurance companies, and other database objects will be created later.

2. Follow the startup procedure outlined in Unit 2 to load Windows and enter Access.

3. To begin the process you must first open a new database in Access. Use the Open Database command from the File menu to open the database. Give the name PMC for this database.

4. To continue the process, you must next create a new table called New Patients. Click on the New button in the Database window to open a new table and then on the New Table button in the New Table dialog box.

5. Next, you should enter field definitions for the New Patients table. Remember that Access suggests that you enter four items for each field: field name, field type, field size, and the definition for each field. That information is shown in the table below. The first field will be the primary key.

Field Name	Field Type/Size	Definition
Patient Number	Text/9	9-character patient identification number (SS #)
First Name	Text/18	Patient's first name followed by middle initial
Last Name	Text/20	Patient's last name
Address Line 1	Text/20	First line of patient's home address
Address Line 2	Text/20	Second (optional) line of patient's home address
City	Text/20	Patient's home address city
State	Text/2	Two-letter abbreviation of patient's home state
Zipcode	Text/9	Patient's home zip code (Zip+Four format)
Date of Birth	Date	Patient's date of birth
Employer Name	Text/30	Patient's primary employer
Insured Name	Text/25	Name of insured holder of health insurance
Insurance Name	Text/20	Patient's health insurance company name
Insurance Policy	Text/20	Patient's health insurance policy number

6. After saving the table definition, you discover you have left out a few fields. Add these two fields to the end of the table definition, then save the results.

Field Name	Field Type/Size	Definition
Insurance Filed	Yes/No	Indicates whether an application is currently on file with the insurance company
Balance Forward	Currency	Current balance owed on clinic account

7. Using *your own information*, open the New Patients table in Datasheet view and add two records to the table. The first record should be your own record as head of household. Make the second record be that of a dependent of yours who will use your own health insurance policy. You may use imaginary data for the patient number and policy number.

8. After saving the information, print the contents of the New Patients table. What is "wrong" with using the normal Access print facility for this table? What would you recommend to resolve the printing problems?

Building a QBE Query

This unit will illustrate the use of Access queries to display data from one or more tables that meets specific conditions called criteria. You will create a simple select query and use the query to sort records and provide totals for groups of records within the database. The unit contains a detailed list of Access expressions and functions that can be used in queries as well as in other Access objects.

Learning Objectives

At the completion of this unit you should know

1. the types of queries available in Access,
2. what kinds of expressions and functions can be used in queries.

At the completion of this unit you should be able to

1. create a simple select query,
2. build a criteria expression for selecting records,
3. sort records and prepare group totals for the dynaset,
4. print the query result,
5. use the Expression Builder to create a query.

Important Commands

+, & operators

date separators

[ ] brackets

Edit | Delete

File | Print Preview

File | New | Query

File | Save Query, File | Save Query As

Query | Run

View | Totals

Query Basics

Access queries provide an easy way to select data that meets certain criteria that you set up. You specify the conditions in the form of an example, hence the name QBE or query-by-example. You choose which fields are retained by the query by dragging the field names from the data tables to the query. Once the query is prepared, you can use the resulting data as the basis for a form, report, graph, or another query.

You can use a query to *link* two or more tables that share common data values. For example, suppose you wanted to link a Department table with the Employees table, showing just those employees who are members of that department. Or you might want to link the products from a particular vendor with information from the Vendor table that is not stored in the Products table. One of the strongest features of Access is its ability to create queries that link two or more tables. Coverage of relational databases and linked tables via queries appears in Unit 8 of this book.

Types of Queries

The *select query* is most common. It provides for selection of records that meet the criteria you specify. After you run the query, the records that meet the criteria are displayed in a datasheet called a *dynaset*. The dynaset's name represents the fact that the *set* of records that match the criteria is *dynamic*; that is, the dynaset changes if the underlying table values change. The dynaset is not a regular data table, although its current contents can be saved as one, if desired.

When you want to make changes to your data, use an *action query*. You can make changes to a selected set of records with one query command. There are four kinds of action queries:

- An *update query* can make changes to an existing table.

- An *append query* can append records to a table.

- A *make-table query* creates a new table with modified records from the query's dynaset.

- A *delete query* is used to delete selected records.

We will not cover action queries in this unit. Action queries are covered in Unit 8 of this book.

A *parameter query* allows you to create a query, save it, then rerun the query whenever desired with *new* QBE grid values. For example, suppose you build a query that specifies a particular department of the store. Each time you run this query, it will select records that match that department. If you make that value a parameter, Access will allow you to input a new value for the query's department criteria without modifying the original query.

Crosstab queries are used to categorize data into groups. Access shows the record count or field sums for the records in each group in a two-dimensional manner. We will not cover crosstab queries in this unit. Crosstab queries are covered in Unit 8 of this book.

The Query Window

Figure 4.1 shows the query design window for a select query. At the top are the tables used in the query. At the bottom of the window is the *QBE grid*. Its columns represent the fields you have added to the query. Each column provides for the field name, sorting instructions, a *show box* for that field, and rows for the QBE *criteria expressions*.

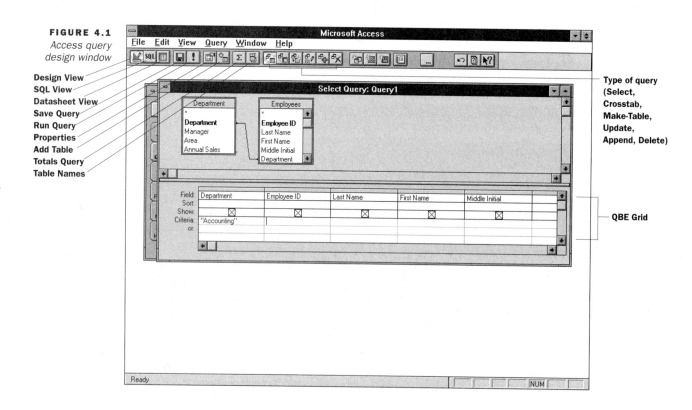

FIGURE 4.1
Access query design window

Building a Select Query

In this section we will discuss how to create a simple select query. There are five steps in building a simple select query in Access. Each step is discussed below.

- Open the Database window and choose New in Query mode.

- Add one or more tables to the query.

- Drag the fields to be added to the query from the tables to the QBE grid.

- Specify field criteria in the QBE grid for inclusion in the query dynaset.

- View the results of the query.

Creating a New Query

The first step is easily accomplished. Once the Database window is open, click on the Query button and then click on the New button. Alternatively, you could click on the New Query button in the toolbar, or use the File | New Query command from the menu bar. You can choose the Query Wizards, new to Access 2.0, or build one of your own. After choosing a new query, you will see the blank query in its Design view.

Adding Tables to the Query

Access shows you a table and/or query list from the current database in the Add Table window. Access 2.0 lets you choose whether to view tables, queries, or both in this window. Select the tables and/or queries that you want to add to this query. Only the fields from these selected tables and queries will be available in the query. Of course, you can add more tables at any time by modifying the design of the query. Figure 4.1 shows two tables in the query, linked by the common Department field. We will cover linked queries in Unit 8. When you are finished adding tables, click the Close button.

Adding Fields to the Query

You can add to a query *all* the fields from a table at one time by double-clicking on the table's title bar, then dragging them to the QBE grid. You can add *individual* fields to a query by dragging them from the table box to the QBE grid. Most users will select specific fields rather than the entire table. Because fields will appear in the dynaset in the order they are listed in the QBE grid, you should consider order when dragging fields to the grid. Access will also let you rearrange the field order after the query has been created, as discussed later.

You may want to add an expression involving several fields in the Field row of the QBE grid. For instance, you could place an expression consisting of the city, state, and zip code for an address. Or you could place both first and last names in the same query field box. For more details on this procedure, see the section "Concatenation Operators," later in this unit.

If you do not want the field value to appear in the dynaset, click on the show box to erase the X that Access places there. By default the fields in a query will display. All five fields in the query of Figure 4.1 will appear in the dynaset.

Creating Simple Criteria Expressions

Next, you should add the criteria expression to the query. The query will display only those records that match the criteria provided. A *simple* query uses a criteria expression for one field. For example, you might place a particular vendor's name in the Vendor field in the criteria row. Only those records from that vendor would appear in the dynaset. If no criteria are supplied, *all* records will match the criteria and appear in the dynaset. As seen in the criteria expression of Figure 4.1, only records from the Accounting department will appear in that dynaset.

The most common simple query uses a constant value as the criterion, such as the vendor name above. You can also enter a more elaborate expression to indicate a condition. If the field name contains a space or other punctuation, you must enclose it in brackets; brackets are optional for other field names. Examples of criteria expressions are shown in Table 4.1.

We will cover Access expressions in more detail in a later section of this unit.

Creating Compound Criteria Expressions

A *compound* query uses criteria expressions for two or more fields in the same query. If you provide criteria expressions for more than one field, Access will process the query in the following manner:

- If the expressions are on the same row of the grid, *all* conditions must be true in order for the record to qualify for the dynaset. This is known as an *And condition*. Remember that you can create a compound condition in which no records will appear in the dynaset.

- If the expressions are on different rows of the grid and *any* condition is true, the record will qualify for the query's dynaset. This is known as an *Or condition*.

We will prepare a compound criteria query later in this unit.

Running the Query to View the Results

After creating the query and its criteria, click on the Exclamation (Run Query) toolbar button or click on the Datasheet toolbar button. Access will process your query and display the results in a table called a dynaset. The Dynaset view looks just like Datasheet view from the table window. Only the records that match your query are displayed in the dynaset, as demonstrated in Figure 4.2.

Saving the Query Design

As with other Access objects, you can use the File | Save Query command to save the query design. You will be asked to supply a name for the query. If you want to

TABLE 4.1 *Typical criteria* *expressions*	**EXPRESSION**	**MEANING**
	"Johnson"	This field's value must be the text value, Johnson.
	="Johnson"	Same as the previous expression.
	<=50	The field must be less than or equal to 50.
	Quantity>10	The Quantity field must be greater than 10.
	Between 10 and 50	The field must be at least 10 and no more than 50. *(Includes 10 ? 50)*
	[Order Date]<#1-Jan-95#	The Order Date must be earlier than January 1, 1995.
	Between #1-Oct-94# and #3-31-95#	The date must be between these dates.
	(Open+Close)/2>=30	The average of opening and closing prices must be at least 30.
	[Name] is Null	The Name field is ***null***, meaning it is empty and has no value.
	"Sports" or "Other"	Allows use of either the Sports department or the Other department.
	S*	The field must start with the letter S.

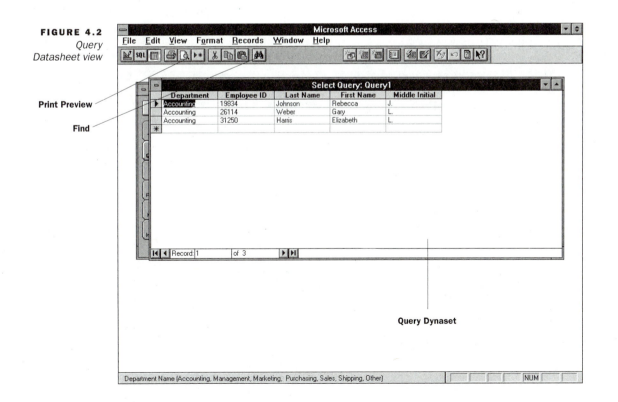

FIGURE 4.2
Query
Datasheet view

Print Preview

Find

Query Dynaset

save the query under a *different* name, use the File I Save Query As command. After saving the query, you may close the query design window and return to the Database window, or go to Datasheet view to view the dynaset that the query has produced.

GUIDED ACTIVITY 4.1

Creating a Select Query

In this Guided Activity you will use the Products table of the HUNT database to prepare a simple select query.

1. Start Windows and Access as usual. Open the HUNT database.

2. At the Database window, click on the Query button to switch to Query mode. Then click on the New button and click New Query to open the select query design window.

3. Access will display the Add Table window, shown in Figure 4.3. Click on the Products table line, then click on Add.

4. We'll just use a single table for this activity, so click on Close to complete the add table portion of the query design.

5. Next you must select the fields for the QBE grid. For this simple query, we'll pick three fields. With the mouse, drag the Description field to the first column of the QBE grid. That is, move the pointer to that field in the Products table, then hold down the left mouse button and drag the field to the first column of the grid, and finally release the left button.

FIGURE 4.3
Query Add Table window

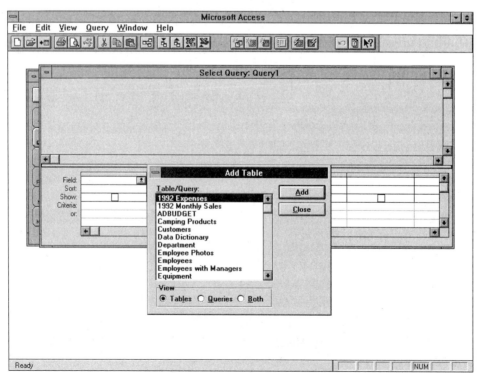

FIGURE 4.4
*Query window
after step 6*

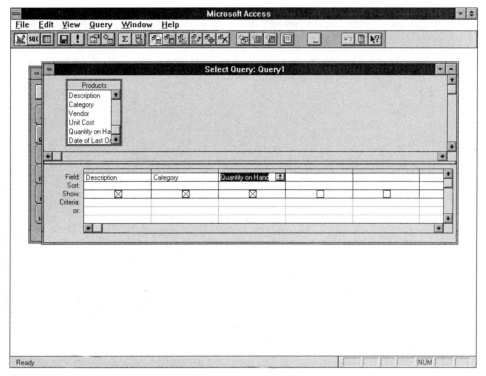

6. Repeat the process, placing the Category field and the Quantity on Hand field in columns 2 and 3. Your screen should look like Figure 4.4.

7. If you click on the Datasheet button in the toolbar, Access will display the records in the dynaset that match the query. Notice that all records qualify because no criteria condition was specified.

NOTE *You can also click on the exclamation point toolbar button or select Query/Run to execute the query and view the dynaset.*

8. Click on the Design button in the toolbar to return to the query design. This time specify `Camping` in the criteria row in the Category column of the QBE grid. Notice that Access will automatically place quotes around the Camping text value when you press the [Enter] key.

9. Again, click on the Datasheet button to see the new dynaset, shown in Figure 4.5.

CHECKPOINT 4A Which records would appear in the dynaset if you put `Camp` in place of `Camping` in the criteria row?

10. Use the File | Save Query command to save the query from step 9. Give it the name `Camping Overstock`. We will modify this query in the next activity, where we demonstrate how to create a more complex query.

FIGURE 4.5
*Results of query
after step 9*

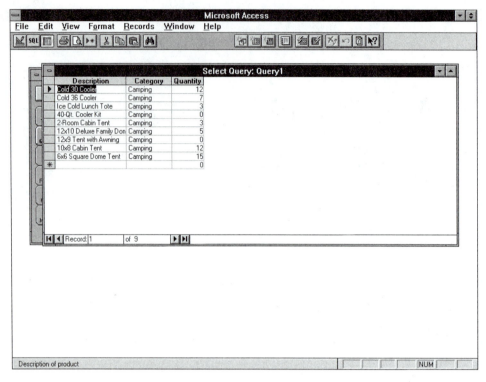

Access Expressions and Built-in Functions

Earlier in this unit we saw sample expressions available in Microsoft Access. In this section we will elaborate on expressions and functions available for Access queries, forms, and reports. Much of the material here is included for *future* reference when you use Access for real database systems.

Parts of the Expression

Access provides a general format for expressions. Suppose we have an *expression*:

```
[Date of Last Order]<Date()-30.
```

This expression asks the question: is the Date of Last Order field more than 30 days before the current date? Each part of the expression is explained below.

- [Date of Last Order] is called an *identifier*, which describes a data field or other data source. If you refer to an identifier that contains spaces or punctuation, you must surround it with brackets.   *(left side)*

- The < sign is called an *operator*, meaning *less than* in this case.

- Date( ) is a *function*, referring to the current system date within the computer you are using.   *(Could use Now())*

- The minus sign (–) is another operator in this example.

- The 30 is a *literal*, which can represent a number, a string of text characters, or a date. A Yes/No literal is known as a *constant*.

Rules for Access Expressions

Access expressions follow algebraic rules similar to what you have used before. This section contains a summary of the rules for expressions.

ARITHMETIC OPERATORS

Access uses the usual +, –, *, and / *arithmetic operators* to represent addition, subtraction, multiplication, and division. Exponentiation is denoted by the ^ character. The \ operator is used for integer division; 7 \ 4 would divide one integer by another and return an integer answer, in this case 1. The Mod operator returns the remainder of a division operation; 7 Mod 4 would return 3.

COMPARISON OPERATORS

Access uses combinations of <, =, and > *comparison operators* to compare pairs of values. < means less than, <= means less than or equal to, and so on. <> is used to denote not equal. The result of a comparison operation is True or False.

Another group of operators can be useful when comparing two items. Like, In, and Between are simpler to use than building compound conditions. Examples are shown in Table 4.2.

LOGICAL OPERATORS

You may use *logical operators* to make conjunctions between pairs of logical (Yes/No) expressions in a similar fashion to the compound criteria described earlier in this unit. And and Or are the most commonly used. The And operator implies that both expressions must be true for the overall expression to be true. The Or operator

TABLE 4.2
Like, In, and Between operators

EXPRESSION	MEANING
Like "Camp*"	Finds a field that begins with "Camp". * is the wild card character that means any number of characters can follow.
Like "3????"	Finds a field of five characters that begins with a 3. ? is the wild card character that matches any other character in that position.
Like "X[A-C]##"	Finds a field starting with letter X, then any letter between A and C, followed by two digits. # is the wild card character that matches digits.
Like "*/*/95"	Finds a date field in 1995.
In("IN","IL","OH")	Finds a field that matches "IN", "IL", or "OH".
Between 2 and 4	Finds a field whose value is at least 2 and no more than 4.

implies that either expression may be true for the overall expression to be true. For example, X=6 And Y=4 is true *only* if both parts of the expression are true. Likewise, X=6 Or Y=4 would be true if either, or both, parts of the expression are true. Access uses the ***not condition*** operator to reverse the meaning of a condition. For instance, Not "IN" implies the field cannot have the value of "IN". You can search for Logical Operators in on-line Help to see more examples of these and other logical operators.

CONCATENATION OPERATORS

Access uses the ***concatenation operator*** to join two text strings. Suppose you keep last name and first name in separate fields. You can join (concatenate) them with the expression: First+Last or First&Last. Both the + and & operators perform the same task in Access. Access trims trailing blanks from the two text strings, and does not place a space after the First field. Thus, the words in the concatenated fields will appear run together. To solve this, use First&" "&Last to insert a space between the concatenated strings.

You could place the First&" "&Last expression in the Field row of the query to place both first and last name fields in the query. Remember that field names with embedded spaces must be enclosed in brackets.

IDENTIFIERS

You may need to specify more than a field name in an Access expression. You can use a form or report name, table name, field name, and other identifiers as part of the expression. Separate each with an exclamation point. For example, the expression Forms![Product Entry]![Quantity on Hand] refers to the Quantity on Hand field from the Product Entry form. [Products]![Category] refers to the Category field from the Products table. In the latter example, brackets are not needed because neither identifier contains spaces or other punctuation. You may specify just the field name if you are referring to a field from the current active data object.

Access Functions

Functions return a value to the expression in which they are used. There are more than 100 functions in Access. We will discuss a few of the more common functions in this section. For a complete list, search Access Help for Functions, lists of.

MATH FUNCTIONS

Access provides 13 mathematical and trigonometric functions. Common math functions are shown in Table 4.3. Trigonometric functions (Atn, Cos, Sin, Tan) use radians as the parameter and return angle answers in radians.

DATE AND TIME FUNCTIONS

Access can provide the current system date and time, as well as extract the individual components from any date or time number. There are nearly 20 date and time functions. Common functions are shown in Table 4.4.

TABLE 4.3	FUNCTION	MEANING
Math functions	Abs( )	Absolute value. Example: Abs(–4.3)=4.3
	Exp( )	Exponential of value. Example: Exp(2)=7.38906
	Int( )	Integer part of value. Example: Int(9/2)=4
	Log( )	Natural log of value. Example: Log(4)=1.386294
	Rnd( )	Random number between 0 and 1. Example: Rnd( )=0.77474
	Sqr( )	Square root of value. Example: Sqr(16)=4

TABLE 4.4	FUNCTION	MEANING
Date and time functions	Date( )	Current system date and time as a date field subtype 7. Example: 3/25/94
	Date$( )	Current system date and time as a date field subtype 8. Example: 25-Mar-94
	DateDiff( )	Difference between two dates. You can specify whether that difference should be expressed in seconds, minutes, hours, days, weeks, months, quarters, or years. Example: DateDiff("d",Now( ), #12/25/94#) will return the number of days between now and December 25, 1994. *(Test w/ your B-day)*
	DateSerial( )	Number of days since December 31, 1899. (Same as Lotus 1-2-3)
	DateValue( )	Allows you to enter date as string and converts to date type. Example: DateValue("3/25/94")
	Day( )	Integer day of the month for a specified date value, between 1 and 31. Other functions are Month( ) and Year( ), which also return integer answers. Example: Day(#7/16/94#) returns 16
	Hour( )	Integer hour of a specified time. Other functions are Minute( ) and Second( ), which return integers between 0 and 59.
	Now( )	Current system date and time. Example: 3/25/94 10:30:06
	Time( )	Time portion of system clock as date field subtype 7.
	Time$( )	Time portion of system clock as a string.
	TimeValue( )	Allows you to enter time as a string and converts to date field type. Example: TimeValue("10:30:06")
	Weekday( )	Day of the week for a specified date value. Answer is between 1 and 7, beginning with Sunday. Example: Weekday(#12/25/94#) returns 1, meaning Christmas in 1994 is on Sunday.

TABLE 4.5 *Financial functions*	**FUNCTION**	**MEANING**
	DDB( )	Double-declining balance depreciation. Example: Ddb(10000,2000,4,3) returns 500, the depreciation for year 3 for an asset that costs $10,000 with a salvage value of $2,000 and a life of 4 years.
	FV( )	Future value of an investment based on a series on constant payments.
	IPmt( )	Interest portion for a particular payment on an installment loan or annuity.
	IRR( )	Internal rate of return for an investment with periodic cash flow amounts. MIRR( ) will calculate the modified rate of return.
	Nper( )	Number of payments necessary to pay off a loan.
	NPV( )	Net present value of an annuity.
	Pmt( )	Amount of the periodic payment for an installment loan or annuity. Example: Pmt(.08/12,3*12,-5000,0,0)=156.68 or the monthly payment for $5,000 loan for 3 years at 8% annual interest.
	PPmt( )	Principal portion for a particular payment on an installment loan or annuity. Example: PPmt(.08/12,5,36,-5000,0,0)=126.67 or the amount of principal paid in the fifth of 36 payments on a $5,000 loan at 8% APR.
	PV( )	Present value of an annuity paid in equal installments.
	Rate( )	Interest rate of a loan or annuity based on equal installments.
	Sln()	Straight line depreciation of an asset for a single period. Example: Sln(10000,2000,4)=2000 or the annual depreciation for an asset that costs $10,000 with a salvage value of $2,000 and a life of 4 years.
	Syd()	Sum-of-years' digits depreciation of an asset for a specified period. Example: Syd(10000,2000,4,3)=1600 or the depreciation for year 3 for an asset that costs $10,000 with a salvage value of $2,000 and a life of 4 years.

FINANCIAL FUNCTIONS

Functions that pertain to the time value of money are built into Access. Functions for depreciation and payments are included. Table 4.5 shows some of the most common functions. You can look up the specific syntax of these functions by searching Access help for the particular function name; examples of some of the more popular functions are shown.

TEXT MANIPULATION FUNCTIONS

These functions work with text field type data, also known as *strings*. The most common text manipulation functions are shown in Table 4.6.

TABLE 4.6
Text manipulation functions

FUNCTION	MEANING
Asc( )	ASCII numeric code for a particular character string. Asc("M") returns 77.
Chr( )	Character for a particular ASCII code. Chr(77) returns "M".
Format( )	Formats an expression according to format code. Format(Date( ),"dd-mmm-yy") returns 3-Mar-94.
InStr( )	Position of one string within another. InStr("ABCD","C") returns 3.
LCase( )	Lowercase version of a string. UCase( ) returns uppercase version.
Left( )	Left-most characters of a string. Left("ABCDEF",3) returns "ABC". Right( ) returns right-most characters from a string.
Len( )	Length of characters in a string, as an integer. Len("ABCDE") returns 5.
LTrim( )	Trims leading spaces from a string. RTrim( ) trims trailing spaces from a string.
Mid( )	Returns a portion of a string. Mid("ABCDEFGH",3,2) returns "CD".
Str( )	Converts number data value to a string. Val( ) converts a string to a numeric value.
Trim( )	Trims leading and trailing spaces from a string. Trim("ABC ") returns "ABC".

MISCELLANEOUS FUNCTIONS

Access provides other functions for miscellaneous purposes, as shown in Table 4.7.

TABLE 4.7
Other functions

FUNCTION	MEANING
Choose( )	Returns a value from a lookup list based on the sequence in the list. Choose(Key,"ounce","pound","ton") would return one of the three strings based on the value of Key (1, 2, or 3).
IIF( )	Returns one value if the expression is true, another if the expression is false. IIF(Hours>40,Rate*1.5,Rate) will return Rate*1.5 if Hours is greater than 40, and Rate otherwise.
IsEmpty( )	True if the indicated field is a noninitialized value, false otherwise. Access can distinguish between the Null value and a noninitialized value.
IsNull( )	True if field is null, false otherwise.

FIGURE 4.6
Query Design view with compound criteria

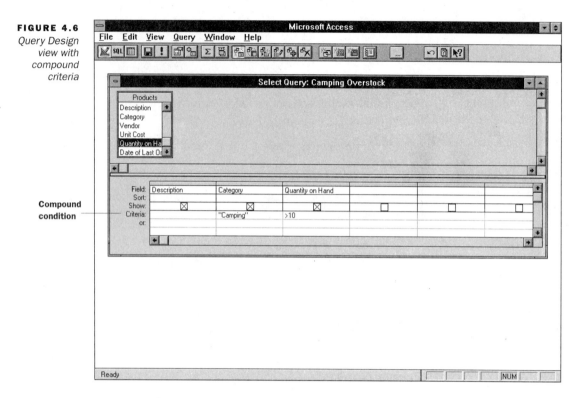

Compound condition

Creating a Compound Query

In this Guided Activity you will create a more complex query with multiple criteria expressions. We will start with the query from step 10 of the previous activity.

1. Go back to the Design view for the Camping Overstock query.

2. Leave Camping in the Category column, and add >10 to the criteria row of the Quantity on Hand column. Make sure both criteria expressions are in the *same* row of the QBE grid, shown in Figure 4.6.

3. Now go to the Datasheet view to see the records in the current dynaset. You should see three products that are both Camping *and* whose balances are greater than 10 units.

CHECKPOINT 4B Without running the query, can you tell which records would qualify if you had placed >15 in the Quantity on Hand criteria expression?

4. Go back to the query Design view. This time place the expression Other in the criteria row directly beneath Camping. You are now specifying that Camping products whose balances are greater than 10 units *or* Other products will meet the criteria in your query.

5. Go to the Datasheet view to see the new dynaset.

CHECKPOINT 4C How would you modify the query to require that Other products must also meet the greater-than-10-units condition?

6. Go back to the Design view and delete all of the criteria conditions. You can easily do this by moving the pointer slowly at the beginning of the Criteria row in the QBE grid. When the pointer changes to a right-pointing arrow, click once to highlight the entire grid row. Then press the [Del] key to erase the criteria expressions. Repeat with the next criteria row in the grid.

7. Go to the Quantity on Hand field cell and enter the following expression: [Quantity on Hand]*[Unit Cost] and press [Enter]. Put >=250 in the Criteria row. This condition specifies that the cost of the current inventory be at least $250. Click on the Run Query button to view the new dynaset. How many records now qualify?

8. Now go back to the Design view again. Let's add another field to the query. Instead of dragging the Date of Last Order field from the Products table to the QBE grid, click on the Field row of the first blank column in the QBE grid. Access will display a pull-down list box; click on the arrow to display the list. Click once on the Date of Last Order field to place it in that row.

9. On the *same* row as the expression from step 7, place this criteria expression in the field you just added: < #1-Jan-93# and press [Enter]. The # signs surrounding the date tell Access you have entered a date expression rather than a text string.

10. Run the query and examine the resulting dynaset, shown in Figure 4.7. Access should display all records that were last ordered before January 1, 1993, and whose current inventory value is at least $250. Close the query but do not save it.

FIGURE 4.7
Results of query

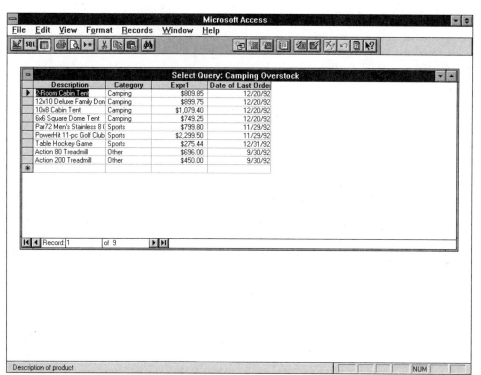

CHECKPOINT 4D How would you tell Access to display items that were last ordered in the first three months of 1993?

Sorting Records in a Query

It is possible to give sorting specifications in the QBE grid for a query in Access. Each field has a Sort row in the QBE grid. The default is no sorting, so the dynaset records appear in *natural order*, the order they were entered in the underlying table.

You can choose an *ascending sort* in which values appear in increasing order. The *descending sort* would place items in decreasing order. For number and currency data types, these types of sorts are obvious. For text items, you can substitute alphabetical order for ascending, and reverse alphabetical order for descending sorts. For dates and times, Access will use chronological order for ascending and the reverse for descending sorts. Yes/No fields cannot be sorted.

If you specify sorts for more than one field, Access uses the left-most sort field as the primary sort key, with remaining sort fields used to break ties in higher-level sort keys. If your query's primary sort key is not left-most among sort fields, rearrange the fields in Design view to the proper order. The next Guided Activity will demonstrate this procedure.

To choose a sort type, click once on the Sort row in a field's QBE grid. Click on the pull-down arrow and choose Ascending or Descending. To remove the sort command, choose the (not sorted) line in the Sort row of the QBE grid.

NOTE *Access 2.0 introduced the QuickSort feature for sorting records in tables and forms. QuickSort is not available in Query mode.*

Making Changes to the Query

You may find that the query is not quite correct. You can rearrange fields, insert new fields, and delete fields in a manner similar to that which you learned with Access tables in Design view.

Rearranging the Fields

You can easily rearrange the fields in a query by highlighting the field's column and dragging it with the mouse. Click on the field selector area at the top of the column to select the column. Then drag the column to the desired location in the QBE grid. If Access leaves the field in the wrong position, you can easily repeat the process to correct the error.

Inserting a New Field

From the field list in the upper section of the query window, select the field you want to insert. Then drag the field to the desired location and release the left mouse button. Access will insert the field into the QBE grid and move other fields over.

Deleting a Field

Click on the field selector area of the field's column that you want to delete. When it is highlighted, press the [Del] key. Or choose the Edit | Delete command from the menu bar.

GUIDED ACTIVITY 4.3 ✳
_____

Sorting Records in a Query

In this Guided Activity you will add sort commands to a query.

1. Use the Camping Overstock query created in Guided Activity 4.1. Select Design view for this query.

2. Highlight the Camping criteria in the Category column and press the [Del] key to _remove_ the Camping restriction.

3. Click once on the Sort row of the Category field. Pull down the sort menu and choose Ascending.

4. Run the query and view the records in the dynaset. Notice that the product records now appear in alphabetical order by Category.

5. Next, go back to Design view and click once on the Sort row in the Description field. Set up an Ascending sort for this field.

6. Run the query and view the records in the dynaset.

CHECKPOINT 4E   Was this a useful sort? Remember that Access uses the left-most sort field as the primary sort key.

7. We need to move the Description field so that it appears _after_ the Category field. Switch back to Design view. Move the pointer to the field selector border just above the Category field column. The cursor will change to a down arrow. Click once to highlight the Category column.

8. With the pointer in the field selector area, drag the Category field to the Description field and release the mouse button. Access will switch the two fields' positions in the query. Figure 4.8 shows the new column order. Note the shape of the mouse pointer in the column border area of the Category column.

9. Run the query and examine the record sequence. With Category first, you should see an alphabetical listing of products within each category.

10. Use the File | Save Query As command to save this query as Sorted Products by Category.

FIGURE 4.8
Move query column in Design view

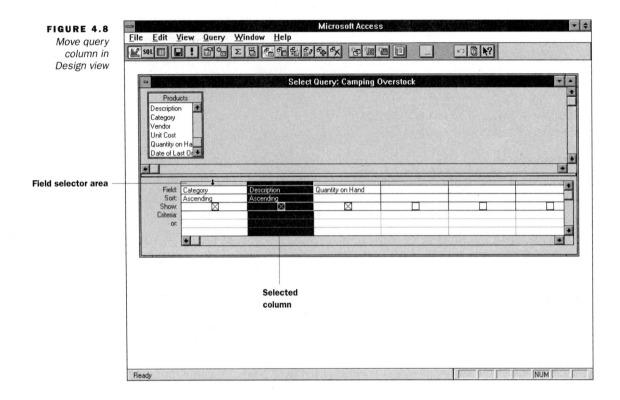

Field selector area

Selected column

Totals for Groups of Records

Microsoft Access queries can also group records that share a common value and can provide totals as well as perform other calculations on fields in those groups. Calculations are done only on records in the dynaset from the query, so you can provide specific criteria if desired.

Types of Calculations

You can do the following types of calculations on Number, Counter, Currency, Date/Time, and Yes/No fields in a query. The operation is specified by typing its name into the Total row in the QBE grid for a particular field.

Calculation	Meaning
Sum	Total of all values in the field
Avg	Arithmetic mean average of all values in the field
Min	Minimum value of the field
Max	Maximum value of the field
StDev	Standard deviation of all values in the field
Var	Variance of all values in the field
Where	Specify a particular value for the field

The following types of calculations can be done to Number, Counter, Currency, Date/Time, Yes/No, Text, Memo, and OLE Object fields:

Calculation	Meaning
Count	Number of non-null values in the field
First	Field value from the first record
Last	Field value from the last record

Calculations on All Records

You can find summary information for all records in the table or dynaset. The basic procedure has four steps:

- Create a new query and drag all the fields to be totaled to the QBE grid.

- Click on the Totals button in the toolbar (a capital sigma or summation sign). You may also choose View | Totals from the menu bar. You will see a new Total row appear in the QBE grid with the words Group By under each field.

- In the total row under the field(s) you want to total, replace Group By with Sum, or the appropriate calculation name.

- Run the query to view the dynaset that results from the query. Access will display names in the columns that reflect the type of calculation done on each field. You will see the results of the group totals calculation in a single row of the dynaset.

Calculations on Groups of Records

This procedure is very similar to the All Records procedure. The major difference is that you must also drag the "Group By" fields to the QBE grid. For example, you might want to find the average salary of employees in each department. In this case, the Department field is the Group By field, and the Salary field would be the totals field. You might also want to know the oldest Last Order Date in the Products table for each category.

You cannot group by memo fields or by OLE object fields.

Calculations for One Group

In this application you create the query as before, but add a criteria expression that defines the group for which you would like totals. When you run the query, only those records that match the criteria will be selected for totals.

You can also establish criteria for the total field. For instance, you might want to know the average number of units in stock but only for those products that have non-zero Quantity on Hand values. In that case you would specify >0 as the criteria in the Quantity on Hand field, as well as entering Avg in the Total row for that field.

Calculations for Subgroups

You may want to break groups down into subgroups for total purposes. This procedure is analogous to sorting on more than one field. Access will take the first group by field it encounters from the left side of the QBE grid and make it the primary group. It will then subdivide that group by the next group by field it finds, proceeding from left to right.

Suppose you wanted to count the number of products from each vendor within each product category. The left-most group by field would be Category, and the next group by field would be Vendor. We will demonstrate this feature in the next Guided Activity.

GUIDED ACTIVITY 4.4 ✳

Creating a Query with Total Calculations

In this Guided Activity you will build a simple totals query, then modify it for several situations.

1. Open the HUNT database and change to Query mode. Click on the New button, then click on New Query.

2. At the Add Table window choose the Products table, then Close the window.

3. Drag the Quantity on Hand field to the QBE grid.

4. Click on the Totals button (the summation sign) in the toolbar. You will see the Total row appear in the QBE grid.

5. Replace the Group By expression with Sum in the Total row.

6. Run the query and examine the dynaset. You will see a single row labeled SumOfQuantity on Hand with the value 310.

CHECKPOINT 4F Why is there just *one* row in the resulting dynaset?

7. Click on the Design button to return to the query design.

8. Drag the Category field to the QBE grid, then run the query to view the dynaset, shown in Figure 4.9.

CHECKPOINT 4G Why do you see four records in the dynaset at this time?

9. Return to the Design view and place the criteria expression Camping in the criteria row of the Category field.

10. Rerun the query. You should now see only the total for the Camping products.

11. Return to Design view and remove the Camping criteria from the Category field.

12. Drag the Vendor field to the QBE grid, and place the expression Count in the Total row under the Quantity on Hand field. Group By appears in the Total row under the Vendor field.

FIGURE 4.9
*Result of the
totals query
after step 8*

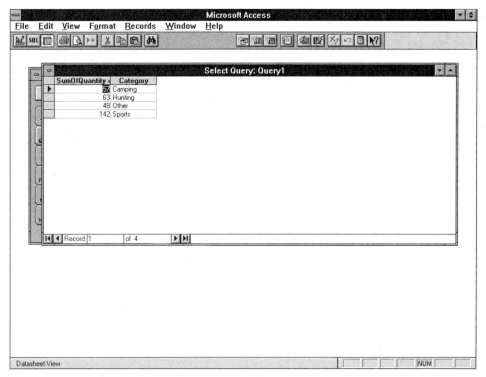

13. Run the query.

CHECKPOINT 4H   You should see 14 records in this dynaset. What do the numbers in the
`CountOfQuantity on Hand` column mean?

14. Use the File | Save Query As command to save this query under the name
`Product Count by Vendor`. In the next section you will learn how to print
the contents of the dynaset for this query.

Printing the Query

As with Access tables in Datasheet mode, you can print the dynaset resulting
from the query. Open the Database window and switch to the Query view. Highlight
the query you would like to print, and click on the Print Preview button, or use the
File | Print Preview command from the menu bar. Access will prepare the print job,
then display the first page of the output on the screen. You can use the magnifying
glass pointer to zoom in on a portion of the output. If you want to send the output to
the printer, click on the Print button. Click on Close if you wish to cancel the Print
Preview command.

You can also send the output directly to the printer, without previewing, if you
choose the Print button in the toolbar.

GUIDED ACTIVITY 4.5

Printing the Query's Dynaset

In this Guided Activity you will print the dynaset resulting from the query of the previous activity.

1. Open the HUNT Database window and click on the Query button.

2. Click once on the Product Count by Vendor query in the Database window. If you already have the query window open on the desktop, go to the next step.

3. Click on the Print Preview button in the toolbar, or give the File | Print Preview command from the menu bar.

4. After a few seconds, Access will show you the first page of your print output on the display screen. Use the magnifying pointer to zoom in on a portion of the output.

5. If a printer is attached to your computer, click on the Print button to send the output to the printer. Otherwise, click on Close to cancel the Print Preview command. The print preview output is shown in Figure 4.10.

    If you are not continuing with the Exercises, you may exit from Access.

FIGURE 4.10
Sample query print preview

Command Review

+, & operators   Concatenation operators, joining two text strings into one

# # date separators	Used to mark a date entered in text format, as #9-Apr-1995#
[ ] brackets	Surround data object name containing spaces or punctuation
Edit I Delete	Delete a field that is highlighted.
File I Print Preview	Preview the printed query dynaset.
File I New I Query	Create a new query.
File I Save Query, File I Save Query As	Save the query design.
Query I Run	Execute a query, view results in Datasheet mode.
View I Totals	Create a totals query in Design view.

Exercises

Use the Hunter River database contained in the HUNT.MDB file on the Student Data Disk for these exercises. *Be sure to identify any printed output with your name and the Exercise and part numbers.*

1. Create a select query that includes the following fields from the Employees table in the sequence given: Last Name, Department, Salary. Write the appropriate query expression on the output for each part. Modify the query to solve each part below.

   a. Print the query for *all records*.

   b. Print the query for Accounting department *only*.

   c. Print the query for Accounting *or* Sales department employees.

   d. Print the query for all employees having at least $15,000 annual salary.

   e. Save the query under the name Exercise 4-1.

2. Prepare another select query for the Employees table. This query should contain *all* fields from the table, in the default order of the table definition. Modify the query to solve each part below. Write the criteria expressions on the printed output for each part so your instructor can see how you got your answer.

   a. Print the query for employees whose last name begins with the letters A–M.

   b. Print the query for employees hired during 1993.

   c. Print the query for employees hired during 1993 *and* who are in the Sales department.

   d. Print the query for employees hired *after* January 1, 1992, *and* who are *not* in the Sales department.

    e. Print the query for employees whose *monthly* salary is from $1,000 to $1,500. Show only the last name and annual salary fields. Save the query as Exercise 4-2.

3. Write the query criteria expressions using fields from the Employees table that would match the following conditions. Do not run the query unless you want to test your expressions.

    a. Employees hired during the month of March.

    b. Employees hired during the first quarter (January–March).

    c. Employees who have worked for the Hunter River store for at least 24 months; use the current date when you solve this problem. (*Hint*: Use the DateDiff() function.)

    d. Employees whose salary is above the average salary for all employees in the table. (*Hint*: Use the Davg() function.)

4. Prepare a query that will accomplish the following parts. Modify the query for each part and print each part individually. Include Last Name, First Name, Department, Salary, and Date Hired fields from the Employees table in the query.

    a. Alphabetical listing of all employees

    b. Alphabetical listing of employees broken down by department; departments should appear in alphabetical order

    c. Same as part (b) except that first and last names should appear within one field (*Hint*: Use the concatenation operator in the Field: row of the QBE grid.)

    d. Listing of employees by salary, in descending order

    e. Listing of employees by salary broken down by department, in ascending order; save this query as Exercise 4-4

5. Prepare a totals query that will accomplish each of the following parts. Include fields from the Employees table. Print each part individually.

    a. Calculate the sum of all salaries.

    b. Calculate the average salary for each department.

    c. Add the Salary field twice to the QBE grid and show both the minimum and maximum salaries values for all records.

    d. Count the number of employees in each department.

    e. Calculate the average salary for those people hired in 1993. Save this query as Exercise 4-5. (*Hint:* Use the Where calculation in the Total row to select only 1993 hires.)

6. Prepare a query that will accomplish each of the following parts. Include fields from the Products table. Print each part individually.

    a. Show the products that were last ordered in the month of November.

b. Show the products that were *not* ordered during 1993.

c. Show the products whose current inventory value (unit cost multiplied by quantity on hand) is between $20 and $100, inclusively.

d. Show the products that were *not* ordered during 1993 and that are currently out of stock.

7. For this query select any table as the data source but do not drag any fields to the QBE grid. Use the QBE grid Field row to key in the appropriate Access function to answer each of the following questions. Write down the function expression and provide the answer. For example, write `Pmt(.08/12,3*12,-5000,0,0)` in the Field cell, then run the query to find out that the payment should be $126.67.

a. Find the monthly payment for borrowing $7,000 for 4 years at 9% per year. Remember to enter the *monthly* interest rate and number of months for the loan.

b. Find the depreciation for year 6 of a 10-year asset whose initial cost was $75,000 and whose salvage value is $15,000. Assume the double-declining balance method.

c. Find the day of the week for your own birth.

d. Find the number of days since your own birth using the DateDiff function.

Review Questions

Delete - can delete records from query
Update - can update information from query
Action - performs an action based on query
Append - appends information from query
Select - basic query
Crosstab - uses more than 1 table ; creates crosstab query.

1. Discuss the six types of queries available in Microsoft Access. Give an example for use of each query type.

2. Describe the purpose of each of the following rows of the QBE grid:

a. Field — *the name of the field*

b. Total — *allows standard functions such as group by, sum, etc.*

c. Sort — *allow ascending, descending, or not sorted*

d. Show — *will see in query or not*

e. Criteria — *specify a particular value*

f. Or — *Ex. James or Anderson (not And) means one "or" the other*

3. Define the following query terms:
   a. Dynaset ~ results of a query
   b. Compound criteria - combines several specific values needed
   c. Logical operator - And, or
   d. Group By - groups records by select order
   e. Concatenation - joins fields Ex: 3

4. Explain the use of each of the following Access functions:
   a. Log() Natural log of value
   b. Date$() Current system date
   c. DateValue() allows you to convert date format
   d. SLN() Straight line of depreciation
   e. Mid() Returns the middle function of a string

5. Discuss the differences between a *simple* criteria expression and a *compound* criteria expression. Give an example of each type of expression.
   Has criteria for simple, compound reads a function uses criteria for 2 or more fields

6. Give the *precise* meaning of each of the following Access expressions.
   a. `In("ACCT","MKTG","MIS","MGT")` - find records with whats in ( )
   b. `"Microsoft"&"Access"` Create field for 2 fields into one
   c. `Like "MIS3??"` Look for records MIS3 + any other last 2 char.
   d. `Like "MIS[1-4]##"` First part matches MIS, then could be a 1-4, and any other 2 char.
   e. `Reports![Camping Overstock]!Category` Category field from camping overstock report.

7. Suppose you have created a query and find that the fields are in the wrong order and there is one field whose value should not be shown. How can you remedy these problems?

Key Terms

Action query	Crosstab query	Link table
And condition	Delete query	Literal
Append query	Descending sort	Logical operator
Arithmetic operator	Dynaset	Make-table query
Ascending sort	Expression	Mathematical function
Comparison operator	Expression Builder	Miscellaneous function
Compound condition	Financial function	Natural order
Concatenation operator	Function	Not condition
Constant	Identifier	Null
Criteria expression	Input mask	Operator

Or condition
Parameter query
QBE grid
Query

Select query
Show box
Simple condition
String

Text manipulation
    function
Update query

Documentation Review

Use the printed documentation and on-line Help available with Microsoft Access to answer the following questions. If you use one of the manuals, provide the page number for your reference in the manual.

1. Are Cue Cards available for use with Microsoft Access queries?

2. Use the on-line Help system to find the help screen titled "Functions Reference." Print a copy of this help section.

3. Look up the specific syntax of the function called Pmt( ). Give the precise function to find the monthly payment for a loan of $7,350 borrowed for 3 years at 9% annual percentage rate.

4. Discuss the use of the Expression Builder in creating a complex query expression. How do you invoke the Expression Builder?

5. Although the link operation is not covered in this unit, explain how it can be used to link two tables in an Access query. (*Hint*: Use Cue Cards.)

Physicians' Medical Clinic*
(III): Using a Select Query

Dr. Greenway and the hospital board are very concerned about the effects of the national health program on PMC. They have asked you to prepare some select queries to examine patient statistics. Using the PMC database, create a select query, display and print the dynaset, modify the query, and repeat the process as specified below. Indicate clearly which printed output goes with which part of the application.

1. You have been asked to provide a list of patients from the Patients table in patient number order. The following fields are requested: Patient Number, First and Last name as one field with a space between, Employer Name, and Date of Birth. Print this list.

2. Modify the query from step 1 of this application to select only those patients *from the State University* employer. Print this list.

3. Prepare a query to select patients from any employer who are *younger than age 18.* Use the current date to determine actual age. Print this list in *descending age* order, oldest first.

4. Prepare and print another list showing names, home address fields, and employer name for those patients having *no insurance company* listed. This list should appear in alphabetical order.

5. Finally, prepare a list of patients who are insured by the *US Insurance Company* or by the *Municipal Insurance.* Print this list in order of insurance company and within each company by patient number. Include the patient number, last and first names, and insurance name.

6. Save your query.

Building a Form

This unit will illustrate the use of Access forms to display data from a table or a query. You will learn the basics of forms, including the types of forms available with Access Form Wizards. You will create a simple form using the Form Wizards, then use that form to view data and add data to a table. The unit concludes with the development and printing of a more complicated main/subform form.

Learning Objectives

At the completion of this unit you should know

1. the various types of forms used in Access,

2. the advantages of using a form to display data.

At the completion of this unit you should be able to

1. create a form using the Access Form Wizard,

2. use the form to display data from a table,

3. add data to a table using a form,

4. print the data with the form.

Important Commands

Edit | Delete

Edit | Tab Order

File | Save Form

Records | Data Entry

Form Basics

Access forms provide a visually attractive means of presenting data on the screen, usually one record at a time. You can arrange the record's data fields in any location on the desktop and format the fields as desired. Fields can be arranged in a specific order in the form to make data input easier and more accurate.

Form Controls

Forms are composed of the standard Windows graphical objects for displaying data. Called *controls*, these graphical objects include such items as labels, text boxes, lines, rectangles, check boxes, drop-down option lists, graphical objects, and the like. Samples of these controls are shown in the Orders form of Figure 5.1. Note that the Salesperson pull-down list has been pulled down to illustrate this feature. The Northwind logo in the bottom corner is an OLE object. Similar controls are also used in Access reports.

FIGURE 5.1
Sample Access form controls

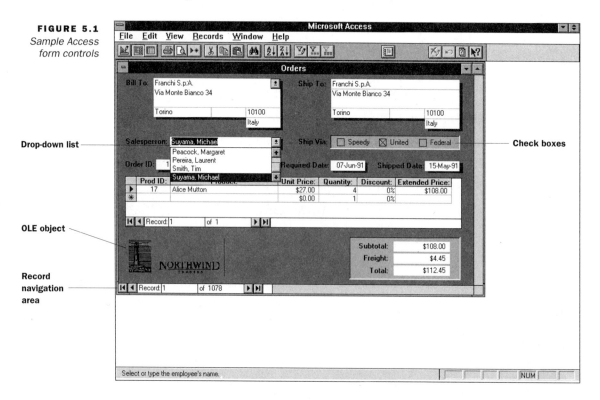

Drop-down list

Check boxes

OLE object

Record navigation area

FIGURE 5.2
*Form toolbar
(Datasheet view)*

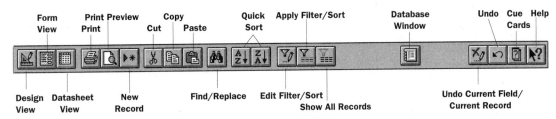

For many forms you can use the Form Wizards to automatically build the form. This unit looks at forms created with the Form Wizard. You don't need to work with the controls on forms created with the Form Wizards unless you want to make changes to the form. For more customized forms, you may need to learn more about controls. Units 9 and 10 will cover use of controls in manually creating and editing customized forms.

The Form View Toolbar

The *Form view* toolbar is shown in Figure 5.2. It uses many of the same tool buttons as the table Datasheet and Query views, listed in Table 5.1. There is a slightly different toolbar for *Form Design* view. The Form Design view is covered in Unit 10 of this book.

TABLE 5.1
*Form view
toolbar buttons*

BUTTON	MEANING
Design View	Make changes to the form design, without displaying values
Form View	View the form with data values in Form view
Datasheet View	View the table or query in Datasheet view
Print	Print the form
Print Preview	Display Print Preview view for the form
New Record	Display a new blank record in the form
Cut	Cut selected text and place in Clipboard
Copy	Copy selected text and place in Clipboard
Paste	Place contents of Clipboard into current form
Find/Replace	Display Find window when searching for data
Filter/Sort	Several buttons used for applying data filters and sorting records
Database	Display Database window
Undo Current Field/Record	Undo changes made to current field (or record)
Undo	Cancel the most recent change to the form
Cue Cards	Activate Cue Cards
Help	Activate Access Help system

Designing a Form

In this section we will discuss the types of forms and various styles available via Access Form Wizards.

Types of Forms

Access provides an easy-to-use tool called **Form Wizards** for creating forms. The Form Wizards lead you through an interview process, asking questions about what kind of form you would like to build and the appropriate information for the form. There are five main types of forms in Form Wizards, described next.

SINGLE-COLUMN FORM

A *single-column form* displays the field values from a record down the screen in one column, one field per line. Preceding the field is a label, defaulting to the field name or the caption you provided as a field property for that field when you defined the table. It is also possible to "snake" extra fields into two columns, newspaper-style. That is, the fields go down the first column, then continue at the top of the second column. Figure 5.3 shows a single-column form.

TABULAR FORM

The *tabular form* presents fields in row and column format, similar to the Datasheet view. You can display multiple records with a tabular form, as shown in

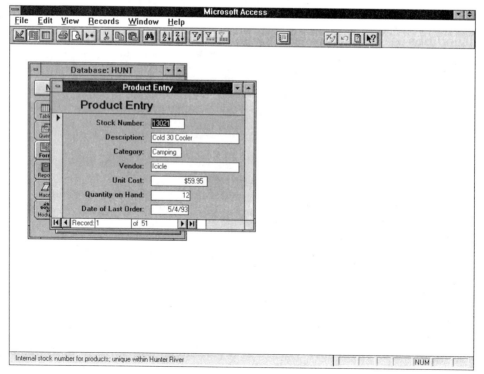

FIGURE 5.3
Single-column form in Standard style

FIGURE 5.4
*Tabular form
with Standard
style*

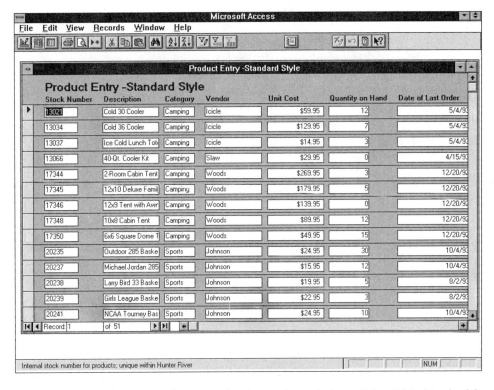

Figure 5.4. Fields proceed across the form, from left to right. This kind of form is useful when there are fewer fields to display. Long fields can be displayed over two or more lines.

GRAPH FORM

A *graph form* depicts numerical data in a graph. Figure 5.5 shows a color graph form but is reproduced in gray shades in this book. It is easier to distinguish employees with a color monitor. If you customize forms, it may be appropriate to combine this type of form with one of the others in a comprehensive screen.

MAIN/SUBFORM FORM

You may want to link two tables that contain matching field values. For instance, you might have a department table and an employee table; these tables can be linked by matching their department name fields. A *main/subform form* is used to display matching records from the two tables together. In this example, the top portion (main) of the form in Figure 5.6 contains information about the department. The bottom portion (subform) shows all of the employees in that department.

AUTOFORM FORM

This new form type was introduced with Access 2.0. The *AutoForm* Form Wizard will automatically create a single-column form, place all the fields in it from the selected table or query, place the name of the table or query data source in the form

FIGURE 5.5
*Graph form
(color graph
appears in
gray here)*

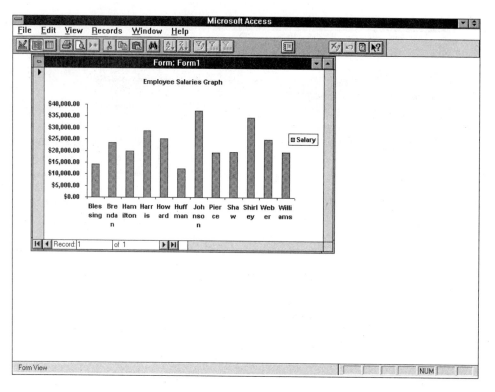

header, and open the form with data in it. The form is not yet saved, however;
you must save it and give it a form name. This is the quickest way to create an
Access form.

FIGURE 5.6
*Main/subform
form example*

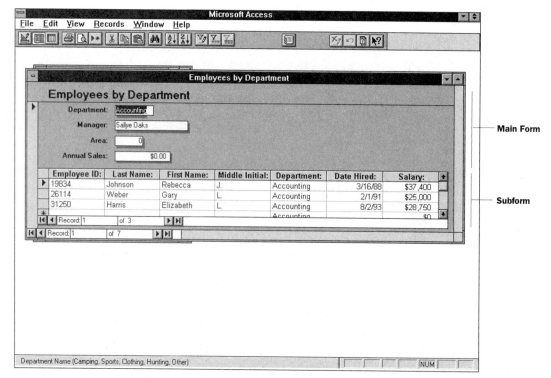

FIGURE 5.7
*Form styles
dialog box*

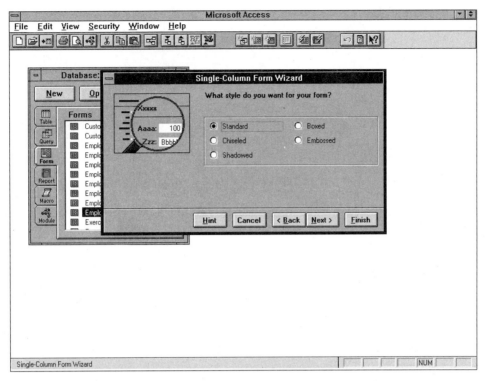

NOTE *You can modify the default settings for the AutoForm with the File/Add-ins command, not described here.*

Field List

You must decide which fields to place in the form, and their sequence, called *tab order*. Many people will add data to the form from a paper document, so field sequence ought to mimic the order of fields in the paper document. When you have finished with a field, the Tab key will take you to the next field on the form. Shift Tab will take you to the previous field. You can override the tab order with the Edit | Tab Order command. Search Access help for Tab Order for more information.

You may decide to add all of the record's fields to the form, or to select a subset of fields. For example, you might use a supervisor version of a form with all fields available, but use a separate form for lower-level employees that does not include certain sensitive fields such as salary and date of birth.

Form Styles

After you specify the type of form, Form Wizards will ask you what style you want to use. These styles do not affect the data or form itself, only the way fields appear on the screen. In each case, the field name appears as a label next to the field text box. Figure 5.7 shows the Form Wizard dialog box for choosing the style. You can click on each style button in this box to see a preview of the style in the left portion of the box.

The usual style is *Standard* with the field label to the left of the field value box. The *Chiseled, Shadowed*, and *Embossed* styles add three-dimensional characteristics to the form. The *Boxed* style places the field name *above* the field box, but otherwise these five styles are similar.

Using the Form Wizards

This section will cover use of the Access Form Wizards to create a form. The subsequent Guided Activities will help you to easily build your own forms.

Steps in Building a Form with Form Wizards

The Form Wizards help you create the form by presenting a series of questions. As you fill in the answers to these questions, the form is created automatically. You don't have to remember long steps on your own when using the Form Wizards to build a form.

Although the form created in this process is complete, you may want to make some changes to its design. You may use the Form Design view to make corrections manually. But because Form Wizards are so easy to use, we recommend that you create a new form with the Form Wizards at least until you have more experience with Access. This unit does not cover making manual changes in Form Design view.

Before starting the Form Wizards, you should open the Database window for your database, then select the Form mode in the Database window. To create a form, click the New button. Then answer the questions presented by Form Wizards.

When using the Form Wizards, you must provide the following information:

- Which table or query the form will use for its *data source* (the table or query from which the form gets its data values)

- Type of form to build (Single-Column, Tabular, Graph, Main/Subform, AutoForm)

- Order of fields to place in the form

- Which style to use (Standard, Chiseled, Shadowed, Embossed, Boxed)

- Title to appear at the top of the form

After you have specified this information, Access will give you a chance to open your form or to make changes to its design. You can also use Cue Cards to make changes to the form's design. After examining the form, you must give the form a name and save it in the database.

GUIDED ACTIVITY 5.1

Creating a Form with Form Wizards

In this Guided Activity you will use the Form Wizards to create a single-column form.

1. Start Windows and load Access.

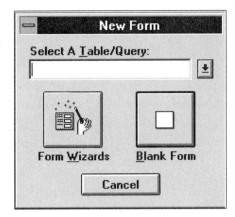

FIGURE 5.8
The New Form dialog box

2. Use the File | Open Database command to open the HUNT database. This database can be found on the West Student Data Disk that accompanies this book.

3. Click the Form button in the Database window.

4. Click the New button to open the New Form window.

5. Click on the selector button to the right of the Select A Table/Query combo box in the New Form window, shown in Figure 5.8. Access will display an alphabetical list of all the tables and queries associated with the current database. Click once on the Products table but *do not* press ⏎Enter. The Products table will become the data source for this new form.

CHECKPOINT 5A What would happen if you *double-clicked* the table name in step 5?

6. Click on the Form Wizards button in the New Form window.

7. Access will display a window with the various types of forms and reports you can build with the Wizards. At the right side is a list of the five form types. Select Single-Column, then click OK. See Figure 5.9.

8. Next Access will display the Form Wizard window with a picture of your form type at the left and a list of your fields on the right. You can add fields one at a time, in the desired order, or click on the >> button to add all the fields from the Products table in the order they were placed in the table definition.

FIGURE 5.9
Main Form Wizards window

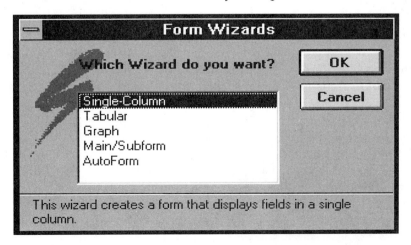

9. For this example, click on the >> button to add all the fields to the form, and click on Next to go to the next step.

CHECKPOINT 5B What could you do if you accidentally added the wrong fields to the form?

10. The Form Wizard window now shows the five form styles, with a picture of the currently selected style in the left side of the window. Choose Standard, then click on Next.

11. In the form title box, key in `Product Entry`. This title appears at the top of the form whenever it is used.

12. Click on the Finish button to open the form with data in it, shown in Figure 5.3 earlier in this unit. Notice that `Product Entry` appears in the title bar of the form window.

13. You may use the navigation buttons at the bottom of the form to scroll through the records in the Products table.

14. When finished examining the data from the Products table, use the File I Save Form command to save the form's design. Use the name `Product Entry` for the form.

15. Double-click the form's Control-menu box to close the form. (Or use the File I Close command.) If you neglected to save the form in the previous step, Access will ask whether you want to save the results before closing the form window or to cancel the close command.

Form Design View

Although we will not explain how to make changes to form design in this unit, you may be interested to see what Access uses to represent the form design. While the Product Entry form is active, you can click on the design button to see the Design view, shown in Figure 5.10.

The title of the form appears in the form *header section*, while the fields appear in the form *detail section*. The form *footer section* is empty. You can pull down the bottom border of the window to see the footer section. Surrounding the form are the horizontal and vertical *ruler bars*, used to indicate placement of the boxes on the form.

The boxes within the detail section are called controls, mentioned earlier. Adjacent to each text box is a label, in this case the field name. You will also see the *Control Toolbox* in the lower-left portion of the screen. The buttons in this toolbox are used to place different kinds of controls into the form design. An experienced Access user is able to manipulate controls individually and can customize the form. Development of custom forms is covered in Units 9 and 10.

In the next Guided Activity we introduce a more complicated form, again created with Access Form Wizards.

FIGURE 5.10
Design view of the Product Entry form

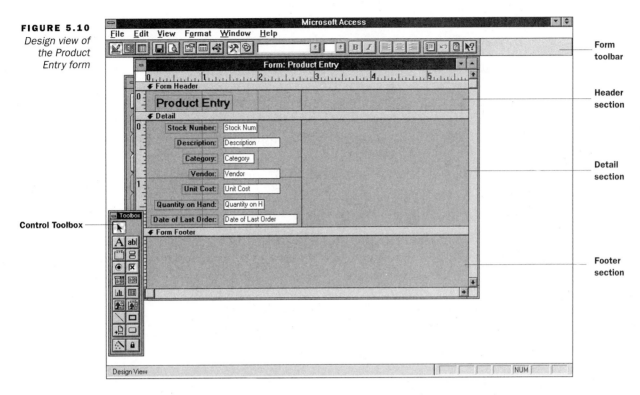

GUIDED ACTIVITY 5.2

Creating a Main/Subform

In this Guided Activity you will use the Form Wizards to create a more complex form that shows the Hunter River departments at the top and employees belonging to each department at the bottom.

1. Make sure you are at the HUNT Database window.

2. Click on the Form button and click on New.

3. At the New Form window choose the Department table, then click on the Form Wizards button.

4. Select the Main/Subform Access Wizard (form type) and click on OK.

5. You will be asked which table or query contains data for the subform. Choose the Employees table and click on Next.

6. Next, specify which fields from the main form table should be placed in the form. Click on the >> button and go to the Next window.

7. Next, select all of the fields from the Employees table for the subform by clicking on the >> button, then click on Next.

8. Use the Shadowed style in this form, and go on to the Next step.

9. In the title box, enter Employees by Department. Then click on the Open button to view the new form.

10. Access will prompt you to give a name for the subform before it will show you the result. Enter `Employee Subform`, then click on OK.

11. Next you will see the finished main/subform, shown in Figure 5.6 earlier in this unit. The fields from the Department table appear as a single-column main form, while the fields from the Employee table appear in the tabular subform at the bottom of the form window. Each part of the form has its own record selector area. We will work with this form shortly, in Guided Activity 5.4. Save this form as Employees by Department.

Viewing and Editing Data with a Form

In this section you will view and edit data from the Hunter River database using several Access forms. A form generally displays a single record at a time, and you can use the navigation buttons to move data from the table through the form window. Any changes made to data in the form are automatically made to the underlying table, even if you have used a query as the form's data source.

NOTE *If a field or expression is **read-only**, you will not be able to make changes to its value in the form. Some applications may require that users only view data.*

Viewing Field Values

Ordinarily the form consists of a set of field labels, each with an attached text box that contains field values. The form opens with the pointer in the first field of the first record. You can move from field to field in the form by pressing the [Tab] key, or by clicking on the field you would like to see. If there are more fields than will fit in the window, you may need to use the vertical and horizontal scroll bars to see them.

When you open the form, Access will size the window just large enough to display all of the fields unless there are more fields than can fit on the screen. You can resize the form window by dragging the corners or sides of the window. You can also use the minimize and maximize buttons to change the window size.

Moving the Record Pointer in the Form

With the single-column form, you will see the fields from a single record at a time. You can scroll through the records by using the *navigation buttons* at the bottom of the form window. They work just like the navigation buttons in the datasheet's table window—the inner arrow buttons move one record backward or forward, and the outer arrow buttons move to the first or last records, respectively. You can also use the [PgUp] and [PgDn] keys to scroll from record to record, or the Records | Goto command from the menu bar to go to a specific record.

With a tabular form, you will see several records at one time, displayed across the screen. You can move the record pointer by clicking on the record selector button, or by using the navigation buttons in the status line, the [PgUp] and [PgDn] keys, or the Records menu bar.

Adding Data with a Form

Working with the form is very similar to working with the datasheet. If you want to add new records to the underlying table, use the Records | Data Entry command (or click the New Record button in the toolbar) to display a blank form. Another method is to move to the last record with the navigation buttons. Then click on the next record button (or press `PgDn`) and Access will display a new blank record on the form. You can key in new values on the form and they will be stored in the underlying table.

Editing Data with a Form

To edit data with the form, position the record selector to the desired record, then click on the field that you want to change. Make changes to the values as necessary, then go to the next record to be changed. Access will display a pencil icon in the record selector area in the left portion of the form window while you are making changes to the record, indicating that the changes have not yet been committed to the database. When you move to a different record, the new values are automatically saved in the table, just as in Datasheet mode. You can undo changes to the current record with the Undo button in the toolbar.

Deleting Records with a Form

To delete the current record, click in the record selector area. Then press the `Del` key or use the Edit | Delete command from the menu bar. Access will ask you to confirm that you want to delete the highlighted record(s). *Remember that deletions are irrevocable*—once you have deleted the record and confirmed it, the data are gone. You will have to key them in again if the deletion was in error.

GUIDED ACTIVITY 5.3

Working with Data Using a Form

In this Guided Activity you will use a form to make changes to the HUNT database.

1. Start Access and open the HUNT Database window.

2. Click on the Form button, then open the Product Entry form.

3. Notice the size that Access picked for the form window. Use the mouse to decrease the box size, working with the lower-right corner.

CHECKPOINT 5C What happened to the window when you reduced the size so that not all of the fields appear within the form window at one time?

4. Use the mouse to resize the window to its original size. Alternatively, you can close and reopen the form to regain its original size.

5. Use the navigation buttons to directly move the record pointer to record 8. Reduce the quantity on hand by one unit. Notice that Access displays the pencil icon in the record selector area.

CHECKPOINT 5D   What is the purpose of the pencil icon in the form?

▶| ✗6. Click on the last record button, and examine the contents of this record. Access is able to move the record pointer there very quickly.

7. Next enter the Records | Data Entry command to display a blank form. The navigation buttons should say Record 1, even though there are many more records in the table.

8. Add the following record:

```
63050  5" Combination Knife  Hunting  Swick  $14.70  9  1/15/93
```

9. When you have entered all the fields, close the form by double-clicking on the Control-menu box.

10. Open the form again and click on the last record button. You should see the record that you just added to the Products table.

11. Click on the record selector area of the form, then press the [Del] key to delete the record you just added. Confirm the change when Access prompts you.

The next Guided Activity will explore use of the main/subform form that you created earlier in this unit.

GUIDED ACTIVITY 5.4

Working with Data in a Main/Subform

In this Guided Activity you will work with data using a main/subform.

1. Return to the HUNT Database window and open the Employees by Department form, previously shown in Figure 5.6.

2. The main form uses the Departments table as its data source. Because this table is indexed by its primary key, department name, the departments will appear in alphabetical order. The Accounting department is listed first, along with its three employees. The Employees table is indexed by employee number, and its record appears in that order.

3. Click on the next record button in the navigation area in the *middle* of the form window to move to the next employee of the Accounting department. Remember that the main form has its own navigation buttons at the bottom of the form.

4. Click on the next record button two times in the navigation area at the *bottom* of the form window. You should see the next department (Marketing) and its employees appear in the form. If you had accidentally pressed the Employees navigation button, you would see the second employee of the Accounting department.

5. Let us add new employees in Marketing at this time by using the Records | Data Entry command and filling in fields in the subform. The new employee data is shown below.

```
23111 Oak       Sally M.      Marketing      9/10/89    42,500
```

Figure 5.11 shows the form with this new entry in the Marketing department.

✗6. Manipulate the navigation buttons to find the fourth employee in the Sales department.

✗7. Form windows can be moved like any other window. Use the pointer to drag the window's title bar to a new location so that you can view other objects on the desktop.

Printing the Form

Although forms are primarily designed for displaying data values on the screen, Access provides a way to print them. Unfortunately, Access may not keep all fields from one form together on a single printed page. Thus, the printed form output may leave something to be desired. Access reports are usually a better way to print information.

It is possible to modify the form properties to force Access to print each form on a separate page. The default is to place forms together, one after another, until the printed page is full and the output spills to the next page.

As we did with printing the table in Datasheet view, you can use the Print Preview button to see how the printed output will look. To do this, open the Database window and switch to forms. Click once on the form you wish to print, and click on the Print Preview button. Access will show you a reduced view of the printed form.

FIGURE 5.11
Employee form with new record

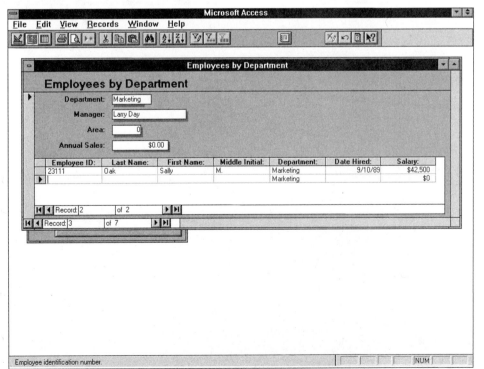

You can place the magnifying glass pointer on any part of the reduced page and click once to zoom in on that portion. You can click on the Print button to print the form as is, or click on the Close button to return to the Database window.

GUIDED ACTIVITY 5.5

Printing a Form

In this Guided Activity we will print a form on the printer. If your computer is not able to print, you can still preview the output and see how the printed page would appear.

1. Start Access and open the HUNT Database window. Click on the Form button to display the forms in this database.

2. Select the Product Entry form by clicking once on it. You don't have to open the form to print it.

3. Click on the Print Preview button and Access will create a print preview on the screen. You should see four or five forms repeating on one page. A sample appears in Figure 5.12.

4. You can use the magnifying glass pointer to zoom in on a portion of the page. Move the pointer to the desired location and click the left mouse button to zoom in on the desired part of the report.

FIGURE 5.12
Form Print Preview output, zoomed out

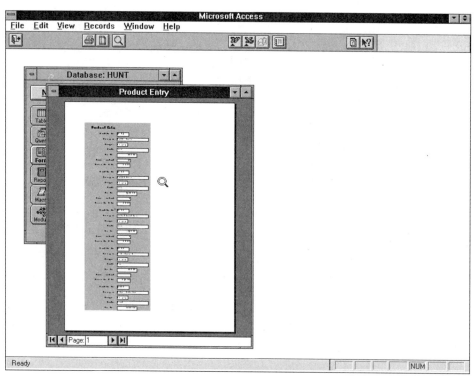

5. If a printer is attached to your computer and configured to print in Windows, click the Print button to print the output. Otherwise click Close to return to the Database window.

6. This is the final Guided Activity for this unit. If you are finished working with Access, close it by double-clicking on the Control-menu box or use the File | Exit command.

Command Review

Shift Tab	Move to the previous field.
Tab	Move to the next field.
Edit	Delete	Delete the highlighted field value.
Edit	Tab Order	Change field order in a form.
File	Save Form	Save the form design.
Records	Data Entry	Use the form to add new record values.

Exercises

Use the Hunter River database contained in the HUNT.MDB file on the West Student Data Disk for these exercises.

1. Create a single-column form with all fields for the Employees table using the Embossed style. The name of the form should be Employee Information. Print a copy of the form with data from the Employee table.

2. Create a tabular form for the Products table. Use the Boxed style. Place only the following fields in the form in the order given, not the order in the table definition. Print just one page of this form.

    Stock Number   Vendor   Unit Cost   Quantity on Hand

The name of the form should be Exercise 5-2.

3. Use the 1992 Expenses table to prepare a single-column standard form. Use all fields in the default order. Print a copy of the data in the form. Save the form with the name Exercise 5-3.

4. Use the Vendors and Products tables to prepare a main/subform form for the Hunter River management. Which table should be used for the main portion of this form? Which vendors do not have any products in the current Products file? Can you tell whether there are any products that do not have a matching vendor in the Vendors file? Save the form with the name Exercise 5-4.

5. Use the AutoForm Wizard to create a Customer form. Print a copy of the data in the form. Save the form with the name Exercise 5-5.

Review Questions

1. Explain the purpose of the Form Wizards in creating Access forms. *To speed up process to create forms. Uses all fields*

2. Discuss the five types of forms available with Form Wizards. Explain the purpose of each type of form. *Single-Column, Tabular, Main Subform, Autoform, Graph*

3. Discuss the use of the field list screen in Form Wizards. *Lists all fields for use in specific table*

4. Suppose you create a form with Form Wizards that is not quite correct. What steps would you follow to make corrections? *Switch to design view and make changes.*

5. Describe the form's possible data sources. *Table, query, both.*

6. Is it possible to make permanent changes to the data values displayed in the form? Explain how this is done. *yes, record, data entry for new, or go to records make changes to old.*

7. Discuss the purpose of the following tools and buttons in an Access form:

   a. Vertical scroll bar *so side to side*

   b. Next record button *go to next record*

   c. Record selector *shows record*

   d. Control Toolbox *turns on & off lets you use auto controls*

8. Explain how you would delete a particular record while using a form.

Key Terms

AutoForm form	Footer section	Read-only
Boxed style	Form Design view	Ruler bar
Chiseled style	Form view	Shadowed style
Control	Form Wizards	Single-column form
Control Toolbox	Graph form	Standard style
Data source	Header section	Tab order
Detail section	Main/subform form	Tabular form
Embossed style	Navigation button	

Documentation Research

Use the printed documentation and the on-line Help available with Microsoft Access to answer the following questions. If you use one of the manuals, provide the page number for your reference in the manual.

1. How would you change the tab order in an existing form?

2. Describe the kinds of headers available with an Access form.

3. Use Cue Cards to learn more about Access forms.

4. Learn how the Add-ins Manager can be used to change the default style and format of an AutoForm Form Wizard.

Physicians' Medical Clinic (IV): Building a Form to View Data

In this exercise you will create a form to view, add, and edit data using the concepts from previous units. You will open the PMC database, create a form using Form Wizards, view data, add new data, edit data, and print the results. Read the directions carefully. Clearly identify which output goes with which part of the application.

1. Start Windows and enter Access. Open the PMC database.

2. Because of the large number of lengthy fields in the Patients table, Dr. Greenway has requested that you create a form to facilitate data entry. All fields in this table must be included in the form, but you have some latitude in the sequence and placement of fields on the form. Remember that the sequence should follow the order in which data is obtained from the patient. Design your form on paper first, then use the Form Wizard to create the form. Save a copy of the form's design. Use the Records | Data Entry command, then print a copy of the blank form.

3. Use the form to enter the following information for one patient. Do *not* type the hyphens in the Patient Number field.

   ```
   555-12-9876    Henry, Kelsey J.    1552 Fifth Avenue     Paris, IL 61944
   02/01/1950     State University    US Insurance Company  B-35524-9867
   ```

   Print the form for this patient.

4. Locate the patient whose patient number is 123-45-6789. Change the employer to Graphics Design and Typography. Print the form preview showing this record.

5. Suppose you were told that it takes too long to enter all of the information for new patients, and had to streamline the data entry process. You know that most patients are from a single city and state, that there are four major employers that employ probably 75% of new patients, and that three health insurance companies cover 80–90% of patients. How would you modify the design of the form to make use of this information?   *List Box*

NOTE *Do not make changes to the form to accommodate these changes now.*

Building a Report

This unit will illustrate the use of Access reports to display printed data from one or more tables. You will learn the report basics, including the types of reports available with Report Wizards. You will create a simple report using Report Wizards, then view that report in Print Preview view. You will learn how to make manual changes to the report design. The unit concludes with a section on mailing label reports.

Learning Objectives

At the completion of this unit you should know

1. the types of reports available in Access,

2. the advantages of using a report to display data,

3. the uses of the report sections.

At the completion of this unit you should be able to

1. create a groups/totals report with Report Wizards,

2. make minor modifications to the report design,

3. build a sorted report,

4. create a mailing labels report.

Important Commands

File | Open Database

File | Print Preview

File | Save

Report Basics

Access *reports* provide a visually attractive means of presenting data in printed form, usually for all records in a table or query's dynaset. You can arrange the sequence of the data fields used and format the fields as desired. You can combine fields and create calculated fields. Totals and subtotals are available in Access reports.

Reports Versus Forms

Reports and forms are very similar. Both show records from one or more tables, but reports provide more control over how printed data will appear. Reports also give more flexibility for handling summarized data than forms. While forms require you to create a main form with a related subform (each with its own table or query) to show detailed data, reports can group data with a single table or query.

As with forms, reports allow you to combine graphical information and Access controls. Most of the techniques used to build forms can also be used with reports, including Cue Cards and Report Wizards. However, reports are designed expressly for printing. They can only be viewed on the screen in Print Preview fashion. You cannot use a report to input or edit data, as you can with a form.

The Report Design View Toolbar

Figure 6.1 shows the Report Design view toolbar. It shares some buttons with Table Datasheet view and Form view. The Report Design view is covered in Unit 11.

FIGURE 6.1
Report Design view toolbar

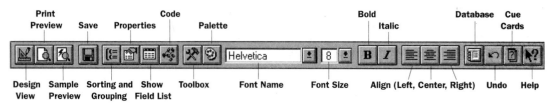

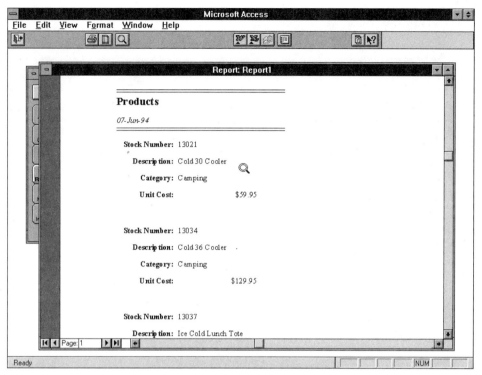

Designing a Report

In this section we will discuss the types of reports and styles available via Access Report Wizards.

Types of Reports

Access provides an easy-to-use tool called **Report Wizard** for creating reports. The Report Wizard leads you through an interview process, asking questions about what kind of report you would like to build and eliciting the appropriate information for the report. There are seven main types of reports in Report Wizards, described next.

SINGLE-COLUMN REPORT

The **single-column report** is similar to the single-column form look, with fields going down the page in one long column. At the left side of the column is the field name or caption as a label, and on the right side is the field value. Each field appears on a different line. Single-column reports are used with long field values. An example of a single-column report is shown in Figure 6.2.

FIGURE 6.3
Groups/totals report

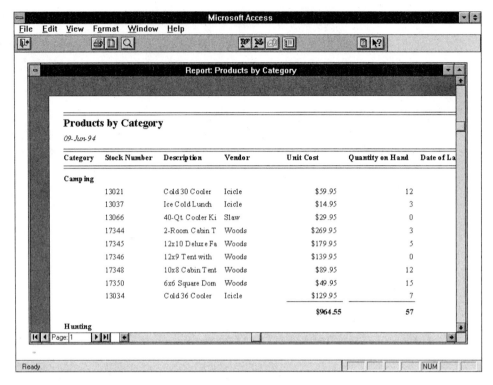

GROUPS/TOTALS REPORT

The *groups/totals report* resembles the datasheet or tabular form, but without boxes around cells. (You can request that values appear in boxes.) Field name or caption labels appear as column headings, spread across the page. Field values appear beneath the headings, one row per record. This report type is particularly useful for showing groups of data with subtotals and totals. It is not necessary to specify a group field with this report, so it can be used to prepare ordinary tabular reports. The groups/totals type is the most common report used with Access. Figure 6.3 shows a groups/totals report.

MAILING LABELS REPORT

The *mailing labels report* combines both previous types. Field values appear like a mailing label, usually one per row, although there can be one or more labels across the page in a grid, depending on the size of the label and the paper used. Access does not print field labels with this report type. Mailing labels reports are particularly useful when printing mailing labels, but are also useful for displaying short blocks of related data on regular paper when the other two types are not appropriate. An example of a mailing labels report is shown in Figure 6.4.

SUMMARY REPORT

The *summary report* organizes data into groups and prints subtotals and totals for groups of data. It is similar to the groups/totals report except that it does not

FIGURE 6.4
Mailing labels report

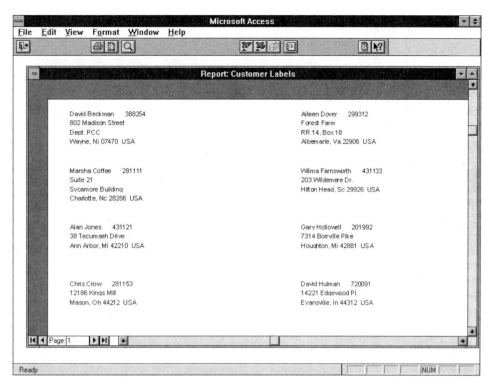

print the detail records in the report, only the summary. This Report Wizard is new to Access 2.0.

TABULAR REPORT

The *tabular report* displays data in columns, from left to right, similar to a tabular form. Each record appears in a new row. Labels appear at the top of each column. This Report Wizard is new to Access 2.0.

AUTOREPORT REPORT

The *AutoReport report* automatically creates a single-column report with each field on a separate line and the field name to the left of the field value. You can change the style of the AutoReport Wizard with the File I Add-ins command.

MS WORD MAIL MERGE REPORT

The *MS Word Mail Merge report* can be created automatically by this Report Wizard. It will assemble the data necessary to do merge printing with Microsoft Word 6. You must have MS Word installed in Windows on your computer in order to print the report.

Report Fields

As with Access forms, the next step is to specify the fields for the report. You can select them one at a time with the > button, or choose all fields with the >> button.

Report Styles

After you specify the report fields, Report Wizards will ask you what style you want to use. These styles do not affect the data or the fields in the reports, only the way they appear on paper. As you create the report with the Report Wizards, Access will show you a preview of the style in the report type you have chosen. In most cases you can "back up" by clicking the Back button and change your selection to a different style.

The default style is *Executive*, with the field label appearing in bold text. The *Presentation* style underlines the field name label that appears in bold. In *Ledger* style the fields appear in cells with boxes around them; the field labels appear in bold. Access may use different fonts in different styles. The best way to choose among report styles is to print a page in each style and select the one that fits your application. You can also choose between portrait orientation (upright) and landscape (sideways) page orientation.

Using the Report Wizards

This section will cover use of the Access Report Wizards to create a report. The subsequent Guided Activities will help you to easily build your own reports.

Steps in Building a Report with Report Wizards

The Report Wizards help you create the report by presenting a series of questions. As you fill in the answers to these questions, the report design is created automatically. You don't have to remember long steps on your own when using the Report Wizard to build a report.

Although the report created in the process is complete, you may want to make some changes to its design. You can use the Report Design view to make corrections manually, or use the Report Wizards and build a new report with the desired features. This unit does not cover making manual changes in Report Design view. Unit 11 will cover creating reports manually, without Report Wizards.

Before starting the Report Wizard, you should open the Database window for your database, then select the Report button in the Database window. To create a report, click on the New button. Then answer the questions presented by the Report Wizard.

When using the Report Wizard, you must provide the following information:

- Which table or query the report will use for its data source; this **binds** the report to its data source. You can use a query to limit reports to certain records.

- Type of report to build (single-column, groups/totals, mailing labels)

- Order of fields to place in the report

- Fields to group by and sort on, depending on which report type is chosen

- Which style to use (Executive, Presentation, Ledger) and orientation (Portrait, Landscape)

- Title to appear at the top of the report and other report options that vary by type of report

Previewing and Printing the Report

After you have specified this information, Access will give you a chance to preview your report or to make changes to its design. The procedure is essentially the same as with other Access data objects: after selecting the report to preview, click on the Print Preview button in the toolbar. Access will generate an image of the report for the screen and allow you to zoom in any portion for scrutiny—say, a *subtotal*. The navigation buttons at the bottom of the preview window can be used to select other pages of the report. You may want to check the last page to see end-of-report *grand totals*. You can then send the report to the printer or cancel the preview command and return to the report window.

If you have saved a report in the database, you can still preview the report before printing it. In the Database window, highlight the report's name, then click on the Preview button in the Database window.

Saving the Report

Finally, you must give the report a name and save it in the database. The File | Save command is ordinarily used to save the report design. If you close the report window without saving the report design, Access will prompt you to save the report or cancel the close command.

GUIDED ACTIVITY 6.1

Creating a Report with Report Wizards

In this Guided Activity you will use the Report Wizard to create a group report and preview it on the screen.

1. Start Windows and load Access.

2. Use the File | Open command to open the HUNT database. The HUNT database can be found on the West Student Data Disk that accompanies this book.

3. Click the Report button in the Database window to switch to Report mode.

4. Click on the New button to open the New Report window, shown in Figure 6.5.

5. Click on the selector button to the right of the Select A Table/Query box. Access will display an alphabetical list of all the tables and queries associated with the current database. Click once on the Products table but *do not press* Enter.

FIGURE 6.5
*The New Report
dialog box*

6.   Click on the Report Wizards button in the New Report window.

7.   Access will display the window shown in Figure 6.6 with a list of the seven report types. Select Groups/Totals, then click OK.

FIGURE 6.6
*Main Report
Wizards window*

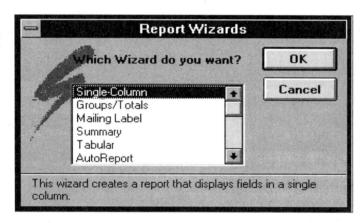

8.   Access will display the Report Wizard window with a picture of your report type at the left and a list of the fields in the right. You can add fields one at a time, or click on the >> button to add all the fields from the Products table in the order they were placed in the table definition. See Figure 6.7.

9.   For this example, click on the >> button to add all fields to the report. Click on Next to go to the next step.

CHECKPOINT 6A   What could you do to remedy the situation if you accidentally added the wrong fields to the report?

10.   Next, Access will ask you to specify a field to group the report by. Highlight the Category field and click on the > button. Click on Next to go to the next step, and click on Next again to accept the Normal group by criteria.

11.   Access will ask you to specify fields to sort on. We'll skip this step, so click on Next.

12.   The Report Wizard window will next show you the three report styles, with a picture of the currently selected style in the left portion of the window. Click on Executive, and keep the Landscape orientation. Click on Next to go to the last step.

FIGURE 6.7
The Report Wizard Field List dialog box

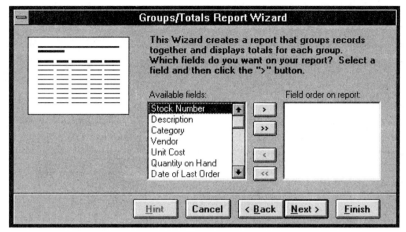

Groups/Totals Report Wizard

This Wizard creates a report that groups records together and displays totals for each group.
Which fields do you want on your report? Select a field and then click the ">" button.

Available fields:

Stock Number
Description
Category
Vendor
Unit Cost
Quantity on Hand
Date of Last Order

Field order on report:

>
>>
<
<<

Hint   Cancel   < Back   Next >   Finish

NOTE   *Access chose the Landscape (sideways) orientation because you have so many fields in the report. If you choose the Portrait orientation, there are too many fields to fit on one page.*

13.   In the report title box key in Products by Category. The title appears at the top of the first page of the report, along with the system date when the report is printed. Click on the Calculate percentages line to *remove* the group percentages.

14.   Click on the Finish button to see a preview of the printed version on the screen, shown earlier in Figure 6.3.

15.   You can use the magnifying glass pointer to zoom in or out on a section of the report. Use the navigation buttons at the bottom of the window to scroll to different pages of the report.

16.   If your computer has a printer attached, click on the Print button to send the output to the printer. Otherwise click on the Cancel button to return to the report window.

CHECKPOINT 6B   Examine the output of the report carefully, particularly the two subtotal figures. Is it appropriate to total the Unit Cost and Quantity fields?

17.   Use the File | Save command to save the report's design. Use the same name, Products by Category.

18.   Double-click on the Control-menu box to close the report window. (Or use the File | Close command.) If you neglected to save the report in the previous step, Access will ask whether you want to save the report before closing the report window, or to cancel the close command.

Report Design View

You may be interested to see what Access uses to represent the report design. Figure 6.8 shows the Design view for the Products by Category report of the previous Guided Activity. The Controls Toolbox covers up a small portion of the last few report sections. You can drag the title bar of the Toolbox to a new location that does not hide a part of the design that you want to work with.

FIGURE 6.8
*Design view for
groups/totals
report*

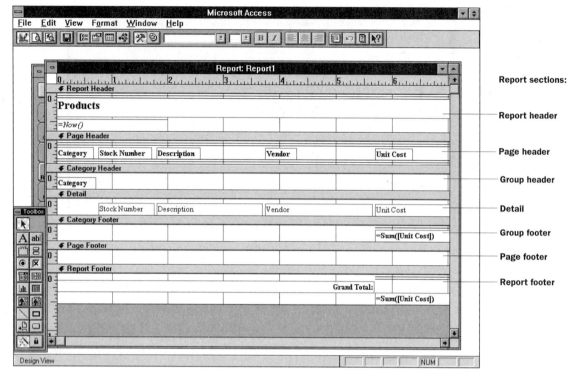

Report Sections

Like many other database management products, Access uses a *report section* structure to hold parts of the design. There are seven sections in the Products by Category report, described below. All but the two Category sections (header and footer) are standard in all reports. The Category sections are present because we asked the Report Wizard to produce a group report, grouped by that field.

Report sections help you organize the information that goes into the report. Fields and other controls are placed in the sections as needed. A control's section will determine where and how often that control is printed in the report. A discussion of each section follows.

REPORT HEADER SECTION

The *report header section* contains information that is printed only on the first page of the report. The standard groups/totals Report Wizard will place the report title and system date fields in the report header section, along with horizontal rule lines that separate the title from the rest of the report. You might want to place a logo or other graphic in the report header section as well.

PAGE HEADER SECTION

The *page header section* appears at the top of every page of the report except the first page, where it appears just beneath the report header. Place column headings in this section for tabular reports.

GROUP (CATEGORY) HEADER SECTION

The *group header section* appears at the beginning of a new group of records. The field name used for grouping (in this case, Category) is displayed in the Design view. Access substitutes the value of the group by field in the actual report output. Access usually leaves a blank line before a new group begins, but you can override that to start a new group on a new page. You will see this in Guided Activity 6.3.

DETAIL SECTION

The *detail section* contains the values for fields you have chosen for the report, one record per line in the detail section. Tabular reports display fields side by side, so a long field will take up considerable room in the detail section. You might choose to display less than the full field, or spread the field over two or more lines, in such a case.

GROUP (CATEGORY) FOOTER SECTION

The *group footer section* appears at the end of a group of records. You can add group totals in this section, or display a count of the number of records in the group.

PAGE FOOTER SECTION

The *page footer section* appears at the bottom of each page in the report. You can use it for page numbers, as well as additional information not contained in the report title. Not all users will need a page footer.

REPORT FOOTER SECTION

The *report footer section* appears at the end of the report, on the last page. You can use it for report totals and record counts. Note that the report footer section appears before the page footer on the last page of the report.

Making Changes in Report Design View

Although we did not discuss manual changes in forms in Unit 5, it may be necessary for even casual users to make some slight modifications to the report design provided by the Report Wizard. For example, it is not appropriate to show group and report totals for the Unit Cost field from the previous example.

To make changes to the report's design, highlight the report name and click on the Design button in Report mode of the Database window. You can move, resize, or delete controls in the design by clicking on their corresponding Design view. The following Guided Activity will show how to make a few changes to the design without going into detailed Report Design view instructions. Further modification techniques are covered in Unit 11.

GUIDED ACTIVITY 6.2

Changing the Report Design Manually

In this Guided Activity you will make four small changes to the Products by Category report design created by the Report Wizard in the previous activity.

1. In the HUNT Database window, switch to Report mode.

2. Highlight the Products by Category report name. Click on the Design button to open Report Design view. You should see the same screen as in Figure 6.8.

3. With the mouse, click once on the label box containing the title of the report in the Report Header section. Wait a second, then click once more. The insertion point cursor should be blinking at the end of the title. If a report property box appears instead, click one more time in the label box to open the label box for editing.

4. Use the arrow keys (or the mouse) to move the pointer to the letter b in by. Change this letter to a capital B and press [Enter].

5. Next click once on the box in the Category Footer containing =Sum([Unit Cost]).

CHECKPOINT 6C   What do the handles at the edges of this box represent?

6. Press the [Del] key to remove this control field from the report design.

7. Repeat the process to delete the same box in the Report Footer section of the design.

8. Notice that there are two thin horizontal lines remaining above the control box you deleted in the previous step. Carefully click on one line with the mouse; you should see its move handles appear. Press the [Del] key to remove the Unit Cost underscore line from the design.

9. Repeat step 8 to remove the remaining horizontal line.

10. To view your efforts, click the Print Preview button. (Or use the File | Print Preview command in the menu bar.)

11. You should see that the report title has been modified, and that the two totals for the Unit Cost field are gone.

12. Use the File | Save command to save the changes made to the report design, and close the report window.

The following activity will give you a chance to build a more complicated groups/totals report with the Report Wizard.

GUIDED ACTIVITY 6.3

Building a Sorted Groups/Totals Report

In this Guided Activity you will use the Report Wizard to create a report with two group levels.

1. Open the HUNT Database window and change to the Report mode.

2. Click on the New button to create a new report.

3. At the Select A Table/Query combo box of the New Report window, select the query called Inventory Value. Only records that match this query will appear in the report.

4. Click on the Report Wizards button.

5. Choose the Groups/Totals report type.

6. Add these fields in the order specified: Category, Vendor, Description, and Expr1. We will not use the Date of Last Order field. The Expr1 field is an expression, calculated in the query as [Unit Cost]*[Quantity on Hand] for each product in the Products table. Click Next to go to the next screen.

7. At the next Report Wizard window, click on > to specify these fields to group by, in the order given: Category, Vendor. Click Next to go to the next step.

8. We'll use the default grouping of Normal for both group fields, so just click on Next at the next window.

9. Let's sort by the Expr1 field, so that items will appear by order of inventory value within each group and subgroup. Click Next to go to the next step.

10. Use the Executive style for this report and Portrait orientation, then click Next.

11. The report title should be Inventory Value Group Report. Click on the Calculate percentages line to omit percentage calculations.

12. Click on the Finish button to view your report.

CHECKPOINT 6D Are you satisfied with the label Expr1 as the column heading for inventory value?

13. Use the File | Save command to save the report under the same name, Inventory Value Group Report. Close the Print Preview window and return to the Database window.

14. From the Database window, be sure that this report is highlighted, then click on the Design button.

15. You will see the design that the Access Report Wizard created for your report. Click two times slowly on the box containing Expr1 in the Page Header section. (Be certain that you do not click on the similar box in the Detail section.)

16. Use the [Del] key to delete the letters Expr1. Then key in Inventory Value. The box will expand to contain your new column heading label. Press [Enter] when finished.

FIGURE 6.9
*Print Preview for
Group Report*

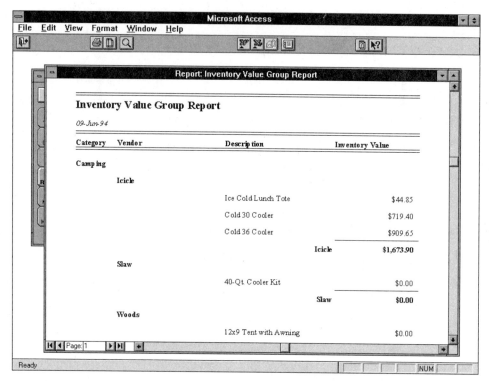

17. Click on the Print Preview button in the toolbar, and Access will show you the modified report. If a printer is attached to your computer, print the report. Figure 6.9 shows the Print Preview window for this report. Close this window.

18. Finally, use the File | Save command to save the changes to your report. Close the report design window and return to the Database window.

Creating a Mailing Labels Report

The mailing labels Report Wizard requires more effort than single-column and groups/totals reports. Although the basic approach is the same, you must specify which fields are to be placed on each line of the label design, as well as provide the dimensions of the labels to be used.

Using the Mailing Labels Report Wizard

Figure 6.10 shows the mailing label format screen in the Report Wizard sequence. At the left is a picture of the general format of a label report. The center of the window shows the field list, with > and < buttons to add or remove those fields from the report design. The punctuation buttons are beneath the field list. These buttons insert punctuation symbols such as spaces or commas into the report design. The Newline button represents the hard return key on the keyboard, and sends you to the next line of the label format. At the right is a box that shows the label appearance as you

FIGURE 6.10
*Completed label
format*

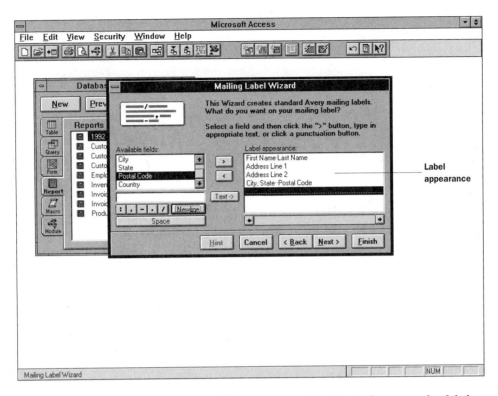

add fields and punctuation to it. You can type in a text phrase and add that to the label format.

As you build the label format, the Report Wizard will create a report design similar to those for single-column and groups/totals reports. In fact, when you preview the mailing labels report, Access will display the report design before showing the print output. Only three report sections appear in a mailing labels report design, and two of those are closed. The page header and page footer sections appear with no space allotted for them. Only the detail section has field values in it.

Making Changes to the Design

You can make changes to the report design as needed. For instance, some laser and inkjet printers are unable to print on the top ½-inch of the page. Access may "chop off" the top portion of the labels if printed with that printer. To remedy this problem in Design view, drag the border of the page header section down about ½", creating a blank header for the top of each page. The laser printer will skip down about ½-inch before printing the first row of labels. Of course, you must properly align the blank labels in the printer to ensure that they line up with the printed label. Dot-matrix printers are usually able to print to the edge of the page and don't suffer from the chopped-off effect. (See more about margins in the next section.)

Adjusting the Printer Setup

With the Print Setup window you can choose the printer for your report, and tell the printer whether you want the report orientation to be *portrait* or *landscape*.

FIGURE 6.11

Print Setup window

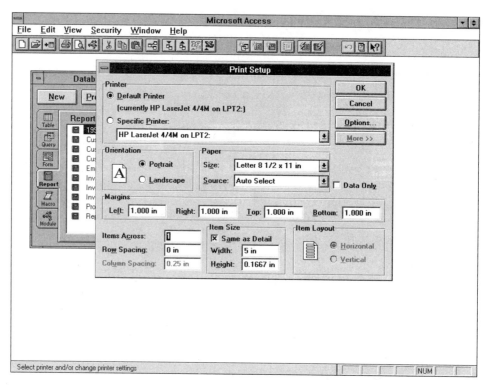

Landscape (horizontal) orientation will print the page sideways, or 11"×8½"; the default is portrait (vertical), or 8½"×11". Not all printers are capable of printing in landscape mode.

You can also make changes in the ***page margins*** for a particular report. Highlight the report name in the Database window, and give the File | Print Setup command from the menu bar. The Print Setup window is shown in Figure 6.11. You can change left, right, top, and bottom page margins in this window. To see additional choices for mailing label report, click on the ***More*** >> button. Access will display information about the number of columns in the mailing labels grid along with the column and row spacing for the grid. You can also choose whether to use the standard ***horizontal layout,*** or a ***vertical layout*** in which the labels are printed down the page rather than across the page. Any changes made here are stored in the report design.

Printing the Labels

When you print the mailing labels report, Access will substitute the values from each record into the report, filling in the labels from left to right if you have selected a label design with multiple labels per row. Trailing blanks in text fields are automatically trimmed when they are inserted in the report. If the entire row of a label is blank, Access will skip that row and move lower rows up in its place. For example, you may need to keep two lines for street addresses; the first line might be used as an office or suite number, and the second line for a building name or a street address. If a record does not need the second line, Access will simply omit it from the label report. The following Guided Activity will demonstrate this feature.

Creating a Mailing Labels Report

This Guided Activity will demonstrate how to create a mailing labels report using the Report Wizard.

1. Open the HUNT Database window and switch to Report mode.

2. Click on the New button to create a new report.

3. Select the Customers table in the New Report dialog box, then click on the Report Wizards button to design the mailing labels report.

4. Choose the Mailing Label report type, and click on OK to go to the next screen.

5. Access will display the label formatting screen and ask you to select fields for the label. Select the First Name field, and click on the > button to place that field on the first row of the label. Notice that Access shows you this field in the box on the right of the window.

6. Click on the Space button to place one space after the First Name field. Then add the Last Name field to the first row of the label. If you make a mistake, use the < button next to the field list to remove the last item placed in the label format.

7. Click the Newline button to go to the second line of the label.

8. Select the Address Line 1 field and place it on the second line of the label. Click the Newline button to go to the third line of the label.

9. Select the Address Line 2 field for the third line of the label. Click the Newline button to go to the fourth line.

10. On the fourth line place the following fields and punctuation. Remember to press the > key after you select each field.

    ```
    City<comma><Space>State<Space><Space>Postal Code<Space>
    Country<Newline>
    ```

11. Figure 6.10 shows the completed label format. Review the Label appearance box and make any corrections. When finished, click the Next button to go to the next step.

12. Access will ask for fields to sort the output on. Select the Postal Code (zip code) field and click on the > button to sort on the postal code field. Click Next to go to the next screen.

13. Next, you should specify the dimensions of your labels. Access provides the Avery brand label stock codes for nearly 60 different sizes of labels. First select the Continuous label type button, then scroll through the list until you find the correct size. In this case, we will use the second label, Avery 4144 $^{15}/_{16}$"×2½"×3 across. This means there are 3 labels across (called "3 up") with each label $^{15}/_{16}$" high and 2½" wide. With standard fonts, you can print approximately 5 or 6 lines on each label, with about 25–30 characters on each line. With smaller, proportionally spaced fonts, you can squeeze more information onto each label.

FIGURE 6.12
*Print Preview for
mailing labels*

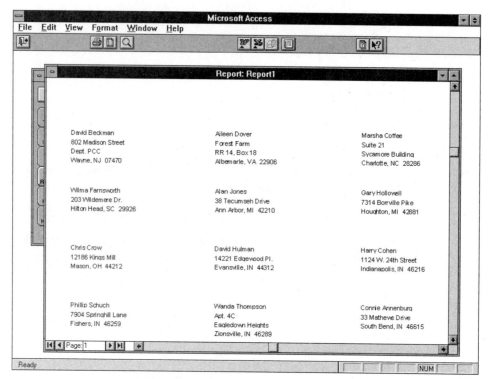

14. After you have highlighted the Avery 4144 label, click on Next to go to the next step. Click Next again to select the default font size and color.

15. Click the Finish button to view the labels that Access prepares. If a printer is attached to your computer, print the labels. Figure 6.12 shows the labels from this report.

16. Save the mailing labels report as 3-Up Customer Labels.

Command Review

File | Open Database	Open a database file from the Access startup menu.
File | Print Preview	Open the Print Preview window for the specified report.
File | Save	Save the report.

Exercises

Use the Hunter River database contained within the HUNT.MDB file on the Student Data Disk for these exercises.

1. Use the Employees table to prepare a tabular report. Include all of the fields in the report, but do not present groups or totals. Use a suitable title for your report. Print the report. Save the report design as Exercise 6-1.

2. Use the Report Wizard to prepare a group report showing employee salaries by department. Within each department, sort alphabetically. Save the report design as Exercise 6-2.

3. Create a group report for the Customers table based on the State field. Include all fields except Customer Number and Country. Print the report and save a copy as Exercise 6-3.

4. Create a set of mailing labels for the Customers table, but limit the labels to Indiana and Illinois only. Labels should appear in Postal Code (zip code) order. Print the report and save a copy as Exercise 6-4. (*Hint*: Use a query.)

5. Use the AutoReport feature to create a report for Vendors. Print the report and save a copy as Exercise 6-5.

Review Questions

1. Explain the differences between forms and reports. When is each useful, and why? *Forms- Data Entry, view records. Reports- show information, view several records*

2. Discuss the seven types of reports that you can create with Report Wizards. Give an example of each kind of report using the Employees table. *Autoformat, Mailing, Tabular, Single Column, Groups/Totals, Summary, mail merge*

3. List the general steps in creating a report with the Report Wizard. *Report tab, New, Choose data source, choose wizard, choose type, follow directions.*

4. Explain how you would remove a meaningless total field from a groups/totals report created with Report Wizard. *Go to design view, click field, press delete key*

5. Describe the differences between the term "group by" and the term "sort by" as used in Access reports. *Group puts things together based on a criteria, a sort put things in order.*

6. Give the purpose of each of the following report sections:

   a. Detail *— main information*

   b. Group footer *— shows end of each new group*

   c. Report header *— title, pertinent info for first page*

   d. Page header *— shows each page at top*

   e. Group header *- beginning each new group*

7. Explain how you could print a report that considered only employees whose annual salaries were less than $20,000 and who were hired within the past two years. *Run query, specify criteria Salary <20,000.00 & date of hire within past 2 years, then new report - report wizard. Tabular.*

Key Terms

AutoReport report
Bind
Detail section
Executive style
Grand total
Group footer section
Group header section
Groups/totals report
Horizontal layout
Landscape orientation

Ledger style
Mailing labels report
More button
MS Word MailMerge
  report
Page footer section
Page header section
Page margin
Portrait orientation
Presentation style

Report
Report footer section
Report header section
Report section
Report Wizards
Single-column report
Subtotal
Summary report
Tabular report
Vertical layout

Documentation Research

Use the printed documentation and the on-line Help available with Microsoft Access to answer the following questions. If you use one of the manuals, provide the page number for your reference in the manual.

1. Use Access Cue Cards to learn about creating a report. Describe the sample report used in the "See what a report is" Cue Card screen.

2. Search Access Help for information about the resize and move handles for report controls. Draw a sketch to show where they are placed in a control box.

3. Use Cue Cards to learn how you can keep groups of records together on the same page.

4. Describe how you can use the File | Add-ins command to change the default report settings used for the AutoReport Wizard. List the current choices.

Physicians' Medical Clinic (V): Creating a Report

In this exercise you will create a report to show information in various ways. You will open the PMC database, create a report with the Report Wizards, print the report, make changes and print the new report, and repeat the process. Read the directions carefully. Clearly identify which output goes with which part of the application.

1. Dr. Greenway has asked that you create a group report that shows all of the patients within each insurance company, sorted alphabetically. Include the patient name fields, zip code, patient number, date of birth, insurance company, and policy number. Print the report, and save its design.

2. After presenting the report to the administrator, you learn that he is really only interested in the patients from the US Insurance Company. Create an appropriate query and repeat the report from step 1. Of course, you will not have to use the group report type, but you should show the insurance company name in the report title.

3. The insurance office asked that you create a set of mailing labels for all patients having a positive balance forward. These should be 2-across labels and should show the name and address fields, and they must include the patient number. Sort the labels in zip code order.

Intermediate Database Management with Access

■ **PART TWO** continues the development of database objects using Microsoft Access. While Part One focused on creation of tables, queries, forms, and reports with Cue Cards and the Wizards, Part Two examines customized database objects. In Unit 7, you will learn how to make changes to the design of objects created with the Wizards. Unit 8 introduces the concept of relational databases and linked tables. Because similar Access controls are used in forms and reports, Unit 9 discusses working with these controls. Finally, Units 10 and 11 deal with how to create and edit custom forms and reports.

7 Finding Data, Applying Filters, and Sorting

In this unit you will learn how to use the Find command to locate a specific value within a table. You will use the Replace command to locate data and replace it with other values. The Filter concept is introduced and compared with an Access query. Finally, the unit will cover sorting data in a table.

Learning Objectives

At the completion of this unit you should know

1. the use of the Find and Replace commands,

2. how to use Access wild cards in Find and Replace expressions,

3. the advantages of using a Filter instead of a Query.

At the completion of this unit you should be able to

1. find data that matches specified values,

2. replace data in several places at once with a new value,

3. sort data within a filter,

4. save a filter as a query,

5. convert a query into a filter.

Important Commands

Edit | Find

Edit | Replace

Edit | Undo

File | Save As Query

File | Load from Query

Records | Edit Filter/Sort

Records | Apply Filter/Sort

Using the Find Command to Locate Data

Suppose you wanted to find the record that matches a specified value. Although you could prepare a query, that is cumbersome. Access provides the *Find command* in the Edit menu to allow you to specify the field and match condition, after which Access will move the record pointer to that record. You can repeat the Find command to search for subsequent occurrences of the value.

The Find Dialog Box

You can use the Find command to search the active table or dynaset in either Form view or Datasheet view. First move the cursor to the field in which you want to find a specific value. To activate the Find box, press the Find button in the toolbar (binoculars icon) or use the Edit | Find command from the keyboard. Figure 7.1 shows the Find dialog box for the Customers table in the HUNT database. Notice that the pointer was in the Customer Number field when the Find command was given.

FIGURE 7.1
The Find dialog box

Find

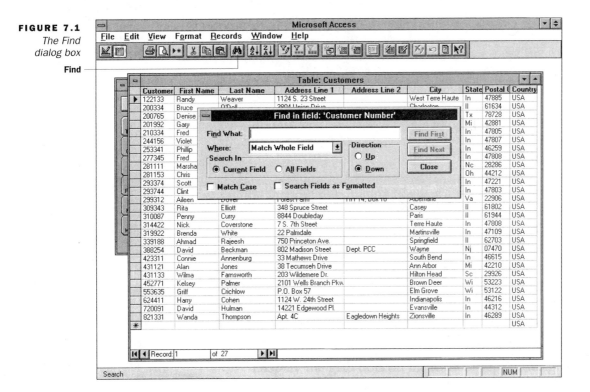

If you want to search on a different field, click on the Close button and move the pointer to the field of interest. Then issue the Find command again. Specify the Find What condition by giving a value for that field to match. The ***Where box*** qualifier specifies whether the value must Match Whole Field (default), be at the Start of Field, or be in Any Part of Field. Click on the arrow at the end of the drop-down box to see the other choices. If the target value occurs at the beginning of the field, select the Start of Field option for this box, to increase search speed.

The ***Search In check box*** choice defaults to the Current Field; Access will search in the current field much faster with this option than if you specify All Fields. If you choose the Match Case option, the find value must match uppercase and lowercase characters exactly as typed; most users will leave this box *unchecked*. The default is to find matches regardless of capitalization.

When you search formatted fields, the value may display in a different manner than it is actually stored in the table. Examples of formatted fields include Numeric, Date | Time, Currency, and Yes/No fields. If you want to search fields the way they are displayed (formatted), rather than the way they are stored in the table, select the Search Fields as Formatted box. For instance, suppose you are searching a date/time field that is formatted as Medium Date, or `12-Apr-95`. The actual storage of that field in the table is somewhat different. To find dates that occurred in April, you can enter `Apr` in the ***Find What box*** and select Any Part of Field. Then, click on the Search Fields as Formatted check box and click on Find First to find dates that occurred in April.

The default ***search direction*** is Down, from the current record to the end of the table. The first time you use Find to locate a new value, click the Find First button. Access will search in the desired direction to locate the *first* occurrence of the match string in the table or dynaset. It will move the record pointer to the record that matches the find command. To find *additional* records that also match the find value, click the Find Next button. If there are no other instances of the find value, Access will ask if you want to continue the search from the beginning of the table. Click the Close button to close the Find dialog box.

GUIDED ACTIVITY 7.1

Using the Find Command

In this Guided Activity you will use the Find command to locate values in a table.

1. Start Windows and load Access as usual. Open the HUNT database.

2. For this example, we will open the Employees table in Datasheet view.

3. With the Employees table open, move the pointer to the Last Name field and click anywhere in that field.

4. Next, click on the Find button in the toolbar, or issue the Edit | Find command. Access will display the Find dialog box.

5. If you have used the Find command earlier during this Access session, the Find box will contain the selections used earlier. Be sure that the Where box contains

FIGURE 7.2
Found Johnson last name

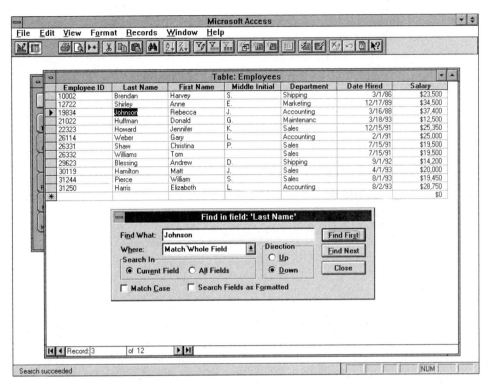

Match Whole Field, and that neither Match Case nor Search Fields as Formatted is checked.

6. In the Find What box, enter `Johnson` and click on the Find First button. Access will quickly move the record pointer to the third record, Rebecca Johnson.

7. To better see the datasheet, use the mouse pointer to drag the title bar of the Find box to a position below the datasheet, as shown in Figure 7.2.

8. Next, we will search for a portion of the Last Name field. Delete the current Find What field value and type `Will` in the box. In the Where box, select Start of Field.

CHECKPOINT 7A Why did you select Start of Field instead of Match Whole Field in the Where box?

9. Click on the Find Next button. Access will move the record pointer to the Tom Williams record.

10. Click on the Close button to close the Find box. Position the pointer in the Department field *in the same Tom Williams record* and click once.

11. Click on the Find button in the toolbar (or issue the Edit I Find command). Then specify `Marketing` in the Find What box.

12. Click on the Find Next button. Access will not find any instances of the Marketing department before it reaches the end of the table, and will display the warning box, asking if you wish to search from the beginning of the table. Click on Yes.

13. Access will locate the second record, for Anne Shirley, who works in the Marketing department.

14. Searching on dates is also possible. Close the Find box, then select the Date Hired field of the first record with the mouse. Click on the Find button in the toolbar to display the Find dialog box.

15. Because the Date Hired field is not formatted, you *cannot* specify `Dec` when looking for December hires. Instead, you must look for the `12` at the start of the field. Specify this in the Find What box, and select Start of Field in the Where box. Click on the Find First button to locate the record for Anne Shirley, who was hired on 12/17/89.

16. Click on the Find Next button to locate the next matching record, for Jennifer Howard, hired on 12/15/91. Click on the Find Next button once more and Access will reach the end of the table without finding a third December hire.

17. Close the Find box and close the Employees table.

Using the Replace Command

The Find command allows you to locate individual occurrences of a specified value in a table or dynaset, for browsing or informational purposes. The *Replace command* is similar, but more active in that it allows you to Find the value and replace it with another value. If you need to change the same data in several locations within the table, the Replace command makes it easy. You can look at each value before replacing it, or make all the changes with a single command. There is no Replace toolbar icon; move the pointer to the desired field, then use the Edit | Replace command from the menu bar to start the replace procedure.

The Replace Dialog Box

The Replace dialog box shown in Figure 7.3 is similar to the Find dialog box. There is a Find What box in which you give the expression you wish to replace. The Replace With box specifies the new value for the field. You can Search In the Current Field (default) or All Fields. There are check boxes for Match Case and Match Whole Field. The three action buttons are Find Next, Replace, and Replace All. The Find Next button skips to the next occurence without replacing; the Replace button replaces the current record with the new value; the Replace All button replaces all remaining instances with the new value (*use this one with care*).

Find and Replace Wild Card Characters

You can also use *wild card characters* in both the Find and Replace commands. Similar to those presented for queries, the wild card characters let you specify just a portion of the Find What value. The asterisk (*) stands for any number of characters in the asterisk position and following; unlike the DOS asterisk wild card, in Access you *can* specify characters that follow the asterisk. The question mark (?) stands for any single character in its position. A number sign (#) stands for a single numeric digit in its position. Square brackets [ ] allow you to specify several matching

FIGURE 7.3
The Replace dialog box

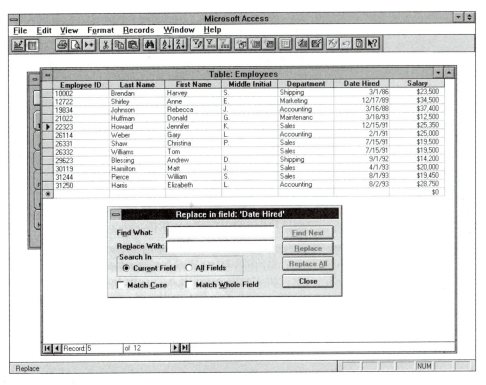

characters for a single position. The exclamation point (!) is used to define characters that you *don't* want to match. For example, if you specify [! X], Access will find all characters in that position except the letter X.

Examples of wild card expressions that can appear in the Find What box appear in Table 7.1.

GUIDED ACTIVITY 7.2

Using the Replace Command

This Guided Activity will illustrate how to use the Replace command to change a group of values at one time.

1. Retrieve the HUNT database and open the Old Customers table.

2. Move the pointer to the Country field on the first line and click once.

3. Choose the Replace command from the Edit menu bar to open the Replace dialog box.

4. In the Find What box key in USA, then press [Tab] to move to the Replace With box.

5. Key in US in the Replace With box. Neither Match Case nor Match Whole Field should be checked.

6. Click on the Find Next button. Access will move the pointer to the second record, highlighting the USA value.

TABLE 7.1	**FIND WHAT**	**MATCHING VALUES**
Typical wild card expressions	MIS*	MIS 320, MIS 276, MIS Major
	MIS 3??	MIS 320, MIS 399, MIS 3FH (but not MIS 276)
	*ville	Charlottesville, Evansville (but not Hovilles)
	MIS 3##	MIS 320 (but not MIS 3FH)
	MIS [34]##	MIS 376, MIS 400, MIS 476 (but not MIS 276)
	MIS [3-5]##	MIS 376, MIS 580 (but not MIS 276)
	M[IG][ST]	MIS, MGT, MIT, MGS (but not MIG)
	M[!G][!T]*	MIS 475, MIS Major (but not MGT)

7. Click the Replace button to replace that instance. You could continue this replacement one-record-at-a-time, or do it all in one batch. We'll choose the latter. Click on Replace All, and Access will rapidly replace all of the remaining values until it reaches the bottom of the table.

8. When Access reaches the end of the table, you will be asked whether to continue the replace operation from the beginning of the table. In this case we started at the top of the file, so click on No.

9. Just before the Replace results are committed to the database, Access will ask you to confirm the replace operation. You would not be able to cancel the changes with the Edit | Undo command if you specify OK to continue. In this case, we want to continue, so click on OK.

10. Close the Replace box. Close Old Customers table.

Access Filters

An Access *filter* is used to temporarily limit or restrict the records that you see in a form. Filters work *only* with forms. The Filter window is very similar to the Query window: you must specify the sort order and criteria for the form in use. Access will then display only those records that match the filter conditions. You can easily change the filter conditions and return to viewing the data.

Find can only be used to find an instance of a specific value of one field. Find cannot be used to create complex criteria expressions involving more than one field. Rather, a filter can be used for such criteria expressions, just like a query.

Filters Versus Queries

Because filters and queries perform similar work, you might ask when it is appropriate to use each. Remember that a query will copy to its dynaset records that meet the criteria. To work with those qualifying records, you must work with the dynaset, not directly with the query. If you change the criteria often, it is somewhat cumbersome to go through multiple steps: you must modify the query according to the new criteria, then run the query, and only then use the resulting dynaset to view or print the matching records.

A filter is your best choice when you want to temporarily filter out records that don't pertain to your current work. You can successively narrow the set of records seen in a form with a filter. You can easily change the filter criteria so that a different subset of records can be examined. Finally, a filter can be used to quickly sort the records in a different order than is normally used with the form. It is possible to save the filter as a query, discussed later in this unit. Because a filter can only be used with a form, it may be necessary to work with a query if you are *not* using a form.

A query can be used with forms, with reports, or with a datasheet. It provides more flexibility for selection of tables or other queries as the data source. A query can link two or more tables together, based on a common field value. You can create update queries that perform updates to the underlying tables. Certain simple queries can be converted to filters, discussed later in this unit.

Creating the Filter

First you must open the form for viewing the data. The Form toolbar is shown in Figure 7.4. The three Filter/Sort buttons are shown in the middle. Each has a funnel icon, representing the Filter. The first is *Edit Filter*, used to create and make changes to the filter. The middle button is *Apply Filter*, comparable to running a query and restricting the viewer to those records that match the filter condition. The right-most button is *Show All Records*, equivalent to removing the filter altogether.

FIGURE 7.4
Form View toolbar with Filter/Sort buttons

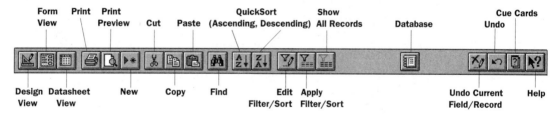

Click on the Edit Filter/Sort button in the toolbar to open the Filter window, shown in Figure 7.5. At the top of the Filter window is a box containing the fields created in the form. As with a query, you drag fields to the filter grid in the lower part of the window. Each field's column contains *criteria rows* for a criteria expression and a *sort row* to specify sort instructions.

Add only those fields to the filter grid for which you intend to provide criteria or sort specifications. Unlike the query, the filter column has no Show Field check box. The form design itself will determine which fields will appear on the form and in which order. You can also create expressions in the Filter grid; these expressions use fields already available in the form. For instance, you can calculate the inventory value for each product by multiplying the Unit Cost field by the Quantity on Hand field.

Once fields are in the Filter grid, you may enter the sort and criteria expressions. Remember that *compound criteria* will be entered in more than one column of the

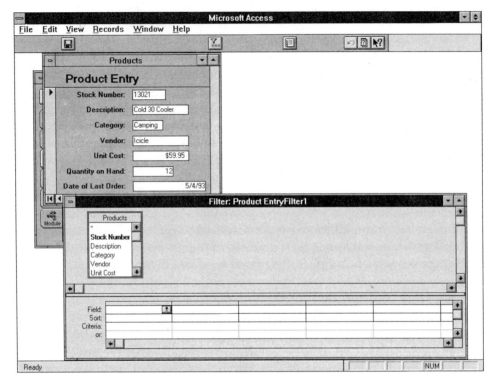

grid. Suppose you have two conditions: if both conditions are on the *same* Criteria line, both must be true for the record to qualify; if the conditions are entered on *different* lines, either or both may be true for the record to qualify for the filter.

Applying the Filter

Once the filter is created, you can apply the filter by clicking on the Apply Filter/Sort button in the toolbar, or by using the Records | Apply Filter/Sort command from the menu bar. Access will immediately apply the filter, removing records that don't match the criteria and sorting the qualifying records according to your sort instructions. Use the record navigation buttons at the bottom of the form to view records according to the filter. Note that the record numbers shown in the form's record navigation area may *not* be the original record numbers, but represent the new order if you have applied a filter or sort.

Notice that the Filter window remains open on the desktop while you work with the form window. If you want to change the Filter grid, use the pointer to make changes. Click on the Apply Filter/Sort button to see the results of the new filter condition.

Saving the Filter

We have not mentioned how to save the filter. Because filters are designed for temporary conditions, Access does not provide a means of formally saving the filter when you close the form. If you need to use the filter again in the future, it is easy to re-create the filter after opening the form.

However, you may want to save the current filter as a query. From the File menu, choose Save As Query and give a name. In the future, you can use this query in two ways: use it as a normal query, or convert it to a filter. To do the latter, first open the form. Click on the Edit Filter/Sort button in the toolbar. Then issue the File | Load from Query command. Access will present a list of query names; select the appropriate query and click on the OK button. Then apply the filter as usual.

Removing the Filter

If you no longer want the filter to be applied, click on the Show All Records button in the toolbar, or choose the Show All Records command from the Records menu. Access will remove the filter and sort conditions; then all records from the form will appear in their original order. Access does not change the Filter grid when you remove the filter. To reapply the filter, click on the Apply Filter/Sort button.

GUIDED ACTIVITY 7.3 ✳

Building a Form Filter

In this Guided Activity you will open a form and create a filter for the records.

1. Be sure that the HUNT database is open in Access. Click on the Form button to change to Form view in the Database window.

2. Highlight the Product Entry form and click on the Open button.

3. Next click on the Edit Filter/Sort button in the toolbar. Access will open a Filter window in the lower part of the screen. Use the mouse to drag the title bar of the Filter window so that you see portions of both the form and the filter window. See Figure 7.5.

4. For the first filter operation, drag the Category field to the Filter grid.

5. In the Criteria row, specify Sports and press Enter.

6. Click on the Apply Filter/Sort button in the toolbar (or use the Records | Apply Filter/Sort command) to activate the filter. Then use the form's record navigation buttons to examine the records. Notice as you cycle through the records that only Sports category products appear.

7. Click on the Filter window, then place Hunting in the Or: criteria row directly beneath the "Sports". Click on the Apply Filter/Sort button to activate the filter.

CHECKPOINT 7B   How many records now qualify for the filter?

8. The auditor has asked how many vendor orders were placed during the last month of a quarter. To get an idea, you prepare a filter to look at the Date of Last Order field to see whether the month was 3, 6, 9, or 12. Remove the first column in the Filter grid, and replace it with the Date of Last Order field.

9. In the Criteria row, enter the following expression. (You might want to press Shift F2 to open a zoom window to type in the entire expression.) Be careful to match the (and [characters as shown below:

```
Month([Date of Last Order]) In(3,6,9,12)
```

10. Activate the filter by clicking on the Apply Filter/Sort button, then examine the records in the form window.

CHECKPOINT 7C   What does *each* part of the expression in step 9 mean? Is there another way to create this filter?

11. Leave the form open. We will use it in the next Guided Activity.

Sorting Data with a Filter

You can sort records in the form by using a filter. The sort instructions are similar to query sort instructions. You can choose *Ascending order*, *Descending order*, or *(not sorted)* order for each field in the Filter grid. As a shortcut, you can enter an A or a D in the Sort row; when you press Enter, Access will fill in Ascending or Descending for you.

If sort instructions are given for more than one field, the left-most field will be the primary sort field. If the field order in the Filter grid is not appropriate, highlight its column and move it to the proper location by dragging its field border at the top of the column.

NOTE   *You can use the Quick Sort feature, new to Access 2.0, to temporarily sort a form or table without sorting with a filter. Move the pointer to the desired sort field and click one of the two QuickSort buttons in the toolbar. Only one field can be used as a sort key, however.*

GUIDED ACTIVITY 7.4

Sorting a Form with a Filter

In this Guided Activity you will sort the records that appear in a form, using a filter.

1. We will begin with the previous Guided Activity's Product Entry form. Open that form now if it is not already open.

2. Click on the Edit Filter/Sort button to open the Filter window for this form. We did this step in the previous activity and the filter should still be there.

3. Remove any previous columns from the filter grid, if any. A shortcut way to do this is to highlight the column by clicking once in the column border. Then press the Del key to remove the field, sort, and criteria expressions from this column.

4. Drag the Date of Last Order field to the filter grid.

5. In the Sort row of the first column, type D and press Enter. Access should fill in the word Descending for you.

6. Click on the Apply Filter/Sort button in the toolbar, then examine the records in the form window. You should see all 51 records (click on the last record button) in this window, sorted in reverse chronological order, most recent record first.

7. Next, we'll add a second sort field *before* the Date of Last Order field. Drag the Category field from the Products table to the left-most edge of the first column, then release the left mouse button. Access should move the Date field to the second column and make room for the Category field.

8. Enter an A in the Sort row of the Category field and press ⏎. Click on the Apply Filter/Sort button (or use the Records | Apply Filter/Sort command) to view the new results.

CHECKPOINT 7D   In what order will the records now appear? How would you arrange the fields and sort instructions to have the primary key be the Date of Last Order, and within that order break ties with the Category field?

9. Close the Product Entry filter and the Product Entry form.

The following Guided Activity will explore a more complicated filter with compound criteria and sorting.

GUIDED ACTIVITY 7.5

Building a Compound Filter with Sorting

We will build a more complex filter in this Guided Activity with compound criteria and sorting. You will also save the filter as a query, then convert the query back to a filter in a later activity.

1. Open the HUNT Database window in Access and switch to the Form mode.

2. Open the Tabular Customer Form saved in the HUNT database.

3. Click on the Edit Filter/Sort button in the toolbar. Your screen should resemble Figure 7.6.

4. Now drag the State field to the Filter grid. In its Criteria row enter the following expression: In("IN","IL","OH"). We'll leave the Sort row empty for now.

5. Drag the Last Name field to the Filter grid. In its Criteria row place "[A-M]*" and press ⏎.

NOTE   *If you leave off the quote characters, Access will not be able to understand your expression and will give a syntax error message.*

CHECKPOINT 7E   What did Access substitute for your expression? Precisely what does the criteria expression in step 5 mean? Give examples of text strings that would *not* match this expression.

6. Click on the Apply Filter/Sort button to activate the filter. You should see customers with last names starting with letters A through M from the three midwestern states listed. See Figure 7.7.

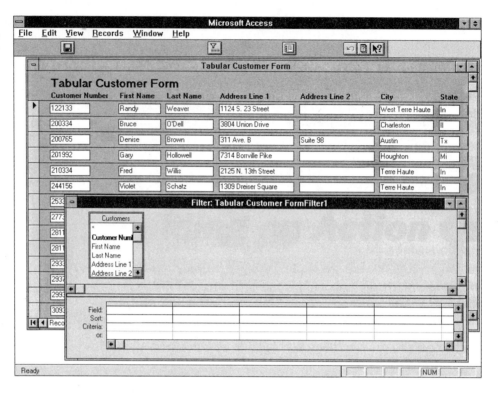

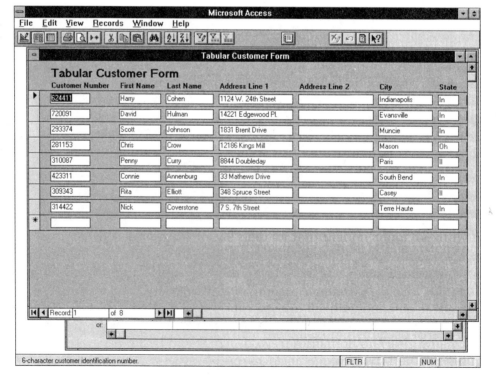

FIGURE 7.8
Dynaset of Customer Filter saved as query

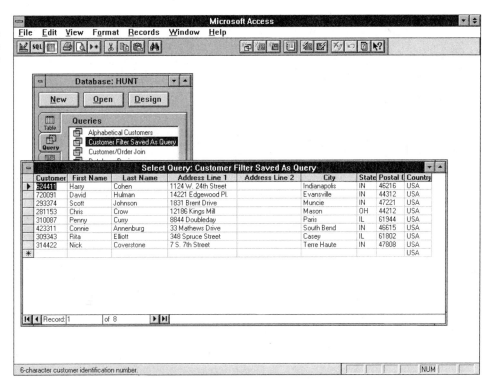

7. To give you practice, we will save the filter as a simple query. First click on the Filter window to make it the active window. Then issue the File | Save As Query command. When prompted for the name, key in `Customer Filter Saved as Query`.

8. To test your filter as a query, close the filter and form window. Then click on the Query button in the Database window.

9. Highlight the Customer Filter Saved as Query line, then click on Open. You should see customers with last names starting with letters A through M from Indiana, Illinois, and Ohio, as shown in Figure 7.8.

10. Close the query window.

Converting a Query to a Filter

Although a filter is designed as a temporary tool, you may want to reuse it in a future session. We spoke earlier of how to save a filter as a query. This section will describe how to convert a simple select query into a filter.

The query must be based on the same underlying table or query as the form you will use it with. The query cannot include totals, and must not refer to any other tables or queries. The query must be a simple select query, not a crosstab or action query.

To start the process, open the desired form and click on the Edit Filter/Sort button. From the File menu, choose the Load From Query command. Specify the correct query name from the dialog box and click the OK button. Then click on Apply Filter/Sort as usual. The following activity will illustrate this procedure.

GUIDED ACTIVITY 7.6

Converting a Query into a Filter

This Guided Activity will show you how to convert a saved query into an Access filter.

1. With the HUNT database open, change to the Form mode.

2. Open the Standard Employee Form.

3. Click on the Edit Filter/Sort button to open a filter window, then give the File | Load From Query command. Figure 7.9 shows the desktop with the windows moved so that you can see each box.

4. Choose the Salary by Department query from the Applicable Filter dialog box.

5. Access will convert the query Sort and Criteria expressions into the filter format and place those in the Filter grid. In this case, the query will sort on the Department field as the primary key and do a descending sort on the Salary field.

6. To activate the filter, click on the Apply Filter/Sort button. Access will display each employee record in the form by department, and within department by decreasing salary. Use the form's record navigation buttons to confirm that this sort has occurred.

7. This is the final activity of this unit. You may close the form window.

FIGURE 7.9
*Filter dialog box
based on query*

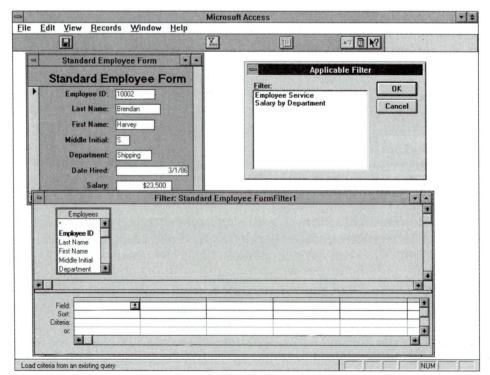

Command Review

Edit I Find	Activate the Find window for a form or datasheet.
Edit I Undo	Cancel the effects of the last command.
Edit I Replace	Activate the Replace window for a form or datasheet.
File I Save as Query	Save the filter as an Access query.
File I Load from Query	Convert a query into a filter.
Records I Edit Filter/Sort	Open the Filter window for a form.
Records I Apply Filter/Sort	Activate the filter for a form.

Exercises

Use the Hunter River database contained within the HUNT.MDB file on the West Student Data Disk for these exercises.

1. Use the Find command with the Customers table in the HUNT database to answer the following questions. Write the name and customer number of each record that meets the specified condition.

    a. Find the first occurrence of a customer from Martinsville. *Brenda White*

    b. Find all the customers whose zip codes begin with 478. *Nick Coverstone, Randy Weaver, Fred Willis, Violet Schatz, Fred Whalen, Clint Williams*

    c. Find the *third* customer from Illinois.

    d. Find the *last* customer from Indiana. Is there a simple way to do this with just one Find command? *Penny Curry*

    e. Find the customer whose first name is Kelsey. *Kelsey Palmer*

2. Replace all of the State fields in the Customers table with lowercase versions. In other words, IN would become In, MI would become Mi, and so on. Print a copy of the new table's datasheet after making this change.

3. For this exercise, use the Products table from the HUNT database.

    a. Using the Find command, count the number of products with 0 units in stock. *4*

    b. Count the number of products whose Stock Number begins with 60. *13*

    c. Find the *first* product whose vendor is Scandavia. *Pro Cross Country Skier*

    d. Find the *third* product whose vendor is Bishop. *50mm Binoculars*

    e. Find the product whose description begins with ST. *ST 55 Stepper*

4. For this exercise, use the Tabular Inventory Form contained in the HUNT database. Prepare filters for each step and print a copy of the resulting form. The steps are independent of each other.

    a. Prepare a filter to limit records to Camping or Sports.

    b. Limit records to Sports only, and sort the form in descending order by the Expr1 field, which is Unit Cost multiplied by Quantity on Hand.

    c. Records qualify for this filter if their last reorder occurred in 1992 or before, and if their inventory value (Expr1) is more than $350. Sort the filter by Vendor.

    d. Modify your filter from step c. so that parts qualify if *either* condition is true.

5. Using the Tabular Inventory Form from the HUNT database, create a filter that sorts the records by Vendor in ascending order as the primary key, and descending Date of Last Order as the secondary key. Only use Hunting records. Save this filter as a query and print the resulting dynaset from this query.

Review Questions

1. Explain what happens when the Find command is used. How is it different from the Replace command?

2. Suppose you start in the middle of a table, say record 15, and want to find all of the occurrences of a certain value in the table. Give at least two ways to be certain you have searched through records 1–14 as well as the lower part of the table.

3. Discuss reasons for clicking the Search Fields as Formatted box in the Find window. Give an example of where this option would be helpful.

4. Give the precise meaning of the following Find What expressions:

    a. *C

    b. C*

    c. A??D

    d. [AD]##

    e. [!B]###

5. Discuss the three choices in the Where box in the Find window. Why is it important to select the best choice with large databases?

6. The Find and Filter commands are related. Describe the differences, and explain when each would be used.

7. A filter is similar to an Access query. Explain the advantages of using each procedure.

8. Explain why you cannot "save" an Access filter. Discuss ways to circumvent this restriction.

9. Suppose you wanted to sort on two fields and view the results in a form. Explain how you could use a filter for this purpose. Discuss sort order and placement of fields in the filter grid.

Key Terms

Apply Filter button	Filter	Search In check box
Ascending order	Find command	Show All Records button
Compound criteria	Find What box	Sort row
Criteria row	(Not sorted)	Where box
Descending order	Replace command	Wild card characters *, ?,
Edit Filter button	Search direction	#, [ ], !

Documentation Research

Use the printed documentation and the on-line Help available with Microsoft Access to answer the following questions. If you use one of the manuals, provide the page number for your reference in the manual.

1. Is it possible to use Cue Cards with the Find or Replace commands, or to create an Access filter? You may have to search Cue Cards to locate these features.

2. Search the Replace Command section of Access Help. What does Access recommend if you want to replace a large number of records or to replace values with an expression?

3. What is the shortcut function key method for the Edit | Replace command? What is the shortcut function key method for the Edit | Find command? These are not shown in the Access menu bar.

Relational Database Concepts and Advanced Queries

This unit will extend the knowledge you gained from Part One to create customized queries. It will formally introduce the relational database concept and show how tables can be joined together with a query. The unit covers action queries in which changes to tables are made through the Query view. A section on crosstab queries illustrates preparation of queries in tabular fashion. The chapter concludes with a brief discussion of SQL, the industry-standard Structured Query Language.

Learning Objectives

At the completion of this unit you should know

1. the overall concept of a relational database,

2. how Access queries can join multiple tables,

3. what kinds of action queries Access supports,

4. the purpose of a parameter query,

5. the use of a crosstab query,

6. how to use the built-in Access SQL support.

At the completion of this unit you should be able to

1. join tables with a query,

2. create an update query to make changes to a group of records,

3. use a delete query,

4. create a crosstab query.

Important Commands

Edit | Relationships

File | Save Layout

Format | Column Width

Query | Update

Query | Delete

Query | Crosstab

Query | Parameters

Query | Make Table

Query | Append

Query | Run

View | SQL

View | Table Names

Relational Database Concepts

Thus far in this book we have dealt primarily with individual tables. Real-world applications frequently involve multiple tables that must be joined to retrieve appropriate information. In fact, the Hunter River database is a good example of a *relational database*, in which we store data in numerous two-dimensional tables that can be linked by matching common data values in several tables. For instance, we store permanent information about departments in a Department table rather than storing that information in the Employees table; by joining the Department table to the Employees table, we have access to that store of information when dealing with an employee of that department.

Joining Separate Tables

Although there is a large body of formal mathematical literature concerning relational databases, they can be described more simply in common-sense terms. We want to establish a *separate table* for each entity in the system. That is, we want to store information about a single type of data object in a table for that data object. If there is information that is shared across most or all of the members of the data object group, we should place that information in a different table. Hence, we store information about individual employees in the Employees table; this includes employee number, name, address, date of birth, salary, and department name. Information about departments such as department manager, department address, and department telephone number should go into the Department table and not be *duplicated* for each member of that department. Both tables must contain a common value, department name, so that information about that department can be linked to the employee.

So far we can describe the following tables in the Hunter River database: Products, Employees, Department, Customers, and Vendors. Products can be linked with the Vendors table by matching vendor name. Employees can be linked with Department by matching department name. We can introduce a table called Orders that will contain information about customer orders. It can be joined to the Customers table by matching customer number. You might be tempted to use the customer name field for matching these two tables, but proper names are notoriously poor for providing *unique* identifiers. Is there someone at your university with the same name? We will develop the Hunter River relational model in more depth later in this unit.

Deciding What Fields Go into What Tables: Normalization

Database students always have some difficulty at this point in the database design. Most database textbooks use a confusing procedure called ***normalization*** that begins with all fields in one huge table. Through the normalization process, fields are methodically moved into successively smaller tables until certain conditions have been met. Each stage of the process results in a normal form such as First normal form, Second normal form, Third normal form, and so on. We will discuss the goals of the normalization process before giving some example of the normalization result.

REPEATING GROUPS

We often encounter ***repeating groups*** of fields in a database. For instance, one customer may place several orders over a period of time. We could store all information about customers, including their orders, in a single table. But how can we define fields that describe an unknown number of orders? It becomes impossible to work with this data unless the order information is moved to a separate table. Thus, the Customers table contains permanent information about the customer that doesn't change from order to order (until, say, the customer moves). The Orders table would contain information about each order such as order date, order number, customer number (but not customer name, which is contained in the customer table), total amount of the order, and the like. If one customer places five orders, there would be five records in the Orders table, one per order for that customer. As part of the normalization process, move repeating groups of fields to their own separate table.

ANOMALIES AND REDUNDANCY

A normalized database is easier to work with than one that is not normalized. Certain ***anomalies***, or irregularities, can occur when records are added to, modified, or deleted from nonnormalized databases. Suppose *all* the data about departments were stored only in the Employees table. If Hunter River were to change a department manager's name, *every* employee record belonging to that department would have to be modified. By placing departmental data in a separate Department table, however, we need only change the manager's name in one place. Having the department manager's name in every employee record is redundant and should be avoided. Examine your tables for redundant information that can be placed in a separate table.

CALCULATED FIELDS

It is generally accepted that calculated fields are *not* stored separately in a table. Rather, when needed these fields should be calculated from the underlying values that are stored in that record. For instance, the calculation for grade point average is given as total points divided by total credit hours. It is necessary to store the latter two items. When the GPA is desired, do the operation. By eliminating redundant calculated fields you will save storage space in the database. There are instances, however, when storing a calculated field is desirable. In the GPA example, schools frequently group or sort by GPA. In that case it would have to be calculated and stored, at least temporarily. Use your judgment when deciding whether to eliminate calculated fields from tables.

PARTIAL DEPENDENCY

Each field in a table should depend on the whole primary key, not just a portion of that key. Suppose you had a table in which a **concatenation** (combining) of two consecutive fields was the primary key. To do this in Access, drag the pointer across the field selector buttons of the adjacent primary key fields, then click on the key button in the toolbar. Access will place the key icon in front of both fields and treat their concatenation as the primary key.

For example, you might have an Order Items table that contains the individual products in one customer order. A customer purchases a basketball, a basketball rim and backboard, and a basketball goal pole. Although this represents a single order, the order would have three repeating groups and thus the line items in the order should be placed in a separate table. The primary key for the Order Items table would be the concatenation of order number and product number.

If the table is properly normalized, all of the nonkey fields should depend on the *entire* concatenated key and not just one of the key fields. If you placed the unit price field in the Order Items table, it would depend on the product number but *not* on the order number. Thus, there is a partial dependency in the Order Items table design. To resolve this problem, remove the unit price from the Order Items table and place it in the Products table where the price depends only on the primary key, the product number. Can you think of an instance where the unit price *would* depend on both the product number and the order number? In other words, when you would have a different price for this particular order than the standard price given in the Products table?

Putting It All Together

My database design advice for beginning students is to develop tables that meet the three normalization criteria. First, remove repeating groups and place them in their own table; look for redundant, duplicated information and place it in a master table where information can be looked up when needed. Second, eliminate calculated fields that can easily be recalculated. Finally, examine each table to be sure that the entire primary key uniquely identifies each field in that table. If not, consider moving the field to another table in which it only depends on the full key. Other normalization rules can be found in database management textbooks. For a more thorough treatment, read more about this issue there. The three normalization criteria are as follows:

Normal Form	Description
First Normal Form	Use a flat file structure without repeating groups.
Second Normal Form	Data is in first normal form and there are no partial dependencies.
Third Normal Form	Data is in second normal form and contains no transitive dependencies.

Normalizing a database results in more tables with fewer fields in each one. Most applications require that you join two or more tables to make use of the information at one time. As you pursue normalization, remember that it will take a short time for the computer to join the tables. Some database designers are willing to accept a slightly less normalized design in order to eliminate some of the links necessary when joining tables. However, with today's faster hardware most database designers prefer the modeling advantages of normalized data structures.

The Hunter River Relational Model

This section will describe the tables used in the Hunter River relational database model. We can describe the base tables with their table names and field names, with the primary key coming first. For purposes of this book, the primary key field(s) are shown in italic. It is not necessary that common fields used to link tables have the same name; rather, they must have the same value in order for the match to occur. By convention, we frequently use the same name in the table design, although it is not strictly necessary. For instance, we can use both Stock Number and Product Number to refer to the same field in different tables. Because Access permits use of long, descriptive data names, we can accurately describe our fields. Some database packages restrict data names to ten characters or fewer, making it more difficult to understand the precise definition of a field.

The base tables are as follows:

CUSTOMERS (*Customer Number*, First Name, Last Name, Address Line 1, Address Line 2, City, State, Postal Code, Country)

ORDERS (*Order Number*, Customer Number, Order Date, Employee ID, Total Order Amount, Taxable Sale, Method of Payment)

ORDER ITEMS (*Order Number, Product Number,* Order Quantity)

PRODUCTS (*Stock Number*, Description, Category, Vendor, Unit Cost, Quantity on Hand, Date of Last Order)

EMPLOYEES (*Employee ID*, First Name, Last Name, Middle Initial, Department, Date Hired, Salary)

DEPARTMENT (*Department*, Manager, Area, Annual Sales)

VENDORS (*Vendor Name*, Address Line 1, Address Line 2, City, State, Zip Code, Contact Person, Telephone Number)

Suppose we wanted to prepare an invoice for a customer order. At the top of the invoice would come the order number, order date, and customer information (name, address, and so on). In the middle of the invoice would be the items purchased for this order, one line per item. Each line would contain the item number, its description, the number of units purchased, the cost per unit, and the extended cost obtained by multiplying the number of units by the unit cost. At the bottom of the invoice would be a subtotal for the items ordered, plus the sales tax information.

How would we obtain this information? First decide which table is the most important. Because we are preparing an invoice for a specific order, the Orders table is most important. Notice that the Orders table can be joined to the Customers table by the Customer Number field in each table. Next, we want only those Order Items that match this order number. Notice that the Order Number field is present in both the Orders and Order Items tables. Finally, for each line item we will need to look up the description and unit cost from the Products table, matching Product Number in the Order Items table with the Stock Number in the Products table. These relationships are summarized graphically in the database diagram shown in the query window of Figure 8.1.

The PMC Relational Model

Recall the Physicians' Medical Clinic (I) application from Part One of this book. You were asked to design a database that met the needs of patient medical data, billing, and insurance. This section will sketch out a possible relational model that meets these needs. Not all the details are given; the rest are left as an exercise for you. This model is similar to the Hunter River model.

The main tables are Patients, Visits, Payments, Procedures, Insurers, and Doctors. The Patients table corresponds to the Customers table from the Hunter River example. The Visits table corresponds to the Order Items table; we can assume that a patient visit represents a single line item such as a checkup, X-ray, or the like. The Procedures file corresponds to the Products file and represents the list of possible procedures, their descriptions, and costs. When a patient comes to the clinic, the doctor fills out a form and checks off the procedure just completed. If you wanted to allow more than one line item per visit, break the Visits table into two tables, Visits and Visit Items. The Payments table includes payments and insurer reimbursements.

FIGURE 8.1

Database design for Hunter River database model

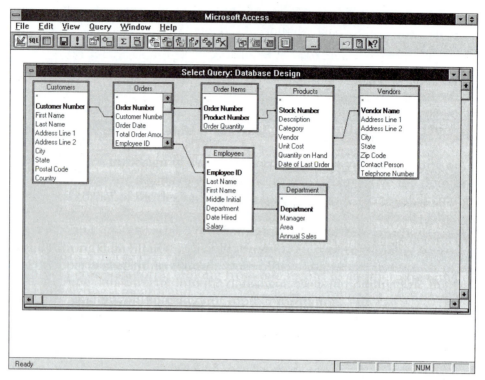

How will we relate the tables? Patients are linked to the Visits table by matching the patient number. The Visits table contains a procedure number that allows a look-up in the Procedures table. To prepare an insurance billing, the patient's insurance company from the Patients table can be used to look up the matching name in the Insurer table.

Joining Multiple Tables with a Query

In Part One we saw how a simple select query can select records from one or more tables. The tables appear in the top portion of the Query window. We can use the ***drag method*** to join the two matching fields; Access will draw a line between these fields, representing the fact that the tables are now joined. As you move the pointer in one datasheet, Access will attempt to move the pointer in the other table so that the linked fields maintain the *same*, common values. The best way to illustrate this is with an example, shown in the guided activity below.

GUIDED ACTIVITY 8.1 ✳

Using a Query to Join Two Tables

In this Guided Activity we will create a query that joins the Employees and Department tables.

1. Begin Windows and load Access as usual. Open the HUNT database.

2. Click on the Query button and choose the New button. Then click New Query to manually create a new query. The Query Wizard can only be used for some of the advanced queries, discussed later in this unit.

3. Add the Employees table and the Department table in the Add Table dialog box. Click Close to signify that you are finished adding tables.

4. Because they have the same name, Access will automatically draw a line between the two Department fields, as shown in Figure 8.2. This link is called a *join line*. If the fields to be joined have *different* names, you could drag one field onto the other table, then release the left mouse button, to create the join line.

NOTE *In earlier Access versions, you had to make the link manually.*

FIGURE 8.2
Joined tables in the query window

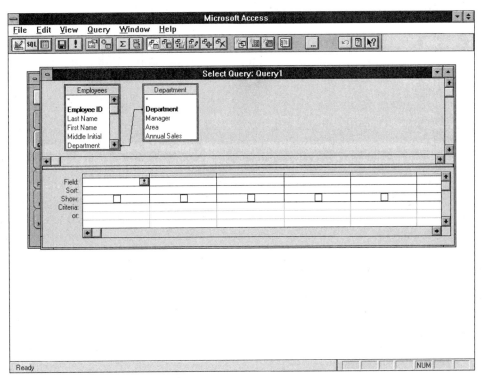

5. Select the following Employees table fields for the QBE grid: Department, First Name, Last Name, and Salary. Drag each to the QBE grid.

6. Drag the Manager field from the Department table to the QBE grid.

7. Run the query by clicking on the exclamation point button in the toolbar (or click on the Datasheet button in the toolbar). The resulting dynaset in Datasheet view is shown in Figure 8.3. Notice that Access has pulled the correct manager for each employee's department, as a result of the join you created above.

8. Save this query as Employees with Managers, then close the Query window.

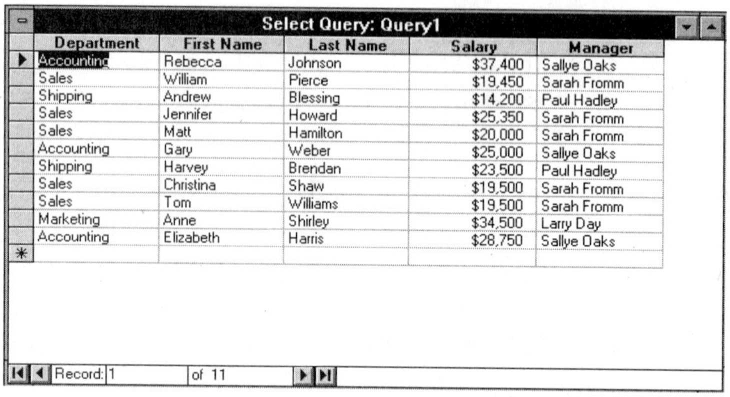

FIGURE 8.3
Dynaset from query joining two tables

Department	First Name	Last Name	Salary	Manager
Accounting	Rebecca	Johnson	$37,400	Sallye Oaks
Sales	William	Pierce	$19,450	Sarah Fromm
Shipping	Andrew	Blessing	$14,200	Paul Hadley
Sales	Jennifer	Howard	$25,350	Sarah Fromm
Sales	Matt	Hamilton	$20,000	Sarah Fromm
Accounting	Gary	Weber	$25,000	Sallye Oaks
Shipping	Harvey	Brendan	$23,500	Paul Hadley
Sales	Christina	Shaw	$19,500	Sarah Fromm
Sales	Tom	Williams	$19,500	Sarah Fromm
Marketing	Anne	Shirley	$34,500	Larry Day
Accounting	Elizabeth	Harris	$28,750	Sallye Oaks

Select Query: Query1

Record: 1 of 11

Types of Joins with a Query

Three kinds of joins are possible with Access queries—equi-joins, outer joins, and self-joins. You can control whether records that *don't* match are included in the query, as explained below.

EQUI-JOINS

Unless otherwise instructed, Access will match up all combinations of matching records in the two tables. Called an *equi-join*, this join creates as many rows in the resulting dynaset as there are matching combinations in the two joined tables. In the previous example, there are 11 employees and 7 departments. There are 11 rows in the dynaset: each employee has a matching department, so all employee records were selected. If one of the employee records had a department that did not exist, that employee would *not* appear in the equi-join.

NOTE *Records may not appear in the same order in various versions of Access.*

OUTER JOINS

Not all the departments appear in the equi-join—only four of the departments are now represented by employees. The three departments without listed employees—Management, Purchasing, and Other—are not shown. To include these departments without matching employees, you can create an *outer join*. To create this type of join, double-click the join line between the two tables to bring up the Join Properties dialog box shown in Figure 8.4. Clicking on choice 3 will display all departments whether or not there are employees that match. Choice 2 would display all employees whether or not there are departments that match. Choice 1, the default, produced the equi-join we created in the previous example.

FIGURE 8.4
*Example for
outer join
showing Join
Properties
dialog box*

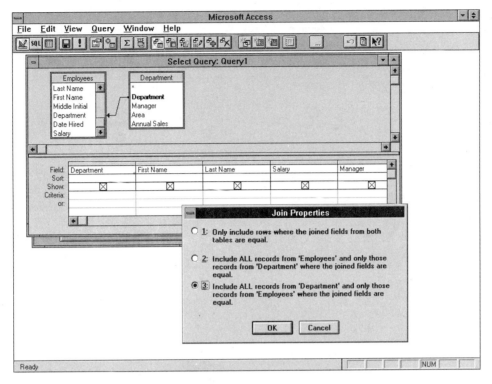

FIGURE 8.4
Example for outer join showing Join Properties dialog box

SELF-JOINS

This type of join relates values within the same table. For example, you might have a table showing both employees and managers. In this scenario, you would have a Reports To field in the Employees table that gives the employee ID of the manager. You can use a *self-join* to determine which employee reports to which manager. To have access to the name of that manager employee, add a second copy of the Employees table to the query, then link the Reports To field in the first Employees table to the Employee ID in the second Employees table. You can drag the appropriate fields to the QBE grid and view the resulting dynaset. Figure 8.5 shows the query window for this type of join. (Note that the Hunter River Employees table does not include managers.)

Defining Table Relationships

Access provides another way to define join relationships between tables. Using the Relationships dialog box, you can create a permanent link between two tables. This relationship is automatically transferred to subsequent queries, forms, and reports using the tables so that you can view data from both tables at the same time. Create table relationships *before* you build queries using the tables.

For instance, if two tables are joined in a relationship, Access will automatically draw a join line between them if they are added to a query. If the tables are used in a main/subform or main/subreport, Access will display the proper matching records in the subform or subreport.

FIGURE 8.5
Example of self-join

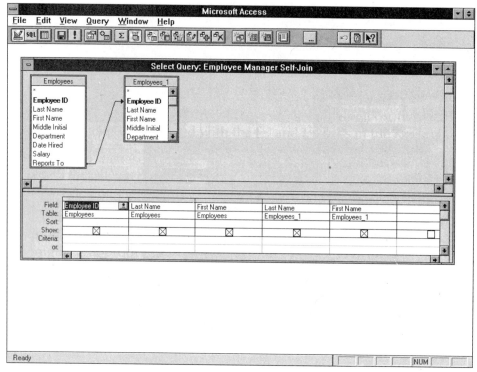

The Relationships Dialog Box

To create a relationship in a database, switch to the Database window and choose the Relationships command from the Edit menu. Double-click on the join line between two tables. The Relationships dialog box is shown in Figure 8.6. You should identify a primary table and a related table. The primary table is the master table, such as the Department table from the previous Guided Activity. The related table contains one or more records that match some or all of the records in the primary table, such as the Employees table from the previous example.

The key field in the primary table is compared with the specified field in the related table to join the two tables. In this example, both tables contain a field named Department. It is not necessary that the tables be joined on fields with the same names. An exercise appeared earlier in this book that asked you to produce a main/subreport report listing the Vendors and the Products supplied by each vendor. In the Vendors table (primary table), the key field was Vendor Name. In the Products table (related table), the matching field was Vendor. There is a relationship between these two tables in the HUNT database.

Join Type refers to equi-join (default), outer join, or self-join as discussed in the previous section. By default, only records that have matching values in the linked fields will appear.

Referential integrity refers to the requirement that any record placed in the related table *must* have a matching record in the primary table. If you choose to enforce referential integrity with the check box in the Relationships dialog box, any changes to either table must not violate referential integrity. For example, Access would prevent you from deleting the parent record from the primary table if it has a

FIGURE 8.6
*The
Relationships
dialog box*

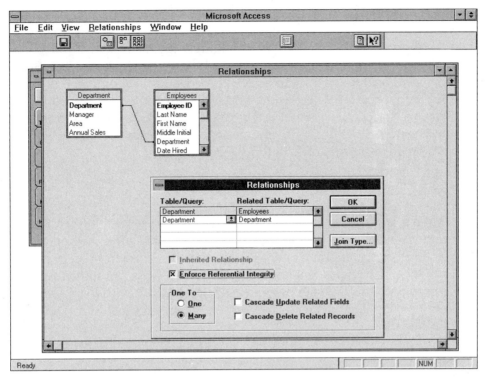

matching record in the related table. Similarly, Access would not allow you to add a record to the related table if a matching parent record does not already exist in the primary table. In this case, because we already have some Employees records without a matching record in the Department table, Access will not let us require referential integrity in this relationship.

The relationship can be one-to-one or one-to-many. In one-to-many relationships, a record from the primary table can match more than one record in the related table. The one-to-one relationship type states that only one record from the related table can match a record from the primary table. In this case, there can be more than one employee from a particular department, so the one-to-many type is appropriate.

To complete the relationship, specify whether referential integrity should be observed. Click the Create button to create the relationship, or OK if you are editing the relationship. Then use the File | Save Layout command to save the relationships in the database.

Building Action Queries

In Part One of this book we created simple select queries that determined which records qualified for the dynaset. The query itself did not make any changes to the underlying tables. In this section we will discuss how to create queries that perform some type of action based on the criteria in the query.

Types of Action Queries

When you run an *action query*, changes are made to the underlying tables. To help remind you that these queries can be dangerous, Access places a small exclamation point next to the query symbol in the Database window. It is generally a good idea to first create a select query to test the effects, without jeopardizing your data. Once the select query is working properly, you can convert it to an action query.

The four types of action queries are briefly described below. Following that discussion are examples of each type of action query.

UPDATE QUERIES

An *update query* can be used to change every record in the underlying table(s) that meets the criteria conditions of the query. Similar to the Replace command of the previous unit, an update query is more flexible, allowing you to specify expressions with most field types, not just with text fields. There are some restrictions on update queries with multiple tables—refer to Chapter 13 of the *User's Guide* for more details about multiple-table queries. An update query appears in the Database window as a pencil icon.

DELETE QUERIES

The *delete query* will cause a group of records that meet the criteria conditions to be permanently deleted from the database. This is much faster than manually deleting each record. The *User's Guide* suggests that you can delete records from only a single table at a time unless the cascade delete option is set in the Relationships window. A delete query appears in the Database window as a script X.

CAUTION   *Use delete queries with care! Once deleted, data is gone forever.*

MAKE-TABLE QUERIES

The *make-table query* will save in a new table those records that match your criteria. These records also remain in the original table. You can select a subset of the fields for the new table, which will have the effect of making any forms or reports using the new table run faster. The make-table query will save records as of a certain point in time; subsequent changes to the original tables will *not* be reflected in the new table unless you run the make-table query again to extract the appropriate records. A make-table query appears in the database window as a table icon.

APPEND QUERIES

You can use an *append query* to add certain records from one table to the end of another existing table. Only records that meet the criteria will be appended to the other table. The appended records also remain in their initial table. This is a good method for copying some or all records from one table to another table. An append query appears in the Database window as a plus icon.

Creating an Update Query

In this section we will discuss how to create an update query to make changes to an existing table. There are four steps in creating an update query. First, create a select query as usual with the proper selection criteria expressions. Run the query to view the dynaset in Datasheet view to be certain the correct records have been selected. Second, switch back to Query Design view and choose the Query | Update command from the menu bar. The name of the window will change to Update Query, and Access will insert an Update To row in the QBE grid. The third step is to insert the new expression in the proper column of the QBE grid. Finally, run the query to make the changes. Remember that these changes will be permanent if you click the OK button after Access performs the update. If you do not want to commit the changes to the database, click the Cancel button instead. The following activity will illustrate the preparation of an update query.

GUIDED ACTIVITY 8.2

Creating an Update Action Query

This Guided Activity will illustrate how to create an update action query to mark down prices for a clearance sale.

1. Close any open windows and return to the HUNT Database window. Change to the Query view.

2. Click the New button to create a new query design, then click New Query.

3. At the Add Table dialog box, add the Final Sales Merchandise Table and close the Add Table box.

4. Drag the following fields to the QBE grid: Stock Number, Unit Cost, Quantity on Hand, and Now on Order.

5. In the Quantity on Hand column enter the criteria expression >0. In the Now on Order column enter the Criteria expression No in the same criteria row. You are creating a condition for marking down prices of closeout units that are in stock and not now on order.

6. Click on the Run Query button in the toolbar to execute the select query. Notice which products qualify, and write down the unit cost for the first and last products. Six records should qualify.

7. Return to Design view. Now we will convert this select query into an update query. Select the Update command from the Query menu, or click the Update Query button in the toolbar. Access will insert an Update To row in the QBE grid.

8. Beneath the Unit Cost column, enter [Unit Cost]*0.85 in the Update To row, as shown in Figure 8.7.

9. Run the query by clicking on the exclamation point button in the toolbar (or use the Query | Run command in the menu bar).

FIGURE 8.7
*Update query
window*

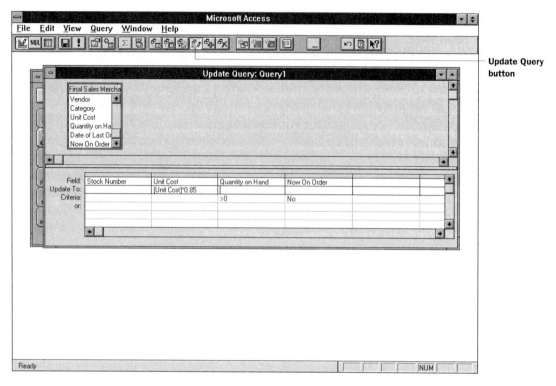

10. Before making the changes permanent, Access will ask you to confirm the update. Click on OK to commit the changes.

11. Close the Update Query window. You do not have to save the query design.

12. Switch to the Table view and open the Final Sales Merchandise table. You should see the changes to the unit cost fields.

CHECKPOINT 8A   Notice that 40-Qt. Cooler Kit still has its original price. Why is this so?

13. To reverse the effects of the price change, prepare the same select query, and use the Update To expression [Unit Cost]/0.85 to run the query.

Creating a Delete Query

The process of creating a delete action query is similar to creating an update query. First, create a select query with the correct criteria for those records to be deleted. Then choose the Delete command from the Query menu and Access will convert the query window into a Delete Query window. When you run the query, Access will delete all those records that meet the criteria. As with the Update query, you are given a chance to cancel the command before its changes become permanent.

Creating a Make-Table Query

With a make-table action query, all records that meet the criteria are copied to a new table. First, create a select query with appropriate fields. Only those fields included will be copied to the new table. Establish criteria expressions if necessary.

Run the select query to confirm the settings in the QBE grid. To convert the select query to a make-table query, give the Query | Make Table command. You will see a Query Properties box in which you specify the name of the table in the current database. There is a check box to specify that the table belongs in a different database. The following activity will show how to create a make-table action query that joins two tables.

GUIDED ACTIVITY 8.3

Creating a Make-Table Query

This Guided Activity will show you how to copy records from joined tables to a new table, using a make-table action query.

1. Close any open windows and return to the HUNT Database window.

2. Open a new query in New Query mode.

3. Add the Employees and Department tables to the query and close the Add Table window. Access will automatically place a join line between the Department fields of these two tables.

4. Drag the following fields to the QBE grid: First Name, Middle Initial, Last Name, Department (all from Employees), and Manager (from Department).

5. Select the Make Table command from the Query menu, or click the Make-Table button in the toolbar. Your desktop should look like Figure 8.8.

FIGURE 8.8
Make-table query window

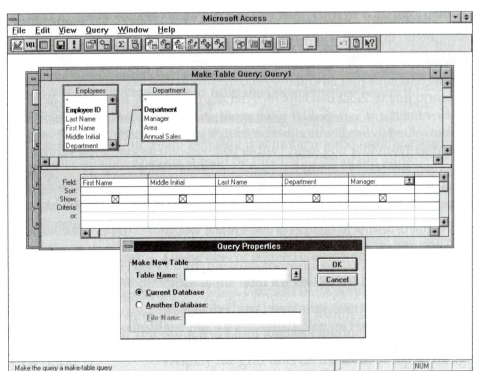

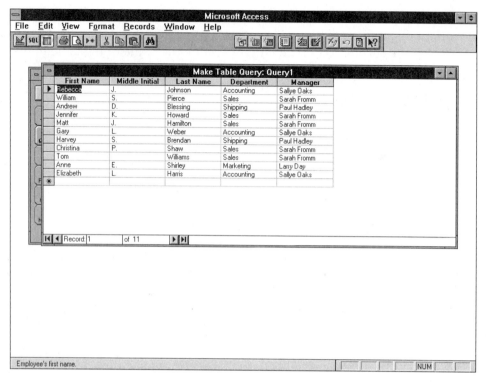

6. In the Table Name box, specify `Employees with Managers` and press [Enter].

7. Run the query to create the new table. Access will ask you to confirm the creation of the new table. Click OK. Its datasheet is shown in Figure 8.9.

8. Close the Make Table Query window. Do not save the query design. Switch to Table mode to see the Employees with Managers table.

Creating an Append Query

Not surprisingly, the append action query works in much the same manner as the other action queries. The first step is to create a select query with the appropriate fields and criteria. Only those fields that are included in the query will be copied to the other table. Next, select the Append command from the Query menu. Access will display the Query Properties box in which you can specify the name of the existing table to which you wish to append records. To complete the procedure, run the query. The extracted records are placed at the end of (are appended to) the existing table.

If you were to accidentally execute the same append query two times, the records would be added *twice* to the existing table. There is a check box in the Query Properties box for unique values only; if it is checked, Access will examine the primary key value and only append records whose primary key does *not* already exist in the table.

Using a Parameter Query

There may be occasions when you want to reuse a previous query several times, making changes in the criteria each time. You can speed up the process by saving the query as a *parameter query*. When you run a parameter query, Access will display a dialog box and ask you to enter the criteria as a parameter. The query then runs normally. This way you can specify the criteria whenever you run the query without having to formally change its design in a query window.

Parameter queries can be useful when printing reports for a specific time period. For instance, use a parameter query as the basis for a monthly report, and specify the month in the parameter box. Access will print the report, including just the records for that month.

To create a parameter query, first prepare a select query as usual. In the criteria cell you want to use as a parameter, enter the parameter name surrounded by *square brackets*. This may be entered as an imperative statement, such as `[Enter the Department name:]`. You may have more than one parameter in a single query. Save the query normally.

When you run the query (or open a form or report that uses the query as its data source), Access will display the parameter box with your prompts and ask you to fill in the entry. Your responses are transferred into the query, and the resulting dynaset reflects the same criteria that would have been input directly into the query design window.

Creating a Crosstab Query

The final query in this unit is useful when tabulating results *across* groups of records. The *crosstab query* will present summaries of these groups in a two-dimensional, crosstab format. In one dimension appears one variable (field value) and in the other dimension appears the other variable, both in groups. The crosstab format is easier to read than the long list that results from a select query.

The method to create a crosstab query is similar to the previous queries. First, create a new query and add tables to the query window. Drag appropriate fields to the QBE grid. Choose Crosstab from the Query menu. Access will add two new rows to the QBE grid: Total and Crosstab. The crosstab cell is used to specify which fields will become the horizontal and vertical headings in the crosstab matrix, and which field is to be summarized. The Total cell for the summarized field specifies the type of summary calculations (Sum, Avg, Min, Max, Count, StDev, Var, First, Last, Expression, and Where). Then run the query to view the crosstab dynaset.

The following example will illustrate the Access crosstab query.

FIGURE 8.10
Query Wizard window showing crosstab structure

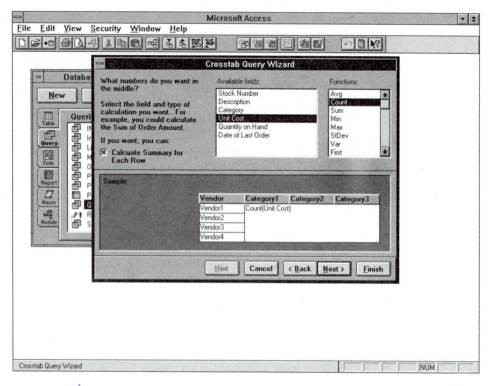

GUIDED ACTIVITY 8.4 ✳

Creating a Crosstab Query

In this Guided Activity you will use the Query Wizards to create a crosstab query for the Products table.

1. Close any open windows and return to the HUNT Database window.

2. Switch to Query view and click the New button, then click Query Wizards.

3. Choose the Crosstab Query and click OK.

4. Choose the Products table for the query and click Next.

5. Select the Vendor field for the row headings and click on the > key. Click Next to go on to the next step.

6. Choose the Category field for the column headings and click Next.

7. Pick the Unit Cost field for values in the middle of the table. At the right side of this window, select the Count function, as shown in Figure 8.10. Click Next to go to the next step.

8. In the next step use the default crosstab name and click Finish to see your crosstab query, shown in Figure 8.11.

9. Close the Query window without saving it.

CHECKPOINT 8B What do the numbers in the query's dynaset cells represent?

FIGURE 8.11
Crosstab query dynaset

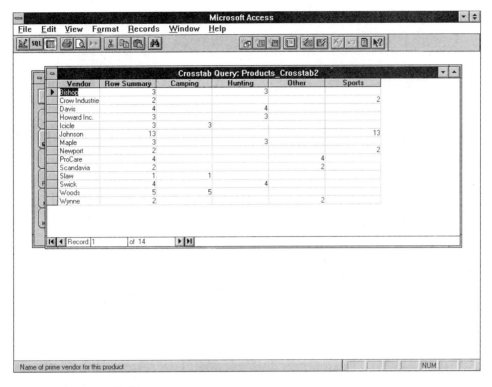

Other Crosstab Features

CHANGING THE QUERY DESIGN

Figure 8.12 shows the Design view for the previous query. Notice that the Total row and the Crosstab row have been added. The Query Wizard placed the appropriate values in those cells for row and column heading, with Group By in the Total row. Unit Cost is the value in the Field cell; Count in the Total row means to display the number of products for a particular vendor and category. The optional Row Summary column was added by the Query Wizard to show the count of entries in each row. You can make changes to your crosstab query here, or use the Query Wizard to create a new crosstab query.

CROSSTABS WITH JOINED TABLES

It is possible to use joined tables in a crosstab query. After joining the tables in the top portion of the query window, drag the relevant fields down to the QBE grid. You may wish to turn on the table names in the QBE grid by giving the View | Table Names command while in Query Design view. Access will add one more row to the QBE grid to designate which table that field came from.

USING DATE HEADINGS

You might want a crosstab query with annual, monthly, or quarterly column headings. The Access Format function can be used to extract the month name from a

FIGURE 8.12
Design view for crosstab query

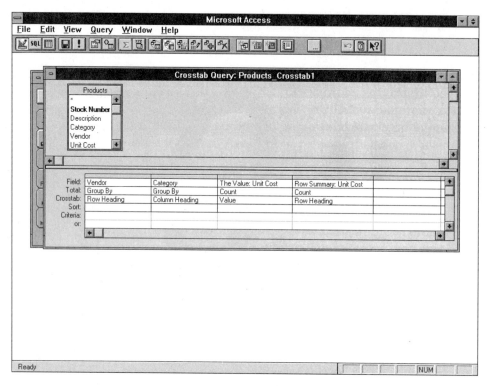

date field type. Instead of entering just the field name, substitute the expression `FORMAT([datefieldname],"mmm")` for the date field and Access will display Jan, Feb, and so on, instead of the full date. Other choices include `"yyyy"` for year and `"q"` for quarter number. (Insert the name of the date field into the preceding expression.)

You can use the Query Wizard to create fixed column headings for date fields. Use the same approach as in the previous activity, but specify Date of Last order for the column heading field. The Query Wizard will ask how you want the date field to appear, and you can choose from Year, Quarter, Month, or Date settings. Access will sort the columns chronologically when you run the query. The rest of this is left as an exercise. The query's dynaset is shown in Figure 8.13; the column widths have been adjusted to show all of the months on one screen.

TIP *To adjust all of the column widths in a datasheet or dynaset at one time, drag the pointer across all of the field selector bars above each column, highlighting the fields. Give the Format/Column Width command from the menu bar, and specify the proper column width in characters. In this case, we chose 9 as the column width for the month fields; the Vendor field was expanded to 18 characters wide to display long vendor names.*

SQL—Structured Query Language

Structured Query Language is a common language used with many database management systems to retrieve information, using near-English queries that are more comprehensible. SQL queries are procedural in nature—you must explain what to do with an SQL command verb, listing each field involved and any selection

FIGURE 8.13
Fixed column crosstab query with row summary

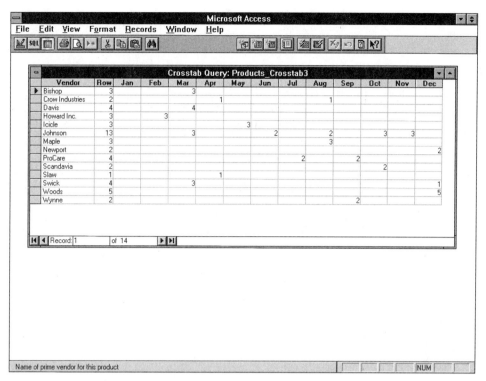

Vendor	Row	Jan	Feb	Mar	Apr	May	Jun	Jul	Aug	Sep	Oct	Nov	Dec
Bishop	3			3									
Crow Industries	2				1				1				
Davis	4				4								
Howard Inc.	3		3										
Icicle	3					3							
Johnson	13			3			2		2		3	3	
Maple	3								3				
Newport	2												2
ProCare	4							2		2			
Scandavia	2										2		
Slaw	1				1								
Swick	4			3									1
Woods	5												5
Wynne	2									2			

criteria within the query statement itself. Complicated queries can result in an extremely long SQL statement.

Most users will not find it necessary to know or use SQL statements. Access translates your query into the SQL language before submitting it to the database engine for processing. The database engine breaks the SQL query down before applying it to the database. Because Access must work with data from sources other than itself, its ability to translate queries into standard SQL statements makes it compatible with a great many database systems.

Viewing the SQL Box in an Access Query

In the event that you are curious enough to view the SQL statement that is equivalent to your own Access query, choose the SQL command from the View menu in Query Design view or click the SQL button in the toolbar. Access will display the SQL statement in a box. Figure 8.14 shows the SQL statement corresponding to a select query. Can you pick out the purpose of the various parts of the SQL statement that correspond to the Access query? The answer is left to the reader as an exercise.

Making Changes to the Query with the SQL Box

If you know how to use SQL, you can make changes to queries by modifying the SQL statements in the SQL box. Make changes directly to the statements in the box. If you want to add a new line, press [Enter]. When you exit from the SQL dialog box, Access will make changes to the query to reflect the SQL statement.

FIGURE 8.14
*SQL statement
corresponding
to an Access
query*

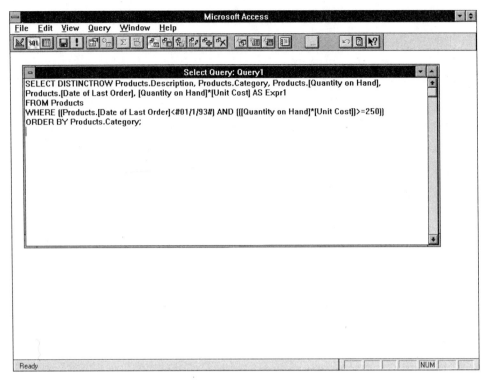

FIGURE 8.14
SQL statement corresponding to an Access query

It is possible to use SQL statements in Access program modules. Refer to the Access *Programming Reference Manual* for more details about modules.

Command Review

Edit I Relationships	Add, change, or delete relationships between tables.
File I Save Layout	Save relationships in the database.
Format I Column Width	Change column width of the selected column(s).
Query I Parameters	Convert a select query into a parameter query.
Query I Crosstab	Convert a select query into a crosstab query.
Query I Update	Convert a select query into an update query.
Query I Delete	Convert a select query to a delete query.
Query I Make Table	Convert a select query to a make-table query.
Query I Append	Convert a select query to an append query.
Query I Run	Execute the query and display the dynaset in Datasheet view.
View I SQL	View the SQL statements for an Access query.
View I Table Names	Display the table names in a QBE grid (useful with joined tables).

Exercises

Use the Hunter River database contained within the HUNT.MDB file on the West Student Data Disk for these exercises.

1. Design a relational database for a university student information system. Your database should store information about students, classes they took, grades received, courses available within the university, and instructors that teach those classes. Be sure to consider how the tables will be joined to produce desired forms and reports.

2. Prepare a query that links the Orders and Order Items tables.

   a. Print the resulting dynaset for the orders.

   b. Prepare a groups/totals report using your query so that all of the order lines that relate to a particular order appear together as one group.

   c. *Optional*: To document your query from step a., open the query in Design view and press [PrtSc] on your keyboard. This will copy the screen to the Windows Clipboard. Immediately return to the Program Manager window and open a word processor such as Windows Write. To copy the contents of the Clipboard into Write, choose the Paste command from the Edit menu. Then print the Write document on your printer.

NOTE *Access 2.0 users might want to try the File/Print Definition command for more detailed documentation about your query.*

3. Create a make-table action query for the Employees table. Only employees who were hired prior to January 1, 1993, should be included in the new table. Use all fields. The new table should be called Plan I Employees. Print a copy of the datasheet for this new table.

4. Use the Plan I Employees table from the previous exercise. Create a new currency field called Bonus. Prepare an update query in which each employee whose salary is below $20,000 receives an 8% bonus; employees at $20,000 or above will receive a 6% bonus. This will take two different update queries. Remember to enclose the field name in square brackets if you use it in an Update To expression. Print a copy of the resulting datasheet.

5. Create a parameter query for the Customers table, using the State field as the parameter. Save the query as the name Customer State Parameter Query, then execute the parameter query and substitute IN for the state. Print the resulting dynaset.

6. Use the Query Wizards to create a crosstab query that has Vendor as the row header and Date of Last Order as the column header. Count the number of orders placed each month. Reduce the width of the columns and print the resulting datasheet. Save the query as Monthly Product Orders.

7. Prepare a crosstab query that shows the breakdown of customers by state.

Review Questions

1. What is meant by the term *relational database*? How is working with a relational database different from working with a single table?

2. Describe the process of normalization. What are the general guidelines to follow when designing normalized tables?

3. Discuss the following terms as they pertain to the normalization process.

    a. Repeating groups

    b. Data redundancy

    c. Partial dependency

    d. Calculated fields

4. Are there any *disadvantages* to using a normalized database with many tables to be joined? Explain.

5. Compare the three kinds of joins that Access can do in a query. Which one is the default choice? Give an example where each type of join could be used. Don't repeat examples from this book.

6. Describe the steps to follow in joining two tables together and showing all of the fields from both tables in the resulting dynaset.

7. Discuss the four types of action queries supported by Access. Give an example of each type, using the PMC database tables.

8. It is recommended that a user build a select query before converting it to an action query. Why is this good advice?

9. What is a parameter query, and how is it useful in Access?

10. Describe the contents of a crosstab dynaset, and explain how it is used to present data summaries.

11. Examine the Access query shown in Figure 8.14. The SQL statement that corresponds to the query is shown in this figure. Give the meaning of the following parts of the SQL statement. You may have to search Help for some of the items.

    a. SELECT DISTINCTROW Products.Description

    b. WHERE ((Products.[Date of Last Order]<#01/1/93#) AND (([Quantity on Hand]*[Unit Cost])>=250))

    c. ORDER BY Products.Category;

12. What is SQL? How can knowledge of SQL be relevant for Access users?

Key Terms

Action query	Equi-join	Repeating group
Anomaly	Join line	Self-join
Append query	Make-table query	SQL (Structured Query
Concatenation	Normalization	Language)
Crosstab query	Outer join	Update query
Delete query	Parameter query	
Drag method	Relational database	

Documentation Research

Use the printed documentation and the on-line Help available with Microsoft Access to answer the following questions. If you use one of the manuals, provide the page number for your reference in the manual.

1. We introduced the Format function in this unit. Look up this function in the on-line Help system and list the kinds of formats available. Give reasons for using this function.

2. Describe the Run with Owner's Permission option in an Access Query Properties box. Why would it be used in an action query?

3. An action query does not produce a dynaset as a select query does. How can you view the results of an action query?

4. Search the Access Help system for "Microsoft Access SQL Reserved Words." Compare the WHERE and HAVING clauses in the SQL language.

5. What do the Cascade Update Related Fields and Cascade Delete Related Records options in the Relationships dialog box mean? Give an example using the Employees and Department tables.

Physicians' Medical Clinic (VI): Building an Action Query

In this exercise you will create several queries for tables in the PMC database, using the material covered in previous units. You will open the PMC database, join several tables with a select query, create several action queries, and print a patient billing statement report using data from these queries. Read the directions carefully. Clearly identify which output goes with which part of the Application.

1. Start Windows and enter Access. Open the PMC database.

2. As preparation for preparing a patient statement report, you have been asked to create a query that joins the appropriate tables from the PMC database. You know that this query will need information about patients, visits, payments, procedures, and insurers as described in Unit 8. Assume that there is no more than one procedure per patient visit, but that a patient will probably have several visits over the billing period, one calendar month. Sketch out the format for the patient billing statement, but do not create a report format at this time.

3. Create a make-table action query from the join query you created in the previous step. Copy all of the records that fall in the April month into this temporary table. Use an appropriate name for the new table to reflect its contents. Make sure that you have all the fields necessary to create the patient billing statement. Print a copy of the datasheet corresponding to this new table.

4. Finally, use the Report Wizards to prepare a tentative groups/subtotals report for the clinic. Use the new table you created in the previous step as the data source. Because of the limitations of the Access Report Wizards, you may not be able to design a customized report that shows information precisely where you want it. We will modify this report design in a later application after learning how to prepare custom report designs. Print a copy of the report for the April patient visits.

Working with Access Controls in Forms and Reports

This unit acts as a building block for the ultimate preparation of customized Access forms and reports. The unit describes the types of controls available for Access data objects. You will learn how to add, move, and resize controls that are used in forms and reports. There are sections on use of the Access Toolbox to place new controls in a form or report. The unit contains a discussion about control properties.

Learning Objectives

At the completion of this unit you should know

1. the definition of an Access control,

2. the various types of controls,

3. the differences between bound, unbound, and calculated controls,

4. the settings that can be modified with the Control Properties box.

At the completion of this unit you should be able to

1. move a control,

2. resize a control,

3. add a control with the Access Toolbox,

4. create a calculated control,

5. display and change control properties.

Important Commands

Format | Align

Format | Size | to Fit

Format | Snap to Grid

View | Field List

View | Form

View | Form Design

View | Grid

View | Palette

View | Properties

Control Basis

Controls are graphical objects used to display text, lines, boxes, data values, or graphic images on a form or report. When you used the Wizards to create forms and reports in Part One of this book, Access generated the controls for you and placed them on the design surface for you in predefined ways. In those units we suggested that you would probably find it easier to re-create the data object with the Wizards than to make the changes manually by adding, moving, and resizing controls.

In this unit we discuss how to work directly with those controls to create custom forms and reports. Some users will still prefer to let the Wizards build the form or report, then make manual changes to the design. Other users would rather start with a blank screen and add the controls necessary for the final design. In this unit we will discuss controls themselves. In future units you will learn details on how to use these controls with forms and reports.

Classes of Controls

There are three general classes of controls in Access. Bound controls and calculated controls depend on field values, whereas unbound controls are not connected with fields. Each is described below.

BOUND CONTROLS

Bound controls are those that show data from tables or query dynasets. We say that the controls are *bound* or connected to a field from the table or query. Each record in the table or dynaset will have a different field value for that control. Bound controls include text, number, date/time, yes/no, memo, counter, and OLE data types.

UNBOUND CONTROLS

Unbound controls show text, lines, rectangles, or OLE pictures and are not bound to a field of a table or dynaset. Unbound controls can include messages or anything that remains unchanged from record to record in the table or dynaset. Unbound controls are used to highlight forms and reports, as well as to provide messages and prompts that are not based on particular field values.

CALCULATED CONTROLS

Similar to bound controls, *calculated controls* get their data values from an expression of fields. As you navigate through the table or query, the value of the calculated control will change as the expression is recalculated. In an earlier unit we created an inventory value expression that multiplied Unit Cost by Quantity on Hand. In a form or report this would be considered a calculated control.

Types of Toolbox Controls

The *Toolbox* is a collection of icons that is automatically displayed when you open a form or report in Design view. Shown in Figure 9.1, the Toolbox is a normal window that can be moved or closed by double-clicking on the Control-menu box.

This section will discuss the types of controls that are accessible through the Toolbox. Use of the Toolbox appears in the following section.

FIGURE 9.1
Access Control Toolbox

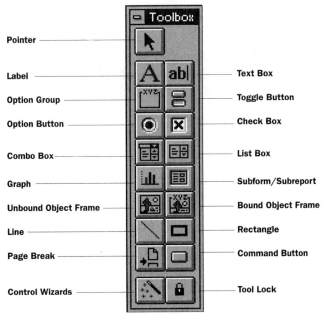

Pointer

Label — Text Box

Option Group — Toggle Button

Option Button — Check Box

Combo Box — List Box

Graph — Subform/Subreport

Unbound Object Frame — Bound Object Frame

Line — Rectangle

Page Break — Command Button

Control Wizards — Tool Lock

POINTER (SELECT OBJECTS)

The *pointer* tool is used to select commands from a menu and to select, move, size, and edit objects in the design window. This is the default tool when the Toolbox is opened.

LABEL

The *label* tool is used to place a descriptive text phrase on the screen. Examples include report title, column headings, and explanatory messages. The label is not to be confused with the text box, which is described next. A label is an unbound control.

TEXT BOX

A *text box* is used to enter or display data of all types, including text, numbers, and pictures. A text box control is usually associated with a field, whereas a label is an unbound control. A text box can have scroll bars.

OPTION GROUP

An *option group* control is used to create a group of buttons or boxes in an option group. Only one button in an option group can be selected at a time. In Access 2.0, the Control Wizards can help you create an option group.

TOGGLE BUTTON

A *toggle button* is used to select a response from a group of values. It may be used by itself to select a Yes/No value. The toggle button, option button, and check box all do the same thing and differ only in their appearance.

OPTION BUTTON

Similar to a toggle button, the *option button* can be used in an option group to select one response from a set of values. These are sometimes referred to as *radio buttons* because they resemble a round knob on a radio. The option button may be used by itself to select a Yes/No value. When selected, the option button appears as a small filled-in circle and means "Yes."

CHECK BOX

Similar to toggle and option buttons, the *check box* can be used in an option group to select a response from a set of values. When used by itself, it may be used to select a Yes/No value. It is a rectangular box and, when checked, appears with a small "x" in the box, meaning "Yes."

COMBO BOX

A *combo box* lets you select a value from a list by choosing it with the pointer, or lets you fill in the value in the box. Many Windows dialog boxes use a combo box for user responses, such as when you save a file and specify the file name. In Access 2.0, the Control Wizards can help you create a combo box.

LIST BOX

With a *list box* you can choose a value from a list. Although a list box is similar to a combo box, you cannot enter a value by keying it into a list box. In Access 2.0, the Control Wizards can help you create an list box.

GRAPH

The *graph* tool is used to place a graph control in the form or report. Using this tool will cause the Microsoft Graph application to begin.

SUBFORM/SUBREPORT

The *subform/subreport* tool is used to place a subform within a main form or a subreport within a main report.

UNBOUND OBJECT FRAME

The *unbound object frame* tool is used to hold an unbound OLE object in the form or report. An unbound OLE object is a picture or graphic image.

BOUND OBJECT FRAME

The *bound object frame* tool is used to hold an OLE object that is bound to a field in a table. The OLE object is usually stored within the database.

LINE

The *line* tool is used to add a straight line to the form or report. The line is an unbound object. Lines are used to separate portions of the form or report and can make the output appear more like a printed document. You can use the Palette button in the toolbar to change the width and color of the line.

RECTANGLE

The *rectangle* tool is used to place a rectangle in the form or report. Rectangles can highlight items from one group and can produce a shadow effect when placed beneath another control. The color of the rectangle can be changed with the Properties sheet (discussed later) or the *Palette box*.

PAGE BREAK

The *page break* tool is used to place a page break in the form or report, causing the printer to begin a new page. This tool is used with the screen and with a printed page.

COMMAND BUTTON

The *command button* tool can be used to insert a command button in a form. You associate the command button with an Access macro. The command button executes a set of commands when pushed.

CONTROL WIZARDS

The *Control Wizards* tool is used to turn Control Wizards on or off. If this button is pushed, the Control Wizards will assist you when adding an option group, combo box, or list box control. You can also use the View | Control Wizards command to toggle the Control Wizards.

TOOL LOCK

The *lock button* tool will keep active the tool you selected until you select another tool. This is useful if you want to add several controls of the same kind to a database object.

Adding a Control from the Field List

Before we learn how to insert the custom controls with the Toolbox, we should discuss the method to insert field text boxes directly into the form or report from the field list. Open the form or report in Design view, then click on the Field List button in the toolbar. (Or use the View | Field List command from the menu bar.)

Using the mouse, drag a field from the field list to its desired location on the design screen. Access will create *two controls* for each field—a label containing the field name and a text box bound to the field value. Access will copy the field properties you created when you designed the table to the Control Properties sheet. Thus field properties such as format, validation information, and default value are consistent wherever you use that field.

NOTE *If you change a field property after the control using that field has been created, that property will not be transferred to the control as well. Access 2.0 will check validation rules, however, even if you add one after the control was created.*

GUIDED ACTIVITY 9.1

Adding a Control from the Field List ✳

In this Guided Activity you will create a control in a form by dragging it from the field list.

1. Start Windows and load Access. Open the HUNT database file.

2. Change to Form mode and click the New button to open a new form.

3. Choose the Customers table in the New Form dialog box. Click on the Blank Form button to open the Form Design view.

4. If the *grid dots* are not already present, use the View | Grid command to display the placement grid. These dots do not appear in the final form or report. Notice that Access also places light gray grid lines at one-inch intervals to help you place controls in the form.

CHECKPOINT 9A   What is the purpose of the grid dots in the design screen?

5. If the field list is not already present, click on the Field List button in the toolbar or issue the View | Field List command from the menu bar. Access will display a window containing the field names from the Customers table. Move the Field List window to the side, out of the way, by dragging its title bar.

6. Drag the Last Name field from the Field List to the design grid so that the text box is approximately 0.5 inch down and 1.5 inches across, according to the rulers in the Form Design window. The crosshairs pointer indicates the location for the text control, *not* its label. Release the mouse button. If you placed the boxes in the wrong location, press the [Del] key to delete these two controls and repeat this step.

7. Access will create two controls as shown in Figure 9.2. The left control is a label that contains the field's name; the right control is a text box that is bound to the Last Name field. Access always places the upper-left corner of the text box control at the location you indicate with the pointer.

We will discuss the purpose of the handles that appear at the edges of these controls in the next section. Leave the form design on the screen at this time and we will add more to it in a later activity.

Moving and Resizing Access Controls

After placing a control on the design screen, you may want to move it or change its size. The *control handles* that appear at the edges of the control box are used for these purposes. In Figure 9.2 you can see that the Last Name text box on the right has eight handles around its edges. Use these handles to move and resize this box. Note that when you move or resize the text box control, its accompanying label does *not* change. Each box must be adjusted separately. If you want to move both boxes, it might be easier to delete both boxes and drag them again to the desired location.

FIGURE 9.2
*Add a control
from the field list*

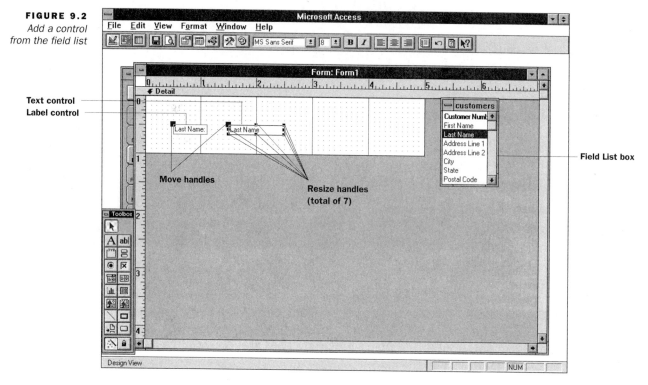

Moving a Control

The upper-left corner handle is larger than the others. This is the *move handle*. You can move the control by dragging its move handle. Slowly move the pointer on this handle until it changes to a small hand shape. Then drag the control to its new location. When you release the left mouse button, Access will redraw the control with its upper-left corner at that location.

Resizing a Control

The other seven handles on the control are *size handles*. The top and bottom size handles are used to expand the box size up or down, while the left and right handles can be used to expand the box sideways. The three corner handles are used to change the size in two directions at once, just like dragging the corner border of a window. Notice that the label control does not have any size handles. It can be expanded in the horizontal direction when you edit the text in the label box. This is covered later.

The Grid System for Aligning Controls

Access uses a grid system in the form and report design screens. The grid appears as a series of evenly-spaced dots, usually 10 horizontal and 12 vertical dots per inch. Use the View | Grid command to turn them on or off. Access uses the grid system to help you align controls horizontally and vertically. Horizontal and vertical gridlines appear at 1-inch increments in Access 2.0.

If the Snap to Grid command in the Format menu is checked, Access will *snap* all four corners of the control to the nearest grid coordinates. That is, when you add, resize, or move the control, it will be aligned horizontally and vertically with the grid dots. You can't place the control's location between the dots when this command is on. You can toggle the grid alignment off by using the Format | Snap to Grid command again. You can temporarily defeat the grid by holding down the Ctrl key while you complete the control move or resize operation.

Access defaults to Snap to Grid, but your computer site may have changed this setting. Use the Format menu to see the current setting. You can also change the spacing of the dots with the form or report property sheet. Search Help for "Changing the Grid's Fineness." You can turn off the grid with the View | Grid command, but the Snap to Grid setting remains active even when the grid is not visible.

The Format | Align command is helpful in aligning a group of selected controls. You can specify that one or all of the edges of the selected controls align to a control or a certain point on the design grid. Thus, you can align a column of controls, or a row of controls, so that they match. This is particularly useful after you have made a series of changes to the controls and they are out of alignment. We will demonstrate this in a future activity.

GUIDED ACTIVITY 9.2

Moving and Resizing a Control

In this Guided Activity you will practice moving and resizing an Access control.

1. We will start with the custom form started in the previous activity. If you have not already completed the activity, do so at this time. Refer back to Figure 9.2.

2. First we will move the text box control on the right. Be sure it is selected so that its handles appear. If the handles are not present, click once on the control to select it.

3. Position the mouse pointer on the move handle at the upper-left corner of the control on the right so that the pointer turns into the hand icon with a single pointing finger.

4. While pressing the left mouse button, drag the control to the right until the pointer is at the 2-inch mark on the ruler. Notice that Access displays a shadow of the box in the new position while you are dragging it. Release the mouse button to move the box.

5. Repeat step 4, but this time try to move the box to a point *between* the grid dots. When you release the mouse button, the box will snap to the nearest grid dot.

6. Next, you will resize the box. Position the mouse pointer on the lower-left resize handle until the pointer turns into a diagonal arrow with two heads.

7. While pressing the left mouse button, slowly drag the left border to the left to increase the size of the box. When the left edge of the box reaches the 1.5-inch mark, release the mouse button. Access will resize the box to your specification.

CHECKPOINT 9B   How would you make this control box taller?

The next activity will illustrate how to align two controls on the same form.

GUIDED ACTIVITY 9.3

Aligning a Group of Controls

In this Guided Activity you will add another control and align it with the previous control already in the form from Guided Activity 9.2.

1. We will begin with the form from the previous activity. If you have not already completed that activity, do so at this time.

2. Examine the form from the previous activity. The Last Name text box control should start at the 1.5-inch mark.

3. Use the pointer to drag the First Name field from the field list box to the form. Place its upper-left corner 0.25 inch down and 2 inches across on the grid. Your design screen should look like Figure 9.3.

4. Select the First Name label and drag the move handle of the First Name label so that it aligns with the Last Name label just beneath it.

5. Click on the pointer tool in the Toolbox if it is not already selected. Then move the pointer to a point about 0.125 inch down and 1.25 inches across. While holding down the left mouse button, drag the pointer to draw a rectangle to enclose a

FIGURE 9.3
*Unaligned Form
Design screen*

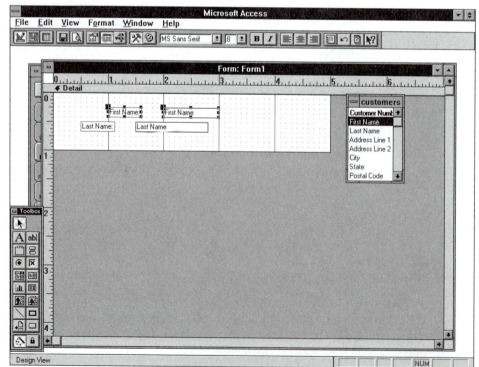

FIGURE 9.4
*Aligned controls
in the Form
Design screen*

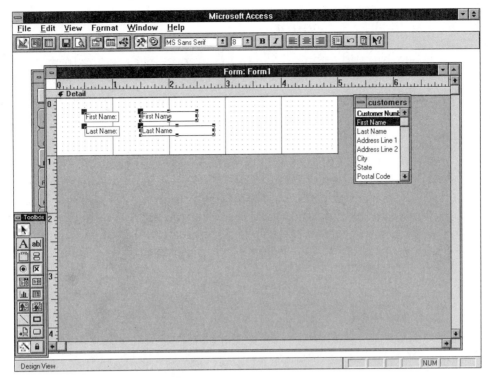

portion of both of the text boxes. This is one way to select more than one field in the form or report design screens. (The other way is to hold down the [Shift] key and click on each item to be selected, then release the [Shift] key.)

6. Choose the Align command from the Format menu. From the submenu, choose Left with the pointer. Access will align the two fields at their left edges. The screen should look like Figure 9.4.

7. Close the Form Design window without saving the form.

We will address more custom form design issues in the next unit of this book.

Size to Fit Option

Ordinarily, you will specify the size of the control when you add it to the design. If you choose the *Size | to Fit* command from the Format menu, Access will automatically adjust the size of the control to fit the item it contains. For instance, if you change the font size in a label, command button, or toggle button, the control's height and width can be adjusted to fit its contents. This command will adjust only the height of a text box, list box, or combo box if the font size of text within is changed. You must resize the box to change the width of the box.

Using the Toolbox to Add a Control

When you add a control to a form or report by dragging from the field list box, Access will create only label and text box controls. In this section you will learn how to use the Toolbox to insert other types of controls in a form or report.

General Procedure to Add a Control

First switch to Design view for the form or report you're working on. Use the pointer to select the desired tool from the Toolbox, then move the pointer to the upper-left corner of the desired location for the control. Access will change the pointer shape to reflect the tool you selected. Use the mouse to drag the control box to the desired size and release the left mouse button. Access will place the control in that location. Then fill in the details about the control, and make changes to the control's property sheet if necessary.

Viewing the Property Sheet

There are three ways to display the property sheet for a control, form, or report. The easiest way is to double-click on the object and the property sheet will appear. To use the other ways, you must first select the object by clicking once on it in the design screen. Then click on the Properties button in the toolbar or use the View I Properties command from the menu bar. Once a property sheet window appears, Access will display the appropriate property sheet when you select a different object. After you save the form or report, Access will usually "remember" that you have the property sheet displayed when you work on the same form or report in a future session. You can close the property sheet window or move it out of the way to make more room on the desktop.

Fill in the Property Sheet

The details about the control depend on the type of control you insert. Label controls contain text phrases. A text box is tied to a specific field or calculated value. Toggle buttons, option buttons, and check boxes are also tied to a particular field. Combo and list boxes are tied to a field and must be given a set of values to choose from. Object frames are associated with a graphic image or other OLE object. Line and rectangle controls are drawn directly on the design screen, using the mouse pointer.

Although there are properties for nearly all of the options for each control, you may find it easier to use the toolbar and other tools to fill in some of the properties. For instance, we saw in Part One of this book that you can use the Palette box to choose colors and line widths for controls. You can select a font, font size, and other features such as bold or italic from the toolbar. These settings are automatically transferred to the appropriate property. We will cover properties later in this unit.

GUIDED ACTIVITY 9.4

Adding a Line Control with the Toolbox

In this Guided Activity you will add a line control to a form with the Toolbox.

1. We will begin with a new form, so close the previous Form Design window and return to the HUNT Database window.

2. Click on the New button in Form view in the Database window. Specify the Products table in the New Form box, then choose Blank Form.

3. Drag the bottom edge of the form screen down about 2 inches to make more room in the form. You may want to drag the Toolbox over to the right side of the desktop so that the entire form design surface is visible.

4. We need to place a title in the upper portion of the form. Click on the Label button in the Toolbox. In the Form Design toolbar click the font size drop-down list box and choose 14 points. This will produce a large font for the top of the form.

5. Then position the pointer at about 0.25 inch down and 0.5 inch across the ruler lines. Press the left mouse button and drag the box to the 0.5,4.0-inch coordinates, then release the mouse button. Access will create a label control and leave the pointer blinking inside.

6. You can key in the desired heading for the form. Notice that the pointer is taller than normal, indicating your use of the 14-point font. Key in Sample Custom Form Heading Label and press Enter. Your screen should resemble Figure 9.5.

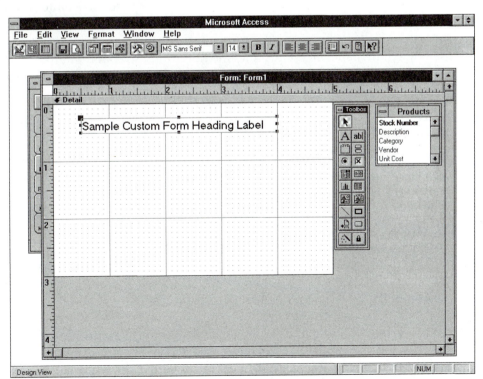

FIGURE 9.5
Custom Form Design window

FIGURE 9.6
*Line control
added to
custom form*

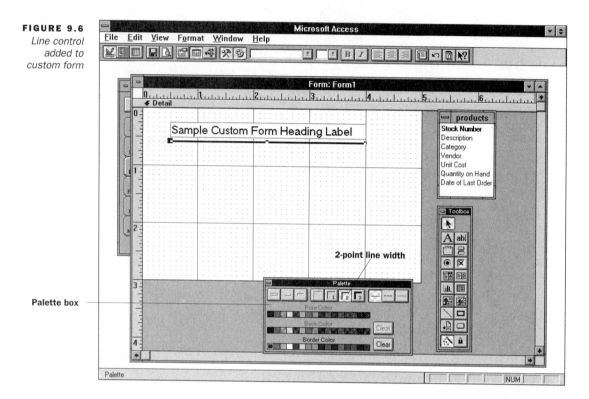

Palette box

CHECKPOINT 9C What happens to the width of a label control when you enter a phrase that is wider than the current width of the control?

7. Next, click on the Line button in the Toolbox. Move the pointer to the grid location just beneath the lower-left corner of the heading label. Depress the left mouse button and drag the line to the right until it just lines up with the right edge of the label box. Keep the line horizontal so that it aligns with the grid dots. Release the mouse button.

8. Access will draw the line in the indicated location, using the default thin line width. Click on the Palette button, or give the View | Palette command, to display the Palette box. Click on the Width button marked 2 (2 points) to make the line heavier. Figure 9.6 shows the form design to this stage.

9. Close the Palette window. Leave the form design on the screen, as it will be used in the next Guided Activity.

Adding a List Box Control

We could use a similar procedure to add a list box that shows several values for the record. Select the List Box control tool from the Toolbox, then drag the desired field from the field list to the form design. Access will create two controls—a label attached to the list box and the list box itself. However, to use the list box to display data, you must fill in details in the control's Properties sheet.

With the list box control selected, click on the Properties button in the toolbar to display the Properties sheet for the control. You must specify the number of columns (usually one) for the list box and indicate where Access can find the row values to be displayed in the box.

There are three Row Source Types for the list box control: Table/query, Value list, and Field list. The Table/query type assumes that the data comes from a table or a query named in the Row Source line, and is the default setting. The Value list type assumes that the data comes from a list of values typed into the Row Source line. The Field list assumes that the data is a list of field names from the table or query named in the Row Source setting.

Access 2.0 introduces the List Box Control Wizard that will make creating the list box much simpler. The following activity will illustrate how to add a list box control to the form, using the Value list row source for the Category field of the Products table.

GUIDED ACTIVITY 9.5 ✳

Adding a List Box Control with the Toolbox

In this Guided Activity we will add a list box control to the form started in the previous activity. The list box will make it easier to enter the product category.

1. This activity will add on to the form design begun in the previous activity. If you have not completed that exercise, do so at this time.

2. Be sure that the Control Wizard button is pushed in the Toolbox. Click on the List Box tool in the Toolbox.

3. Drag the Category field from the Field List box to the form screen, placing it at the 1,1-inch coordinates.

4. After a few seconds, the first List Box Wizard window will appear, as shown in Figure 9.7. You can have Access get the list of values from a table or query, or from a fixed list. Because we are going to use values from a table, click Next to go to the next step.

5. Access will ask which table or query contains the values for the list box. Choose the table Category and click Next. Click the > key to select the Category field. Access will display the values from the Category table and ask how wide you want the column to be. Accept the default and click Next.

6. At the next screen click Next to signify that you will store the value in the Category field of the Products table. Then click Finish to use the default label and return to Design view.

7. To view the results of your form, click the Form view button in the toolbar, or issue the View | Form command from the menu bar. Figure 9.8 shows the form with the list box for the first record and a portion of the second record.

8. You can use the record navigation buttons at the bottom of the window to move to different records. The list box will show the value of the Category field for each record. Don't make any changes on the form at this time—the new values would be saved in the Products table!

FIGURE 9.7
*List box
Control Wizard*

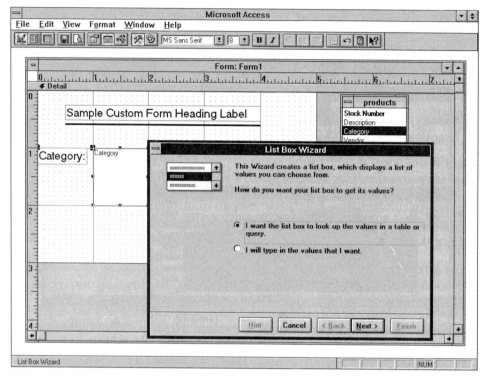

9. The label for the Category field is too large—it used the same size as the form heading label you selected. Click on the Design View button in the toolbar to return to Design view. (Or use the View I Form Design command from the menu bar.)

10. Click once on the Category label (*not* the list box) to select it. Notice that the label box now has handles at all corners, and the list box control has only a move handle.

11. With the label control selected, click once on the font size button in the toolbar and choose 10 points. Access will immediately change the label to this font size in the design screen. Although we will not illustrate it here, you can select a different font from the font box adjacent to the Font Size box in the toolbar.

12. The list box is also a little larger than necessary. Click once on the list box control to select it, then drag the bottom middle handle up to about the 1.7-inch mark. Click the Form View button to see how the list box appears.

13. Close the Form Design window without saving the form.

Properties of Controls

Although each type of control has different properties, they are similar. To view the property sheet for a control, select the control and click on the Properties button in the toolbar (or issue the View I Properties command from the menu bar). You can also double-click a control to bring up its property sheet. To view the default properties for a type of control, double-click its button in the Toolbox.

FIGURE 9.8
*Form view of
list box control*

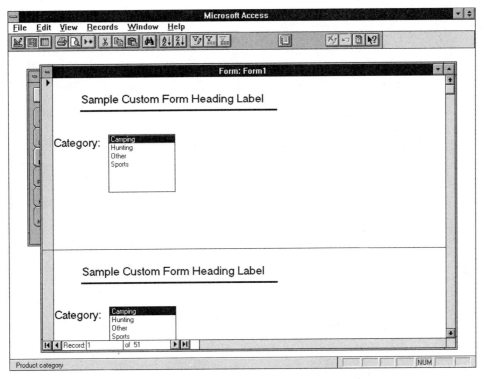

Properties for Label Controls

Figure 9.9 shows the full property sheet for the label control. Ordinarily, you cannot see all of the choices at the same time. Access 2.0 introduced a way to view a subset of the properties; in this case, all properties are displayed. The Properties sheet is a box like other Windows objects and can be moved or resized as desired.

The *Name* gives the name of the control. It must be unique for this form or report. If you drag a field from the field list box, Access will use the field name as the control name. If you create an unbound control, Access will assign a unique name. In this case, Text5 represents an unbound label.

The *Caption* property reflects the label contained within the control itself. If you change the caption property, the form will also change. Likewise, if you change the name on the form design, the property sheet will reflect that change.

The *Visible* property describes whether the label appears. The default is Yes, but you may want to control this property based on a condition within the data itself. For example, if a customer payment is past due, you might display a warning message on the form. You can make changes to Access properties in macros.

The *Display When* property can be used to always display the field, or to display it only on the screen form or on the printed form.

The next few properties reflect the location and size of the control. In this case, the left edge of the label is at the 0-inch mark and its top is at the 1-inch mark. If you move or resize the control, your changes are stored in the property sheet.

The following few properties are used less frequently. *Back Style* allows you to create a transparent control that permits other controls in the same location to

FIGURE 9.9
*Label control
property sheet*

Property box —

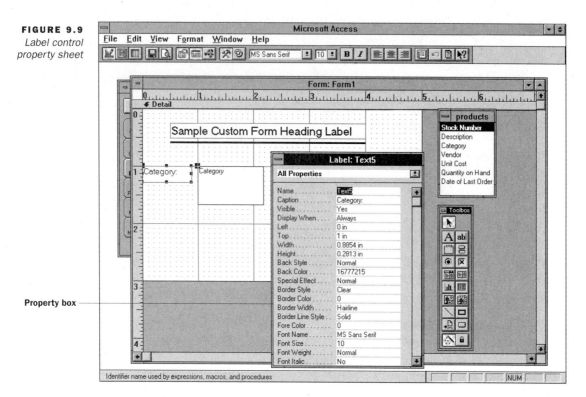

appear, such as in an option group where the *option group control* contains other buttons or boxes. The *Special Effect* property implies whether the item is to be normal, be raised, or have a sunken appearance. The colors are shown as Access codes; to make changes to colors or special effects, use the Palette box.

The *font properties* can be adjusted more easily with the buttons in the toolbar. You can choose the font name and size; select from bold, italic, and underline; and choose text alignment (general, left, right, center). General alignment means that character values are left-aligned while number and date values are right-aligned.

Properties for Text Box Controls

With a *text box control* on the form, Figure 9.10 shows its resized property sheet. Ordinarily, you would use the scroll bar to view the choices in the property sheet. Many of the properties are the same as the label control properties, but there are some new properties described below. Not all of these appear in the property window; to see them, use the scroll bar.

Several of the properties for this control are taken directly from the table design. Format, Decimal Places, Input Mask, Default Value, Status Bar Text, and the Validation Rule properties follow what has been defined for the field to which this control is bound. Status Bar Text defaults to the field Description in the table definition.

The *Before Update* and *After Update* properties describe Access macros or user functions that are to execute before and after, respectively, the data in the text control updates the field value in the underlying table. Typical applications for these macros or user functions are validation procedures that are too complicated for a single validation expression.

FIGURE 9.10

*Text box control
property sheet*

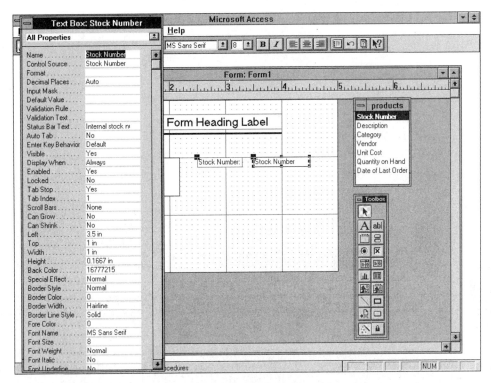

The *On Enter* and *On Exit* properties describe a macro or user function that is to execute when that control receives the *focus* (when it becomes the active control). The on enter procedure executes when the control first gets the focus; the on exit procedure executes when the control is about to lose the focus.

The *Locked* property makes a field read-only. That is, it will display data but will not allow you to change data in the field using that control. This is useful in applications where the user has the authority to read the value but not to erase or change the data in the field. In this example, the control is not read-only.

The *Scroll Bars* property allows you to define whether horizontal, vertical, or either type of scroll bars appear with the control. The default is no scroll bars.

The *Can Grow* and *Can Shrink* properties describe how Access will handle data values that are too big or too small for the current control box size. The default is No for both properties, meaning that values that are too large to fit are truncated (shortened). Items that are smaller than the box result in a box with blank space.

The *Help Context ID* property allows you to identify a particular custom help topic for this control. When the user presses the [F1] key, Access will check the help-context ID property for the control that has the focus. If available, your own custom help message will appear. See Access Help for assistance on this property.

Properties for Other Controls

Earlier in this unit we described the property sheet for list boxes. In fact, most of the Access form controls share similar property sheets. If you have questions about a particular property, highlight that line and press the [F1] key to display help screens.

Access Help contains examples of most of the properties. Coverage of bound and unbound OLE object controls appears in Unit 12 of this book.

Adding Controls to a Report Design

Forms and reports share many features, including use of controls in the design screen. Of course, forms permit you to add or edit data, while reports only permit you to *display* data values. Although most of the controls covered earlier in this unit apply equally to forms and reports, the most common for reports are label, text box, and line controls.

Recall from Unit 6 that Access report designs are broken into sections. The Page Header section contains the report title, page number, date, and column headings. The Detail section contains actual data values for records. The Page Footer section may contain explanatory information such as footnotes. Other sections may be used in reports to accommodate grouped data, title/cover page, and report summaries. We will focus on report controls for these three report sections in this unit. Unit 11 will cover custom reports in more detail.

When you drag a field from the field list box, position the pointer where you want the text box to be located. Access will place an attached label in front of the text box. In most reports you will delete the attached label and use column headings in the Page Header section to identify the text box values. Click once on the box you want to delete, then press the Del key.

You can drag the section borders to adjust the space. If there is any room above or below the controls in the detail section, Access will duplicate that space above and below the data values in the report. Most users will want to eliminate that blank space. The following activity will show how to create a simple custom report by placing controls directly in the design.

GUIDED ACTIVITY 9.6

Adding Controls to a Report

This Guided Activity will demonstrate how to create a report by adding controls directly to the report design.

1. Close any open windows and return to the HUNT Database window.

2. Switch to Report mode and click on New to create a new report.

3. Choose the Products table for the data source and click on Blank Report.

4. If the Toolbox is not visible, use the View | Toolbox command. If the field list dialog box is not present, use the View | Field List command.

5. Click on the Label control button in the Toolbox. Then move the pointer to the page header section and create a box from 0.25 inch across to 3 inches across. In this box type Hunter River Product List and press Enter.

6. With the label control selected, change the font size to 14 points for the report title.

7. You will have to drag down the bottom border of the page header section to allow the title and headings to fit. Make this section approximately 0.75 inch tall.

8. Next, issue the Format command and select Size I to Fit. Access will enlarge the box to hold the title.

CHECKPOINT 9D Is it simpler to use the Format I Size I to Fit command or to resize the box manually to fit the larger text into the control?

9. Add another label control to the Page Header section for Product Number under the previous label control. While this control is still selected, click on the Bold button in the toolbar. Issue the Size I to Fit command in the Format menu to resize the control.

10. Repeat step 9 with another label control for Product Description, just to the right of the Product Number label. While this control is selected, click on the Bold button in the toolbar. Then issue the Size I to Fit command from the Format menu.

11. Click the text box button in the Toolbox, then drag the Stock Number field from the field list to the detail section. Select the attached label by clicking on it once, then press [Del] to remove its label from the Detail section. Place the text box right below the Detail section border so that it aligns with the Product Number heading, then release the mouse button. (Do *not* remove the Product Number label you placed in the Page Header section.)

12. Repeat step 11 with the Description field. Remove its attached label from the Detail section and make it align with its column heading.

13. Finally, drag the Page Footer section border up to reduce the size of the Detail section. Your screen should look like Figure 9.11.

14. To preview your report, click the Print Preview button in the toolbar or choose the Print Preview command from the File menu. See Figure 9.12.

15. Close the Report window without saving the report.

Command Review

Format I Align	Align selected controls by left, right, top, or bottom edges.
Format I Size I to Fit	Allow control box to expand or shrink to fit the enclosed value.
Format I Snap to Grid	Cause new or resized controls to align to grid.
View I Field List	Display the field list box on the design screen.
View I Form	Switch to Form view.
View I Form Design	Switch to Form Design view.
View I Grid	Display the grid dots on the form or report design screen.

FIGURE 9.11
*Report design
with controls*

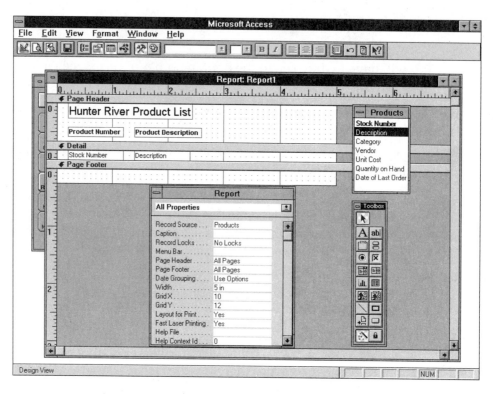

FIGURE 9.12
*Print Preview for
custom report*

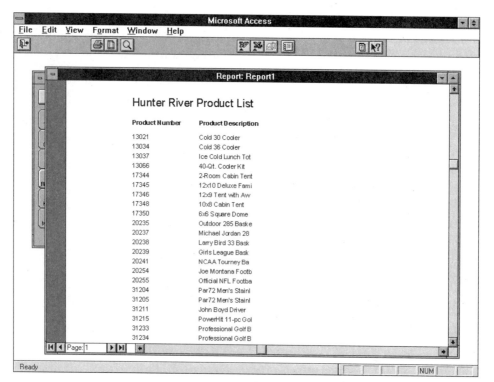

| View | Palette | Display the Palette box on the design screen. |
| View | Properties | Display the property sheet for the selected control, form, or report. |

Exercises

Use the Hunter River database contained within the HUNT.MDB file on the West Student Data Disk for these exercises.

1. Create a form with the following control specifications. Use the Customers table. Print a copy of your completed form.

   a. Place a 14-point label containing CUSTOMER ENTRY FORM at the top of the form. Be sure to return the default label font size to 8 or 10 after you create this label box.

   b. Place *two* horizontal lines beneath the label. Use the default line width.

   c. Drag the First Name field to the form.

   d. Drag the Last Name field to the form, beside the First Name text box.

   e. Change the prompt for the First Name field to Cust Name: and resize the label box as needed to fit.

   f. Delete the Last Name label box.

   g. Move the Last Name text box to place it closer to the First Name text box.

2. Continue with the form you created in the previous exercise. Add the following elements, then print a copy of the completed form.

   a. Drag the Address Line 1 field to the form, allowing one row of grid dots between the name and the Address field.

   b. Drag the Address Line 2 field to the form, placing it directly beneath the previous Address field box. Delete the label for this field.

   c. Drag the City field to the form, placing it directly beneath the previous Address field box. Delete the label for this field.

   d. Drag the State field to the form, placing it to the right of the City text box. Delete the label for this field.

   e. Drag the Postal Code field to the form, placing it to the right of the State text box. Delete the label for this field.

   f. Reposition the State and Postal Code text boxes so that there is a single grid dot between fields.

   g. Change the Address Line 1 label box to read Address: and move the box so that its right edge aligns with the Cust Name label box.

3. In this exercise you will create a custom report. Use the Customers table. Follow the directions below.

    a. In the Page Header section, place a title `Customer List`. With the box still selected, change the font size to 14 points in the toolbar. Use the Format | Size | to Fit command.

    b. Drag the Customer Number field to the Detail section. Delete the attached label.

    c. On the same row of the Detail section, create a text box. Delete its attached label box. Within the text box, enter the expression `=[First Name]+" " +[Last Name]` and press the ⏎ Enter key. This tells Access to concatenate (combine) the customer's first and last names with one space between. Don't forget the equal sign, which tells Access to create this calculated field.

    d. Add suitable column headings to the Page Header section. They should appear in bold.

    e. Adjust the space in the sections to match the example in Guided Activity 9.6, then print a copy of your report.

4. Create a blank form using the Employees table. Prepare a suitable form title, then add the Employee ID, First and Last names, and Department fields. The Department field should be in a list box that uses the Department table as its data source.

Review Questions

1. Explain the purposes of Access controls. Why are they useful for forms and reports?

2. Briefly explain the purpose of the following controls:

    a. Bound control

    b. Text box control

    c. Combo box control

    d. Check box control

    e. Line control

3. Discuss the differences between a label control and a text box control.

4. Discuss at least three methods for selecting Access controls in the design screen.

5. Explain how you can move an Access control to a new location.

6. Discuss how the grid system can be used to align controls in a form or report. Are there any other ways to align groups of controls? Explain.

7. How do you resize an Access control?

8. Describe the use of the Palette box with controls such as line and rectangle. Can this box be used with any other control types?

9. Briefly describe the purpose of the following control properties:

   a. Row Source Type

   b. Visible

   c. Font Alignment

   d. Locked

   e. Can Grow

   f. Help Context ID

Key Terms

Back style
Before/After Update
   property
Bind
Bound control
Bound Object Frame
   control
Calculated control
Can Grow/Can Shrink
   property
Caption property
Check Box control
Combo Box control
Command button
Control
Control handle
Control Wizards
Display When property

Focus
Font property
Graph control
Grid dots
Help Context ID property
Label control
Line control
List box
Lock button tool
Locked property
Move handle
Name property
On Enter/On Exit
   property
Option Button control
Option Group control
Page Break control
Palette box

Pointer tool
Rectangle control
Row Source control
Scroll Bars property
Size handle
Size to Fit
Snap
Special Effect property
Subform/Subreport tool
Text Box control
Toggle Button control
Toolbox
Unbound control
Unbound Object Frame
   control
Visible property

Documentation Research

Use the printed documentation and the on-line Help available with Microsoft Access to answer the following questions. If you use one of the manuals, provide the page number for your reference in the manual.

1. Use the [Shift][F1] command to convert the pointer into a question mark. Then click on the Control Source property of a control to bring up help for that property. List the choices for this property.

2. What is the use of the Hide Duplicates property for text box controls?

3. How do you change the *default* properties for a type of control?

Customizing a Form
10

This unit covers preparation of customized Access forms. It builds on the discussion of controls found in the previous unit and the forms introduction in Part One of this book. You will learn how to modify an existing form design as well as how to format text and controls. Advanced form features are covered, including the design and construction of complex forms that take advantage of the graphical user interface elements available in Access.

Learning Objectives

At the completion of this unit you should know

1. the five steps in creating a custom form,
2. the purpose of form sections,
3. the advantages of using yes/no controls instead of a text box in a form,
4. methods to improve the usefulness of a form,
5. how a main form and subform are linked together.

At the completion of this unit you should be able to

1. modify an existing form,
2. create a custom form using the blank form method,
3. create a list box control,
4. create an option group control,

5. set the font, font size, style, and alignment of text in a control,

6. change the tab order in a form,

7. create a main/subform form with a calculated subtotal.

Important Commands

Edit | Tab Order

Format | Form Header/Footer

Format | Page Header/Footer

View | Options

View | Toolbox

Designing the Custom Form

We touched on the design of forms in Part One of this book. With Form Wizards you can prepare a single-column form, a tabular form, a graph form, or a main/subform. While these form types provide some flexibility, you may need to prepare a combination of these types for use in a particular application. Our study of controls from the previous unit indicated that check boxes, toggle buttons, list boxes, and a variety of other helpful controls can make it easier for you to understand and work with the database. This section will show you how to create a custom form that incorporates these controls.

Steps in Creating the Custom Form

There are five steps in creating a custom form, described below. Starting with understanding the information needs, this process emphasizes how the user will work with the form.

UNDERSTAND THE PURPOSE OF THE FORM

The first and most important step is to understand the purpose for the form. Is it to enter data? Will the data be transferred from paper records? Is the form simply to show records? Will the form be used for making changes to (editing) the data? Who will be using the form? How many records will be examined? How much data should be presented on the form? What fields should appear on the form?

The answers to these and other questions will make it easier to design a form that meets the needs of the organization. Remember that these needs are often not stated precisely by the users. In fact, you will often be called upon to prepare a *prototype* data object, whether it be a form or a report, then you will let the users react to the model and make notes on their observations. Because it is so easy to make changes to Access data objects, you can quickly cycle through several iterations (versions) to be certain that the form meets the organization's needs.

CREATE THE DESIGN ON PAPER

You should sketch out a few rough ideas on paper, before you sit down before the computer. Although some people can create excellent forms directly on the screen, we generally recommend that you develop ideas first on paper. From the previous step you will know what information is to be displayed on the form. This step provides feedback on how to display and work with that data. For instance, if there are a great many fields, it may be necessary to use scrolling text boxes to reach them all or even to have multiple screens that are associated with one form.

Look for examples of good form design in other forms used by your organization. Some paper forms have been carefully crafted and can serve as a guide for your computer forms. Consider the tab order sequence of data on the form. Do you want to give users choices in list or combo boxes, or provide buttons or check boxes to choose? Do you want to provide validation rules for certain fields so that incorrect values can be eliminated at the source of data entry? We will talk more about form designs when we introduce form sections.

BUILD THE FORM DESIGN

You can either start with a Form Wizard design, then make changes, or create the form yourself by placing controls in the blank design screen. Because it is so easy to place fields on the screen, you will probably choose the latter. Our first activity will show how to make changes to an existing form design. Later activities will start with a blank form.

Main/subform forms combine two forms. First build the main form portion and save it. Then build the subform form. Finally, add the subform to the main form and save the combined form as one unit.

TEST THE DESIGN

This important step involves presenting the form to users and asking for their feedback. Expect them to "take it for a test drive" as they try to use the form with realistic data. This step usually results in valuable feedback about changes that should be made. Also expect users to tell you things that they neglected to mention earlier in the process. Experience shows that once a user can do hands-on work with the real object, good progress is made toward the development of the best design for that object.

TIP   *Use copies of realistic data rather than the real data itself, because at this point the form is not ready for use in making permanent changes to the database.*

MODIFY THE DESIGN

After receiving feedback from the users, rebuild the form with corrections and enhancements. Retest the design with the same users to be certain that the revised form meets their needs. It is not unusual to go through several cycles at this stage.

Form Sections

Like reports, Access forms also have *sections*. The *Detail section* contains the text boxes and command buttons that the user manipulates while working with the form. So far, all of our custom form examples have used the detail section for all of the form elements.

The *Form Header* appears one time per form, at the beginning. The form header contains titles, instructions for the user, and other preliminary information about the form. It may also contain command buttons that accomplish certain tasks such as bringing up a second form. The *Page Header* appears at the top of each printed page. Likewise, there are *Form Footers* and *Page Footers*. Page headers and footers do not appear in Form view, but will appear when the form is printed. The page header and footer are used for column headings, date and time, page number, and other information that is pertinent for printed output.

Form headers and footers are added as a pair, using the Form Header/Footer command of the Format menu. Likewise, page headers and footers are added as a pair using the Page Header/Footer command of the Format menu. Once active on the design screen, you can drag the lower portion of the section borders up or down to shrink or enlarge the size of the section. Figure 10.1 shows a form design that uses sections.

In this case, the form was prepared by the Form Wizard in Part One of this book. The form header contains the form title in a label box. The detail section contains the seven fields in the single-column format. The form footer is empty. From the form property sheet window, the *Default View property* is Single Form, meaning that the form for only one record will appear on screen at a time. Figure 10.2 shows the Form view for this form.

Use of Controls in Form Designs

As we discussed in the previous unit, Access uses controls to represent labels, data values, OLE objects, lines, and other features that appear on forms. The Form Wizards use labels, text boxes, and lines when Access creates forms automatically. You might want to add other kinds of controls to your forms. While the previous unit covered types of controls, in this unit we will discuss how to *apply* those controls to enhance your forms.

TEXT BOXES VERSUS YES/NO CONTROLS

Suppose we are looking at the Category field in the Products table. Its value, Camping, is displayed in the text box of Figure 10.2. When adding new records or

FIGURE 10.1
*Form design
showing form
sections*

Design View
Form View
Datasheet View
Save
Print Preview
Properties
Field List
Code
Toolbar
Palette

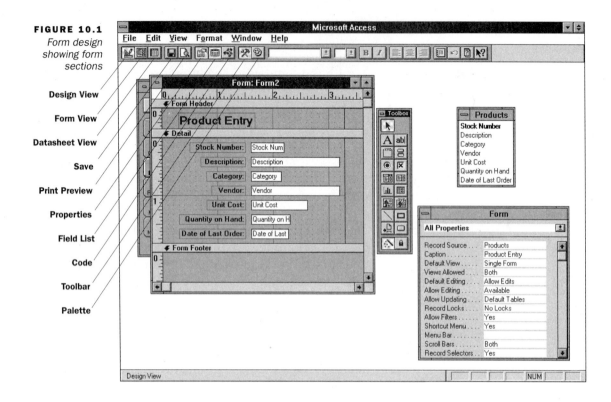

FIGURE 10.2
Single Form view

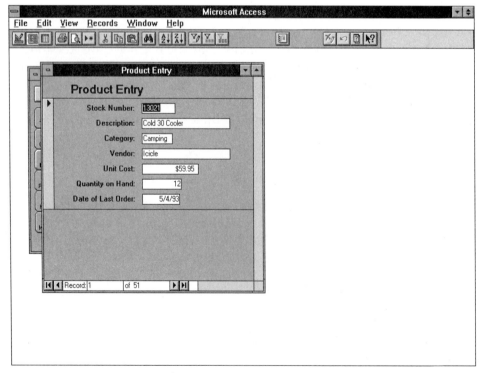

changing the category for a particular product, the user must key in the entire name of the department. It must be spelled correctly to match other tables.

Because there are only a few product categories, it might be simpler to design a form with an option group containing a check box (or perhaps option buttons or toggle buttons) for *each* category. The user can then simply click on the box representing the category for that product, saving time and increasing accuracy. Access will make sure that only one check box in the option group is turned on at a time (making it, in effect, a Yes/No control). The major limitation of an option group is that the values returned by clicking one of the check boxes must be numeric. You might have to redesign the table in order to make use of such values. For instance, Camping could be 1, Hunting 2, and so forth.

TEXT BOX VERSUS A LIST BOX CONTROL

The list box control provides a drop-down list of values from which the user can choose. This control would also be suitable for the product category. The user must move the pointer to the proper choice, then click. For anything more than a few choices, the list box is more efficient than an option group of separate check boxes. With four current product categories, the list box would be a useful substitute for an option group of four boxes or buttons. We will later demonstrate how to replace a text box with a list box control.

TEXT BOX VERSUS AN OPTION LIST CONTROL

Although similar to the Category field in the previous discussion, the Vendor field is less predictable. Thus, we might have a new vendor that is not already in the list. An option list control provides a list of items to choose from, but also allows the user to key in a new value *not* in that list. Thus, an option list control would be necessary for the vendor field unless there were a way to guarantee that the vendor was already in existence *before* the user adds a product to the database. We will later demonstrate how to add an option list to the form.

Creating a Custom Form

After the design is complete, it is time to build the form. If you start with a Form Wizard form design, you can go to Form Design view and manipulate existing controls to match the design. Certain kinds of custom forms are easier to build this way: if the Form Wizard can come close to your design, save yourself some effort and adopt this method. For other forms, it would be more trouble to make changes to the Form Wizard version than to start from scratch. We will demonstrate both methods in this unit.

GUIDED ACTIVITY 10.1

Modifying a Form Design with a List Box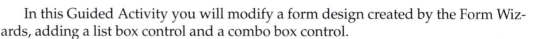

In this Guided Activity you will modify a form design created by the Form Wizards, adding a list box control and a combo box control.

1. Start Windows and load Access. Open the HUNT Database window. Switch to Form mode and highlight the Product Entry form.

2. Click the Design button. If they are not already present, use the View menu to add the Toolbox, field list, and property sheet boxes. Drag the right side of the form window border to about the 5-inch mark.

3. Select the Category text box by clicking within its box. Press the [Del] key to delete this control and its attached label control.

4. Next, we will manually add a list box control for the Category. Click once on the List Box button in the Toolbox. Make sure that the Control Wizard button is *not* pushed. Then drag the Category field from the field list box to the detail section, placing it to the right of the other fields, about 4 inches over.

5. Access will create two controls: the list box itself and an attached label control.

6. You should reduce the size of the list box by dragging the size handle. Make it about ¾-inch tall.

7. In Guided Activity 9.5 in the last unit we created a list box with the Control Wizard. Here we must manually modify the list box property sheet to contain the values for the departments. Click once on the list box to select it.

8. In the property sheet, make the following changes. The Row Source Type should be `Value List`. On the Row Source line, type `Camping, Hunting, Sports, Other` and press [Enter].

9. To preview the results, click once on the Form View button in the toolbar. Click on the Category label to give that field the focus. The Camping choice is outlined, signifying that the first record is from that Category. Your screen should resemble Figure 10.3.

10. Next, we will replace the Vendor field with a combo box with help from the Control Wizard. Return to Form Design view. Select the Vendor text box and press the [Del] key to remove it and its attached label.

11. Click on the combo box button in the Toolbox. It is to the left of the list box button, and directly below the "bull's-eye" icon. Make sure the Control Wizard button is pushed.

12. Drag the Vendor field from the field list box to the detail section, placing it beneath the Description field where the Category field used to be. Align the combo box with the other fields.

FIGURE 10.3
*Form view with
list box control*

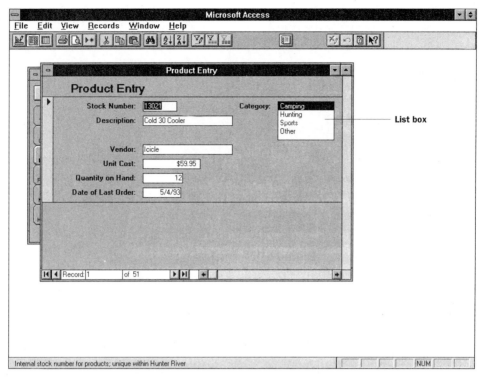

13. The Combo Box Control Wizards screen will appear after a few seconds. Click Next to have the combo box look up values from a table. At the next screen select the Vendors table and click Next.

14. At the next step click the > button to select the Vendor Name field. Click Next to go on.

15. Click Next to accept the default column spacing. Click Next again to store the value in the Vendor field of the Products table. Finally, click Finish to add the combo box to your form.

CHECKPOINT 10A What are the differences between a list box and a combo box in an Access form? Why is the Vendor control better as a combo box?

16. Click on the Form View button in the toolbar to view your form. It should look like Figure 10.4.

17. Close the Form window without saving the revised design.

Advanced Form Features

This section will present several advanced features possible with Access forms. We also discuss how to build custom forms from scratch, starting with a blank form.

FIGURE 10.4
*Form View with
combo box*

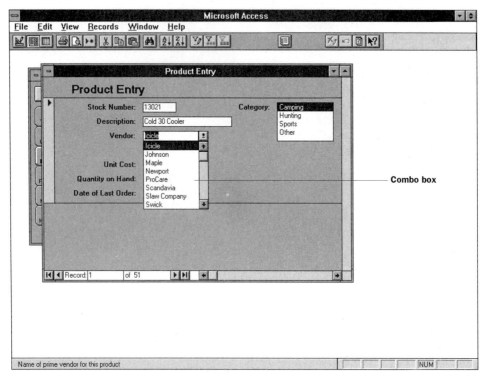

Combo box

Creating an Option Group

As mentioned previously, an option group is a control that contains several yes/no choices or options, represented by check boxes, option buttons, or toggle buttons. Only one choice can be selected (yes) at a time; all the other choices are (no). The option group control returns the numeric value associated with the selected yes/no control, storing that value in the field it is bound to.

The option group Control Wizard procedure is similar to that used for other form controls. Build the form as normal, adding other controls as needed. When you are ready for the option group, click on the option group button in the Toolbox. With the Control Wizard's button pushed in, drag the field from the field list that is to be bound to the option group. Place that field in the form design screen, most likely in the detail section. Access will create two controls—a label with the name of the field bound to the option group, and the option group itself, represented by a large rectangle.

First type in the labels for each value in the option group. The Control Wizard presents a grid that resembles the datasheet. Then choose whether to have a default value for the option group, and specify the values used for the various options. They are usually 1, 2, 3, and so forth. Specify which field in the form's data source (underlying table or query) will receive the value from the option group; typically, it will be the field you dragged to the form for the option group.

Next, select the style and yes/no control type that will represent the choices in the form. After choosing the label text for the option group, you are finished with the Control Wizard and you can see the design. The following example will show how to create an option group in a custom form.

FIGURE 10.5
Order Entry preliminary form design

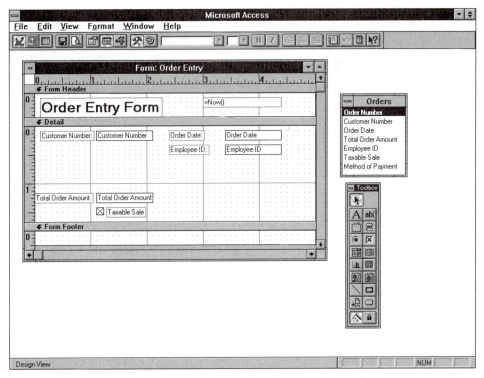

GUIDED ACTIVITY 10.2

Adding an Option Group to a Form Design

In this Guided Activity you will use the Control Wizards to add an option group to a form design.

1. Close all open windows and return to the HUNT Database window.

2. Switch to the Form mode and select the Order Entry form in Design view. It should resemble the design shown in Figure 10.5.

3. If necessary, move the field list box and property sheet out of the way. Use the View | Toolbox command to make sure that the Toolbox is displayed.

4. Make sure the Control Wizard button is pushed, then click on the option group button in the Toolbox. It is the rectangle directly beneath the large letter A. Then drag the Method of Payment field from the field list box, placing it at the 1,3-inch coordinates in the Detail section.

5. The Control Wizard will ask you to type in the labels for each option item. The values are Cash, Purchase Order, and Credit. Type each on a separate line, then click Next.

6. You will be asked if you want to select a default value. Click Next to accept the default of no default method of payment.

7. The Control Wizard chooses the values of 1, 2, and 3 for the three option choices. Click Next to accept these values.

FIGURE 10.6
*Order Entry
form design
with option
group*

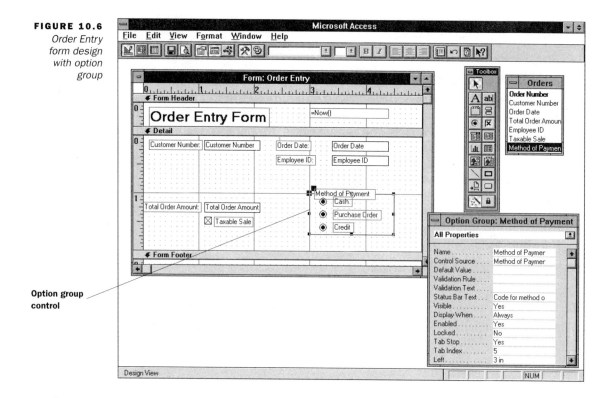

Option group
control

CHECKPOINT 10B How does Access use these values in an option group?

8. Click Next once more to signify that you want Access to store the option value in the Method of Payment field.

9. We will use the Normal style for the option group. Make sure that the Option Buttons choice is selected, then click Next to go on.

10. For the option group's label, enter `Method of Payment` and click Finish to place the option group in the form. Figure 10.6 shows the form's Design view.

11. Finally, we will view the form. Click on the Form View button in the toolbar (or give the View I Form command). Figure 10.7 shows the form for a record in the Orders file.

12. Close the Form window. Save the changes under the same form name.

Improving the Form's Usefulness

It is possible (and desirable) to make the form easier to use by improving its layout and visual image. Rearranging fields, enclosing similar fields with rectangles or lines, adding sunken or raised 3-D special effects, and using color are all techniques that will help the user. Refer to the previous unit or search Help for suggestions in these areas. Some other suggestions follow.

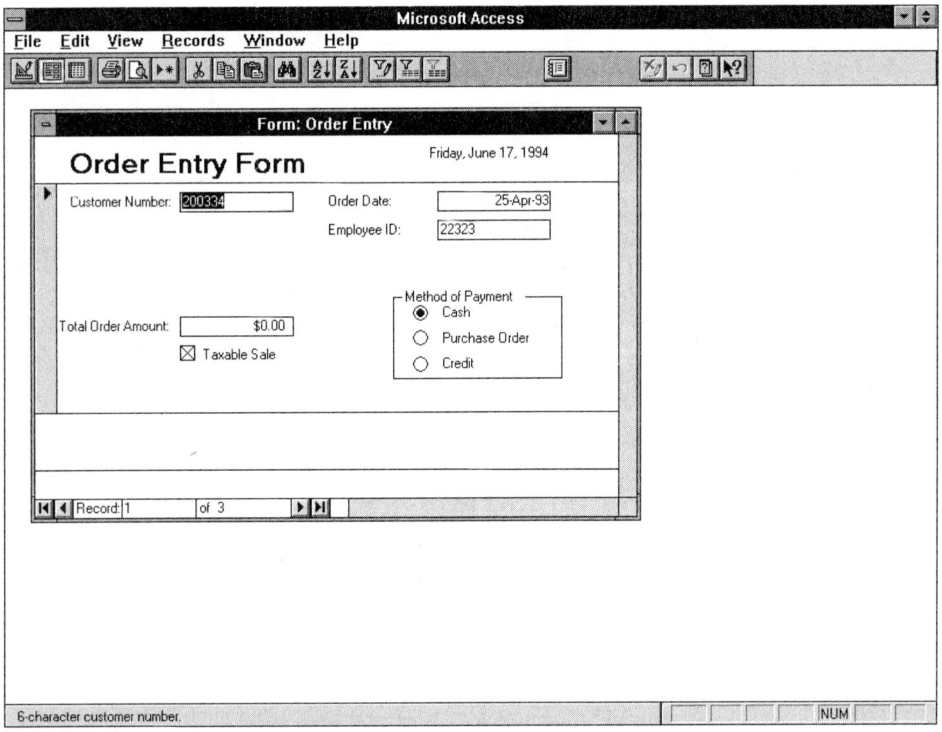

FIGURE 10.7
Order Entry
form view

FORMATTING TEXT: FONT, SIZE, STYLE, AND ALIGNMENT

As mentioned earlier in this book, Access shares many desirable Windows features, including choice of typeface *font* and *font size*. The font refers to the particular typeface used such as Arial, Courier, and Times Roman. Your choice of fonts depends on which fonts were installed on your system. Beginning with Windows 3.1, built-in TrueType fonts are *scalable*; that is, Windows can automatically enlarge or shrink the font to the desired size. TrueType fonts can be displayed on the screen and printed on nearly any printer. Typical font size for a form title is 14 or 18 points. Text box labels may be 8 or 10 points. The Font and Font Size buttons appear in the toolbar whenever a text control is selected.

The text *style* refers to normal, **bold**, and *italic*. To change the style of text in a control, select that control, then click the appropriate style button in the toolbar. You can format a portion of the text in a control by highlighting just the portion that you want to change. As mentioned in the previous unit, you can change a single control or change the default values for all new controls of a specific type.

Text alignment refers to where a value appears within its column. The default text alignment is General, in which numbers and dates are aligned right in the control box, and other values are aligned with the left side of the control box. You can also select Left-Align, Center-Align, or Right-Align. Select the text control, then click on the Left-Align, Center-Align, or Right-Align buttons in the toolbar.

INSERTING A PAGE BREAK

When there are numerous fields, you may need to break the form into several screens. The page break control is used for this purpose. You can move back and forth between the screens of the form as necessary. Create the form as usual, filling the form's detail section with controls. Then click on the Page Break button in the Toolbox. Move the pointer to the location in the form design where you want to put the page break, and click the left mouse button. Access will insert the page break and mark it next to the left ruler with a short dotted line.

CHANGING THE TAB ORDER IN A FORM

Access will sequence the fields in the order you add them to the form. If you have made mistakes or rearranged fields, the *tab order* may not be correct. Recall that the tab order is the order in which a user will go through the fields in a form. You can press the [Tab] or [Enter] keys to go forward through the fields in the form. Press [Shift][Tab] to go in the reverse order. The [→] and [←] keys will usually work in the same manner, sending you to the next or previous field.

TIP *It is possible to change the behavior of the arrow keys, in the Keyboard section of the Options dialog box. Use the View/Options command to display the Options dialog box. Select Keyboard, then change the arrow keys to move a character at a time instead of a field at a time.*

The standard tab order is top-to-bottom, or left-to-right. To change the tab order, open the form in Design view. Choose the Tab Order command from the Edit menu. Figure 10.8 shows the Tab Order dialog box for the previous form. Select the form

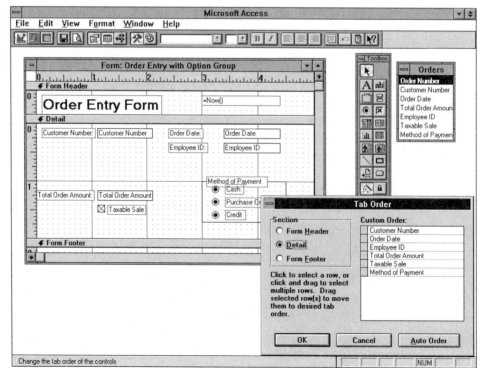

FIGURE 10.8
The Tab Order dialog box

section you wish to change (Form Header, Detail, or Form Footer). To select the standard order, click the Auto Order button. If you want a custom tab order, click the field selector button to the left of the field name to select the field. Then drag that field to the proper sequence and release the mouse button. Access will insert the selected field and rearrange the other fields.

USING A COMMAND BUTTON TO OPEN ANOTHER FORM

From the previous unit you likely will remember that a command button is used in a form to cause some action to occur. The command button is attached to an Access macro or a user procedure. You can use the command button to open another form on demand; that is, you can choose to see another form based on characteristics of the data.

Add the command button control like any other Access control. Then modify the property sheet to indicate what action the button is to take. For example, the *On Click property* can give the name of the macro that runs when the button is clicked. That macro can cause the requested form to be displayed. Macros are covered in Units 14 and 15 of this book.

Creating a Complex Main/Subform Form

We covered preparation of a main/subform design in Part One of this book. That discussion featured use of Access Form Wizards to prepare the form. In this section we will build the order entry form by hand, using a join query as the data source for the form.

Starting with a Join Query

We must join the four main tables for the order form: Customers, Orders, Order Items, and Products. You read about this design in the "Relational Database Concepts" section of Unit 8. The database design is shown in Figure 8.1. We actually need two queries: one that joins the Orders and Customers tables, and another that joins the Order Items and Products tables. These queries are already created and stored in the HUNT database. They are called Customers/Orders Join and Order Items/Products Join. The first one will be used for the main form fields, the second query for the subform fields.

Access will automatically link the main form and the subform if both are based on tables and contain a field with the same name that is also the primary key of the underlying table. If the two forms are based on queries, as they are here, you must use the subform property sheet to name the link fields.

NOTE *If you have created a relationship between the two tables, Access will automatically link the main form and subform.*

Create the Main Form

The next step is to create the main form. In this case, the main form contains the Order information including customer number, order number, order date, and all the name and address information from the Customers table. These fields have been dragged to the query. Remember to leave room for the subform in the lower portion of the screen. Save this form.

Create the Subform

Next, create the subform that contains the individual items with this order. This form will have no header or footer, and should have just a single line in the detail section. In the subform's property sheet select Datasheet as the default view. Save this form with a different name than the main form.

Add the Subform to the Main Form

The final design step is to drag the subform from the Database window to the lower portion of the main form. Access will create a subform control to hold the subform. We will have to link the two forms' Order Number fields through the **Link Child Fields** and **Link Master Fields** *properties* in the subform's property sheet. We'll demonstrate this in the following activity.

GUIDED ACTIVITY 10.3

Creating an Order Main/Subform Form

In this Guided Activity you will prepare an order main form with a subform, beginning with a blank form.

1. Close all windows and return to the HUNT Database window.

2. As described earlier, our form will use two queries that have been saved in the HUNT database. Switch to the Form mode, and click the New button to create the main form. Select the Customer/Order Join query as the data source for this form and click on the Blank Form button.

3. Choose the Form Header/Footer command from the Format menu to create a form header and footer. Increase the size of the form to about 4 inches.

4. In the header section create a label box for the form title. In this box type Hunter River Order Form and press Enter. With the box still selected, choose Bold and make the font size 14 points. If the box does not expand automatically to fit the font size, increase the size of the Form Header section to accommodate this label box.

5. In the detail section drag the Order Number and Order Date fields from the field list. Although placement is not critical, Figure 10.9 provides a suggestion for locations.

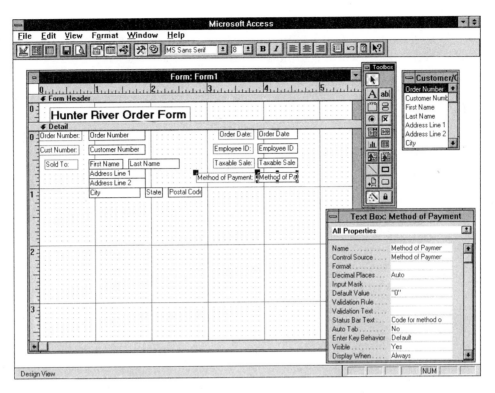

FIGURE 10.9
Main order
form design

6. Repeat step 5 with the Customer Number field, just beneath the Order Number field.

7. Add the First Name field to the form. Change its attached label to read Sold To:. Place the Last Name to the right of the First Name field, then delete its label. Drag the Last Name control over near the First Name field.

8. Add all of the address fields to the form, placing them directly beneath the name controls. Delete all of the attached labels.

9. Also add the Employee ID, Taxable Sale, and Method of Payment fields to the form.

10. Next, we are ready to save the main form. Use the name Hunter Main Order Form. Don't close the main form—we will want to add the subform to it later.

11. Click on the Database window (or press F11) to bring it to the foreground. Click on the New button to create the subform. Access will open another Form window while leaving the previous form window open.

12. Choose the Order Items/Products Join query as the data source for the subform. Choose a blank form.

CHECKPOINT 10C What information is contained in the query of step 12?

13. Drag the following fields to the detail section of the subform, all on the same line: Product Number, Order Quantity, Description, and Unit Cost. Delete each attached label. You will want to resize the fields to fit their contents.

14. We need to add a calculated field to the subform. Click on the text box button in the Toolbox. Then position the pointer to the end of the line and click the left button. Make the attached label of this field `Extended Cost`.

15. Type the expression `=[Unit Cost]*[Order Quantity]` inside the new text box and press `Enter`. Don't forget the equal sign. While this control is still selected, change its Decimal Places property from Auto to 2. Its Name property should be `Extended Cost`.

16. Click in the gray area outside the white area of this form. Access will display the form's property sheet. Change the Default View property to Datasheet View.

17. Save the subform as `Hunter Order Subform` and close its form window.

18. Click on the main form window (or use the Window command from the menu bar) to make it active. Press `F11` to show the Database window. Drag the subform you just saved from the Database window to the lower portion of the main form and release the left mouse button. Access will create a subform control. Drag its lower border down a little to enlarge the subform.

19. With the subform selected, type `Order Number` into both the LinkChildFields and LinkMasterFields properties in the subform's property sheet. That will cause Access to display only records in the subform area that match the order number displayed in the main form.

20. Click on the Form View button to see what your form looks like. Figure 10.10 shows the subform in place in the main form for the first order. You can examine additional orders by clicking on the bottom record-navigation buttons. If one

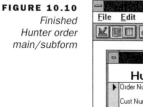

FIGURE 10.10
Finished Hunter order main/subform

Microsoft Access

File Edit View Records Window Help

Form: Form1

Hunter River Order Form

Order Number:	100001	Order Date:	25-Apr-93
Cust Number:	200334	Employee ID:	22323
Sold To:	Bruce O'Dell	Taxable Sale:	Yes
	3804 Union Drive	Method of Payment:	1
	Charleston Il 61634		

Hunter Order Subform:

Product Numb	Order Quantity	Description	Unit Cost	Extended Cos
13066	1	40-Qt. Cooler Kit	$29.95	$29.95
17348	1	10x8 Cabin Tent	$89.95	$89.95
*			$0.00	$0.00

Record: 1 of 2

Record: 1 of 3

6-character sequential order number determined by Hunter River.   NUM

order has a large number of items, the inner record-navigation buttons can be used to scroll through the items.

21. Save the finished main form design.

CHECKPOINT 10D Suppose you later make changes to the subform design that is embedded in the main form. Will Access pick up those changes automatically in the main form, or do you have to modify the design?

Calculating Subtotals

In our last activity we did not place the Total field on the form. We can sum the Extended Cost calculated field and place it in a control on the form. To do this, add a form footer to the subform and place a calculated control in the footer that sums the Extended field. Because the Default View property for the subform is Datasheet View, you will not see any controls that were placed in the subform's header or footer. Create a calculated control on the main form and have it refer to the total field in the subform's footer. The next activity will illustrate this process.

GUIDED ACTIVITY 10.4

Adding a Subtotal Control to the Main/Subform

In this Guided Activity we will take the Hunter River Order Form created in the previous activity and add a control that calculates the total amount of the order items.

1. Close any open windows and return to the HUNT Database window. In Form mode, select the Hunter Order Subform. Click the Design button.

2. Choose the Page Header/Footer command from the Format menu. Although Access will create a form header and footer, they will not display in Form view because we have selected Datasheet View in the property sheet for the subform.

3. Select the text box control in the Toolbox. In the Form Footer section, add a text box control beneath the Extended Cost control found in the Detail section.

4. Select the attached label of this control, then change its caption to Order Subtotal: and press [Enter]. You may have to resize the box or choose Format | Size | to Fit to display all of the text.

5. Select the text box control in the footer section. In its property sheet enter Order Subtotal for the Name property. In the Control Source property, enter =Sum([Unit Cost]*[Order Quantity]) and press [Enter].

NOTE *You cannot sum the Extended Cost calculated field directly in this expression.*

6. Save the subform and close its window.

7. Open the Hunter Main Order Form in Design view.

8. Select the text box button in the Toolbox. Place a text box control beneath the Method of Payment control, around the 1.25,4-inch coordinates.

FIGURE 10.11
*Hunter River
Order Form with
subtotal control*

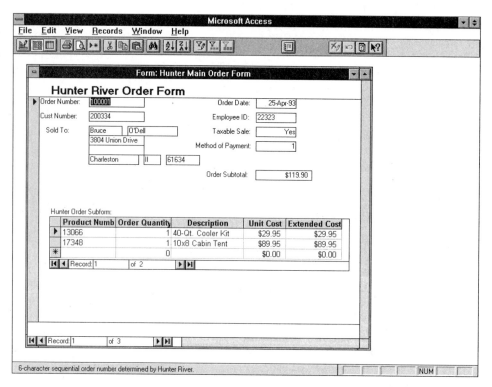

9. Select the attached label, and change its Caption property to Order Subtotal:.

10. Select the text box that you just added and enter the following expression in its Control Source property: =[Hunter Order Subform].Form![Order Subtotal] and press Enter. The *equal sign* signifies that this is a calculated field; the *[Hunter Order Subform].* is the name of the subform control that contains the values used in the calculation; the *Form!* phrase allows access to the subform's controls and properties; and the *[Order Subtotal]* is the name of the control that contains the value we want.

TIP *In Access 2.0 it might be easier to use the Expression Builder window to create this expression. Click on the button with three dots to the right of the property box.*

11. Select Currency for the Format property of this control.

12. Click on the Form View button in the toolbar to see the results, shown in Figure 10.11. Save the form and close the Form window.

Now you can use the main/subform to view existing orders or add new orders for Hunter River, explained in the next section.

Using the Main/Subform Form

Although this form is not yet as complete as it might be, we can demonstrate how it can be used to view existing orders or add new orders to the HUNT database. To improve the form, you might replace the Cust Number text box with a combo box control so that you can search through the customer records for a name. The Order

Number must be filled in for new orders—you could make this a counter field and have Access fill it in for you. You could replace the Taxable text control with check boxes for Taxable and Nontaxable. You could add a vertical scroll bar for the subform, removing the navigation buttons area. You could add a command button to close the order form or move on to the next record.

VIEWING EXISTING CUSTOMER ORDERS

To use the form, open the main form from the HUNT Database window. Access will display the first record in the Orders table and any matching items from the Order Items table. You can use the main form's navigation area to move through the orders one at a time or go directly to the last order. You can see up to three order items in the subform area; to see additional items, use the subform's record navigation area.

ADDING A NEW CUSTOMER ORDER

To add a new order, open the main form from the HUNT Database window. Move to the last record in the main form and click the next record button. Access will display a blank record. Place a number in the Order Number box and press the `Tab` key. You will move to the Cust Number box. Enter a valid customer and press `Enter`; Access will fill in that customer's information in the rest of the boxes. Then fill in the Order Date, Employee ID, Taxable Sale, and Method of Payment fields. Press `Tab` to move to the subform. Fill in the Product Number for the first order item and press `Tab`. Access will automatically fill in the Description and Unit Cost fields. Enter an Order Quantity, and Access will calculate the Extended Cost and Order Subtotal fields. You can add more order items for the current order, or add another order, or close the form. You will add a new customer order as an exercise.

Command Review

`F11`	Display the database window.
Edit	Tab Order	Make changes to tab order of controls in a form.
Format	Form Header/Footer	Add or remove form header and footer to or from a form design.
Format	Page Header/Footer	Add or remove page header and footer to or from a form design.
View	Options	View or change the Access setup options.
View	Toolbox	Display the Controls Toolbox.

Exercises

Use the Hunter River database contained within the HUNT.MDB file on the West Student Data Disk for these exercises.

1. Design a custom form on paper to enter a new employee into the Hunter River database. Use a layout and whatever controls make it easiest to perform this operation. Remember to place similar fields together.

2. Using your design from the previous problem, create a custom Access form. Print the Form view for your form. If possible, also print a copy of the *Design* view of your form. To do this, have the Form Design view on your screen, then press the [PrtSc] key. Windows will place a copy of the screen in the Clipboard. Open a word processor such as Windows Write or your own Windows word processor, then Paste the contents of the Clipboard into a new document. Printing that document may be time-consuming, depending on the speed of your printer and the print resolution you have selected. The output should resemble the screens depicted in the figures of this book.

3. Design a custom form for Hunter River vendors and products. Your form should include vendor information at the top of the screen and a list of products from that vendor in the lower portion as a subform.

4. Using your design from the previous problem, create custom Access main forms and subforms. Be sure to link the forms together. Print the Design view and Form view for your forms.

5. Modify the form from Exercise 4 to include inventory value (unit cost multiplied by quantity on hand) in the subform. Be sure to create a subtotal for all products for a particular vendor.

6. Create a new table called Equipment that contains the computers, cash registers, fixtures, display cabinets, storage bins, and other equipment used by Hunter River to display and account for merchandise and customer sales. Develop fields that would be appropriate to calculate age and annual depreciation. One of the fields is a depreciation type for each piece; its codes are represented by the numeric values 1–5, which stand for the depreciation type. Labels for those types are MACRS, ACRS, Section 168(f)(1), CLADR, and pre-ACRS. Print a copy of the design of this table, using the Clipboard procedure discussed in Exercise 2.

7. Create a form to enter and view information about the Equipment table. It should contain an option group for the depreciation type field. Create at least one record for the equipment table, entering it from your custom form. Print a copy of the Form view and Design view for your form.

8. Use the Hunter Main Order Form you created in Guided Activities 10.3 and 10.4 to add a new customer order to the database. The Order Number is 110003 and the customer number is 281111. Use the current date for the order. The employee making the sale was number 26331. The order consists of a single item, number 20238. The order quantity is 1.

Review Questions

1. Describe the reasons for creating a custom form instead of using the Form Wizards to create the form.

2. Discuss the five steps in creating a custom form.

3. Describe the purpose or use of the following Access form terms:

   a. Detail section

   b. Form Header

   c. Page Header

   d. Form Footer

   e. Default View property

4. Explain why it might be preferable to use a list box control instead of a text box. Are there situations in which a list box is *not* preferred? Explain.

5. Describe the option group control and how it could be useful for a form. Give an example that is different from the one in this unit.

6. Explain the use of fonts for text in controls. How do you select fonts?

7. Why would a page break be needed for a form that is intended only for the screen, and not to be printed? Give an example that is different from the one in this unit.

8. Discuss the procedure for adding a calculated field from a subform in a main form.

Key Terms

Default View property	Form section	Page Header section
Detail section	Link Child Fields property	Prototype
Font	Link Master Fields	Scalable
Font size	property	Style
Form Footer section	On Click property	Tab order
Form Header section	Page Footer section	Text alignment

Documentation Research

Use the printed documentation and the on-line Help available with Microsoft Access to answer the following questions. If you use one of the manuals, provide the page number for your reference in the manual.

1. Search Help to learn about the Access Options dialog box. In particular, note the possible actions associated with the ▶ and ◀ keys in the Keyboard options section.

2. Go to the Microsoft Access *User's Guide* manual and examine the examples. In particular, note the many form examples found in Part 4 of that manual.

3. Examine the form property sheet and describe how the Pop Up property can be used to change how the form appears. Can you think of an example of how this might be appropriate with the Hunter River database?

Physicians' Medical Clinic (VII): Building a Custom Form

In this application you will create a form for data in the PMC database, using the material covered in previous units. You will open the PMC database, create a main form, create a subform, then prepare a form showing patient visits to PMC. Read the directions carefully. Clearly identify which output goes with which part of the application.

1. Prepare a form that shows the patient's permanent information in the top portion of the form. In the bottom part add a subform that shows that patient's visits to the clinic, including the name of the procedure and the cost of that procedure. Remember that each visit should be on a separate line of the subform, in Datasheet view. Print a copy of the form for one patient.

2. Modify the form for this step so that only the *1993 visits* are included in the subform. You will probably create a query for this condition; change the subform's data source to reflect the query instead of the Visits table. Print a copy of the form for one patient.

3. Modify the form for this step so that you display the total charges for that patient's 1993 visits. Print a copy of the form for one patient. Be sure that the subform control is large enough to display all of the charges for that patient's visits.

Customizing a Report

11

This unit covers preparation of customized Access reports. It builds on the discussion of controls found in Unit 9 and on the report introduction in Part One of this book. You will learn how to modify an existing report design, as well as how to format text and controls in reports. Advanced report features are covered, including group reports and linked subreports.

Learning Objectives

At the completion of this unit you should know

1. the steps in creating a custom report,

2. how to work with Access report controls,

3. the use of report sections,

4. the sorting and grouping command options,

5. report properties, including linking a subreport to a main report.

At the completion of this unit you should be able to

1. change the design of an existing report,

2. change section size and section properties,

3. use label, text box, line, rectangle, and page break controls,

4. add a calculated field control to a report,

5. create a group report with multiple groups of records,

6. create a report with a linked subreport,

7. build a report cover page in the Report Header section.

Important Commands

Format | Align

Format | Report Header/Footer

Format | Page Header/Footer

View | Sorting and Grouping

View | Properties

Designing the Custom Report

We touched on the design of reports in Part One of this book. With Report Wizards you can prepare a single-column report, a groups/totals report, or a mailing labels report. You can let the Report Wizard create the report and then make modifications as necessary. You may have a situation in which you must build the entire report yourself from scratch, such as matching a specific format or working with a large number of fields. You can design a custom report for nearly any situation; the Report Wizards are more limited in formatting and field placement.

Steps in Creating a Custom Report

Although reports only allow output of data values, the steps in creating a custom report are very similar to those for creating a custom form. The emphasis is on creating a design that makes it easy for users to work with the information.

UNDERSTAND THE PURPOSE OF THE REPORT

The first and most important step is to understand the purpose of the report and the kinds of information that it is to provide. What fields are to be included? Must you provide detailed data or summaries? What is the proper sequence for records in the report? How frequently will the report be printed? Talk to the users of the report to learn more about the answers to these questions. Be prepared to make changes to the design after users react to prototype reports.

CREATE THE DESIGN ON PAPER

Sketch rough ideas on paper, *before* you sit down at the computer. Although some people can create excellent reports directly on the screen, we recommend that you develop ideas first on paper. This step provides feedback on how to display and fit the formatted data fields on the report. Consider use of different font sizes in this step to emphasize certain parts of the report. Although it is fairly easy to move controls around the report design, your preliminary design on paper should enable you to initially place fields in their approximate locations.

BUILD THE REPORT DESIGN

You can start with a Report Wizard design and make changes, or create a new one by starting with a blank report. We will show Guided Activities for both methods. In either case, Access will place controls in the report design in a manner similar to forms. Of course, some of the controls used in forms are not appropriate for reports. Access reports use five main sections; group reports add group header and footer sections as well. For a complete review on report sections, refer to Unit 6 in Part One. Our first activity will show how to modify an existing report design. Later activities will start with a blank report.

TEST THE DESIGN

This important step involves taking the report to users and asking for their feedback. Expect them to "take it for a test drive" as they print reports with realistic data. This step usually results in valuable feedback about changes that should be made. Expect users to tell you things that they neglected to mention earlier in the process. Experience shows that once a user can do hands-on work with the real object, good progress is made toward the development of the best design for that object.

MODIFY THE DESIGN

After receiving feedback from users, rebuild the report with corrections and enhancements. Retest the design with users to be certain that the revised report meets their needs.

Changing the Design of an Existing Report

We saw how to make minor changes to a Report Wizard report design in Part One of this book. In that instance we removed a calculated subtotal of a number field that was not meaningful for the group report in which it appeared. The report design screen is nearly identical to the form design screen. You can add, move, and resize report controls just as you do form controls. The Report Design View toolbar is shown in Figure 11.1.

The most common type of Access Report Wizard is the groups/totals report in which fields are displayed across the page with similar records grouped together.

FIGURE 11.1
*Report Design
View toolbar*

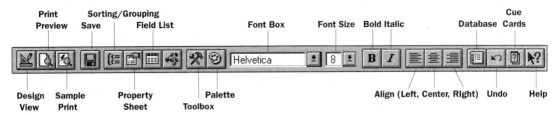

Unless otherwise specified, the field names are used for column headings. Column widths match the field sizes, with one Detail section row per record. Access 2.0 will try to fit wide reports in Landscape orientation. If there are too many fields to fit on a standard 8.5-inch-wide page, the extra fields are printed on another sheet of paper. You may need to make changes to column widths, rearrange fields, use two or more Detail section rows to hold the fields, or add dates and other system functions to the report. You might want to add another level of grouping to the report, or place a graph in the report. Graphs are covered in Part Three of this book.

Selecting Controls

The basic procedure to change the report is to first select the control(s) you want to change, then apply the change. To select a single control, click anywhere within that control's box. To select several controls, hold down the `Shift` key and select the controls by clicking within them. To select a group of adjacent controls, place the pointer outside that group; while holding down the left mouse button, drag the pointer to create a rectangle that goes through a portion of the controls in the group.

Resizing and Moving Controls

As covered in previous units, you can change the size of a control by dragging one of its seven resize handles in the desired location, then releasing the mouse button. Use the Undo button in the toolbar to reverse the effects of the last change made. The upper-left corner of each control box contains its move handle. Drag this handle to move the control. Many controls have an attached label. If you position the pointer between the text box and its label, the pointer will change to a hand with outstretched fingers. Dragging the control in this configuration will move both control and label. If the hand has an outstretched index finger, you will move only one control, not both.

Remember that lines and rectangles are also controls. They can be selected and manipulated in the usual way.

TIP *Sometimes it is simpler to delete a line and add it again than to make changes to an existing line.*

Text Formatting

Access reports offer the same text formatting features that we discussed in the previous two units. You can select a font and size for one or more text controls. You can choose bold and italic styles for all or a portion of the text in a control. You can select underline from the control's property sheet but not from a toolbar button. The alignment for the text in a control can be left, right, or centered. You can also choose General alignment in which numbers and dates are right-aligned and text fields are left-aligned.

Working with Report Sections

As discussed previously, reports contain five or more *report sections*, each with a specific purpose. The *Report Header section* provides a way to place a title page at the beginning of the report. It appears only one time per report. The Page Header appears at the top of each page (except the first page if there is a report header) and can contain a page title, column headings, page number, system date, and other controls. The Detail section displays the field values for each record in the report. The Page Footer section can contain descriptive information or system fields like date and page number. The *Report Footer section* appears at the end of the report and contains report summary fields and totals. The report footer appears before the page footer on the last page of the report. *Group Header* and *Group Footer Sections* are used for introductory and summary fields for groups of records. You could put the value of the group field in the group header section; place subtotals or record counts in the group footer section.

ADDING OR REMOVING HEADER AND FOOTER SECTIONS

Use the Format menu to add or remove headers and footers. There are separate commands for Report Header/Footer and Page Header/Footer. Access will place a check mark next to the command if that particular header/footer pair is active. To remove the header/footer pair, choose the command and the check mark will disappear. By default, a blank report design will contain a page header and footer, but not a report header and footer.

CHANGING THE SECTION SIZE

You can change the height or width of a section by dragging its borders with the mouse. If there is any extra space above or below the controls in the Detail section, that space will appear between records on the report. The default height for a control is ⅙ inch. You can reduce the Detail section height to that size and have records appear with normal spacing between lines.

NOTE *If you choose a larger font size, you may need to adjust the height of the Detail section.*

CHANGING SECTION PROPERTIES

You can view and change section properties in reports and forms. Click anywhere within the section to select that section, then display the property sheet by clicking the Properties button in the toolbar or by giving the View | Properties command. You can also examine the property sheet for the report by clicking in the gray area in the report window (not in a section) and displaying properties. As with forms, some report properties can be changed only in the property sheet, while others, such as size and color, can also be changed directly in the design window. The Palette box will let you adjust the color and special effects of some controls. You can search Help for more details about setting report properties.

GUIDED ACTIVITY 11.1

Modifying a Report Design

In this Guided Activity you will take a report created by Report Wizards and make changes to the design to improve its layout. Some of the explanations may seem cryptic—refer to the figures to understand the effect of the changes you are making.

1. Load Windows and start Access as usual. Open the HUNT Database window.

2. Switch to the Report mode. Select the Product Report By Vendor report and click the Design button. Figure 11.2 shows a portion of this design.

3. Select the Vendor control in the Page Header section. Stretch this control so that it extends to about the 1-inch mark on the ruler.

4. Next, move the Vendor text box control in the Vendor Header section over to the right, about 1 inch. Move the Vendor label from the Page Header section down to the Vendor section, in front of the Vendor text box. Adjust the two Vendor controls so that they are adjacent, nearly touching.

FIGURE 11.2
Report Wizard group report design

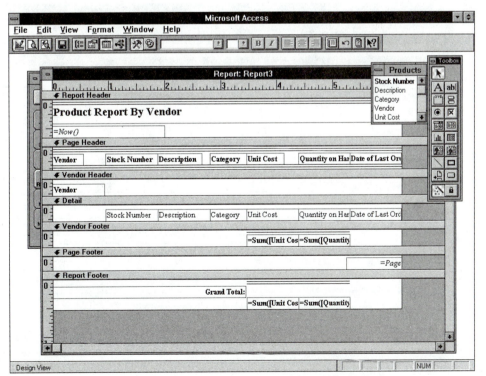

5. Delete the two calculated Sum([Unit Cost]) controls in the Vendor Footer and Report footer sections. Select each field, then press the [Del] key to remove that field. Repeat the process by deleting the thin gray lines above these controls.

6. We want to move some Detail section group of controls over to the left about 1 inch. Place the pointer to the left of the Stock Number field, hold down the left mouse button, and drag a rectangle that includes a portion of the Stock Number and Description controls in the Detail section. This selects all the controls within the rectangle.

CHECKPOINT 11A What other methods of selecting controls are available in Access?

7. With these controls selected, drag the group so that the left-most control appears at the left margin, starting at the 0-inch mark. Click once outside the group to deselect these controls.

8. Repeat step 7 with the Stock Number and Description column heading labels in the Page Header section.

9. We need to improve the column headings used in this report. In particular, the Unit Cost and Quantity on Hand labels are much wider than the fields they represent. Drag the lower border of the Page Header section down to about the 0.75-inch mark to make room for changes.

10. Select the two lines beneath the column headings in the Page Header section. Drag these lines down just below the 0.5-inch mark. You are making room for two-row column headings as shown in Figure 11.3.

FIGURE 11.3
Modified group report design

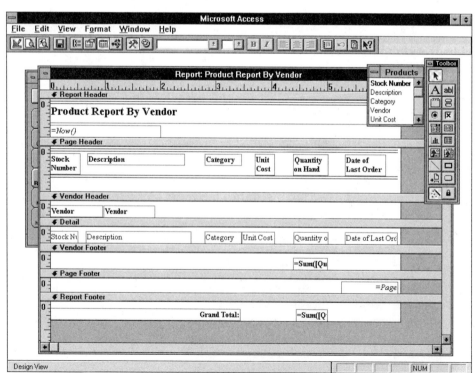

NOTE *Figure 11.3 summarizes the changes you will be making in the remainder of this activity. You can click the Print Preview button after each step to see how your report will look.*

11. Next we will modify the Stock Number label, making it a two-line label with Stock on top and Number on the bottom. Move the pointer just before the "N" in Number and slowly click two times. Then press [Ctrl][Enter]; this will instruct Access to insert a line feed and put Cost on a separate line. Press [Enter] to complete the change and resize the label control. Reduce the width of the Stock Number text box in the Detail section to about ½ inch.

12. Move the Description text box in the Detail section to the left, next to the Stock Number control. Drag the right side of the Description text box control out to about 2.5 inches. Move the Description label in the Page Header section to align with the left edge of the Description text box.

13. Repeat step 11 with the Unit Cost label so that it appears on two lines. Reduce the size of the Unit Cost text box so that its right side is at about the 4-inch mark. Align the Unit Cost label and text box on their *right* sides.

14. Repeat step 11 with the Quantity on Hand label, making it a two-line column heading. Reduce the width of the Quantity on Hand text box to the 5-inch mark, then align the label and text box on their right sides.

15. Next, select the Sum([Quantity on Hand]) controls in the Vendor Footer and Report Footer sections. Move them over so that they align with the Quantity on Hand control in the Detail section. Move the second Sum( ) expression so that it aligns with the Grand Total label.

16. Select the gray line above the Sum([Quantity on Hand]) text box control in the Vendor Header section and delete it. Delete the two similar lines in the Report Footer section.

17. Slowly click twice on the Date of Last Order label, then split the label into two lines. Click once to select the text box in the Detail section, then click on the Left-Align button in the toolbar. This causes the label and its date to align at the left portion of the field. (Dates are normally right-aligned in a text box control.)

18. Click on the Print Preview button in the toolbar to view the revised report. Figure 11.4 shows a portion of this output. Save the revised report and close the active window.

Creating a Custom Report

The 18 steps in the previous activity to modify a Report Wizard design were not hard, but were somewhat tedious. In this section you will create a custom report from scratch, starting with the blank screen and placing controls in the report design precisely where needed. You can design labels that accurately reflect their purpose rather than modifying existing labels.

We will focus on four main controls for most reports: label boxes, text boxes, lines, and rectangles. Yes/no form controls such as check boxes and option boxes are

FIGURE 11.4
*Print Preview for
modified group
report*

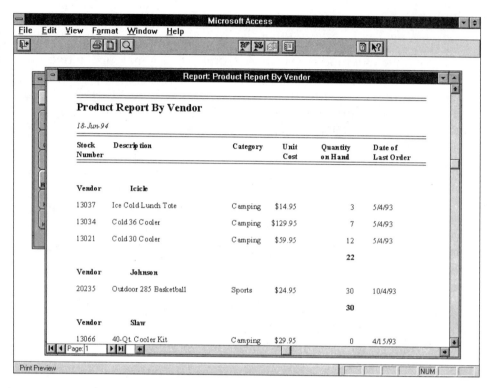

not appropriate for most Access reports. In later sections we will show how to add subreport and page break controls.

GUIDED ACTIVITY 11.2 ✳

Creating a Simple Custom Report

In this Guided Activity you will create a relatively simple custom report without the Report Wizards.

1. Close any open windows and return to the HUNT Database window.

2. Make sure you are in Report mode, then click the New button. Select the Products table as data source, then click the Blank Report button. You should see a blank report design window with three sections on your desktop.

3. In the Page Header section, drag the lower border down to make this section about 1 inch tall.

4. Select Toolbox from the View menu if it is not already present, and click on the label button in the Toolbox. In the upper-left corner open a label box about 2 inches long. In the label box type `Product Catalog` and press `Enter`. Use the Font size box to select 16 points for this label. You may have to resize the box or select Size to Fit from the Format menu.

5. Click on the text box button in the Toolbox, then add a text box control at the 3-inch mark in the Page Header section. Click once on its attached label, then

FIGURE 11.5
*Page Header
section design*

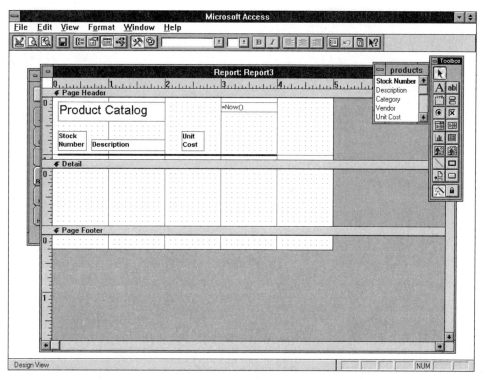

press the [Del] key to delete the label. In the text box type the expression =Now and press [Enter].

6. Next we will add three labels to the lower portion of the Page Header section. Click once on the label button in the Toolbox, then create a small label control at the left portion of the section. In the box type Stock Number and press [Enter]. With this label still selected, click once on the Bold button in the toolbar to make the label bold. See Figure 11.5 for placement of these labels.

7. Create a label for Description and another label for Unit Cost in the Page Header section. Make these labels bold also. Align labels as necessary. You may need to adjust the height of the Description label to make it align.

TIP *Use the Format/Align/Bottom command to align a group of labels by their bottom edges.*

8. Click once on the line button in the Toolbox, then place a horizontal line beneath the column headings. Remember to place the cursor at the beginning of the line, depress the left mouse button, then drag the mouse to the end location of the line. Use the Palette box to give this line a 2-point weight. See Figure 11.5 for placement of these labels.

9. Next, we will place data values in the Detail section of the report. Drag the Stock Number, Description, and Unit Cost fields from the field list box and place them beneath their respective column heading labels. You will have to delete the attached labels for each field.

TIP *It is easier to place these fields in the middle of the section, click on the attached label to select and delete it, then move the text box control to the proper location in the Detail section.*

FIGURE 11.6
Detail section design

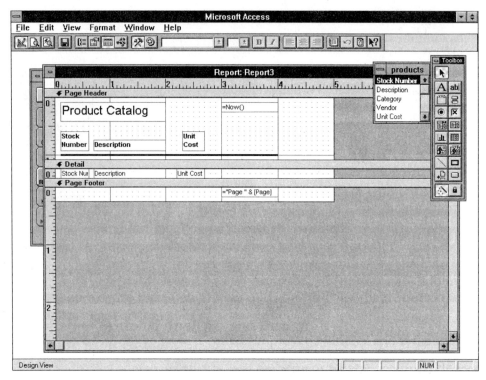

CHECKPOINT 11B Why do we remove the attached labels from fields in the Detail section?

10. Drag the lower border of the Detail section up so that there is no white space below the text box controls.

11. Make the following changes to the size of the Detail section controls: shorten the Stock Number box, lengthen the Description box, and shorten the Unit Cost box. Figure 11.6 shows the proper location and size of the fields for this and the next step.

12. Finally, in the Page Footer section place a text box to contain the page number. Delete the attached label box. In the text box type =" Page "&Page and press Enter. This expression will place the word Page in the report, then concatenate the report page number to it. Notice that there is a single space inside the quotation marks so that the page number is separated by one space.

13. Save the report under the name Custom Product Report.

14. To view the results of this report, click once on the Print Preview button in the toolbar. A zoomed view of the report is shown in Figure 11.7. Notice the placement of the page number in the bottom middle of the report.

FIGURE 11.7
Print Preview for custom report

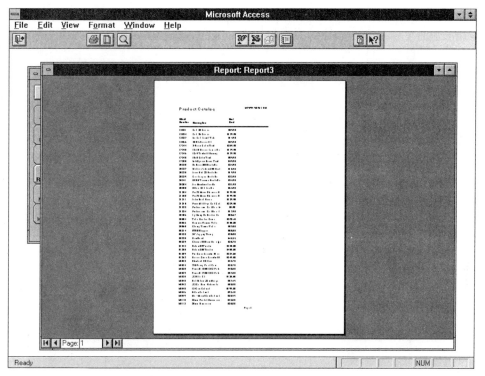

Other Custom Report Options

Most of the customizing techniques we developed in working with forms also work with Access reports. We will first highlight those tools that worked with forms, then introduce new choices.

Format Menu Choices

As with Access forms, you can select page and report headers and footers from the Format menu. In fact, other Format menu choices such as Snap to Grid, Size to Grid, Size to Fit, and Align also exist. These commands affect the size and position of controls in the report design. Refer to Units 9 and 10 for more details on these choices.

Page Break Control

Access ordinarily will print the Page Header section at the top of each page, then print as many Detail section lines as will fit on the page, reserving space at the bottom for the Page Footer section. Some reports have a great deal of information in the Detail section, and you may prefer that each record's Detail section appear on a separate printed page. Place a page break control at the point in the Detail section where you want the printed page to break. This is typically at the bottom of the section, below all the controls in a section. The symbol for a page break control in a section is a group of six dots near the vertical ruler. Access will still print the Page Footer section at the bottom of a page, even with a page break control in the Detail section.

FIGURE 11.8
*The Sorting
and Grouping
dialog box*

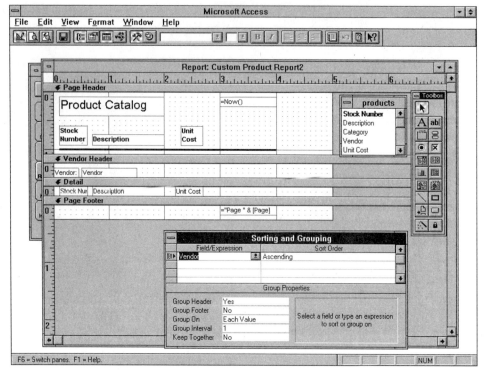

Sorting and Grouping Command

The Sorting and Grouping command from the View menu allows you to specify the sort order for records that appear in the report as well as to determine whether the report will group similar records together. This command produces the Sorting and Grouping dialog box shown in Figure 11.8 with Vendor selected as the first sort field. The upper portion of the box is used for sorting instructions; the lower part describes group properties for each sort expression.

The first column in this box provides the field or expression for sorting the records in the report. The second column is used to declare an ascending or descending sort based on the first column field or expression. The top Field/Expression row will be the primary key for the sort; later rows represent secondary sort keys. You may have up to ten sort and group fields or expressions.

For example, if you wanted to sort by Vendor and group by that field, click once on the Field/Expression row in the Sorting and Grouping box. Choose the Vendor field, and use the default Ascending sort order. Go to the Group properties portion of the box and set the *Group Header property* to Yes. Access will immediately create a group header section in your report design. You can then drag the group field from the field list, placing it in the group header. We will demonstrate this in the next activity.

The other group properties are used to create a group footer section, and to specify whether the grouping is to be done on the entire value (default) or on a certain number of prefix characters. For instance, if part numbers contained a prefix that denoted a certain product class, you could group on just that prefix or use the entire part number.

If you base the report on a query that contains sorted fields or groups, Access will automatically place these instructions in the Sorting and Grouping box. Likewise, if you modify a group report created by Report Wizards, sorting and grouping instructions will already be placed in the dialog box. You can make changes as needed for your report design.

GUIDED ACTIVITY 11.3 ✳

Creating a Simple Group Report

In this Guided Activity you will modify the previous report design to display product records in groups.

1. Select the Custom Product Report you created in the previous activity. If you have not already completed this activity, do so at this time. Open this report in Design view.

2. If it is not already present, display the Sorting and Grouping dialog box by clicking the Sorting and Grouping button in the toolbar or by giving the View | Sorting and Grouping command. Drag the dialog box over to the side of the desktop so that it does not interfere with the report design.

3. In the first row of the upper grid of this box, select the Vendor field and press `Enter`. Access will make this the first sort field and fill in Ascending in the second column of the grid.

4. Set the Group Header property for this row to `Yes`. Access will add a new section to the report, called Vendor Header.

5. Drag the Vendor field from the field list box to the Vendor Header section, placing it at the ½-inch mark. See Figure 11.8.

6. Click on the Print Preview button to view the report. Figure 11.9 shows the results of this group report. Save the report design changes and close the report window.

Other Grouping Features

Access is able to group records in several ways. We have already shown how you can group by a text field's value or a portion of the field. You can also group based on time intervals, or on number or currency ranges, and can even group a fixed number of records together based on the counter value.

The *Group On property* is used to determine how the values are to be grouped. Access will display different choices for this property for each field type. The *Group Interval property* works in conjunction with the Group On property as explained below.

FIGURE 11.9
Custom group report

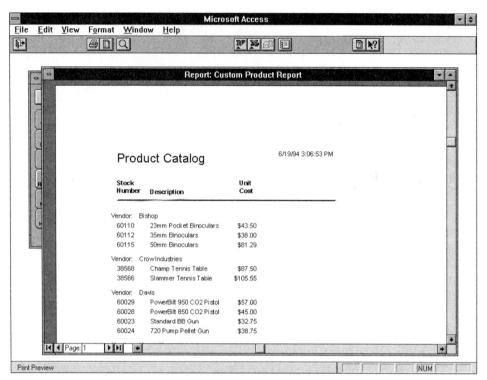

- For text fields, the Group On choices are Each Value (match whole value) and Prefix Characters (match first *n* characters as specified in the Group Interval property).

- For counter, number, and currency fields, the Group On choices are Each Value (match the value) and Interval (match values, starting with zero, whose range is specified in the Group Interval property). For example, if you chose Interval for the Group On property, then specified 10 for the Group Interval property, Access would group records containing number values 0–9, 10–19, 20–29, and so on. For tables containing a counter field, the Interval property can be used to group a specified number of records.

- For date/time group fields, choices for the Group On property are Each Value (match precise date or time), Year, Qtr, Month, Week, Day, Hour, and Minute. Records whose Year, Qtr, or Month, and so forth, match will be grouped together. The Group Interval property is used to determine how many units of the indicated time interval will be grouped together; the default value is 1.

TIP *You can tell Access to print each new group on a different page by selecting the group header section, then displaying the property sheet for that section. Change the Force New Page property from None to Before Section.*

Multiple-Level Group Reports

A ***multiple-level group report*** breaks records into groups and subgroups, using more than one group field. The following activity will show how to create a multiple-level group report that displays Hunter River products broken down by Category and by Vendor within each category.

GUIDED ACTIVITY 11.4

Creating a Multiple-Level Group Report

In this Guided Activity you will create a custom report with multiple group levels.

1. Close any open windows and return to the HUNT Database window.

2. Click on the New button to create a new report. Select the Products table as the data source, then click on Blank Report.

3. For this report we will use the product category as the primary group field and the vendor as the secondary group field. In the Page Header section place a label control that contains the report title, `Inventory Group Report`. Make the text in this label 18 points. Refer to Figure 11.10 for help in sizing and placing controls.

4. Drag the lower border of the Page Header section down to make room for column headings in your report.

5. Create label boxes and enter the following column headings. Use the default font size but make these headings bold. Leave enough room so that the longer product descriptions can be displayed. Remember that you can always move controls later if they are too close together.

```
Stock                                    Inventory
Number              Description          Value
```

6. Place a horizontal line beneath the column headings in the Page Header section.

FIGURE 11.10
Final design for multiple group report

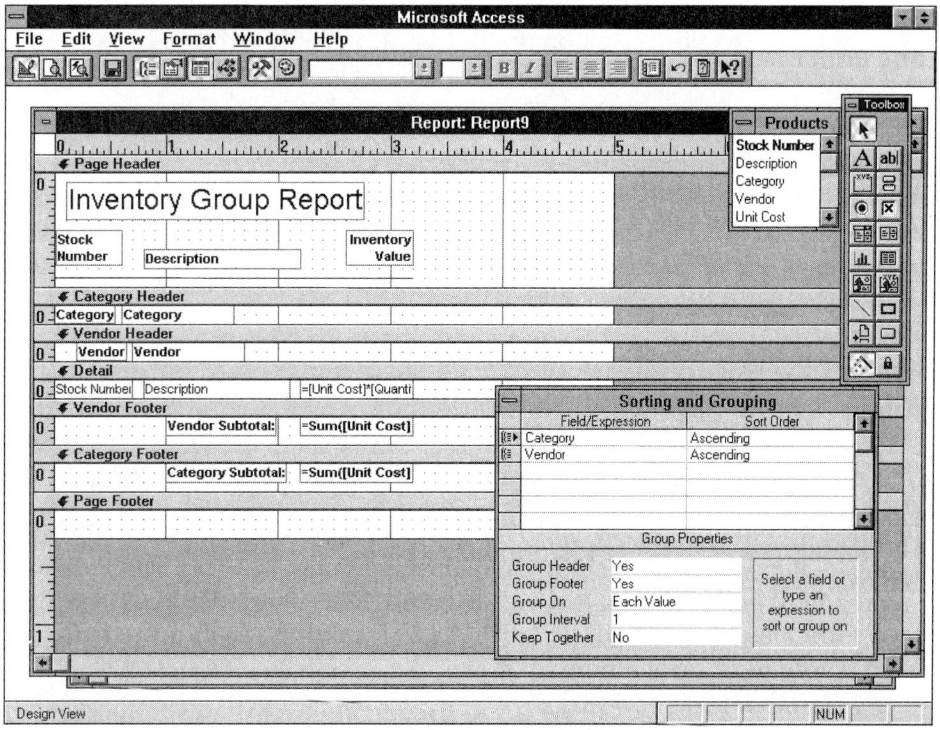

![Microsoft Access window showing report design view. Report: Report9. Page Header section contains "Inventory Group Report" title, with "Stock Number", "Description", and "Inventory Value" column labels. Category Header shows Category fields, Vendor Header shows Vendor fields, Detail section shows Stock Number, Description, and =[Unit Cost]*[Quanti]. Vendor Footer shows Vendor Subtotal: =Sum([Unit Cost]). Category Footer shows Category Subtotal: =Sum([Unit Cost]). Page Footer section. A Products field list box shows Stock Number, Description, Category, Vendor, Unit Cost. A Sorting and Grouping dialog shows Field/Expression: Category (Ascending), Vendor (Ascending). Group Properties: Group Header Yes, Group Footer Yes, Group On Each Value, Group Interval 1, Keep Together No. Design View at bottom.]

7. If it is not already present, display the Sorting and Grouping box by clicking its button in the toolbar or by giving the View | Sorting and Grouping command. Drag the dialog box out of the way so that it does not interfere with the report design.

8. In the first row of the upper grid of this dialog box, select the Category field and press [Enter]. Access will make this the first sort field and fill in ascending in the second column of the upper grid.

9. Set the Group Header property for this row to Yes. Access will add a new section to the report design called Category Header. Also set the Group Footer property for this row to Yes. Access will add a group footer for the Category field.

10. Repeat steps 8 and 9 for the Vendor field. Access will add group sections to the report called Vendor Header and Vendor Footer.

11. Drag the Stock Number field to the Detail section of the report. Remove its attached label. Repeat for the Description field. Enlarge the Description field so that its contents will fit. Adjust the position to fall beneath the column headings.

12. Click on the text box button in the Toolbox, then add a text box control beneath the Inventory Value heading. Remove its attached label. Within the box, type the expression =[Unit Cost]*[Quantity on Hand] and press [Enter].

13. In the property sheet for this calculated control, choose the Currency format. Change the Control Name property to Extended. Also select the Right-aligned text style and position the control so that it aligns with its column heading.

14. Drag the Category field from the field list box and place it in the Category Header section. Click on the Bold button for both the label and the text box. Move the two controls closer together. Drag the lower border of this section up so that there is no extra blank space below the controls.

15. Repeat the previous step with the Vendor field, placing it in the Vendor Header section. Indent the label slightly to the right. Drag the lower border of this section up to remove extra space.

CHECKPOINT 11C Why do we remove this extra space from the group header and footer sections?

16. Click on the text box button in the Toolbox, then place a text box control in the Category Footer section, beneath the Extended field of the Detail section. In this control give the expression =Sum([Unit Cost]*[Quantity on Hand]) and press [Enter]. Use the Currency format. Change its attached label to read Category Subtotal: and adjust spacing so that the controls align.

17. Repeat the previous step, placing another subtotal in the Vendor Footer section. Change its attached label to read Vendor Subtotal: and adjust spacing so that the controls align. Figure 11.10 shows the final design of this report.

18. Click on the Print Preview button to view the finished report. Figure 11.11 shows the print preview. Save this report as Inventory Group Report.

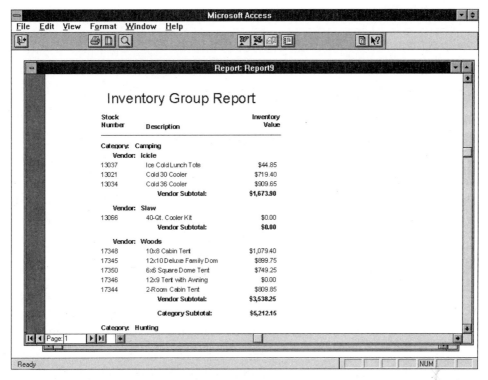

Creating a Report with Linked Subreport

There are instances when it is appropriate to link two or more tables together in a main report with subreport format. This link is accomplished by matching field values. We explored the Hunter River Order Form in the previous unit. We will design a similar report to print order invoices in this section.

The steps to create a custom report with *linked subreport* are similar to those for main/subform forms. First, design both reports on paper. Create the main report, then the subreport. Then insert the subreport into the main report. You can accomplish this by dragging the subreport from the Database window and placing it in the appropriate report section. Then link the reports by setting the *Link Child Fields* and *Link Master Fields properties* as we did with the main/subform form. We will illustrate this process with the Invoice report created in the activity below.

You can also insert an *unlinked subreport* into a main report. This has the effect of placing several short reports together on one or more sheets of paper. Although these reports are not specifically linked by common field values, they contain related information. An example of an unlinked subreport would be a departmental report that appears with an employee report.

GUIDED ACTIVITY 11.5

Creating a Report with Linked Subreport

In this Guided Activity you will create an invoice report that shows the customer order and order items, similar to the order form from the previous unit.

1. Close any open windows and return to the HUNT Database window.

2. Switch to Report mode and click the New button to create the main report. We will use the Customer/Order Join query as the data source for this report. Click on Blank Report.

3. We will create a main invoice report for the order and customer information. Create a label in the center of the Page Header section. In that label place the line Hunter River Sporting Goods. Add a second label control beneath it that contains Wabash Plaza. Add a third label beneath the second that contains Tremain, IN 46263.

4. You will have to pull down the lower border of the Page Header section to make all of these controls fit. Use the pointer to move the controls to center the labels. Make each one appear in Bold by selecting it and clicking the Bold button in the toolbar.

5. Add a fourth label control beneath the third that contains CUSTOMER INVOICE. Make this label appear in a 14-point font. Add a horizontal line control beneath the Customer Invoice control. See Figure 11.12 for location of these labels.

6. If the field list box is not already displayed, click on the Field List button in the toolbar (or use the View | Field List command). Drag the Order Number field from the field list box to the left side of the Detail section. Drag the Order Date field from the field list to the right portion of the Detail section. Adjust the position so that the field is close to its attached label.

7. Drag the Customer Number field from the field list box to the Detail section. Beneath the customer number create a text box control for the customer's name. In the box type =[First Name]+" "+[Last Name] and press [Enter]. Delete the attached label.

8. Pull down the lower border of the Detail section to make room for additional fields. Create additional text box controls beneath the customer name box for the Address Line 1 and Address Line 2 fields. Delete the attached labels for these text boxes.

9. Create an additional text box control beneath the Address Line 2 control. In this text box key in the expression =[City]+", "+[State]+" "+[Postal Code] and press [Enter]. This will create a single concatenated field for the city, state, and zip code. Delete the attached label box. Place a line control beneath the City/State/Postal Code line to separate the invoice header information from the items on the order. Figure 11.12 shows the main report design.

10. Click on the Print Preview button to view your main report. Save this report as Main Invoice Report and close its window.

FIGURE 11.12
Main Invoice
Report design

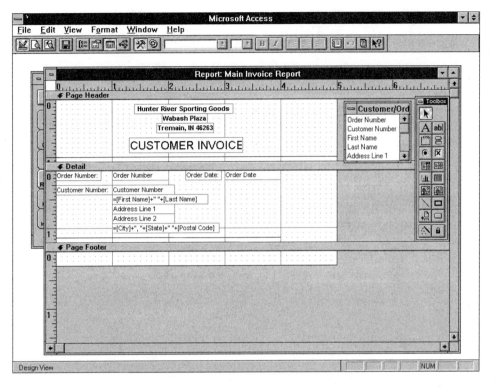

11. ⟩ With Report mode selected, click on the New button in the HUNT Database window. When prompted, select the Order Items/Products Join query as the data source for this subreport. Click on Blank Report.

12. ⟩ We will create a subreport that lists the order items that go with the order information in the main report. Drag the Order Quantity field from the field list to the Detail section. Delete its attached label and move it to the upper-left portion of the section.

13. ⟩ Repeat step 12 for the Description and Unit Cost fields. Delete their attached labels and move them into place. The Description field should be lengthened so that longer descriptions can appear. Access will truncate any description that does not fit.

14. ⟩ We need to add a calculated control for extended cost. Click the text box button in the Toolbox, then place the control to the right of the Unit Cost control. Delete its attached label. In the box type =[Order Quantity]*[Unit Cost] and press `Enter`.

15. ⟩ If the property sheet is not already displayed, use the View I Properties command or click the Properties button in the toolbar. With the calculated control still selected, change the Format property to Currency. Change the Control Name property to Extended Cost.

CHECKPOINT 11D What other methods can you use to display the property sheet for an object?

FIGURE 11.13

Invoice Subreport design

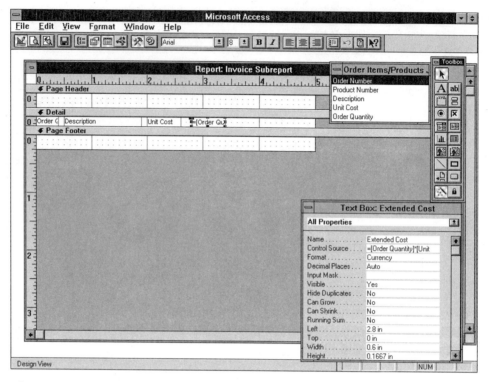

16. Decrease the length of the Detail section so that only these fields are shown. Figure 11.13 shows the subreport design. Save this report as `Invoice Subreport` and close its window.

17. Open the Main Invoice Report in Design view. Drag the lower border of the Detail section down to about the 2.5-inch mark.

18. Press [F11] or click the Database button in the toolbar to display the Database window. Drag the Invoice Subreport to the 0,1.5-inch position of the Detail section of the Main Invoice Report. Change its attached label to read `Order Items:` and press [Enter].

19. Select the subreport control and examine its property sheet. In the LinkMasterFields property enter `Order Number`. Do the same thing for the LinkChildFields property. This will ensure that only the order items that match the order number will appear on the invoice.

20. Click on the page break button in the Toolbox. Place a page break control just beneath the subreport control in the Detail section. This will cause Access to place each new invoice report on a separate page.

21. Click the Print Preview button to view the results of your invoice report. The preview is shown in Figure 11.14. Save the report again and close the Report window.

We will save creation of a Subtotal control for an exercise at the end of this unit.

FIGURE 11.14
Finished Invoice report

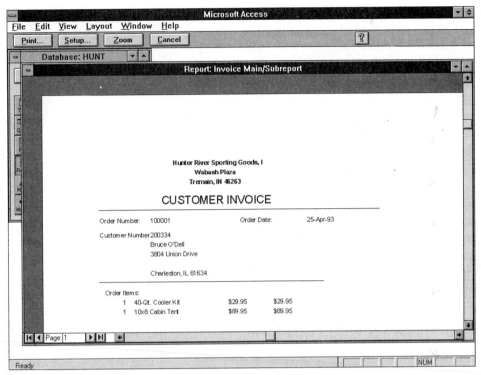

Other Custom Report Features

Access provides numerous options for custom reports that make them look better or convey information more clearly. Some of these features are described below.

Creating a Report Header

Certain reports would be more effective if you created a report cover. Printed just one time per report, the Report Header section serves this purpose. The Page Header and Page Footer should *not* appear on this cover page; you can change the **Page Header property** on the report's property sheet from `All Pages` to `Not with Rpt Hdr` to prevent this from happening.

Suppose you wanted to create a report cover with a large rectangle that sets off the text inside. You might use different fonts and font sizes to highlight certain phrases. Italic and bold styles also help to highlight portions of the text. You might include a date and give credit to the authors of the report. The following activity illustrates this procedure.

GUIDED ACTIVITY 11.6 ✗

Creating a Report Header

In this Guided Activity you will create a Report Header section that prints a cover for a report.

1. Close any open windows and return to the HUNT Database window.

2. Select the Inventory Group Report that was created in Guided Activity 11.4, then click the Design button.

3. Choose the Report Header/Footer command from the Format menu. Access will add sections for Report Header and Footer.

4. We will not need the Report Footer section, so drag its lower border up until the section has no height.

CHECKPOINT 11E Why can't you remove the Report Footer section with a command?

5. Drag the lower border of the Report Header section down to about 7 inches on the vertical ruler. If you drag below the current window, Access will scroll the window and display the lower portion of the report design screen.

6. Click on the rectangle tool in the Toolbox. Starting with the upper-left corner of this control at the 0.5,0.5-inch mark, drag the lower-right corner down to the 6,4.5-inch mark and release the left mouse button. Access will scroll the screen downward if you drag the pointer against the lower window section.

7. Next, click on the label tool in the Toolbox. Create a 2-inch long label control near the upper-left corner of the Report Header section, inside the rectangle. In this box type Hunter River Sporting Goods, Inc. Change it to 12-point size and click on the Italic button in the toolbar. Access will expand the control box to hold the label. Expect it to take two or three lines inside the box.

8. In the center of the rectangle place a second label. In this box type Inventory Report by Category and Vendor. The text in this box should be 18 points and bold. Select the New Times Roman font from the Font box in the toolbar. Resize and move the box manually to fit the text.

9. Below and to the right of the larger box add a text box. Delete its attached label. Inside the text box type =Now() and press ⏎Enter. Access will place the current date and time in this box. The design is shown in Figure 11.15.

10. Finally, click on the Print Preview button to view your report cover as shown in Figure 11.16. Scroll to the next report page to view the regular report. Save the changes made to this report and close the report window.

Adding OLE Object Controls to Reports

You can place bound and unbound OLE (*o-lay*) objects in reports. Unbound objects are frequently used as logos on cover pages or perhaps in a corner of a report page. Bound objects such as employee or product photographs can be added to a

FIGURE 11.15
*Report Header
in Design view*

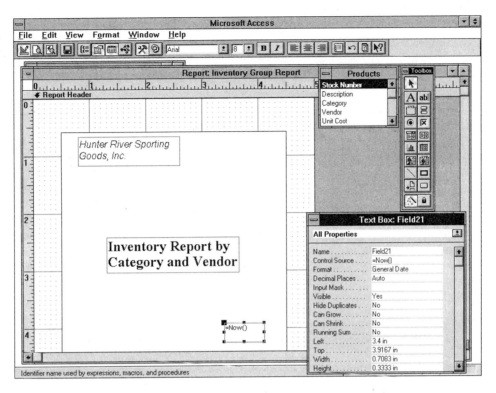

FIGURE 11.16
*Report Cover
print preview*

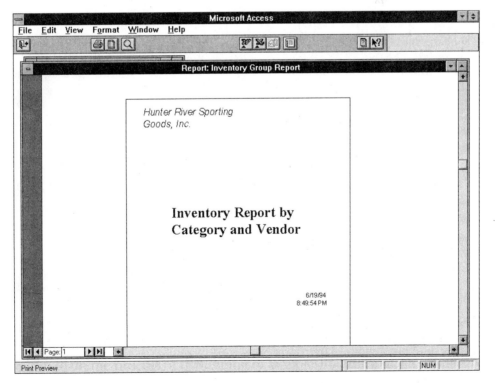

report as well. Access supports use of Microsoft Graph to create graphs for reports. We will not cover these types of controls in this unit. Unit 12 covers use of pictures and graphics in Access reports and forms. Unit 13 shows how to create graphs in reports and forms.

Creating Multi-Column Reports

We learned how to create a *multi-column mailing labels report* with Report Wizards in Part One of this book. In this section we will show how to create a custom mailing labels design, starting with a blank report.

For a mailing labels report, remove the page header and page footer sections. This type of report uses just a Detail section. If you wish, you can add a report cover in a report header section. However, if you print the report on gummed labels the cover page may not print properly. We frequently use the mailing labels format on regular paper.

The Detail section will contain a control for each line of the label. Drag the section borders in so that the section size is equal to the size of one label. Choose the Print Preview button, then click the Setup button in the toolbar of the Preview window. Adjust the Print Setup dialog box settings to reflect the number of printed labels per row and per page.

GUIDED ACTIVITY 11.7

Creating a Custom Mailing Labels Report

In this Guided Activity you will create a 3-across custom mailing labels report, starting with a blank report design. The labels are 1 inch high by 2.5 inches wide.

1. Close all open windows and return to the HUNT Database window.

2. Switch to Report mode and click the New button to create a new report. Select the Customers table as the data source, and click the Blank Report button.

3. Use the Format menu to remove any headers and footers: neither Page Header/Footer nor Report Header/Footer should be checked in this menu.

4. Click on the text box tool in the Toolbox. Create a text box control in the upper-left corner of the Detail section. Remove its attached label. In this box type `=[First Name]+" "+[Last Name]` and press `Enter`.

5. Drag the Address Line 1 field from the field list box to the second line of the Detail section. Delete its attached label. Position it so that it touches the first box.

6. Repeat step 5 for the Address Line 2 field.

7. Create another text box for the fourth line of the Detail section. Delete its attached label. In this box type `=[City]+", "+[State]+" "+[Postal Code]` and press `Enter`.

FIGURE 11.17
Custom mailing labels report design

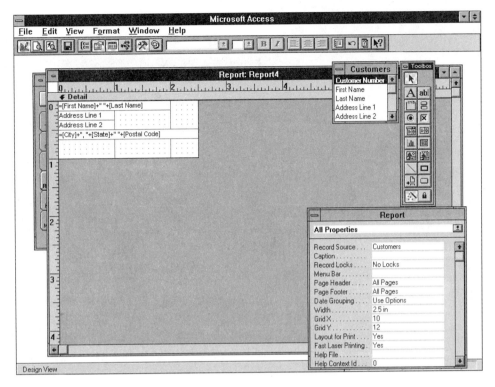

8. Adjust the size of the fields so that none is wider than 2.5 inches, the width of the label.

9. Drag the right border of the Detail section so that it is 2.5 inches wide. Adjust the height of the Detail section to 1 inch, matching the size of the labels. See Figure 11.17.

10. Click on the Print Preview button in the toolbar, then click on the Print Setup button in the toolbar. You will see the Print Setup dialog box. Click on the More>> button to view the Item Spacing choices. The most important item to change is the Items Across box. For 3-across labels, change that value from 1 to 3. We also changed the left and right margins from 1 inch to 0.5 inch to make a little more room for the labels. See Figure 11.18, which shows not only the Print Setup dialog box but also the effects of the changes on the Print Preview screen.

11. Save this report as Customer Labels 3 and close the report window.

Command Review

F11	Display the Database window.
Ctrl Enter	Insert a line feed in a label control.
Format I Align	Align the selected controls.
Format I Report Header/Footer	Display or remove the report header and footer sections.

FIGURE 11.18
*The Print Setup
dialog box with
Print Preview*

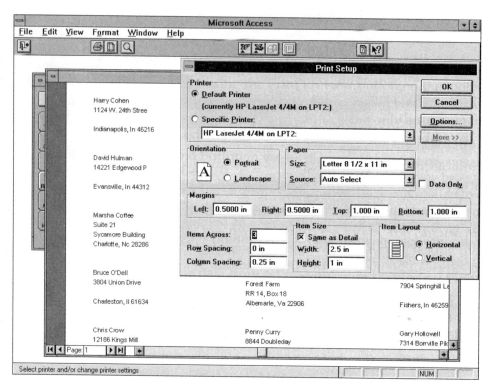

Format	Page Header/Footer	Display or remove the page header and footer sections.
View	Sorting and Grouping	Display the Sorting and Grouping dialog box.
View	Properties	Display the property sheet for the selected object.

Exercises

Use the Hunter River database contained within the HUNT.MDB file on the West Student Data Disk for these exercises.

1. Use the Employees table to prepare a custom tabular report. Include all of the fields in the report, but do not present groups or totals. Use a suitable title for your report. Print the report and save the report design as Exercise 11-1.

2. Using the Employees table, create a custom groups/totals report showing employee salaries by department. Within each department, sort alphabetically by employee last name. Print the report and save its design as Exercise 11-2.

3. Create a custom group report for the Customers table, using all of the fields. Your report should contain two detail lines in a format that makes it easy to read. Leave one blank row between customer names in this report. Print the report and save the report design as Exercise 11-3.

4. Prepare a mailing labels custom report for the Products table. In this exercise you will create a product sales tag. On the first line place the Stock Number field. On the second line put the Description field. On the third line place the Vendor field. On the fourth line place the Unit Cost field, displayed in Currency format and shown in Bold. Change the size of the Unit Cost to 10 points. Arrange the report so that you can print five labels across on a single sheet of paper. Print the report and save the design as Exercise 11-4.

5. Modify the report for Exercise 11-3 so that it has a cover page. The cover page should include the current date, a suitable report title, and your name. The title should appear in a 36-point bold font; your name should be in a 24-point font. Enclose all of this information in a rectangle and center the fields vertically on the page. Print a copy of the cover page. Save the report as Exercise 11-5.

6. Modify the invoice report of Guided Activity 11.5 so that it has a subtotal for the Extended field. You might refer to the similar work done in the order form created in Unit 10. Print a copy of the report and save the design as Exercise 11-6.

Review Questions

1. What are the advantages of building a custom report instead of a Report Wizards report? Are there reasons to use both techniques for a single report? Explain.

2. Discuss the steps in building a custom Access report.

3. Explain how to do the following tasks with Access report controls:

   a. Select a single control.

   b. Select two adjacent controls.

   c. Select two nonadjacent controls.

   d. Line up the left edges of a set of selected controls.

   e. Move both a text box control and its attached label.

4. How do you change the size of a report section? Can you change the report's width?

5. Explain the steps in creating a calculated field control in a report. Assume that the field refers to a currency amount.

6. Discuss the following group properties in the Sorting and Grouping dialog box.

   a. Group Header

   b. Group Footer

   c. Group On

   d. Group Interval

7. Describe the following text formatting features available in Access reports.

   a. Font Name

   b. Font Size

   c. Style

   d. Alignment

8. Describe the differences between a linked subreport and an unlinked subreport. When would each be used?

9. Give the steps used to create a main report with a linked subreport.

10. How would you create a cover page for an Access report?

Key Terms

Group Footer section
Group Header property
Group Header section
Group Interval property
Group On property
Link Child Fields property

Linked subreport
Link Master Fields
   property
Multi-column mailing
   labels report
Multiple-level group report

Page Header property
Report Footer section
Report Header section
Report section
Unlinked subreport

Documentation Research

Use the printed documentation and the on-line Help available with Microsoft Access to answer the following questions. If you use one of the manuals, provide the page number for your reference in the manual.

1. Use the on-line Help system to learn about the Report property sheet. Give a brief definition of each report property.

2. What is the purpose of the Hide Duplicates property for a text box control? Give an example of where it would be useful.

3. How would you tell Access to start each group on a new page of the report without using the page break control?

Physicians' Medical Clinic (VIII): Building a Custom Report

In this application you will create a report from data in the PMC database, using the material covered in previous units. You will open the PMC database, create a main report, create a subreport, then prepare a report showing patient visits to PMC. Read the directions carefully. Clearly identify which output goes with which part of the application.

1. Prepare a custom report that shows the patient's permanent information in the top part of the report. In the lower part of the report list the patient visits to the clinic, including the name of the procedure and the cost of that procedure. Each patient should begin a new page of your report. Patients should appear in alphabetical order.

2. The report should include the total charges for the visits shown for each patient. Your report should include a report summary section to include the total charges for all patients listed in the report.

Advanced Database Management with Access

III

■ **PART THREE** continues the development of advanced database objects using Microsoft Access. While Part Two focused on creation of customized queries, forms, and reports, Part Three applies these advanced database concepts. In it you learn how to add pictures and graphics to your forms and reports. With Microsoft Graph you can create sophisticated graphs, then embed them in Access reports and forms. You learn how to create macros to automate Access commands and expedite your work. You use macros to build a menu-driven custom application. There is a unit on linking other types of data files with Access, including database files from additional popular application programs. Part Three concludes with a unit on administering the database, including the use of Access in a multiuser, shared environment with user accounts.

Using Pictures and Graphics in Access

12

This unit explains how to use OLE objects such as pictures and graphics in Access forms and reports. You will learn how to add a scanned photograph file to a table as a data field. The unit also covers creating a logo with Windows Paintbrush.

Learning Objectives

At the completion of this unit you should know

1. the definition and use of OLE objects in Access databases,

2. the difference between linked and embedded objects,

3. the role of an OLE server,

4. how to capture scanned photographs and place them in an Access database.

At the completion of this unit you should be able to

1. add an unbound object such as a logo to a form,

2. create a simple logo using Windows Paintbrush,

3. embed a bitmap picture file in an OLE field in an Access table,

4. add a photograph to a form.

Important Commands

Access Commands:

> Edit | Insert Object
>
> File | Save Form As

Paintbrush Commands:

> File | Exit & Return
>
> File | Save
>
> Text | Fonts

OLE Objects in Access Databases

We have previously introduced the OLE (object linking and embedding) data type in Microsoft Access databases. *OLE objects* refer to a class of Windows objects that can be linked and embedded in other objects. OLE objects include graphs, sound, pictures, spreadsheets, or other objects that are *OLE-compliant*—that is, compatible with the OLE programming specifications that Microsoft created for both Windows and Access. Many Windows applications are OLE-compliant, and most software developers plan to offer this capability in future versions of their programs. The source application program that creates the OLE object is also known as the *OLE server*.

Linked Versus Embedded Objects

An OLE object can be linked or embedded. An *embedded object* is stored in the database like other data values. If you double-click on the OLE object in a form or report, Access will start the application program that created the OLE object and will display the object for you in that application's window. Any changes made in the object are saved in the database itself when you exit from the application and return to Access. Embedding is the most common way to use OLE objects in Access.

A *linked object* is similar to an embedded object, but the object itself is saved in a separate file, not saved in the database. A link is created between Access and that file. If you double-click the OLE object in Access, the application that created the object will load. Any changes you make to the object must be saved in a separate file created by the source application. Not all OLE-compliant applications support linking.

In linked objects, changes made to the OLE object are automatically passed on to Access without intervention by the database user. The next time you open a form or report that contains an OLE object, you will see the updated version of the OLE object.

Types of OLE Objects

Logos, pictures (photographs and drawings), and graphs are the most common type of OLE objects used in Access databases. Logos are used with forms and reports to identify the organization and provide a more attractive look for the form or report. Look at stationery, business cards, and advertisements for samples of corporate or institutional symbols.

The ability to embed digitized photographs or drawings in the database is an extremely important advantage of Access. You can view an image field directly in the form or report, just like a text or number field. No longer do you have to maintain a separate manual filing system for such images. It is relatively easy to use an optical scanner to convert the picture into a digital computer file. We will discuss this procedure later in this unit. There is a disadvantage in using images, however—the file sizes can be quite large, requiring additional hard drive storage space. Fortunately, the cost of hard drives has been falling in recent years.

Microsoft includes an OLE-compliant graphing package in Access. Microsoft Graph is able to prepare sophisticated charts, using data from Access databases and other sources. The charts can be embedded in Access forms and reports. Use of the Graph application is explained in Unit 13.

It is possible to include objects such as spreadsheets and graphs from spreadsheet applications as OLE objects in Access forms and reports. You may find uses for other OLE objects like sounds and video, particularly with the growing popularity of multimedia applications. *Multimedia* refers to the capability to use sound, still video, and animated video images in a personal computer, typically with a CD-ROM (compact disc, read-only memory) drive. For instance, you might have a database about musical compositions. It is possible to embed or link images of the composer and audio samples of the composition in and to the database. You can also have voice samples in a database.

The Windows Registration Database

Windows includes an internal *registration database* that maps certain file extensions to a particular source application program. Thus, when you double-click a file name in the File Manager with a particular extension, Windows knows what program to start and opens that file within the application. For example, the *.BMP extension* refers to the *bitmap files* used in the *Windows Paintbrush* application. Paintbrush is frequently used to insert objects into Access databases. The .WRI extension refers to Windows Write documents, and .DOC refers to Microsoft Word documents. Files with .WAV extensions are recorded sounds. There are numerous entries in the registration database. As you add a new OLE-compliant application program to your computer, Windows should update the registration database with information about that OLE server.

When you create an OLE object within Access, Windows will consult the registration database and display a list of the types of OLE objects available on your computer. Then, when you select an object type, Access will know which OLE server to associate with that OLE field. We will demonstrate this process in the next section.

Adding a Logo to a Form

This section will demonstrate how to add a color logo to a form. Most Windows users have color monitors but monochrome printers. Color graphics obviously look best when viewed on a color monitor. When you use a monochrome printer to print a form or report containing a color image, some clarity is lost as the printer substitutes shading patterns for colors.

The procedure for adding a logo file to a form is somewhat lengthy. First you must create the basic form with all of the normal controls, leaving space for the logo. We typically place the logo in an unbound frame control in the Page Header section so that it appears at the top of the screen. After creating the unbound frame in Design view, use the Insert Object command from the Edit menu. Access will display the types of object available on your computer. Select the Paintbrush object (or whatever OLE server program you used to create the logo image) and then select the file containing the logo image. Access will embed that object in the frame. To view the object within the form, click on the Form View button in the toolbar.

GUIDED ACTIVITY 12.1

Adding a Color Logo to a Form

In this Guided Activity you will place a logo that was created with Windows Paintbrush into an Access form.

1. Start Windows and load Access. Open the HUNT Database window.

2. Switch to Form mode and select the Hunter Products form. Click on Design.

3. Pull down the border of the Form Header section to make room for the logo. It is about 1 inch tall by 2 inches long.

4. Click the unbound object frame control in the Toolbox. (It is the seventh button down in the left column.)

CHECKPOINT 12A What are the differences between bound and unbound controls?

5. Use the pointer to create a control box in the middle right portion of the Form Header section. The box should be 1 inch by 2.25 inches wide.

6. Access will display the Insert Object dialog box and ask you to select the type of object. Select Paintbrush Picture, then select the Create from File button at the left side.

7. At the next dialog box enter the path and file name for the file. The Hunter logo is stored in the HUNT.BMP file from the Student Data Disk. It is probably located in the Access subdirectory, along with the HUNT.MDB database file.

8. Click OK and Access will embed the logo in the form. If your box is not quite large enough to hold the logo, the Format | Size | to Fit command will enlarge the box to fit the logo. The form design is shown in Figure 12.1.

FIGURE 12.1
*Form with logo
in unbound
frame control*

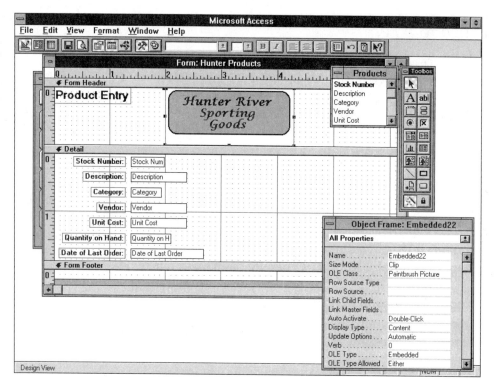

FIGURE 12.1
*Form with logo
in unbound
frame control*

9. To view the form with the logo, click on the Form View button in the toolbar, or give the View | Form command. Figure 12.2 shows the finished form with the data fields from the first record. If you don't have a color monitor, the logo has a light gray background, with a dark gray border. Hunter River is in dark blue, and Sporting Goods is in hunter green.

10. Use the File | Save As command to save this form as Hunter Products Form. Close the form window and return to the HUNT Database window.

Creating a Logo File with Paintbrush

Most logos are created by artists and can be scanned into a computer file. The logo in the previous activity was created by a nonartistic person (the author) in Windows Paintbrush. The technique is not difficult, although it does require some knowledge of the Paintbrush accessory program. If you are not familiar with this product, refer to the Windows *User's Guide* for help. The following activity will guide you through it one time.

GUIDED ACTIVITY 12.2

Creating a Logo with Paintbrush

In this Guided Activity you will learn how to create a simple logo file, using the Windows Paintbrush accessory program. This activity is not necessary for using Access or completing any other guided activities.

FIGURE 12.2
*Finished form
with corporate
logo*

```
┌─────────────────────────── Microsoft Access ──────────────────────── ▼ ◆ ─┐
│ File   Edit   View   Records   Window   Help                                │
│ ▣▣▣ ▣▣▶* ▣▣▣ ▣ ▣▣ ▣▣▣        ▣           ▣▣▣▣                      │
│ ┌──────────────────────────── Products ──────────────────────── ▼ ▲ ─┐    │
│ │                                                                       │    │
│ │  Product Entry          ╭───────────────╮                            │    │
│ │                         │  Hunter River │                            │    │
│ │                         │    Sporting   │                            │    │
│ │                         │      Goods    │                            │    │
│ │ ▶                       ╰───────────────╯                            │    │
│ │          Stock Number:  [13021    ]                                  │    │
│ │          Description:   [Cold 30 Cooler]                             │    │
│ │          Category:      [Camping]                                    │    │
│ │          Vendor:        [Icicle]                                     │    │
│ │          Unit Cost:     [     $59.95]                                │    │
│ │          Quantity on Hand: [    12]                                  │    │
│ │          Date of Last Order: [  5/4/93]                              │    │
│ │                                                                       │    │
│ │                                                                       │    │
│ │ ┃◀│◀│Record: 1   │ of 51 │ ▶│▶┃ │◆│                         ▶│     │    │
│ └───────────────────────────────────────────────────────────────────┘    │
│                                                                            │
│ Internal stock number for products; unique within Hunter River    ▢▢▢ NUM ▢ │
└────────────────────────────────────────────────────────────────────────────┘
```

1. Make sure Windows is loaded. Switch to the Program Manager from the Access window by repeatedly pressing [Alt][Tab]. (Or press [Ctrl][Esc] and choose Program Manager.)

 CHECKPOINT 12B What does the [Ctrl][Esc] command do?

2. Start the Paintbrush accessory located in the Accessories program group. The Paintbrush window is shown in Figure 12.3. The tool buttons are at the left edge of the screen and the color grid is at the bottom portion.

3. Choose the Fonts command from the Text menu. At the Font dialog box, select the Times New Roman font in the first combo box. Select the Bold Italic font style in the second combo box, and choose 14 for the size. Click OK to confirm your selections.

4. Click the text button in the Paintbrush Tools box, the second button in the right column.

5. Position the pointer in the drawing area near the paintbrush button and click once. This locates the beginning of the text to be inserted.

6. Click once on the royal blue button in the lower portion of the Paintbrush window to select this color for your text. Then type Indiana State and press [Enter]. On the next line press [Spacebar] two times, then type University. (You may use the name of your own school, if you wish.)

7. Click on the solid oval tool button in the Tools box, the seventh button down in the right column. Next, click on the light gray button in the Paintbrush color grid.

FIGURE 12.3
*Windows
Paintbrush
window*

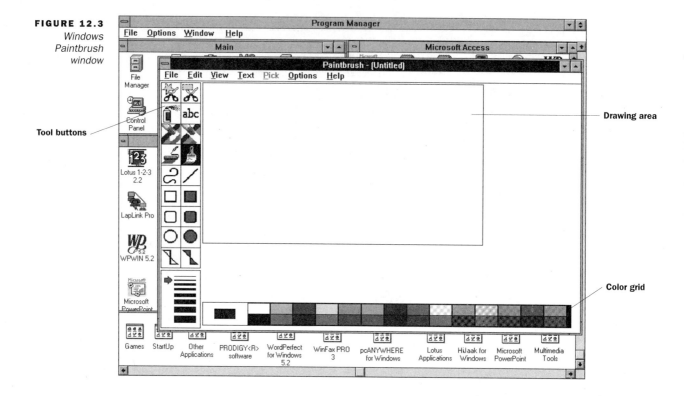

8. Move the crosshairs pointer to a position in the upper-left corner of the drawing area. While holding down the left button, drag the mouse to the right and create an oval that is a little larger than the text you're going to place in it. Be careful not to touch the text with your oval. When you have created the correct size, release the left button. Paintbrush will create a solid gray oval.

9. Click once on the rectangular scissors tool at the top of the right column of the Tools box. Locate the pointer above and to the left of the text, then hold down the left mouse button and drag the mouse to include all of the text in the box. If you make a mistake, repeat the dragging. Figure 12.4 shows the logo so far.

10. Move the pointer into the dotted line box around the text, then hold down the left button and drag the dotted line box on top of the gray oval. Maneuver it until the text is centered over the gray box, then release the button. The text will remain in the scissors box. You can move the dotted line box until you are satisfied with its position.

11. Finally, we will add a black oval border that edges the gray oval. Click on the clear oval tool button, the seventh one down on the left. Click on the black button on the lower portion of the Paintbrush window to select the black color.

12. Using the vertical and horizontal parts of the crosshairs pointer, move to the upper-left corner of the gray oval so that the crosshairs just touch the edge of the gray oval. While holding down the left mouse button, drag the oval to the lower-right corner of the gray oval. Line up the crosshairs with the edge of the gray oval, then release the mouse button.

FIGURE 12.4
*Paintbrush
window for logo*

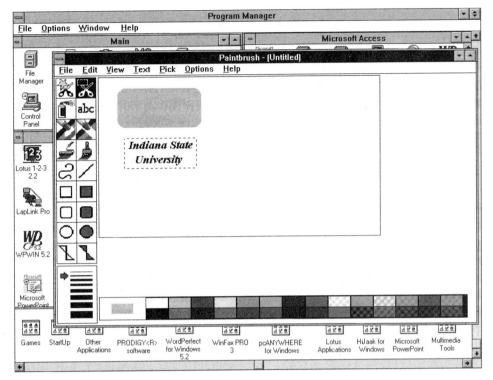

13. Paintbrush will draw a black outline around your logo, as shown in Figure 12.5. To save your logo, choose the Save command from the File menu. When prompted, type in the name ISULOGO or another suitable name for your school. Paintbrush will add the .BMP extension and save the logo file on your disk drive. You can use this logo in an Access form or report. Close the Paintbrush window.

The Paintbrush program has limited drawing capabilities. Other Windows drawing programs like CorelDRAW! offer more sophisticated features and extensive *clip art* collections of predrawn art work that can be incorporated into logos and other graphic designs.

Embedding Bound OLE Objects in Access

The logos from the previous section are unbound objects—that is, they are not associated with a table or record values. We placed them in the Form Header section of the form. This section will explore use of bound objects that are embedded into the Access database as OLE fields. In particular, we will demonstrate how to place color photographs into the Employees table of the HUNT database. Then you can place them in bound object frames in the Detail section of Access forms and reports.

Taking the Photographs

When taking photographs of individuals, your subjects should be well-lit with bright colors. If possible, use a flash mounted on the camera. We recommend that

FIGURE 12.5
*Paintbrush
window with
finished ISU logo*

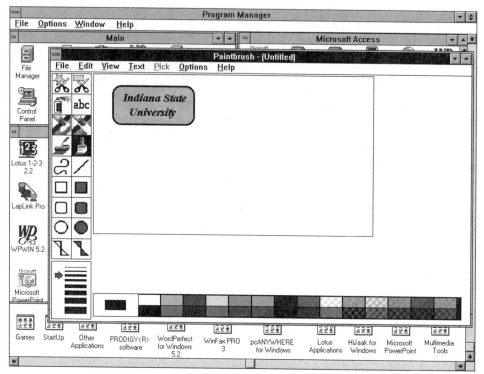

you set the camera in a position to take head and shoulder portraits. By using a tripod you can be sure that each photograph is consistent in content. Use color film for best viewing results with color monitors. The prints can be the normal size provided by your film processor.

Scanning the Photographs

Although we will not illustrate the scanning process in a guided activity, it is useful to discuss how you might accomplish this important process. A *scanner* is an optical device that shines a bright light on the document and converts its image into a digital file for storage on the computer. Typically, a scanner attaches to a special interface card installed in your computer. It comes with software to capture the document and manipulate the image electronically before the image is saved.

TYPES OF SCANNERS

There are two basic types of scanners: hand-held and flatbed scanners. Hand-held scanners require that the user carefully roll the scanner over the image. Rubber wheels underneath the scanner provide a means of keeping the scanner straight as it is drawn across the object, and they also measure the speed at which the scanner is moving. Hand-held scanners are less expensive but can produce good results for small objects. There are more problems associated with larger documents. With a hand scanner you must make several passes and "knit" the images together with the scanning software, a problematic operation for most people.

Flatbed scanners look like copy machines. You place the object to be scanned underneath the cover and command the scanner to begin. The scanner will illuminate the object and adjust the size automatically to match the object's size. The flatbed scanner is able to scan a document as large as its bed permits, usually in one pass. The flatbed scanner is much faster than most hand-held scanners, and is designed for large scanning volumes.

SCANNER SETTINGS

You have some choices to make when scanning the photographs. The image size and number of colors affect the physical size of the scanned image file. Remember that these files can become quite large. Keep the image size small, perhaps 2-by-2 or 2-by-3 inches. Most scanner software can produce images with 16 or 256 colors. Although 256 colors are more pleasant to look at, their files take up far more space than images with 16 colors. This is particularly important for Access OLE fields for which there is an image for every record in a table. You can view 16-color scanned images quite well, even when your Windows video driver is installed for 256 colors. We suggest that you stay with 16-color scanned images.

SCAN FILES

Your scanner will create digital files containing the scanned image. You may have some control over the type of file created. Because you must use an OLE server application to embed the images in Access, use a file type that is compatible with your OLE server. Windows Paintbrush is able to read both .BMP (bitmap) and *.PCX* (PC Paintbrush) format files, two popular scanner file types.

The scanned photographs in the NWIND sample database packaged with Access are approximately 2-by-3 inches; they use 16 colors and occupy about 22KB each if saved as a Paintbrush bitmap file. The files included on the data disk for this book are slightly smaller (2-by-2 inches) and take up about 12KB per image.

Embedding the Image in an Access Table

We assume that the images will be stored in an Access table as OLE fields. You must first define the table and its fields within Access. Select that table and switch to Datasheet view. Then select the record and OLE field to contain the image. Choose the Insert Object command from the Edit menu. As with unbound objects, Access will ask you to select the type of object. Choose Windows Paintbrush, then click the File button. When prompted, key in the path and file name for the OLE image to be embedded in that record. Don't forget to use the file extension, usually .BMP or .PCX with Paintbrush files. Access will save the image in the database itself; you no longer need to store the image as a separate file.

You must repeat this process for each record in the table, inserting the OLE object with the Edit | Insert Object command. After you return to Access from Paintbrush, Access will place the phrase "Paintbrush Picture" in the table, indicating that the value for that field is available in Paintbrush.

Viewing the OLE Images in Datasheet View

To view the OLE object in Datasheet view, select a record and double-click on the OLE field. Access will start the OLE server application that created the OLE image. In our example this would be Paintbrush. We will show how to add the OLE field to a form or report in a later guided activity. The following activity will show how to add a picture to an Access table.

GUIDED ACTIVITY 12.3

Adding a Picture to a Table

In this Guided Activity you will create a small table and insert photographs into that table. The photographs are stored as Paintbrush bitmap files on the data disk.

1. Close any open windows and return to the HUNT Database window in Access.

2. Change to Table mode, click New, and click the New Table button to create a new table.

3. The first field in the table is called Employee Number and is Counter type. Click on the field selector box and click the Key button in the toolbar to make this the primary key for your table.

4. The second field is called Employee Photo and is OLE object type.

5. Use the File | Save command to save this table under the name OLE Example. Click the Datasheet View button in the toolbar.

6. Position the pointer on the Employee Photo field of the first record. Then select Insert Object from the Edit menu.

7. Click on the Create from File button.

8. In the File: text box, enter the file name E1.PCX and click OK. This file contains the scanned image of the photograph. Make sure that the path is set to the same subdirectory that holds the main HUNT.MDB database file.

CHECKPOINT 12C How would you make a change to the file path where the photographs are located?

9. Repeat steps 6–8 for the second record. The photograph file for this record is called E2.PCX.

10. To view the photograph, double-click on the Employee Photo field in either record. Paintbrush will start and display the photograph.

11. When you are finished viewing the image, choose the Exit and Return to OLE Example command from the File menu in Paintbrush.

12. Close the Datasheet window. Your changes are automatically saved in the OLE Example table.

Adding a Photograph to a Form

One important advantage of using a graphical user interface such as Windows is the ability to display photographs in forms and reports. Once you have embedded the photographs in an Access table, those fields can be placed in a form or report just as any Access field can. In fact, you can even use the Form Wizards to create the form. Because the OLE field has been embedded in the table, Access uses the OLE server to display the object.

Whether you use the Form Wizards to build the form or create it manually from a blank form, you will place a bound object control in the Detail section. Remember that a bound object is linked to a particular record in the underlying table or query. Each time you move the record pointer, Access will display the correct photograph in a control box in that form. As with other graphic objects, the time to display the photograph is directly related to the speed of your computer and video subsystem.

GUIDED ACTIVITY 12.4

Adding a Photograph to a Form with Form Wizards

In this Guided Activity you will use the Form Wizards to create a form with photographs, then make some changes to the design manually.

1. Close any open windows and return to the HUNT Database window.

2. Switch to Form mode and click the New button.

3. Select the Employee Photos table, then click on Form Wizards.

4. Select the default form style, Single-column, and click OK.

5. Select the Employee ID field, then click the > button to place it in the form.

6. Repeat step 5 with the First Name, Middle Initial, Last Name, Department, and Photograph fields. They will appear in the form in this tab order. Click Next to go on.

7. In the next dialog box, choose the Standard form style and click Next.

8. Finally, use the title `Employee Information` for this form. Click Finish to open the form with data in it, shown in Figure 12.6. Notice that the default size for the Photograph field is larger than the image.

9. Click the Design View button in the toolbar. Notice that the photograph control box is nearly 3 inches long. Click once to select this box. Using the pointer, drag the lower-right size handle to the left so that the box is approximately 1.5 by 1.5 inches.

10. Click the Form View button in the toolbar to see the photograph in its new aspect ratio. Figure 12.7 shows the finished form in Form view.

11. Use the File | Save Form command to save the form as `Employee Information`. Use the record navigation buttons to examine the remainder of the records with your form. When you are finished, close the active window.

FIGURE 12.6
*Form Wizards
design with
incorrect
photo size*

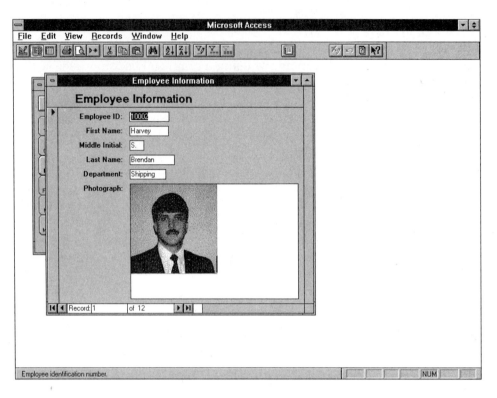

FIGURE 12.7
*Form Wizards
form with
resized
photograph*

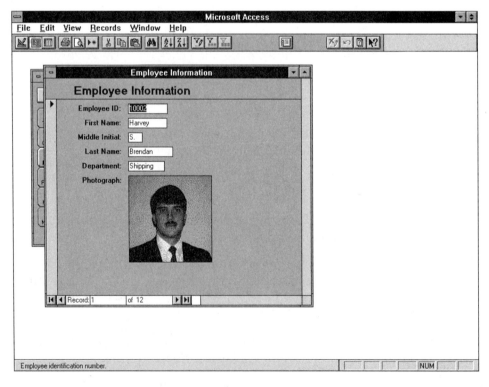

Command Review

Access commands:

Edit I Insert Object	Place an OLE object file into an OLE field in a table.
File I Save Form As	Save the form under a different name.

Paintbrush commands:

Text I Fonts	Choose the font name, style, and size for text in a drawing.
File I Save	Save the Paintbrush drawing as a bitmapped file.
File I Exit & Return	Leave Paintbrush and return to Access.

Exercises

Use the Hunter River database contained within the HUNT.MDB file on the West Student Data Disk for these exercises.

1. Use Paintbrush to create a logo file for the parent corporation, Hunter River Sporting Goods Inc. You may choose the font and any colors used. Print a copy of your logo using the Paintbrush File I Print command.

2. Create a custom form for Hunter River customers. Place the logo from the first exercise in the Form Header section. Print a copy of your form.

3. Continue the work begun in Guided Activity 12.3, adding the next three employee photographs to the OLE Example table. Use the bitmap files called E3.PCX, E4.PCX, and E5.PCX contained on the West Student Data Disk. Print a copy of the datasheet that shows "Paintbrush Picture" in records 3–5.

4. Create a form, using the OLE Example table from the previous exercise. Display the Employee Number and Employee Photo fields in the Detail section. Print a copy of the form for record 4.

Review Questions

1. Describe the advantages of using OLE fields in an Access database. Using a real estate company as an example, describe the kinds of OLE fields that might be used in a multiple-listing service.

2. Constrast linked and embedded objects. Which kind is generally used with Access databases?

3. Describe the importance of the Windows registration database to OLE applications.

4. Explain the procedure used to place a logo in an unbound object frame control in a form.

5. You have created a table that already contains an OLE object field. Explain how you can display the contents of that OLE object field.

6. Describe the general scanning procedure used to convert a photograph into a computer file that can be incorporated in an Access database.

7. Discuss the use of clip art in preparing a logo or other unbound OLE object.

8. How can you add an OLE object field such as a photograph to a form or report? Are the commands needed to handle OLE object fields different from those for other kinds of Access fields?

Key Terms

Bitmap file	Multimedia	Registration database
.BMP extension	OLE-compliant	Scanner
Clip art	OLE object	Windows Paintbrush
Embedded object	OLE server	
Linked object	.PCX extension	

Documentation Research

Use the printed documentation and the on-line Help available with Microsoft Access to answer the following questions. If you use one of the manuals, provide the page number for your reference in the manual.

1. Search on-line Help for information about "Registering an OLE Application." Following the directions in that help screen, run the REGEDIT.EXE file to learn which file types on your computer have been registered with Windows. When finished, close the window.

2. Seach on-line Help for information about "Scaling, Stretching, and Zooming a Picture or Object." Explain the differences between these three choices for the SizeMode property. Which choice is the default?

3. Examine the Paintbrush on-line Help for information about the drawing tools. Give a brief explanation of the purpose of each of these tools:

    a. Scissors tool

    b. Rounded Box tool

    c. Line tool

    d. Paint Roller tool

    e. Color Eraser tool

Physicians' Medical Clinic (IX): Using Graphics in a Form

In this application you will create a form for data in the PMC database, using the material covered in previous units. You will open the PMC database, modify a table to contain embedded graphics, then use that table in a form. Read the directions carefully. Clearly identify which output goes with which part of the application.

1. As a member of the new Total Quality Management program, you have been asked to add patient photographs to the PMC database. You arranged to have photographs taken and then scanned them into .PCX files, using a flatbed scanner. Modify the patient table to hold photographs as an OLE field. If you cannot create your own photographs, you may use the files named E1.PCX...E13.PCX from the West Student Data Disk as your patient image files.

NOTE *There are more records in the Patient table than scanned photographs.*

2. Prepare a new form or modify an existing form (and save it under a different name) that will display patient information along with a small photograph of each patient. Surround the photograph with a clear rectangular box.

3. What other graphic objects would be appropriate for use in the PMC database? Break your list into bound objects and unbound objects. Prioritize each list, and prepare an estimate of the expected number of objects per patient.

13

Graphing with Access

This unit explains how to create graphs with Microsoft Graph 5.0, an OLE utility program packaged with Access 2.0. The unit covers basic graphing terminology, including the types of graphs that can be prepared with Access. You will learn how to add a graph to a form or report using the Graph Wizard, as well as using the Graph menus directly.

Learning Objectives

At the completion of this unit you should know

1. basic graphing terms,
2. the types of graphs available with Microsoft Graph,
3. sources of data for a graph.

At the completion of this unit you should be able to

1. create a simple graph using Graph Wizards,
2. add a graph to a form,
3. add a graph to a report,
4. modify graph settings, using the Microsoft Graph utility program.

Important Commands

Within Microsoft Graph 5.0:

Insert | Axes

Insert | Data Labels

Insert | Gridlines

Insert | Titles

Data | Series

Format | Chart Type

Format | Column Width

Format | Font

Format | Number

Graph Basics

You are already familiar with graphs. We see graphs in the newspaper and on television almost every day. They are a powerful way of visually displaying trends and patterns in numeric data. We use graphs to help interpret the datasheet that contains the actual data values.

Basic Graphing Terminology

The numeric values or *data points* for a graph are found in a *datasheet*. You can use data values from an Access table or even import data from an external application such as Excel or Lotus 1-2-3. We'll talk more about this option later in the unit.

Graphs display values from one or more data series in a chart. A *data series* is a set of data values from one row or column of the datasheet, such as Annual Sales or Annual Expenses.

The data values are plotted on the chart as a symbol called a *data marker*. The data marker is a bar, a shape, or a symbol. In cases where there are multiple data series in the same chart, Access will use different colors, shading patterns, or shapes to distinguish each series.

The *legend* is contained in a box that identifies the colors, patterns, or symbols used with each data series in the chart. The legend gives the name of each data series.

Most Access graphs plot data in a rectangular grid with horizontal and vertical *axis* lines. The Y-axis is known as the *value axis*; data points are plotted on the Y-axis for most chart types. The X-axis is known as the *category axis*; the data categories are printed as labels on the X-axis. 3-D charts use the Z-axis for the value axis; the Y-axis represents data series names, and the X-axis represents category names. Only the pie chart does not use the rectangular grid system. Each axis has *tick marks* that represent a scale or category on that axis.

You may also place labels on the graph to describe parts of the chart. Called *chart text*, these labels may be attached to an item of the graph (such as an axis or data marker) or may stay unattached. Attached text automatically moves with an item when it is repositioned. Unattached text can be positioned anywhere on the chart. Tick mark labels are examples of attached text. You can create a *chart title* to explain the overall contents of the chart. *Axis labels* describe the axis. *Data labels* describe individual data points and may be the value of the data point or some other description.

Types of Charts in Microsoft Graph

Access provides 14 *chart types* for displaying data. The choice depends on the data itself and on what message you are trying to convey with the data. We will look at the chart types and discuss when you might choose each one. After choosing a chart type, you can customize your graph by choosing from a wide range of options.

AREA CHART

The *area chart* shows values over time. It emphasizes the magnitude of the values by displaying them in different shaded regions or areas. If you display multiple data series, the data values are "stacked" one on top of another.

BAR CHART

A common chart is the *bar chart*. Access uses horizontal bars to represent the magnitude of values in different categories. Bar charts are used to compare individual items with other items rather than to the whole.

COLUMN CHART

Similar to a bar chart, a *column chart* uses vertical bars to represent the magnitude of values over time or in different categories. Column charts compare individual items with each other rather than to the whole.

DOUGHNUT CHART

A *doughnut chart* is similar to a pie chart, showing the proportion of parts to a whole. It can show more than one data series, depicted in concentric rings. This chart is common in Asian countries.

LINE CHART

A *line chart* uses a line to connect data values over time. It shows trends or patterns in the data values. Although similar to an area chart, a line chart emphasizes the rate of change rather than the magnitude of the amount.

PIE CHART

A *pie chart* is a circular chart whose pieces are proportional to the magnitude of the data values plotted in it. The pie chart illustrates how a whole is broken into components. A pie chart always contains just a single data series. You can emphasize a single element of the pie by *exploding* it—slicing it and pulling it out slightly—from the rest of the pie.

RADAR CHART

A *radar chart* shows changes or frequencies of data series relative to a center point and to one another. This chart is common in Asian countries.

XY (SCATTER) CHART

The *XY chart* is the traditional graph in which each point's coordinates are plotted against the X- and Y-axis, often looking somewhat scattered. For instance, you might plot Advertising Expenses (X coordinate) against the Sales (Y coordinate) to see the effects of advertising on sales. For XY charts you must have two data values for each point that is to be plotted.

3-D AREA CHART

The *3-D area chart* shows a three-dimensional view of an area chart. Rather than stacking multiple data series on top of each other in a normal area chart, this chart style plots them in separate rows in a 3-D area chart. This way you can see differences in the series.

3-D BAR CHART

The *3-D bar chart* provides a three-dimensional look to the bars plotted in a regular bar chart. However, the data series still appear in the same place in the 3-D version.

3-D COLUMN CHART

Access will use the additional axis in a *3-D column chart* to display additional data series. Each series appears in a separate row to help display the differences in the series.

3-D LINE CHART

The *3-D line chart* displays the data series values as three-dimensional ribbons. The data series are somewhat easier to view, especially if they cross.

3-D PIE CHART

The *3-D pie chart* gives a three-dimensional look to the pie slices plotted in a regular pie chart. The pieces in front are emphasized.

3-D SURFACE CHART

The *3-D surface chart* is similar to the 3-D area chart and can resemble a topographical map. It is used to explore complex relationships between sets of data and is common in Asian countries.

Graph Options

The menus in Microsoft Graph offer extensive customization for most of the chart types. You can add *gridlines* to the chart to help the viewer compare the scale tick marks with plotted points. Data series in bar and column charts can appear side by side or can be stacked on top of each other. Bars can be distinct or can overlap. You can remove the normal space between the categories. For line and XY charts you can select lines, markers, or both for plotted points. You can display line chart data in high/low, high/low/close, or open/high/low/close formats, particularly useful for analyzing stock market price data. You can display the Y-axis as a *logarithmic scale* for data series with high variability. You can see graph samples within the Format | Chart Type menu of Graph. We'll cover Graph later in this unit.

Methods of Creating Access Graphs

There are four ways to create a graph in Access. The simplest way is to use the *Graph Wizards*. The procedure is straightforward but you may not end up with quite what you wanted. Although you can make changes to the graph's design, it is usually simpler to start over again and build a new graph with Graph Wizards.

You can also begin with a blank form or report, selecting the graph control from the Toolbox window. After placing this control in the form or report, you then answer questions presented by the Graph Wizard. This method enables you to add a graph to an existing form or report but has the advantage of simplicity because the Graph Wizard does all the work.

The third way is to call the Microsoft Graph program from within Access and build a graph from scratch. This method is not used as often as the previous two, but can be used to modify the graph design of an existing graph. In the latter case, double-clicking on the graph will start the Graph application. We will cover this in a later section of this unit.

There is one more way to place a graph object in Access. You can link to an OLE graph created outside Access such as in Excel, Lotus 1-2-3, or a separate graphing program like CorelDRAW! or Harvard Graphics. This approach is covered in Unit 12 of this book.

Using the Graph Wizards

The easiest way to add a graph to a form or report is to use the Access Graph Wizards. You don't create a separate graph object. Rather, create a form or report with the Wizards, and select Graph as the subtype. Access then will display the appropriate screens and ask you a series of questions about the content of the graph. After answering the questions, you can view the finished graph. If the graph is not quite correct, you can make changes to the graph settings manually, or create a new graph with the Graph Wizards.

We will assume you are creating a form with an embedded graph. The steps are the same with a report. Switch to Form mode and click on New. The next step is to choose the data source for the graph. You may choose a table or query from the list displayed by Access. Then pick the Form Wizard. At the next screen select the Graph Wizard for the type of form.

Then select the fields to graph and those for labels, as shown in Figure 13.1. Remember that only numeric fields can be graphed; you must include at least one number field to go on to the next step. You will next see a screen with images of some graph types. Click on the desired graph type, then go on to the next screen. See Figure 13.2 for the Graph Wizard chart types.

FIGURE 13.1
Field selection list for Graph Wizard

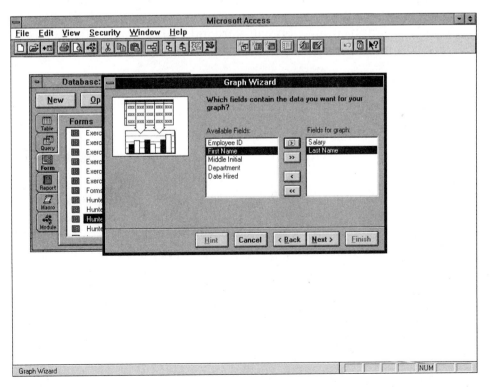

FIGURE 13.2
Graph Wizards chart types

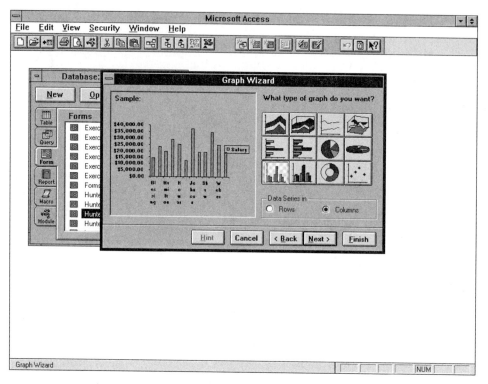

Provide a title for the graph, then click on Finish to view the graph. Access will quickly generate the necessary graph settings and create the graph for you. If you are satisfied with the graph, use the File | Save command and give the form a name. If you are not satisfied with the graph design, switch to Design view. Access will display the graph image for you in Design view. If you double-click on the graph, the Microsoft Graph application will start and you can make changes as needed. Conversely, you can delete the graph and restart with a new form.

GUIDED ACTIVITY 13.1

Adding a Graph with Graph Wizards

In this Guided Activity you will build a form with a graph created by Graph Wizards.

1. Start Windows and load Access. Open the HUNT Database window.

2. Switch to the Form mode and click on the New button.

3. At the next dialog box select the Employees table as the data source and select Form Wizards.

4. Choose Graph from the Form Wizards screen.

5. The Graph Wizard will display a field list and ask you to select fields to be graphed and to appear as legend labels. Select the Last Name field and click the

> button. Select the Salary field and click the > button. See Figure 13.1. Click Next to go to the next step.

CHECKPOINT 13A Why do we need at least two fields for the Graph Wizards?

6. Click Next at the next screen, indicating that you accept the default of adding field values together on the chart.

7. You will see icons representing the types of charts available in Graph Wizards. Select the column chart button as highlighted in Figure 13.2. This is the chart type with vertical bars, shown at the left in the third row of charts. Click Next to go to the next screen.

8. When prompted for the Graph Title, enter `Employee Salary Graph` and click Next to go to the last step. Click the Finish button to see the graph, shown in Figure 13.3. The Salary field is plotted as a vertical bar or column. The X-axis contains the Last Name of the employee receiving that salary.

9. Save the graph with the File I Save command. Use the same name as the title, `Employee Salary Graph`. Close the open window.

Adding a Graph Control to a Report

You can add a graph control to a form or report in the same manner as other Access controls. First open a new form or report, selecting the data source table or query, and choosing Blank Form or Blank Report. Add any other controls as

FIGURE 13.3
Finished Employee Salary Graph

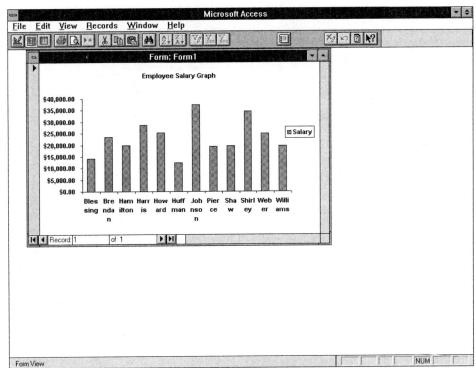

necessary, then click on the graph button in the Toolbox. Use the mouse to open a *graph control* box in the form or report.

At this point the Graph Wizards take over, asking similar questions about the graph. Because you have placed the graph in an existing form or report, Access will ask if you want to link the graph to the other data in the form or report. If you reply affirmatively, you will have an opportunity to specify the link fields, similar to the subform and subreport controls we covered in Part Two of this book. The following example will show how to place a graph in a custom report, along with the data that the graph represents.

GUIDED ACTIVITY 13.2

Adding a Graph Control to a Custom Report

In this Guided Activity we will start by opening a simple custom report, then add a graph control to the report design.

1. Close any open windows and return to the HUNT Database window.

2. Switch to the Report mode and select the 1992 Employee Salary Report. Click on the Design button. The design for this report is shown in Figure 13.4.

3. Use the mouse to pull down the lower border of the Page Footer section to contain the graph. The lower border should be at around 5 inches on the vertical ruler.

4. Click on the graph button in the Toolbox. Use the mouse to create a graph control that fills the entire Page Footer section, starting at the 0,0-inch coordinates.

FIGURE 13.4
Employee Salary Report design without graph control

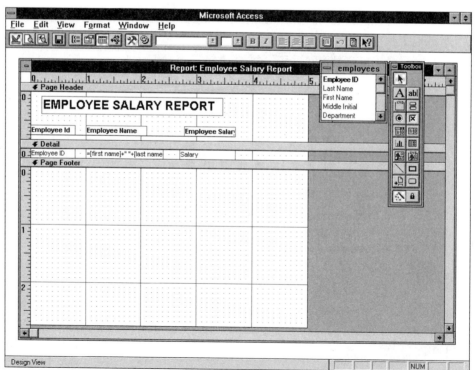

CHECKPOINT 13B Why do you place the graph control in the Page Footer section of the report, and not in the Detail section?

5. After a few seconds, Access will display the opening Graph Wizards screen. In the top portion is a list box that asks for the data source for the graph. Specify the Employees table and click Next.

6. Select the Salary field and click on the > button to add that to the chart. Repeat the process for the Last Name field, then click on Next.

7. In the Link dialog box, click the No button. We will not link this graph to the report records because we are using all of the records in the graph. Click Next again.

8. Click on the column chart type icon in the Graph Wizards screen, then click on Next to go to the next screen.

9. In the next screen enter 1993 Salaries as the graph title. Click the Finish button to return to the report design.

10. Click the Print Preview button in the toolbar to see the report and the graph. Figure 13.5 shows a zoomed-out view of the report with its embedded graph.

11. Use the File | Save As command to save the report as Employee Salary Report with Graph.

FIGURE 13.5
Finished Employee Salary Report with Graph

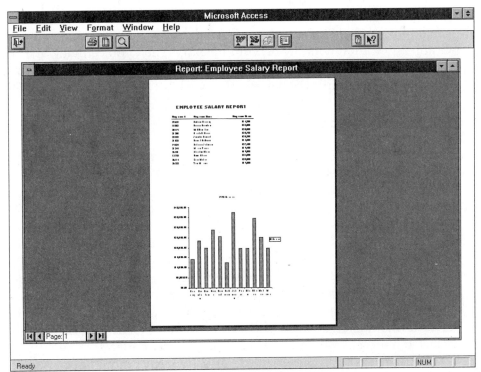

Printing a Graph

You can print the form or report containing the graph as usual, either by issuing the File | Print command or by using the Print Preview button on the toolbar. You may need to experiment with the settings in the Print dialog box to bring out the features of your charts. Remember that most printers can only approximate the full-color shades of your charts when printing in black-and-white gradations.

Importing External Data Into Graph

Microsoft Graph was designed as a separate, general-purpose, Windows graphing application. As a result, it is possible to use data from sources other than Access. You can bring data or a chart directly from a Microsoft Excel spreadsheet or use the File | Import command to use data from other sources. As mentioned previously, you can also type data directly into the datasheet. We will not illustrate this feature here, but you can check on-line Help for more information.

Modifying Graph Settings

When you created a form or report graph with Graph Wizards, Access called up Microsoft Graph in the background to create the settings. To make changes in the graph settings you must use Graph itself. Because Graph is an OLE application, you can double-click on the graph control in Form or Report Design view to bring up the Graph application window on your desktop. Then you can view the current graph settings and make changes as needed. Figure 13.6 shows the Microsoft *Graph window* for the Employee Salary Form we built in the first activity of this unit.

Graph Datasheet Window

In the upper portion of the window is the *graph datasheet*, used by Graph to hold the data values to be plotted. In this case it contains the two columns, Last Name and Salary, that we chose in Graph Wizards. The rows of the graph datasheet represent sample values drawn from records in the Employees table. The Salary values are shown with # symbols, indicating that they are numbers but that the default column width (9) is too narrow to display the currency formatted values, which need 10 characters.

There are three selectable toolbars in the Graph 5.0 window of Figure 13.6. The top one is the Standard toolbar used for making changes to graph and chart settings. The Drawing toolbar is used for drawing lines, arrows, and text. The bottom toolbar is for formatting data values and various parts of chart text. Each toolbar can be selected or deselected with the View | Toolbars command.

You can use the values in the datasheet for the graph, or can type in new ones. It is also possible to import values from other applications using the File menu, discussed earlier in this unit.

FIGURE 13.6
*Graph window
with Employee
Salary Form
Graph*

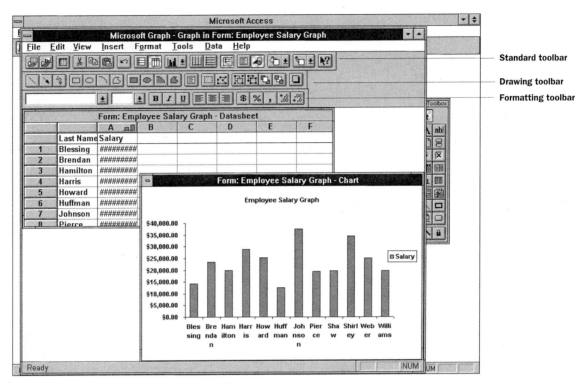

You can move around the datasheet window with the mouse or the arrow keys. The scroll bars let you see cells that are not shown. You can resize the datasheet window as needed to view more of the datasheet. The datasheet in Figure 13.6 has been resized to show the scroll bars.

You may want to select a portion of the datasheet for your graph. You can drag the cursor over the desired cells or use the buttons in the toolbars. To select all the cells in a row or column, click on the row or column selector button at the left or top of the row or column. In most cases you will choose all cells from the datasheet for your graph. If you don't want to use all the data, it is better to use an Access query to limit the records that are to appear in the graph. The *Data menu* lets you specify whether the data to be plotted is in rows or columns of the datasheet. You can also include or exclude portions of the datasheet from this menu.

FORMATTING THE CELLS

Graph will use the field format from the Access table or query as the default for that field in the datasheet. You can reformat selected cells in the datasheet with the Format | Number command or use the bottom toolbar buttons. Cell format affects both the way the values are presented in the chart and the way the scale tick marks appear. You can add dollar signs, insert commas and percent signs, select the number of decimal places, show negative numbers in parentheses, or display numbers in another color. You can create custom formats for numeric and date/time values. Use Graph's on-line Help to view Format menu choices.

Use the Format | Column Width command to change the column width in the datasheet. Remember that Access may require wider columns for large numbers in particular formats. Use the Format I Font command or toolbar buttons to choose the font for text in the datasheet and in the graph. You can select the font, style (bold, italic, underline), and font size with this menu.

Graph Chart Window

In the lower portion of the Graph window shown in Figure 13.6 is the chart resulting from the current graph settings. In this instance the salaries are displayed in a column chart with the employee names shown on the X-axis below the chart. The chart window has been resized and moved to better display both windows. Graph has automatically alphabetized the employee names.

THE FORMAT I CHART TYPE MENU

You can select a new chart type from the *Format menu*. There are 14 basic chart types available, 8 two-dimensional and 6 three-dimensional. Each chart type has multiple "flavors" that are depicted graphically in the Format menu when you select a particular chart type. The 3-D column version of the Employee Salary chart is shown in Figure 13.7. Although the chart appears in full color on the screen (color monitor), this book uses black-and-white shading patterns to approximate its appearance. You can further customize the charts with the Insert menu described next. Changing to a new chart type will cancel any changes made previously, so select the desired chart type first, then make more modifications with the Insert menu.

THE INSERT MENU

In addition to the Format menu choices for chart type, you can modify the chart settings with the *Insert menu*. The Insert I Titles command lets you modify the chart title and titles attached to the axes of the chart. The Insert I Data Labels command is used for placing a data label next to the plotted value of each point. (There are no data labels in Figure 13.6.) The Insert I Legend will remove the legend box from the chart. If there is no legend, the same command will place a legend box in the chart. You can use the pointer to move the legend box to another location on the chart. The Insert I Axes command controls the display of the X-, Y-, and Z-axes in a chart. (All three axes appear in Figure 13.7.) Finally, the Insert I Gridlines command determines whether horizontal or vertical gridlines appear in the chart. (Figure 13.6 uses no gridlines whereas Figure 13.7 displays horizontal gridlines.) Many of the Insert menu choices are also available in the Standard toolbar or by double-clicking on the particular graph component.

Making and Saving Changes in Graph

Microsoft Graph can only be called from a Windows application that is configured to use its objects. Because Graph is an *OLE application*, any graph created by it is *embedded* in the Access database and not saved as a separate file. You can make an unlimited number of graph setting changes while working in Graph. Graph will

FIGURE 13.7

*3-D column
version of
Employee
Salary Graph*

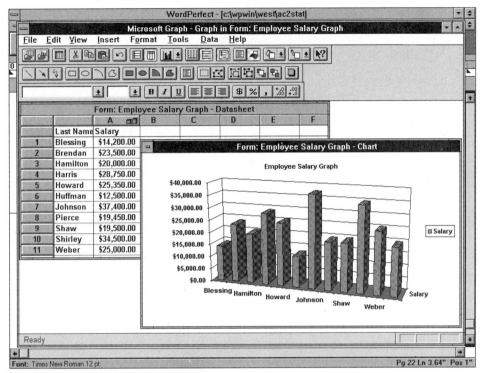

immediately display the new chart. Many users will begin with a Graph Wizards chart, then make embellishments within Graph.

When you have finished work on the graph, use the Exit & Return command from the File menu to return to Access. If you have made changes that have not been updated in Access, you will be asked whether you want to *update* the graph within Access. If you reply affirmatively, those changes become permanent. If you reply negatively, your changes are dropped and the graph will remain in its form prior to your entering Graph. Note that changes made to data values in the Graph datasheet are *not* transferred back to the Access datasheet.

Changes in Underlying Data Values

As with other Access embedded objects, any changes made to the data values in Access will be reflected in the graph the next time it is opened. For instance, if we make a salary change in the Employees table, that change will be reflected in the column chart in the Employee Salary Report.

GUIDED ACTIVITY 13.3

Modifying Graph Settings

In this Guided Activity you will use Microsoft Graph to make changes to a graph created with Graph Wizards.

1. Close any open windows and return to the HUNT Database window.

FIGURE 13.8
*Graph window
for Monthly
Product Sales
form*

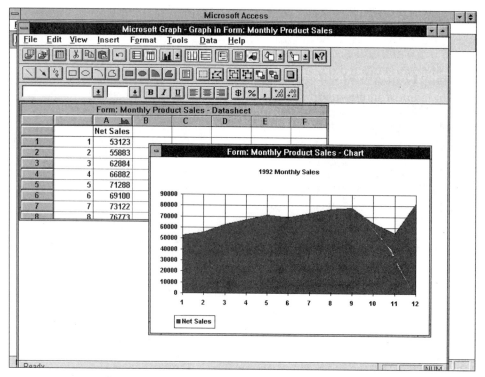

2. Switch to Form mode and select the Monthly Product Sales form, whose graph window is shown in Figure 13.8. Click on the Design View button.

3. While in Design view for this form, double-click on the graph to start Microsoft Graph. After a few seconds, you will see the Microsoft Graph window as shown in Figure 13.8. If the Drawing and Formatting toolbars don't appear, use the View I Toolbars command to turn them on.

4. Notice that the sales amounts in the datasheet and the tick mark labels in the chart are not formatted. Click on the cell in the datasheet above the Net Sales cell to select that column. Issue the Format I Number command and choose the tenth format in the all list: $#,##0_);($#,##0). Click OK.

CHECKPOINT 13C What do the symbols in this format mean?

5. Graph will immediately format the datasheet and change the tick mark labels in the chart. Next we will modify the chart's title. Click on the chart window to make it active, then issue the Insert I Titles command. Choose Category (X) Axis in the Titles dialog box and click OK.

6. Graph will place an X in the box below the X-axis. Type Month and press [Esc]. Graph will replace the title with the word Month. Press [Esc] again to turn off the handles around the title.

7. Click once on the chart title, 1992 Monthly Sales. Then give the Format I Font command. From the Size box choose 14 points, then click OK. Graph will increase the size of the title. Press [Esc] to remove the handles in the title box.

FIGURE 13.9
Modified graph

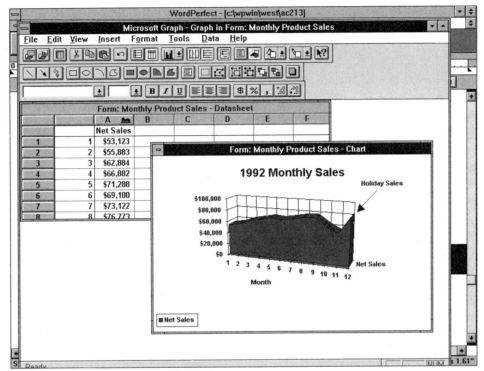

8. Choose the 3-D button from the Format | Chart Type menu. Select the first sample from the dialog box and click OK. Graph will redraw the chart with a three-dimensional effect.

9. Click the Arrow button in the Drawing toolbar to place an arrow in the chart. The cursor will appear as crosshairs. Move the mouse pointer to a point above the chart, then hold down the left mouse button and drag it to the December (Month 12) sales amount.

10. Next, we'll add an annotation to the arrow. Without issuing any other commands, type in the phrase Holiday Sales. Graph will open a window in the center of the chart and place the text in this window. Press [Esc] to close the window.

11. Use the pointer to drag this text window to the end of the arrow. Release the left mouse button, then press [Esc] to remove the handles from the text. Your finished chart should look like Figure 13.9.

12. Choose Exit & Return from the File menu. When you return to Access, you should see the modified graph embedded in the sales form. Close the active form window, saving changes to the form.

CHECKPOINT 13D When you return to Access, any changes made to the chart in Graph are shown on the screen. How can you cancel the changes so that they are not made permanent?

Command Review

Insert	Axes	Display or remove horizontal and vertical axes.
Insert	Data Labels	Display labels with data points.
Insert	Gridlines	Display or remove horizontal and vertical gridlines.
Insert	Titles	Attach text to various portions of the chart.
Data	Series	Indicate which portions of the Graph datasheet are used for the chart.
Format	Chart Type	Choose a chart type from the Graph gallery menu.
Format	Column Width	Change the width of columns in Graph datasheet.
Format	Font	Change the font in Graph datasheet and chart text.
Format	Number	Change the number and date field formats in Graph datasheet and chart tick mark labels.

Exercises

Use the Hunter River database contained within the HUNT.MDB file on the West Student Data Disk for these exercises.

1. Use the Graph Wizards to prepare a graph showing the length of service of each Hunter River employee. You will first have to create a query with a calculated field whose calculation is =Date()-[Date Hired]. You can also use the Access DateDiff( ) function to find the difference between two dates. Use a column chart. Save a copy of the form and print the chart.

2. Prepare a form with a 3-D chart that shows the salary and bonus for the table called Plan I Employees. Your chart should display both salary and bonus as individual data series in three-dimensional form, rather than adding them together. Use appropriate chart text, and print a copy of the form.

3. Prepare a custom report containing the basic data and a pie chart for the following expense data collected by Joleen Branch, the summer accounting intern at Hunter River. The graph control should go in the Page Footer section of the report. Show the percentage (of the total) for each piece of the pie chart. Save and print a copy of the report.

Expense Category	1992 Amount
Salaries	$303,219
Operating Costs	$106,410
Cost of Goods	$445,200
Overhead	$45,331
Taxes	$104,882

Review Questions

1. Choose a chart type for each of the following graphs. Give a brief reason for your choice.

   a. Expense breakdown by category, as a percentage of total expenses

   b. Total sales comparison over the past 48 months

   c. Daily stock price results for the Hunter River common stock

   d. Chart showing 1992 monthly sales of products from top ten vendors

   e. Sales by product category for the last eight quarters

2. Define the following graph terms:

   a. Tick mark

   b. Data series

   c. Value axis

   d. Data labels

   e. 3-D chart

   f. XY chart

3. Explain why it is generally preferable to use the Graph Wizards to prepare a chart in Access.

4. Suppose the chart created by the Graph Wizards is not quite appropriate. Explain your options for making corrections.

5. Discuss the use of the Format menu in Microsoft Graph to change the way values appear. Give examples of the Font and Number commands.

6. Explain how you could place an arrow in a chart to highlight a feature of the chart.

7. If the underlying data values change, will a graph that is embedded in the database automatically reflect those changes? Explain.

Key Terms

3-D chart	Chart type	Doughnut chart
Area chart	Column chart	Embedded
Axis	Data label	Exploding
Axis label	Data marker	Format menu
Bar chart	Data menu	Graph control
Category axis	Data point	Graph datasheet
Chart text	Data series	Graph window
Chart title	Datasheet	Graph Wizards

Gridline	Logarithmic scale	Tick mark
Insert menu	OLE application	Update graph
Legend	Pie chart	Value axis
Line chart	Radar chart	XY chart

Documentation Research

Use the printed documentation and the on-line Help available with Microsoft Access to answer the following questions. If you use one of the manuals, provide the page number for your reference in the manual.

1. Describe how you can combine multiple chart types in a single chart.

2. Explain how you can import data from a Lotus 1-2-3 or Excel worksheet with Microsoft Graph 5.0.

3. Use the on-line Help system to list the types of date formats available in Graph's Format | Number command.

Physicians' Medical Clinic (X): Creating a Report with an Embedded Graph

In this application you will create a report with an embedded graph that displays data from the PMC database, using the material covered in previous units. You will open the PMC database, prepare a group report, and prepare a custom graph. Read the directions carefully. Clearly identify which output goes with which part of the Application.

PMC is preparing to deal with a health insurance program called "managed competition" in which large health care providers must package their services to groups of insured individuals. To help prepare cost estimates, Dr. Greenway has asked you to identify groups of patients by employer and by insurer.

1. Prepare a custom report that shows the total number of patients per Employer and graphs this information in a bar chart on the same page. Include a category for no employer listed.

2. Repeat the first step with the total number of patients per Insurer. Be sure to include a category for no insurer listed.

Introduction to Access Macros

This unit introduces Access macros, in effect miniature program statements you create that save time by automating certain keystrokes and mouse commands. The unit describes how to create a macro, including how to set macro arguments. Several macro examples are given. The unit includes a section on debugging (finding and correcting mistakes in) Access macros.

Learning Objectives

At the completion of this unit you should know

1. why macros are useful in Access,
2. the purpose of macro actions, arguments, conditions, and macro name columns,
3. how to build a macro condition expression,
4. steps in troubleshooting a macro.

At the completion of this unit you should be able to

1. create and run a simple macro,
2. create a macro group,
3. use conditions in a macro,
4. run a macro in single-step mode,
5. use the Action Failed dialog box to debug macro errors.

Important Commands

Edit | Insert Row

Edit | Paste

Edit | Copy

File | Run Macro

File | Save As

Macro | Single Step

Macro | Run

View | Macro Names

View | Macros

View | Conditions

Macro Basics

A *macro* is a list of *actions* or tasks that you want Access to perform that have been saved as a named macro. Access will execute the actions in the order they appear on your list. You can create macros that cause actions to be executed only if certain conditions are true. Once a macro has been created and saved, you can reuse it repeatedly. There is a Macro button in the Database window, just below the Report button. You can select a macro from the macro list, then choose the New, Run, or Design buttons from the window. After describing the advantages of macros, we'll demonstrate how to create a macro.

Advantages of Macros

Macros are efficient—the list of actions, however long, is automatically executed when you run the macro. You don't have to rekey the commands or reissue the mouse commands. In fact, a macro will execute the list of actions much faster than you can do by hand. Needless to say, macros are very accurate. The same commands are executed each time, regardless of the user's experience with Access.

You can place a command button into a form that causes a macro to execute when the button is pushed. That macro can perform some actions, run a query, invoke other macros, print a report, or open another form. The user can choose whether to run the macro from the form.

You can do error checking with a macro, employing more sophisticated rules than are possible with the Validation Rule property of the form or a validation rule attached to a single field in a table. This ensures that the data entered into the form is accurate. You can also use a macro to do special look-ups, setting the value of other fields based upon the values entered into fields on the form. For instance, if a customer order comes into Hunter River from another state, you could use a macro to choose the sales tax rate that is appropriate for that state.

Macros help you automate certain repetitive tasks that are done every time a certain event occurs such as when you close a form or the workday comes to an end. You attach the macro to form properties, as discussed in the next unit.

You can also use a macro to find and filter records in a form. You can attach that macro to a command button so that the user can run the macro at will. You can also transfer data into (import) and out of (export) Access automatically with a macro.

The Macro Window

To switch to Macro mode from the main Database window, click on the Macro button or issue the View | Macros command. The macro icon looks like a scroll on which you could list actions. You will see the list of macros saved in the current database. If there are no macros shown in this window, the Run and Design buttons will be gray. Only the New button can be used at this time.

After switching to the Macro mode, click the New button to create a new macro or click the Design button to modify an existing macro. Access will display the *macro window* shown in Figure 14.1. The first column contains the list of actions in your macro. The second column is used for comments about the macro's actions. The lower section of the Macro window will display the *arguments* for each action. Arguments are similar to properties—they contain additional instructions for carrying out an action. The lower section will be empty if you have not selected any actions for the macro. You can press F6 to move between the top and bottom sections of the macro window.

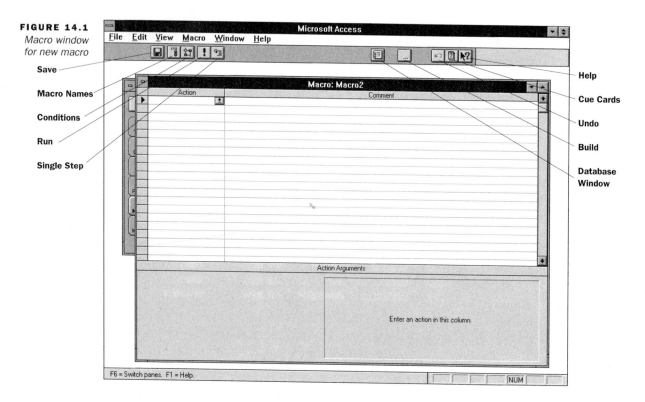

FIGURE 14.1
*Macro window
for new macro*

Save

Macro Names

Conditions

Run

Single Step

Help

Cue Cards

Undo

Build

Database
Window

The *Macro toolbar* accompanying the macro window is shown at the top part of Figure 14.1. You can choose options from this Macro toolbar that open additional columns in the macro window. The Macro Names button lets you assign names to individual macro actions in a macro group. The Conditions button lets you create conditions that determine when a particular group of actions are to be executed. The Run button (exclamation point) will run the macro in the macro window. The Single Step button will cause the macro to run a single line at a time and is used for debugging purposes. We'll discuss the Macro toolbar in more detail later.

Designing a Macro

As with other database procedures, it is helpful to first think through what you want the macro to accomplish. If you go straight to the macro window and start creating your macro, it is easy to overlook some steps and end up with a macro that is more difficult to change. Make a list, on paper, of the desired actions. Leave some blank lines so that you can fill in tasks that you forgot initially. Talk through your steps with a colleague, even speak them out loud if you're alone. Make changes as necessary to fit the situation you are modeling. We will present more about macro design when we get to creating custom applications in Access.

Creating a New Macro

After you click the New button in Macro view in the Database window, Access will open an empty macro window. You can add actions to the new macro in at least two ways: you can select from the action list in the macro window, or drag objects from the Database window to a macro action cell. We'll discuss the first method here.

It is customary to put a blank action in the first cell of the macro and use its comment line to describe the purpose of the macro. Access will ignore the line if there is no action there. You can also use blank actions later in your macro to describe groups of actions that are related.

CHOOSING AN ACTION

The pointer is located in the second cell in the action list of Figure 14.1. If you click on the arrow, the drop-down list of over 45 actions is displayed. Nearly all the commands that you can choose from the menu bar are included in this list, although they may have slightly different names in the macro window. For example, the second entry in the action list is ApplyFilter. This action will apply an Access filter in the same way as the Apply Filter/Sort command from the Records menu in the form window. The Actions: Reference on-line Help screen is shown in Figure 14.2 with the complete list of macro actions. Click on any one for specific help.

SETTING THE ACTION ARGUMENTS

Once you have selected an action for a particular cell, Access displays its arguments in the lower pane of the macro window. You can make entries in the lower

FIGURE 14.2
On-line Help
screen for
Access macro
actions

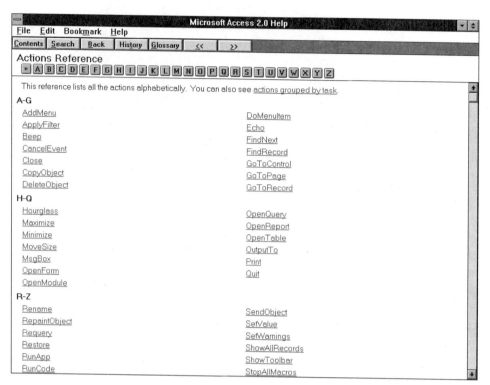

pane to further specify the action. For instance, if you select ApplyFilter as the action, Access shows two action arguments, Filter Name and Where Condition. You must specify the name of the filter in the first argument; it is optional to use the Where Condition argument. If you need help on a particular argument, click once on its line and look at the lower-right portion of the bottom pane for a brief explanation. If you need more assistance, press the [F1] key to invoke the standard Access help system for that argument. Figure 14.3 shows the macro window and the Help screen for the ApplyFilter action at the same time.

You can select arguments from lists that Access presents, or can type them directly in the lower pane. You can also drag database objects to the argument area where appropriate. When you have filled in the arguments for the first action line, move to the second cell and repeat the process of selecting an action and setting its arguments.

If you want to open a form or report, it is easy to drag it from the Database window to the macro window. Rearrange the windows so that both are visible (you can move them manually or use the Tile command from the Window menu). Then switch the Database window to the desired mode and drag the form to the macro window. Access will insert an OpenForm action and automatically fill in the arguments with the name of the form you dragged. If you selected a report, Access will insert an OpenReport action in Print Preview mode. If you drag another macro from the Database window, Access will insert a RunMacro action into the current macro window.

FIGURE 14.3
*Macro window
with Action Help
screen*

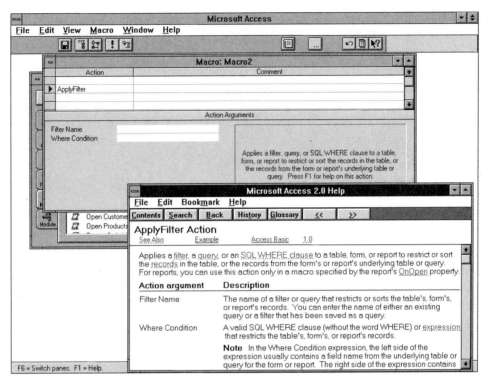

Modifying Your Macro

Creating a macro is somewhat different from other Access activities. In fact, it is more like writing a computer program in which you make small changes and try to run the macro. When it doesn't run, you analyze the problem, make changes accordingly, and try to run it again. This iterative process is normal and should not be a cause of worry. It is rare that your macro will run properly the first time! This section describes how to make changes to the macro in the macro window. A section on troubleshooting macros appears later in this unit.

DELETING, MOVING, AND INSERTING ROWS

If you need to make changes to the macro, Access will let you delete an action or move it to another location. In either case, click the row selector button at the left of the action row. To delete that row permanently, press Del. To move the action to another row, drag it to the desired location and release the left mouse button. To insert a new action row, click on the row selector just below where you want the new row, then use the Edit I Insert Row command.

COPYING ROWS

You can use the Windows Clipboard to copy a single cell, a row, a set of rows, or the entire macro. First you must highlight the text to be copied. In the case of a single row, click the row selector button at the left of the macro window. If you want to select more than one row, hold down the Shift key and click other rows; Access will highlight all the rows you have selected. In the case of a cell, drag the mouse pointer over the text to be copied. Then choose the Copy command from the Edit menu (or use the [Ctrl][C] shortcut command).

Then move the pointer to the macro location where the row(s) are to be copied and click once. Use the Paste command from the Edit menu (or use the [Ctrl][V] short-cut command). Access will insert the contents of the Clipboard in the new location. If you want to copy the Clipboard material into a different macro, open the other macro in the macro window, then use the Edit | Paste command as before.

COPYING THE ENTIRE MACRO

You might want to use a particular macro with more than one database. As with other Access database objects, you can copy or move an entire macro from the Database window. Switch to Macro mode, then highlight the macro you wish to copy. Use the Edit | Copy command (or give the [Ctrl][C] shortcut) to copy the macro to the Clipboard. Then open a different database. Switch to its Macro mode and use the Edit | Paste command to insert the macro from the Clipboard.

Saving the Macro

As with other database objects, use the Save or Save As commands from the File menu to save the macro in the database. Remember that the macro window must be the active window in order for you to see the File | Save command in the menu bar. When choosing a name, use action terms to represent the function of the macro. You must save the macro before you can run it. In fact, if you try to run the macro without saving it, Access will offer to save it for you.

Running the Macro

The method for running the macro depends on where you are in Access. If you are already in the macro window and want to test the current macro, click the Run button in the toolbar or use the Macro | Run command. If you are in the Database window, click the Macro button and select the macro; click the Run button to execute it. If you are in another Access window such as Form, Report, or Query, choose the Run Macro command from the File menu. The macro can run automatically as the result of an event in a form or report, or be attached to a command button in a form. You may want to run the macro in single-step mode for debugging purposes, discussed later in this unit.

GUIDED ACTIVITY 14.1

Creating a Simple Macro

In this Guided Activity you will create and run a simple macro that opens the Customer Entry form.

1. Start Windows and load Access. Open the HUNT database.

2. Switch to Macro mode and click the New button. After a few seconds Access will display the Macro window.

3. Click on the Comment box of the first action line in the top pane. Type `Sample Macro that opens the Customer Entry form.` and press `Enter`. Access will move the pointer to the second action line.

4. Click on the pull-down arrow in the Action column in the second line and scroll down until you see OpenForm. Select this action for the first task.

5. Click once on the Form Name argument. Either type in `Customer Entry-Shadow Style` or choose it from the pull-down list of tables.

CHECKPOINT 14A Is there any other way you could open a form in a macro without picking the Open-Form action from the list? (*Hint*: Use the Database window.)

6. In the comment box for this action, type `Open Customer Entry form,` and press `Enter`. Figure 14.4 shows the macro at this point.

FIGURE 14.4
Sample OpenForm macro

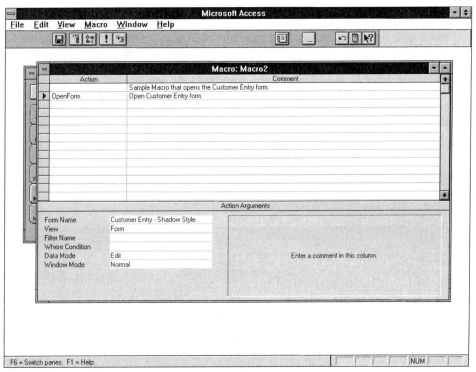

7. Before you can run the macro you must save it. Give the File | Save command and specify `Open Customer Form` as its name.

8. Finally, click the Run button in the toolbar. Access will immediately open the Customer Entry form in Form view and display it on the desktop. Notice that the macro window remains open in the background.

9. You can scroll through the Customer Entry form as usual. Then close the form by double-clicking the Control-menu box or using its File | Close command. You

return to the macro window. We will make a more elaborate macro in the next section. Close the open macro window.

Macro Groups

Some macros can be organized as a ***macro group***, a set of related macros that appear together in the same macro window. When you save the macro group in the database, it appears under the name of the macro group, not the individual macro names within the group. A macro group is useful when you have a group of similar macros for a single form, such as macros attached to command buttons in a menu form. In this example each command button could cause a different form to open or a report to print. These macros would be very similar and can be conveniently combined in a macro group.

Creating a Macro Group

First you must create a new macro. Then click the Macro Names button in the toolbar (or use the View | Macro Names command from the menu bar). Access will open the "Macro Name" column in the macro window, to the left of the Actions column. Next, insert the actions for the first macro as you normally would, setting the arguments and filling in comments as necessary. When you have entered all the actions for the first macro, key its name into the Macro Name column in the first action row. Access will execute the actions in that row and below until it reaches a blank action or a new macro name. You may begin the macro with a blank action and use its comment as a description of the macro.

Go on to insert the actions for the second macro in the group, filling in the Macro Name column with the name of the second macro. Continue this process until all of the actions for each macro in the group have been created and labeled with the correct names. Then use the File | Save command to save the macro group under a single name.

Using a Macro from a Macro Group

Whenever you want to refer to a particular macro within a macro group, use `macrogroupname.macroname` instead. Thus, to refer to the macro named Open Customer Form within the Main Switchboard macro, use the name `Main Switchboard.Open Customer Form`. Otherwise, macros in a macro group are used the same way as an individual macro saved under its own name.

GUIDED ACTIVITY 14.2 ✕

Creating a Macro Group

In this Guided Activity you will create a simple macro group that illustrates how the individual macros work. This is not intended to be an example of a complex macro.

1. Close any open windows and return to the HUNT Database window.

2. Switch to Macro mode and click the New button to open the macro window.

3. Click the Macro Names button in the toolbar, or choose the Macro Names command from the View menu. Access will display the Macro Name column in the macro window.

4. Leave the first action blank, but click once in its Comment cell. Enter the comment `This is a sample macro group.`

5. In the Macro Name column of the second line, key in `First`. In the Comment column for that line enter `This is the first macro in the macro group.`

6. In the next line, click once in the Action cell. Click on the pull-down arrow and select MsgBox from the list of actions. This action will display a Windows message box with your own message text and title bar. You can choose whether to have the computer beep, and can set the relative importance of the information with the Type argument. The next step shows how to fill in those arguments.

7. Press `F6` to move to the lower pane of the macro window. Fill in the following values for the arguments. You can choose the Beep and Type from the pull-down list if desired.

Message `This is the First macro executing`
Beep   `Yes`
Type   `Information`
Title   `Your Custom Message Here`

8. Press `F6` to return to the top pane. Key this into the Comments cell for the same action line: `Display the custom message box with the first message.`

9. Skip one action line and click on the fifth line in the Macro Name cell. Key in `Second` and press `Enter`.

10. In the Action cell type in `MsgBox` or select it from the pull-down list.

11. Press `F6` to move to the lower pane. Fill in the following values for the arguments. You can choose the Beep and Type from the pull-down list if desired.

Message `This is an example of a much longer message that is wider than the width of the box. You can use Shift F2 to open a Zoom box if desired. Access will automatically widen the message box in order to display as much of your message as possible.`
Beep   `No`
Type   `Warning!`
Title   `Title Space is Relatively Short`

CHECKPOINT 14B What are the choices for the message Type argument?

12. Press `F6` to return to the top pane. Type this into the Comment cell of this action line: `Display the custom message box with the second message.`

FIGURE 14.5
Sample macro group

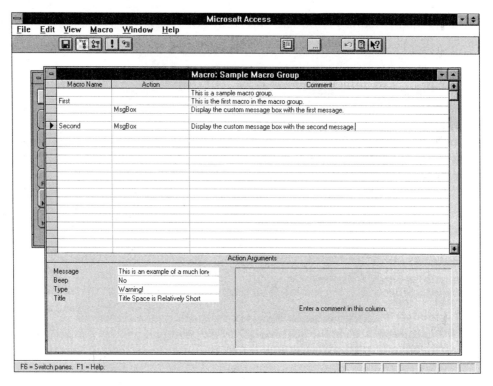

13. ✖ Use the File I Save command to save this macro group with the name Sample Macro Group. Figure 14.5 shows the macro window for this activity.

14. ✖ Because this macro group contains individually named macros, use the File I Run Macro command to run the macro rather than the Run button in the toolbar. When prompted for the name in the Run Macro dialog box, key in Sample Macro Group.First and press Enter. You should see the message box shown in Figure 14.6. The "i" symbol indicates that this is an information message type. Select OK.

FIGURE 14.6
Message box for first macro

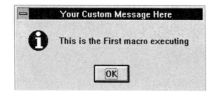

15. Repeat step 14. with the other macro named Sample Macro Group.Second. You should see the message box shown in Figure 14.7. Notice that the "!" exclamation mark warning icon displayed next to the message indicates a higher sense of seriousness for the message. Select OK.

Conditional Macros

Access provides a means of testing conditions in macros using *conditions*, expressions that can be evaluated as True or False. The *conditional expression* goes in the

FIGURE 14.7
*Message box
for second
macro*

Condition column. If the condition on a particular action line is True, Access will execute that action. If the condition is False, Access will not execute that action. If the next line's Condition contains an *ellipsis* (…), Access will apply the same condition as the previous line. In other words, you can conditionally execute a sequence of actions by placing the condition in the first line of the sequence, then writing the ellipsis in each line thereafter that you want to have executed if that first condition is true.

Types of Macro Conditions

In general, you would associate conditional execution of a macro step with control values in the Access object selected. For instance, if the user left blank a particular form control that must be answered, you can have a macro display a message box that instructs the user to make an entry. You can display a message box for one kind of entry and another message box for different entries. You might have a sales tax form that is called up only if the customer is taxable. You can check the number of detail lines used in a form and perform some new-screen actions if that number exceeds a certain count.

Using Control Names in Condition Expressions

Access condition expressions were introduced in Unit 4 of this textbook. Sample expressions with explanations are included in this section. Remember that Access uses the following syntax to refer to control names from forms and reports:

```
Forms!formname!controlname
Reports!reportname!controlname
```

As usual, if any of your names has a space in it, you must enclose the name in square brackets. For a macro to make use of a control from a form or report, that form or report must already be open. The macro can open the form itself, or can test whether it is already open with a macro condition and open it if it is not.

Condition	Explanation
`Forms!Customers!State="IN"`	If the value in the State field in the Customers form is equal to IN…
`[Date of Last Order]<"1/1/95"`	If the Date of Last Order control value on the form from which the macro was run was prior to January 1, 1995…

`Forms!Products!Category ="Camping" AND Forms!Products!Vendor ="Icicle"`	If the value of the Category control in the Products form is Camping and the Vendor control from the same form is Icicle…
`COUNT([Line Number])>=12`	If the total number of entries in the Line Number field on the form from which the macro was run is at least 12…
`[Last Name] Is Null`	If the Last Name field is blank…
`IsLoaded("Customers")`	If the Customers form is already open on the desktop…

The last condition uses a ***user-defined function*** called IsLoaded to determine whether the Customers form is already open in Access. This function was written in Access Basic by Microsoft and is included in the NWIND.MDB sample database packaged with Access. It is included in the HUNT.MDB database on the West Student Data Disk in the module called Module1, and can be copied to your own database via the Clipboard.

GUIDED ACTIVITY 14.3

Creating a Conditional Macro

In this Guided Activity you will create a simple conditional macro that tests to see whether a form has already been opened and displays a message accordingly.

1. Close any open windows and return to the HUNT Database window. If you are not already in Macro mode, click the Macro button.

2. Click the New button to create a new macro.

3. Click the Conditions button in the toolbar, or use the View | Conditions command from the menu bar. Access should open a new column to the left of the Action column.

4. Leave the first action empty, but type in its Comment cell: `Sample macro that uses conditions to check for open forms`.

5. In the second row choose OpenForm as the action. The Form Name argument is `Customers`. Leave the defaults for the other arguments. The Comment for this action is `Open the Customers Form`.

6. Click in the Condition cell of the third line and type: `IsLoaded("Customers")`. Press Enter to complete the entry. Remember to enclose the form name in quotes and to spell the name correctly.

7. In the action cell of the third line select MsgBox as the action. The Message argument should be `Customer is open`. Leave the defaults for the other arguments for this action.

8. The comment for the third line is `If the Customers form is open display Open message.`

9. In the fourth line type an ellipsis (…) into the condition cell, indicating that this action is only to be executed if the previous line's condition is true. The action for this line is Close. The arguments for this action are as follows: Object Type is `Form` and Object Name is `Customers`. The comment for this line is `Close the Customers form.`

10. In the fifth line enter this condition: `Not IsLoaded("Customers")`.

CHECKPOINT 14C   What is the exact meaning of this condition?

11. In the action cell choose MsgBox. In this case the Message argument is `Customer is NOT loaded now`. The comment should be `If the Customers form is not open display Closed message.`

12. Click on the row selector button in the third row. Access will highlight the entire row. Choose the Copy command from the Edit menu. This will copy this row to the Clipboard.

13. Click once on the next empty row. Choose the Paste command from the Edit menu. This will copy the contents of the Clipboard into this new row. We need to make some editing changes in this row.

14. Change `Customers` to `Products` in the condition cell. The easiest way to do this is to drag the mouse pointer across the Customers text, highlighting all of it. Then type `Products` and Access will replace the highlighted text with the new text.

15. Click once on the MsgBox action of this line. In the lower pane change `Customer` to `Product` in the Message argument. The finished macro window is shown in Figure 14.8.

16. Save your macro with the File|Save command. Use the name `Sample Condition Macro`.

17. To run your macro, click the Run button in the toolbar. Access will open the Customers form, then display the message box confirming that it is open. When you click OK in the message box, Access will close the form. Then you should get another message stating that the Customer form is not open. Click on OK and then close the active window.

CHECKPOINT 14D   Will you get a message box corresponding to the last action in the macro?

Debugging the Macro

We use the term *debug* to describe the process of testing and removing errors ("bugs") from the computer program, in this case a macro. As mentioned earlier in this unit, writing a successful macro (program) is an iterative process. You rarely create a macro that works properly the first few times you run it. In fact, we recommend

FIGURE 14.8
Sample conditional macro

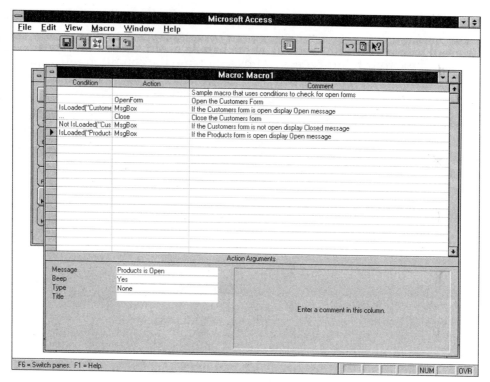

that new Access programmers build complicated macros in pieces. That is, work on a small portion of it at first until it is correct. Then add more actions in small groups, rather than all at once. Experienced programmers may be able to work with larger groups of actions.

Single-Step Mode

Access provides several built-in debugging tools that help you find errors. Perhaps the most useful of these is *single-step mode*. In this mode Access will execute your macro just one action at a time. You have a chance to examine the results after each step. You can use the mouse to switch between Access windows on the desktop, picking up clues about what the macro did (or did not) do on the last step. Access will display the next action to be taken in the macro. You can continue in single-step mode or switch to full speed.

To run your macro in single-step mode, click the Single Step button in the toolbar. Or give the Macro | Single Step command from the menu bar. In either case, next click the Run button. Access will display the Macro Single Step dialog box shown in Figure 14.9. The box shows the macro name, condition, action name, and some of the arguments for the next action. You have three button choices: Step, Halt, and Continue. Step will run the action in the dialog box, Halt will stop the macro, and Continue will run the rest of the macro at normal speed. Note that with any method of turning on single-step mode, Access will remain in single-step mode until you switch it back to run mode.

It is possible to insert actions into the macro that cause it to run at full speed for a portion, then switch to single-step mode, then back to full speed. You can use this

FIGURE 14.9

The Macro Single Step dialog box

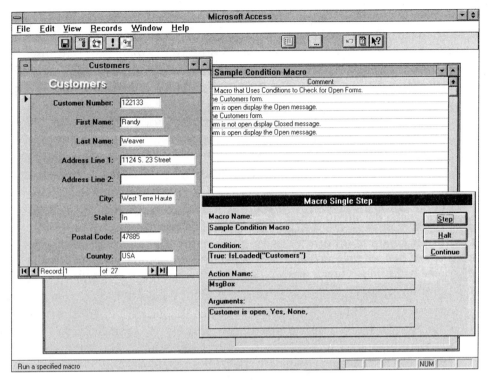

method to check parts of the macro that are not working properly, then to speed past the parts that are working well. The next section will explain how to do this.

You can also switch a macro to single-step mode while it is running by pressing Ctrl Break. This will cause Access to display the Macro Single Step dialog box. You can stop the macro by clicking Halt.

Entering Access Menu Bar Commands in Macros

Nearly all of the menu bar commands are available with the DoMenuItem action, including the Macro | Run and Macro | Single Step commands. The arguments for this action are shown below with an explanation of each one. Remember that you cannot choose a particular menu bar unless a view of that type is active. In other words, you cannot be in Design mode to use the Records menu.

Argument	*Explanation*
Menu Bar	Name of the menu bar window
Menu Name	Name of the drop-down menu from the specified menu bar (this is the word that appears in the menu bar itself)
Command	Command from the drop-down list that you want to execute
Subcommand	Subcommand that you want to execute, if the command has a subcommand; generally indicated by an ellipsis (...) after command name

Thus, to switch to single-step mode inside the macro, insert a blank row and choose the DoMenuItem action. The Menu Bar argument would be Macro, and the Menu Name is Macro. To single step through the macro, the Command argument would be Single Step; to go back to full speed, the Command argument would be Run. The macro will run at the indicated speed until you change the speed with another action or change it manually.

If your DoMenuItem action causes a dialog box to appear, the user can choose a command button from the dialog box. If you want the macro to send something to Access such as choosing a command button in the dialog box, use the SendKeys action in the macro. For more information on this action, search on-line Help.

The Action Failed Dialog Box

Another important debugging tool is the *Action Failed dialog box*. An error box appears when Access detects an error in your macro. When you click OK, the Action Failed dialog box appears, showing the action and its arguments that caused the error. The only user choice available in this box is Halt, equivalent to stopping the macro. You can study the Action Failed dialog box for clues about why the macro failed to run without error. Remember that a single action may work correctly in one place in the macro and incorrectly in another place, often the result of having the wrong Access object active.

Talking Through the Macro

Our experience in other computer languages shows that you can often find your mistakes simply by talking through the macro steps with someone else. By forcing yourself to explain each line, you often see problems before they are pinpointed. The process of speaking the steps out loud may also help you understand a complicated sequence of actions. Don't hesitate to try this. You may even discover features that were omitted from the macro or implemented clumsily. This is one important reason why most programming today is done in teams!

GUIDED ACTIVITY 14.4

Single Stepping Through a Macro

In this Guided Activity you will use single-step mode to work through the previous macro and explore the Action Failed dialog box.

1. Return to the HUNT Database window and select Macro mode.

2. Select the Sample Condition Macro from the previous activity and click the Design button.

3. Click the Single Step button in the toolbar or use the Macro | Single Step command from the menu bar.

4. Then click the Run button or use the Macro | Run command from the menu bar.

5. ↑Access will run the macro and present the Macro Single Step dialog box. Click Step several times until you see the box shown in Figure 14.9, representing the next action to be executed.

CHECKPOINT 14E What information about the macro is displayed in the dialog box of Figure 14.9?

6. ↑Halt the macro, and be sure that the Single Step button is *not* pushed in. Click the Run button in the toolbar and wait until you see the first message box that requires a user response.

7. ↑Instead of clicking OK, press Ctrl Break to turn on single-step mode manually. Step through the next action of this macro, then Halt the macro.

8. ↑Next we will modify the macro. Click on the next open action line and select the DoMenuItem action. Its Menu Bar and Menu Name arguments are Macro. Its Command argument is Single Step. The comment for this action is Enable single-step mode with DoMenuItem action.

9. ↑Add one more action line beneath the DoMenuItem line. Its action is OpenForm and the Form Name argument is Access. Its comment is Open a missing form!

10. Use the File|Save As command to save this macro under the new name of Single Step Macro.

11. Make sure that the Single Step button is not pushed in and click the Run button. Access will run at full speed until it reaches the DoMenuItem action, which places it in single-step mode. Click the Step button to execute the last line of the macro.

FIGURE 14.10
The Action Failed dialog box

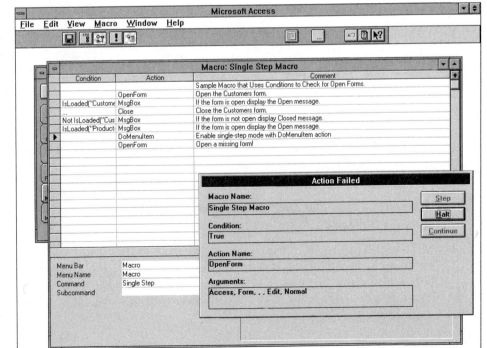

12. When Access tries to open the nonexisting form named Access, it will display an error message. Click OK, and you will see the Action Failed dialog box of Figure 14.10.

13. After examining the contents of this dialog box, click Halt to end the macro and close the macro window.

Command Review

Edit I Insert Row	Insert a new row in the macro window above the selected row.
Edit I Paste	Copy the contents of the Clipboard into the selected object. (Ctrl V)
Edit I Copy	Copy the selected item(s) into the Windows Clipboard. (Ctrl C)
File I Run Macro	Run the macro specified by the user.
File I Save As	Save the contents of the macro window under the new name provided.
Macro I Single Step	Switch to macro execution single-step mode; does not run macro.
Macro I Run	Run macro in macro window.
View I Macro Names	Open Macro Name column in macro window for a group macro.
View I Macros	Switch to Macro mode from Database window.
View I Conditions	Open Condition column in macro window.

Exercises

Use the Hunter River database contained within the HUNT.MDB file on the West Student Data Disk for these exercises.

1. Create a simple macro that opens the Employees form, displays a message box that states a message that the Employees form is open, then closes the form. Be sure to print a copy of the macro. Save it under the name `Open Employees`.

2. Modify the macro from the previous exercise so that it tests whether the Employees form is already open before opening the form. Print a message that is appropriate if the form is already open. Save this macro as `Open Employees2`. When you test your macro, be sure to test it both with the Employees open and not open prior to executing the macro.

3. Create a macro that opens the Inventory Group Report in Print Preview mode. Your macro should display a message box that explains the options available to the user in Print Preview mode. Don't worry about trying to actually print the report. (*Hint:* Don't use the Print action for this macro.) Save this macro under the name `Preview Inventory Report`.

4. Create a simple macro group in which the First macro contains a MsgBox action that gives the name of that macro. Use the Edit | Copy command to copy that macro to the Clipboard, then paste it into the macro group at a lower position. Change the macro name to Second and modify the message box accordingly. Repeat the process with the Third macro. Print a copy of your macro before running it with the File | Run Macro command. Save the macro group with a name of your choice.

Review Questions

1. Define the following macro terms:
   a. Action
   b. Argument
   c. Comment
   d. Condition

2. What are the advantages of using macros in Access?

3. Discuss the procedure of creating a new macro, including the design portion.

4. Suppose you have a terrific macro that you would like to incorporate in another database. Explain ways that you might copy the macro to the new database.

5. Discuss reasons for using a single macro group instead of using separate individual macros. Are there any disadvantages in using the macro group? Explain.

6. Give the use of the following actions. Include a brief discussion of arguments for each action.
   a. OpenForm
   b. MsgBox
   c. Close
   d. ApplyFilter

7. Discuss the reasons for using different types of messages in a MsgBox action. Give an example of each type of message.

8. Explain the process of debugging or troubleshooting a macro, including "talking through" the macro with a colleague.

9. Give the precise definition of each of the following macro conditions:

   a. `Forms!Products!Category="Camping"`

   b. `Not IsLoaded("Employee Salaries")`

   c. `Category="Sports" AND [Date of Last Order]<"1/1/95"`

   d. `Forms!Customer!State In("IN","IL","MI")`

   e. `[Customer Number] Is Null`

10. Explain the information displayed in the Single Step and Action Failed dialog boxes. What user responses are possible with these boxes?

Key Terms

Action	Debug	Macro window
Action Failed dialog box	Ellipsis (…)	Single-step mode
Argument	Macro	User-defined function
Condition	Macro group	
Conditional expression	Macro toolbar	

Documentation Research

Use the printed documentation and the on-line Help available with Microsoft Access to answer the following questions. If you use one of the manuals, provide the page number for your reference in the manual.

1. Use the Access on-line Help system to look up the Actions: Reference screen. Define the following macro actions using that help screen:

   a. GoToControl

   b. MoveSize

   c. Print

   d. SendKeys

   e. SetValue

2. Use the Cue Cards in Access to learn more about macros. Describe the opening example used to introduce macros in Cue Cards.

3. Look up the FindRecord action in the on-line Help and describe all of its arguments.

Advanced Access Macros

This unit extends the basic coverage of Access macros from the previous unit by showing how macros can be used to expedite operations on forms and reports. Macros are attached to command buttons and form properties to automate certain activities. More macro actions are illustrated in the activities. Several macro examples are given, including the creation of an Access macro that executes automatically when the database is opened.

Learning Objectives

At the completion of this unit you should know

1. the arguments associated with the OpenForm action,
2. what events can occur when you use a form,
3. the advantages of attaching macros to properties of forms and controls,
4. the steps in creating and using switchboard forms.

At the completion of this unit you should be able to

1. create a macro that opens a form and positions its window at the correct location,
2. attach a macro to a command button on a form,
3. attach a macro to a property of a form or a control,
4. create an alphabetical look-up macro,
5. print a form or report with a macro,
6. create an auto-execute macro for a database.

Important Commands

Macro | Run

View | Conditions

View | Macro Names

View | Properties

Using Macros with Forms

The most common use for macros is with Access forms. You can use macros in a form menu in which several command buttons are displayed. Clicking the command button runs a macro that opens another form. You can respond to events on forms such as opening the form, moving from one record to another, changing data in a record, deleting a record, and so on. You can synchronize two forms in separate windows by using macros. You can use a macro to set values of controls in forms. You can even print forms with a macro. This section will illustrate many of these macro applications.

Using a Macro to Open a Form

We learned in the last unit that the OpenForm action will open an Access form. We want to create a macro that opens a form and, optionally, changes its size and location. We can also attach this macro to a command button so that pushing that button will cause the macro to run.

OPENING A FORM

The *OpenForm* action causes Access to open the specified form. Its arguments control the Form Name, the View for the form (Form, Design, Print Preview, or Datasheet), and the Filter Name or a Where Condition that restrict the records to appear in the form. You can set arguments for Data Mode (Edit, Add, or Read Only) and Window Mode (Normal, Hidden, Icon, or Dialog). Edit Data Mode permits the user to make changes to existing records. Add Data Mode allows the user to add new records and make changes to existing records. With Read Only Data Mode the user can view the data but cannot make any changes. Hidden Window Mode makes the form invisible when opened on the desktop, and Icon Window Mode opens the form as an icon at the bottom of the screen. Default values for each argument are listed first within each group.

There are two ways to add the OpenForm action to a macro. In the last unit we selected that action from the drop-down list and filled in the arguments as appropriate. In this unit we will show how you can drag the form you want to open from the Database window and place it in the macro. Access will automatically add the Open-Form action and place the appropriate values into the arguments. You can make changes to those settings manually if necessary. This method of dragging a database object to the macro window saves time, especially when you are adding a large number of forms and reports to the macro. It can also reduce errors because you are dragging an existing object instead of typing its name in the argument pane. Of course, if you drag the wrong object it will make the macro incorrect.

MOVING AND SIZING THE FORM

The *MoveSize* action permits the macro to move and/or resize the active window. You may want to place several forms on the same screen to make room for other Access data objects. MoveSize can be used in Form, Design, and Datasheet views.

MoveSize has four arguments. The Right and Down arguments control the position of the upper-left corner of the window, measured in inches from the left and top edges of the window that contains the active window. If you leave these blank, Access uses the window's current settings. The Width and Height arguments specify the dimensions (in inches) of the active box. You can set the default measurement unit to inches or centimeters in the Windows Control Panel.

If you leave the Width and Height arguments blank but change the Right and Down arguments, Access will move the window but leave it in its current size. If you give values for Width and Height but leave the Right and Down arguments blank, Access will resize the window in its current location.

MINIMIZING, MAXIMIZING, AND RESTORING WINDOWS IN A MACRO

The *Minimize* and *Maximize* actions will minimize or maximize the active window, similar to clicking those respective buttons in the upper-right corner of the window. They have no arguments. The *Restore* action will restore a maximized or minimized window to its former size. It has no arguments.

GUIDED ACTIVITY 15.1

Creating a Macro to Open a Form

In this Guided Activity you will create a macro that opens a form and changes its size and position.

1. Start Windows and load Access. Open the HUNT database.

2. Switch to Macro mode and click the New button to create a new macro.

3. In the first line key in `Opens the Customers form and resizes window` in the first Comment line.

4. Press [F11] or click the Database button to display the HUNT Database window at the side of the macro window. Adjust the window positions as necessary to view both at the same time. Click on the Form button in the Database window and locate the Customers form.

5. Drag the Customers form to the action cell in the second line of the macro window. Access will create an OpenForm action and assign Customers to the Form Name argument. Use the defaults for all arguments except the Data mode, which should be Read Only. The comment is Open form.

CHECKPOINT 15A What does the "Read Only" setting for the Data Mode argument mean for the person using the form through this macro?

6. In the third line choose the MsgBox action. Use the default values for its arguments—we will use the box here to pause the macro until you click its OK button. The comment is Pause macro.

7. In the fourth line choose the MoveSize action. In the Right argument enter 3 and for the Down argument enter 1. Leave the Width and Height arguments blank. The comment is Move form.

8. Use the File | Save command to save this macro as `Open Customers`.

9. Make sure the Single Step button is not depressed. Click the Run button in the toolbar or choose Run from the Macro menu. Access will open the form in the normal, upper-left corner position on the desktop.

10. Then Access will display the message box. Click OK and watch where the Customers form moves as the MoveSize action is executed. Close the Customers form active window.

11. Next, copy the actions from steps 6 and 7 as the fifth and sixth lines of the macro.

TIP *You can copy these two actions by using the Windows Clipboard. First select both lines 3 and 4 by dragging on their row selector buttons. Then press the right mouse button to bring up the QuickMenu, and choose Copy. Then click on the fifth line, press the right mouse button, and choose Paste.*

12. The line 6 MoveSize action should leave the Right and Down arguments blank, but use 4 and 2, respectively, for the Width and Height arguments. Its comment line is Resize form.

13. Click the Run button (or choose Run from the Macro menu) and click OK to confirm that you want to save the macro before running it. Watch what happens to the form as the macro executes. The final position of the form, along with the macro itself, is shown in Figure 15.1. Note that your desktop may not look just like this one, particularly if you are running Windows at 640×480 video resolution. To access the portion of the form that does not appear, you must use the scroll bars in the form window.

14. Close the Customers form window and the open macro window.

Using a Command Button to Run a Macro

You can run the macro from the previous activity from the Database window, or directly from the macro window. But as you create custom applications with macros, it sometimes makes sense to attach a macro to a command button in a form. That

FIGURE 15.1
*Macro window
with open form
after move and
resize*

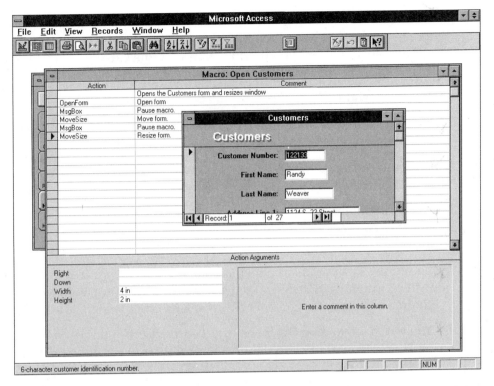

way, whenever the button is pushed, the macro attached to it will run. Thus, the user can determine when the macro executes.

To create a command button that opens a form, first create the macro that opens the form and positions it at the desired location. We did this much in the previous guided activity. Save this macro. Then open the form that will contain the command button in Design view. Remember, you must add the command button to a different form than the one your macro opens. Drag the macro from the Database window to the form in the desired location for the command button. Access will automatically create a command button control and attach the macro to its On Click property. The button will have the name of the macro as its caption. When you open the form in Form view and click the command button, the macro will run and the other form is opened. The following activity will illustrate this procedure.

GUIDED ACTIVITY 15.2

Creating a Command Button that Opens a Form

In this Guided Activity you will create and save a short macro that opens a form, then attach it to a command button in another form.

1. Close any open windows and return to the HUNT Database window.

2. Switch to Macro mode and click the New button to create a new macro.

3. Position the Database window so that it is next to the macro window.

4. Click the Form button in the Database window and locate the Customers form. Drag it to the first line of the macro window and release the left mouse button. Access will create an OpenForm action with the Customers form name.

5. Add a MoveSize action with blank values for the Width and Height arguments. Make the Right argument 3 and the Down argument 1.5.

6. Use the File | Save command to save this macro as Review Customers. Close the macro window.

7. With the Database window still in Form mode, locate the Review Data form. Click the Design button.

8. Click the Database button to display the Database window; adjust its position so that you can see both it and the form window. Click the Macro button in the Database window to switch to Macro mode.

9. Locate the Review Customers macro. Drag it to the form, placing it at the 2,.5-inch coordinates in the grid. Release the mouse button and Access will create a command button to which the Review Customers macro is attached.

10. You will have to drag the lower-right corner of the control to the 3.5-inch mark on the horizontal ruler so that the control is large enough to display its full caption.

CHECKPOINT 15B Is there any other way to adjust the size of the command button to display the full title text?

11. Click the Form button in the toolbar. Access will display the new form with the command button. Click the Review Customers command button to run the macro attached to that button. Figure 15.2 shows the Review Data form with the Customers form open in the right portion of the desktop. Close the Customers form and the Review Data form without saving changes to the form.

Responding to Events on Forms

Access can react to certain things that occur when you use a form, called *events*. You can use a macro to respond to these events when they occur. Events include such things as opening the form, moving from one record to another, double-clicking a control on the form, changing data in a record, and so forth. Typically, the event is described by a property of the form or a property of the controls in a form. A complete list of the events and associated properties is contained in Chapter 25 of the Microsoft Access *User's Guide*. You can also search Access on-line Help for additional help about these properties. A subset is described in this section.

FORM EVENTS These events describe activities that pertain to the entire form. You can attach macros to properties of the form. They apply to both the form and all its controls.

OPENING A FORM The property for this event is called On Open, and it refers to the process when the form is first opened but before the first record is displayed. You could use this event to run a macro that closes another form that is already open.

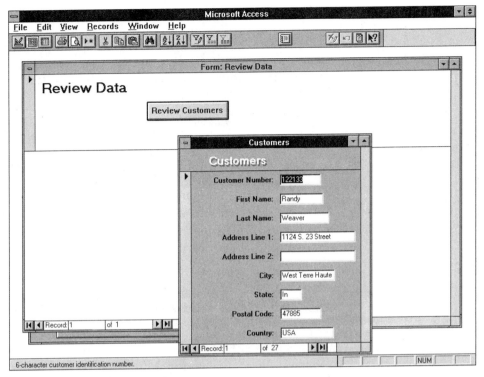

MAKING A RECORD THE CURRENT RECORD The property for this event is called On Current. You could use this to move the focus to a particular control in the form just before the record becomes current.

CHANGING DATA IN A RECORD The properties for this event are called Before Update and After Update. Access will save the changes made to a record after you move out of the record. The time just before the update is performed is called Before Update; the time just after the update is made is called After Update. You can use the Before Update property to run a macro that validates the data just entered before it is saved. That macro can cause other actions to occur if the data prove to be invalid, such as displaying a message box or resetting the value of the control. After the update is performed, you could use a macro to make changes in another form or table that uses the values just changed. This could be a log entry signifying that a change was made to a record in the table.

DELETING A RECORD The On Delete property describes the macro that should be run just before the record is actually deleted from the database. You might display a message box asking the user to confirm that the record is to be deleted, or you might use a macro to make an entry in a transaction log that records the deletion action as well as some user identification and the time.

CLOSING A FORM The On Close property is used to specify what actions are to take place after you have closed the form but before it disappears from the screen. You might make a log entry as to who used the form.

CONTROL EVENTS

These events refer to specific controls. The macro must be attached to properties of an individual control in order for that macro to run. Some control properties are very similar to those used for the form.

SELECTING A CONTROL   The On Enter property refers to the process when you have moved to a control and just before it has the focus. You might use a macro with the property to display instructions for that control. Of course, each control would need different instructions. You might also make the instructions optional by supplying a command button to run the macro instead of automatically running it whenever the control is selected.

CHANGING DATA IN A CONTROL   The Before Update and After Update control properties exist for individual controls as well as for the form as a whole. You can do validation for a specific control when these events occur, or do it for the entire record at once with the earlier events.

DOUBLE-CLICKING A CONTROL   The On Double Click property can be used to start a macro when you double-click a particular control. You could use this event to open another form that displays additional information.

PUSHING A COMMAND BUTTON   Described in the previous section, the On Click property can be used to run a macro whenever a command button control is pushed on the form. This is appropriate for optional user choices.

LEAVING A CONTROL   The On Exit property is used to run a macro when you are leaving a control. You might use this property to run a macro that changes the tab order of the form. This property is less frequently used.

ATTACHING A MACRO TO A PROPERTY IN A FORM

First create and save the macro you want to attach to a form property. Then open the form in Design view. Display the property sheet by clicking the Properties button in the toolbar or by using the View | Properties command from the menu bar. Click the form background to select the form. If you are changing the properties of a specific control, click on that control to select it. The property sheet for the form or control should be open on the desktop. Click once on the On Click property line and select the name of the macro to attach to that property. If the macro is part of a macro group, type in the name of the macro group first, followed by a period, then the individual macro name. Figure 15.3 shows the property sheet for a command button control.

Using a Macro to Synchronize Two Forms

We showed how to synchronize a main form and its subform in a previous unit. When you move to a different record in the main form, Access automatically moves the record pointer in the subform to the matching record. We used common field values in the Link Child Fields and Link Master Fields properties to synchronize the

FIGURE 15.3
*Property sheet
for command
button control*

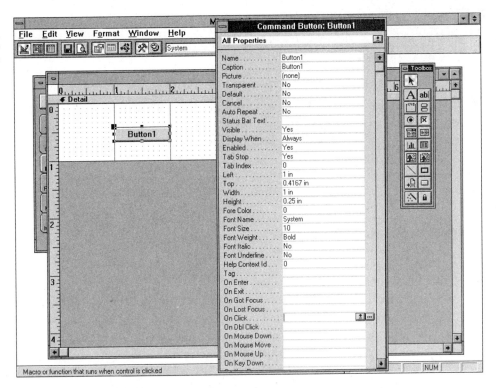

main form and subform within one form window. You do not need a macro to keep the main form and subform synchronized.

There are advantages in using two separate form windows, rather than a single main/subform design. For instance, you might have two separate forms open on the desktop, one for Products and the other for Vendors. If you move to a new record in the Products form, Access can automatically display the form for that product's supplier in the Vendors form on the screen. By having the forms open in their own windows, you can move or resize the forms independently. Here you would need a macro to keep the forms synchronized and in their desired locations.

You can use a macro to display or hide controls in one form based on values in another form. For example, suppose you have a customer form and are checking the account receivable records to see whether that customer is a good credit risk. You might display a previously hidden warning message if that customer has a bad payment history, as well as open another form to show the payment information.

SYNCHRONIZING WITH THE OPENFORM ACTION

You must first decide which form will handle the synchronizing. Typically, this form is the one you will spend more time working with. Call this form the *controlling form*. Attach a macro to a command button in the controlling form that opens the *secondary form* and determines which records to display. It can use the Where Condition argument in the OpenForm action to make sure that the secondary form only displays records that match a control value in the controlling form.

For instance, suppose you made Products the controlling form. Create a macro that opens the Vendors form. The Where Condition argument in the macro would use an expression like:

```
[Vendor Name]=Forms!Products![Vendor Name]
```

In this case the first Vendor Name field refers to a control in the Vendors form that is being opened, and the second Vendor Name refers to the value currently in the Products form. When Access runs this macro and opens the Vendors form, it will only display the records that match this condition. If you move the record pointer in the controlling form and push the command button, it will reopen the secondary form and show records that match the new Supplier ID field value.

KEEPING TWO FORMS SYNCHRONIZED

Access provides the On Current property to keep two forms synchronized as you move from record to record in the controlling form without having to reopen the secondary form. Create a macro to open the secondary form as before, but attach it to the On Current property of the controlling form, instead of a separate command button. Use the same Where Condition in the macro to ensure that the records match. However, this time add a condition to the OpenForm action line in the macro that causes the OpenForm to execute only if the secondary form is already open. That is, if the secondary form is not already open, the macro does nothing. If it is open, the macro repositions the record pointer to match the record values.

To test whether the secondary form is loaded, use the IsLoaded( ) module that was introduced in Unit 14. It is contained in the Module section of the HUNT database and can be copied to your own database as needed. It was written by Microsoft and included as part of the NWIND database as an example of a user-defined function. Inside the parentheses of this function, specify the name of the form in quotes. Access will test whether that form is already loaded and will return True if it is open and False if it is not loaded.

GUIDED ACTIVITY 15.3

Using a Macro to Keep Two Forms Synchronized

In this Guided Activity you will create a macro to keep two forms synchronized.

1. Close any open windows and return to the HUNT Database window.

2. Switch to Macro mode and click the New button.

3. Click the Conditions button in the toolbar (or choose Conditions from the View menu). Access will open the Condition column in the Macro window.

4. In the first Condition cell in the macro window, enter the condition `IsLoaded("Vendors")` and press [Enter].

5. In the Action cell of that same line enter `OpenForm`. The Comment for this line is `Open Vendors form if it is not already open`.

6. The arguments for this action are shown below. Note that the matching fields in the Where Condition don't need to have the same name. In the Vendors table we used Vendor Name, but in the Products table we used Vendor to refer to the same thing.

Form Name	`Vendors`
View	`Form`
Filter Name	
Where Condition	`[Vendor Name]=Forms!Products![Vendor]`
Data Mode	`Read Only`
Window Mode	`Normal`

7. Save this macro as `Show Related Vendor`. Close the macro window.

8. Switch to Form mode. Locate the Products form and click Design.

9. Double-click on the form to open the Property sheet for the form. (Or use the View | Properties command.)

10. In the On Current property, type `Show Related Vendor` and press [Enter]. This will cause Access to run the macro of that name every time a new record becomes current in the Products form. Save the form. Switch to Form view.

11. Without closing the Products form, use the mouse to drag the form's title bar over to the right side of the desktop.

12. Select the Vendors form and click Open to open it. Move it to the bottom of the desktop so that both forms are visible.

13. Click the Products form to make it active. Move the record pointer in this form and watch as Access keeps the Vendors form current with information about the vendor of each product.

CHECKPOINT 15C What happened in the Vendors form when you switched to the fourth record (Stock Number 13066) in the Products form? Can you explain how to solve the problem?

14. Close the active form window.

Filtering Records with a Macro

We can use the Where Condition argument of the OpenForm action to limit the form to records that match that condition. For more complex situations that tend to recur, use a filter instead. The Filter Name argument of the OpenForm action can hold the name of a filter that you have saved as a query. The filter can be used to restrict the records that appear in a form, or to sort the records that appear in the form.

You can also use the *ApplyFilter* action to invoke a filter for a form that is already open. It has just two arguments, Filter Name and Where Condition. You must use one or both of these arguments when you add the ApplyFilter action. If you use both arguments, Access will use the filter first, then apply the Where Condition to the records that match the filter. The ApplyFilter action can be used with Form, Design, and Datasheet views.

One interesting use of the ApplyFilter action is to create a alphabetical filter using command buttons to represent letters of the alphabet. You can set up a single form to look up records in your database based on the first letter of the relevant field or control. We will demonstrate this in the following activity in which you will build a customer look-up macro that displays only those customers in a specific alphabetical letter range.

GUIDED ACTIVITY 15.4

Creating an Alphabetical Look-up Filter

In this Guided Activity you will create an alphabetical look-up macro group that displays customers according to their last name. Each macro in the group will apply a filter for that letter range.

1. Close any open windows and return to the HUNT Database window.

2. Switch to Macro mode and click the New button to open a new macro.

3. Click the Macro Names button (or give the View | Macro Names command) to display the Macro Name column of the macro group.

4. In the Comment cell of the first line, enter Alphabetical filter attached to command buttons in Customer Lookup form.

5. The name of the first macro is A-E. Its action is ApplyFilter. The Comment cell should contain Display customers whose last names begin with "AE".

6. Press F6 to move to the lower pane of the macro window. The Where Condition for this macro is: [Last Name] Like "[ABCDE]*" Thus, any customer whose last name begins with the letters A through E will meet the condition.

7. Press F6 to return to the upper pane. Click the row selector button next to the macro names column to select the row. We will copy this row for the other macros.

8. With the row selected, choose the Copy command from the Edit menu (or use the Ctrl C shortcut command). Access will copy the macro to the Clipboard.

9. Move the pointer to the row below the A–E macro and choose Paste from the Edit menu (or use the Ctrl V shortcut command). Access will copy the A–E macro from the Clipboard back into the macro. Change the name of the second macro to F-K, change the comment cell, and change the Where Condition to [Last Name] Like "[FGHIJK]*"

10. Repeat step 9 for the remaining three letter groups. Use the following groups: L–P, Q–T, and U–Z. Adjust the Macro Name cell, the comment cell, and the Where Condition for each macro.

CHECKPOINT 15D Are there advantages in creating separate macros for each letter of the alphabet? Explain.

FIGURE 15.4
Finished
alphabetical
filter macro
group

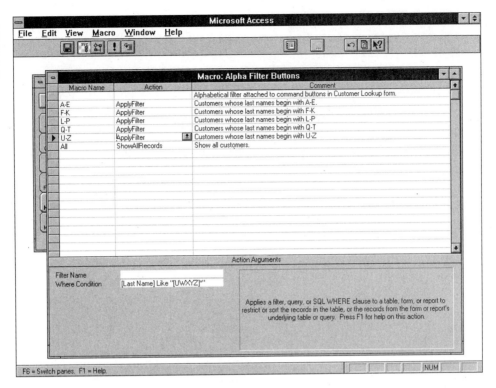

11. When all of the alphabetical letter macros have been created, add one more macro that shows all of the records without applying any filter conditions. Call this macro All, and give its action as ShowAllRecords. This action has no arguments. The comment is Show all customers. The macro is shown in Figure 15.4.

12. Save the entire macro group under the name Alpha Filter Buttons.

13. Close the macro window, then switch to Form mode.

14. Locate the Customer Lookup form and open it in Design view. This form uses a sorted query as its record source. The form already contains the command buttons for the letter groups. You must assign the appropriate macro from the macro group to each button.

15. Click on the A–E command button to select it. If the property sheet is not already displayed, click the Properties button in the toolbar or choose the Properties command from the View menu.

16. Click on the On Click property, then click the pull-down arrow at the right edge of the box. Scroll down until you have located the Alpha Filter Buttons.A-E macro. Press Enter to assign the Alpha Filter Buttons.A-E macro to that button.

17. Repeat step 16 with the other four letter groups, each time selecting the appropriate macro name at the end of the macro group name.

18. Repeat step 16 for the All button. Its On Click property is Alpha Filter Buttons.All. Figure 15.5 shows the form in Design view.

FIGURE 15.5
Lookup form with command buttons and attached macros

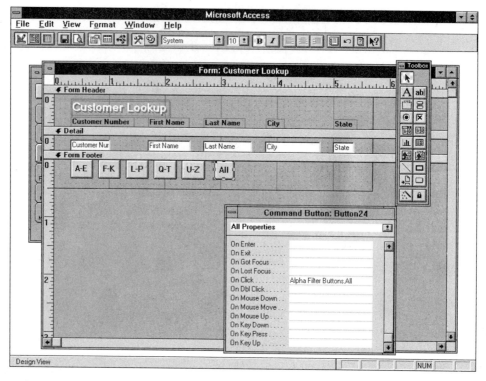

19. Click the Form view button in the toolbar to see the finished form. Figure 15.6 shows the form with the A–E button pushed. Notice that only customers whose names start with the letters A–E are displayed on the form. Save the changes to this form and close the active form window.

FIGURE 15.6
Customer lookup form with A–E macro filter in use

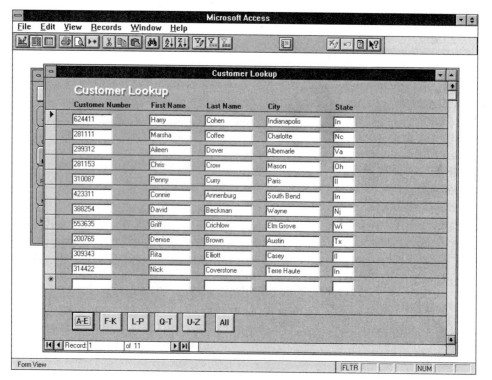

Moving Between Controls in a Macro

You can move automatically between controls and records with your macro. There are three GoTo actions in Access. *GoToControl* lets you move the focus to another field or control in the current table, query, or form. *GoToPage* moves you to the specified page in a multipage form and puts the focus in the first control on that page. *GoToRecord* moves to a specified record or a new record in the current form, table, or query. You can study the arguments for these actions in the on-line Help system.

You might choose to move to a different control than the tab order specifies because of a certain condition in the form. You might skip irrelevant controls or display only controls that the user is authorized to view. You might want to position the focus in a certain control prior to executing another macro action.

Using a Macro to Find a Record

You can use the *FindRecord* action to locate the first record after the current record that matches certain criteria. You can search through a table, a form, or a query. There is an argument for each option in the Find dialog box. For a review of the Find command see Unit 7 of this textbook. You specify the value to search for along with the search direction and other criteria. You can specify whether the entire field or the start of the field must match the search text.

To use this action, have your macro move the focus to the control or field that you want to search. Add the FindRecord action to the macro, then fill in its arguments as shown in Figure 15.7. The Find What argument must be supplied so that

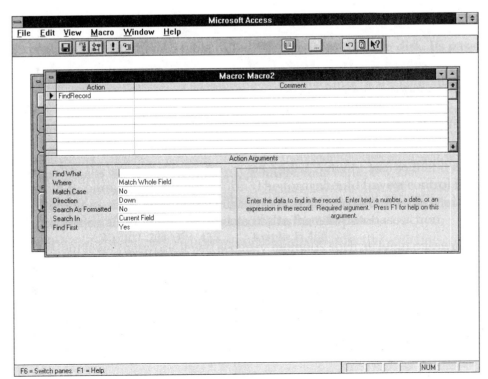

FIGURE 15.7
Arguments of the FindRecord macro action

the action knows what to look for. You can specify text, a number, or a date in this argument. The other arguments are optional; their default values are shown in the figure.

The *FindNext* action can be used repeatedly to find other occurrences of the data matching the previous FindRecord action. For example, you might use the FindRecord action to find the first instance of a particular customer. The FindNext action can cycle through other instances of the same customer.

Using a Macro to Set Values in a Form

You can reduce errors and make work easier for a user by having your macros set values for controls, fields, and properties. You can set the value of a control equal to the value of a different control on this or another form. You can hide or display a certain control based on conditions in the form. For instance, you might have a warning box if the customer's account balance is over a certain limit, or add a message to a report based on a similar condition. You can lock command buttons so that they cannot be pushed if certain conditions are true.

SETVALUE ARGUMENTS

The *SetValue* action is used for setting a value within the macro. This action has two arguments, Item and Expression. Item is the name of the control or property that is to be changed, and Expression contains the new value for that item. If the item refers to a control on the form from which it is called, you can refer to that control by its name alone. If the item refers to a control or property elsewhere, you must give the full name such as `Forms!formname!controlname`.

CONVERTING A CONTROL TO UPPERCASE CHARACTERS

You can use the SetValue action to convert all the characters in a control or field to uppercase values. This is particularly useful when several people input data values inconsistently. Create a macro with a single SetValue action. Its Item argument should be the name of the control you want to convert to uppercase. The Expression argument should be `UCase(fieldname)`. Attach this macro to the After Update property of that control on the form. Whenever someone changes the value of the control, this macro will run and do the conversion. Suppose the field you want to convert is called Type of Insurance. Set the following arguments:

Item   `[Type of Insurance]`
Expression   `UCase([Type of Insurance])`

Note that the square brackets are necessary because the field name contains embedded spaces.

SETTING VALUES FOR NEW RECORDS

You can use a macro to preset values for controls in new records. Suppose you were working with a Vendors form that opens a New Products form to add a new product. The macro can use the SetValue action to set the value of the Vendor Name field in the New Products form to that in the Vendors form. Not only does this save time, but it ensures that relational integrity is maintained between the related tables.

Requiring an Entry in a Control

You may want to be certain that a field in a form always has a value in it. You can create a macro that contains the validation rule and attach the macro to the form's Before Update property. Note that you can't attach the macro to an individual control, because that macro will run only if the user makes a change in the form.

Printing Forms with a Macro

We discussed earlier how to use the OpenForm action in a macro to display a form in *Print Preview mode*. The user can decide whether to print the form. But you may want the macro to make all of those decisions and insulate the user from needing to know how to use the Print Preview window.

The *Print* action can also print the active form, report, query, or table. If the desired print object is not active, your macro can use the *SelectObject* action to make it active; that is equivalent to clicking the object's title bar with the mouse. The Print action contains arguments for all of the options in the Print dialog box except Print to File. You can set the print range, print quality, and number of copies, and can set any collating instructions within the macro arguments.

It is practical to attach a print macro to a button on a form. By pushing that button the user can cause the print macro to run. You can use another pop-up form to let the user make decisions about the various print options, or go with the values already saved in the macro's arguments.

Printing Reports with a Macro

There are two ways to print a report within a macro. The OpenReport action gives more flexibility to the user, including the option to use the Print Preview view. The Print action introduced in the previous section can also be used to print a report when all of the options have been preassigned. Each is described in this section.

Using the OpenReport Action

The *OpenReport* action has four arguments, listed below. Use this action when you want to open the report in Print Preview view, or when you want to apply a filter or a Where Condition that restricts the number of records that print. This macro uses the current values in the Print dialog box for such things as the print range, print quality, and number of copies. If you want to set these items, use the Print action described below.

Argument	Explanation
Report Name	This is the name of the report within the database to print. It is a required argument.
View	The default is Print Preview. You can also select Print, which causes the report to print immediately, or Design view, in which case the user will see the report design.
Filter Name	This is the name of a filter that has been saved as a query, and will restrict the records that qualify for the report.
Where Condition	This allows you to specify a simple SQL Where clause or conditional expression, also limiting which records qualify for the report.

Using the Print Action

The other way to print a report is with the Print action. The Print action will print the currently selected object. This action allows the macro to set values in the Print dialog box such as print range, print quality, number of copies, and collating instructions. The arguments here only pertain to the Print dialog box, not the name of the report. Print will only send the report to the printer, not let the user enter Print Preview view. Use the OpenReport action if you want the user to have the Print Preview option.

There is a way to limit which records qualify for the report and still use the Print action. First use the ApplyFilter action to set a filter, then invoke the Print action in the macro. As with macros of other applications, there are numerous ways to accomplish the same task.

Using a Print Menu

The Access documentation refers to a *switchboard or menu form* as a menu of command buttons or switches that enable the user to choose between several alternative courses of action. You might create a main switchboard with two command buttons—one to View Forms and the other to Print Reports. The macros attached to those buttons can cause other switchboard forms to appear. The print switchboard could contain an option group with radio buttons that let the user choose which report should be printed. The following activity demonstrates creation of a print menu macro.

GUIDED ACTIVITY 15.5

Creating a Print Menu Macro

In this Guided Activity you will create a macro that displays a menu of report names. Then you will create a switchboard form. Pushing a command button on the form will cause a macro attached to that button to run, printing a report.

1. Close any open windows and return to the HUNT Database window.

2. Switch to the Macro mode and click the New button.

3. When the macro window opens, click the Macro Names button in the toolbar (or use the View | Macro Names command) to display the Macro Name column.

4. On the first line enter this comment: This is a macro group that will print reports from the Hunt database.

5. On the second line type Labels as the macro name. The action is OpenReport. Its Report Name argument is Custom Mailing Labels. Leave Print Preview as the view for this report.

6. Repeat step 5 with the Salary macro name. Its report is Employee Salary Report.

7. Repeat step 5 with the Inventory macro name. Its report is Inventory Group Report.

8. Repeat step 5 with the Product macro name. Its report is Product Report by Vendor. Figure 15.8 shows the completed macro.

FIGURE 15.8
Print Switchboard macro group

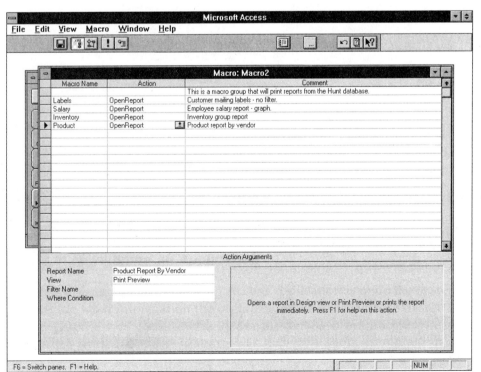

9. Save the macro with the name `Report Switchboard`. Close the macro window.

10. Switch to Form mode, click the New button, then click Blank Form to make the Report Switchboard form.

11. Place a large label control in the upper-left corner of the form. In the box type `Report Switchboard` and press [Enter]. Click the bold and italic buttons. Adjust the size to 18 points and use the Format | Size | to Fit command to make the box fit the text. Pull the bottom border of the Detail section down to 1.5 inches.

12. Make sure the Control Wizard button is not depressed. Click the command button tool in the Toolbox and create a command button control to the right of the form title, near the top of the form. Make it about 1 inch long.

13. Change the name of the control from Button 1 to `Labels`. In the On Click property of that control type `Report Switchboard.Labels`.

CHECKPOINT 15E   What does the Report Switchboard.Labels value mean in this context?

14. Repeat steps 12 and 13 for the other three buttons. Their labels should be the same as the Macro Names (Salary, Inventory, Product). Fill in the On Click property of the three controls with the appropriate macro names (`Report Switchboard.Salary`, `Report Switchboard.Inventory`, `Report Switchboard.Product`). The form is shown in Figure 15.9.

15. Click on the Form button to view your form in action. Click on the Labels button and watch Access display the Print Preview view of the mailing labels report. Try out each of the other reports.

FIGURE 15.9
Report Switchboard form with command buttons

NOTE *If you spell one of the report names incorrectly, Access will display a warning message and the Action Failed dialog box. You will have to go back to the Report Switchboard macro in Design view to make the corrections.*

16. Save the form with the name Report Switchboard. Close any open windows. We will modify this form as an exercise in Unit 18.

Creating an Auto-Execute Macro

If you create a menu-driven application with Access macros, you may want to have an *auto-execute macro* stored in the database that will automatically display an opening menu. This macro is saved as the special name "AutoExec". The next time you open the database, Access will run this macro without user intervention. If the macro displays a main switchboard, the user can pick from custom screens without having to know anything about the Access menu system. Each database you use can have one AutoExec macro stored within it.

If you do not want the auto-execute macro to run when the database is opened, hold down the [Shift] key when you select the database with the File I Open Database command. In this case you will see the usual Database window.

Command Line Auto-Execute Macro Startup Option

It is possible to start Access from the Program Manager's File I Run command with different options. Another way to run a macro automatically is with the /X command line option. That is, add the name of the database file and /X followed by the macro name to the end of the Command Line box in the Program Properties box of the Windows Program Manager. Access will automatically load that database, then execute the macro named. The following command line will start Access, open the HUNT database, and automatically execute the Main Switchboard macro:

```
C:\ACCESS\MSACCESS.EXE HUNT.MDB /X Main Switchboard
```

You can also type that line in at the Run command of the Program Manager's File menu. Access 2.0 adds several new command line startup options: /Compact will compact a database; /Repair will repair a database; /Convert will convert a database; /Ini will cause a different initialization file to be used.

Creating an AutoExec Macro

In this Guided Activity you will create a simple macro and save it as AutoExec, then load the database and have it automatically execute.

1. Close any open windows and return to the HUNT Database window.

2. Switch to the Macro mode and click the New button.

3. On the first comment line type `Runs automatically when you open the database`.

4. In the second line's action cell use the MsgBox action. This will simulate the opening of a menu switchboard that we'll develop in Unit 17.

5. In the Message argument type `This opens automatically!`

6. Use the File | Save command to save this macro as `AutoExec`.

7. Close the macro window, then close the HUNT Database window.

8. Open the HUNT Database window as usual, and notice how the message box appears without further commands. Click OK to clear the message box.

9. For now, we will rename the AutoExec macro so that it does not come up each time we open the HUNT database. Switch to the Macro mode, and click once on the AutoExec macro.

10. Choose the Rename command from the File menu. Give it the new name `AutoExec NOT`.

11. Close the HUNT database and reopen it.

CHECKPOINT 15F Did the auto-execute message box appear when you opened the database the second time? How would you reactivate the auto-execute macro?

Command Review

Macro	Run	Run macro in the macro window.
View	Conditions	Open Conditions column in macro window.
View	Macro Names	Open Macro Names column in macro window.
View	Properties	Display Property sheet in Form mode.

Exercises

Use the Hunter River database contained within the HUNT.MDB file on the West Student Data Disk for these exercises.

1. Create a macro that opens the Employees form in Datasheet view and in Read Only data mode. Move it to the right side of the desktop. Your macro should also open the Managers form in Form view and place it on the left side of the desktop. Save the macro.

2. Modify the alphabetical filter form and related macro group to use more command buttons. Your new form should have no command button with more than three letters.

3. Open the table called Test Values, which has two fields. The first field is called ID and is counter type. The second field is called Text Field and is text type. Create a new form to receive data for this table. Create a validation macro that replaces whatever you type in the Text Field control with the uppercase equivalent. Attach the macro to the proper property of the form. Use the form and try typing in different combinations of lowercase and uppercase values. See what your macro does to those field values.

4. Create a macro that opens the Products form and limits records to Camping category.

5. Modify the macro from Exercise 4 to allow the user to specify which product Category will be displayed.

6. Create a macro that will open the Inventory Group Report in Print Preview mode. Your macro should include only those products that have a positive inventory balance.

Review Questions

1. Describe the choices for the Data Mode argument for the OpenForm action.

2. Why would you want to use the MoveSize action in an Access macro? Give an example of its use.

3. How can you place into a form a command button that runs a macro when it is pushed without using the Toolbox?

4. Discuss reasons why you might want to have more than one Access form open on the desktop at the same time. Give an example.

5. List the advantages of attaching macros to properties of forms and form controls.

6. Explain the use of the Before Update and After Update properties of a control.

7. Describe the purpose of the Filter Name and Where Condition arguments of the OpenForm action. Are you required to use at least one of them?

8. Give the advantages of using an alphabetical look-up filter in Access.

9. Exactly what does the expression [Company Name] Like "[LMN]*" mean?

10. Give a brief explanation of the use of each of the following actions:

    a. FindNext

    b. GoToControl

    c. Restore

    d. SetValue

    e. SelectObject

11. Explain the use of a switchboard in Access.

12. Describe how an auto-execute macro can be used in an Access application. Is there a way to defeat the auto-execution of that macro?

Key Terms

ApplyFilter action	GoToRecord action	Restore action
Auto-Execute macro	Maximize action	Secondary form
Controlling form	Minimize action	SelectObject action
Event	MoveSize action	SetValue action
FindNext action	OpenForm action	Switchboard or menu
FindRecord action	OpenReport action	form
GoToControl action	Print action	
GoToPage action	Print Preview mode	

Documentation Research

Use the printed documentation and the on-line Help available with Microsoft Access to answer the following questions. If you use one of the manuals, provide the page number for your reference in the manual.

1. Use the on-line Help system to learn how Access Cue Cards can be used to design and write a macro. Look through the sample macros in Cue Cards.

2. Search the Help system for information about the AutoKeys macro. Describe how you can assign a macro to a key on the keyboard.

3. Study the following Access macro actions and explain their use:

   a. Echo

   b. Hourglass

   c. Close

   d. SendKeys

   e. StopMacro

4. Create a command button control, then use the Picture Builder feature to learn how to place a bit-mapped picture on the command button. Why would you want to put a bit-mapped picture on a command button?

Physicians' Medical Clinic (XI): Using a Macro to Automate Steps

In this application you will create a macro to automate some processing in the PMC database, using the material covered in previous units. You will open the PMC database and create several forms with some attached macros. Read the directions carefully. Clearly identify which output goes with which part of the application.

One of the analysts in the PMC Data Processing department wants to know how Access macros can be used to automate some steps for the clinic. You have agreed to create a few sample macros.

1. Create an alphabetical filter form that displays patients by their last names. Show several fields from the Patients table.

2. Create a macro that opens a form at a certain location on the desktop and displays all patients for a particular insurer. Your macro should allow the user to specify which insurer is used.

3. List four more macro opportunities that would be appropriate for the PMC database and that would demonstrate some of the power of Access macros.

Linking Access to Other Data Files

In this unit you will learn how Access can exchange data with other compatible applications. Compatible applications include other Access databases, text files, popular spreadsheet programs, other databases, and network SQL server software. The File | Attach Table command lets you open data table files from other applications without first translating them to the Access file format. You will learn how to use the Import and Export commands in the File menu to read and write files from other applications. The unit concludes with a macro that can be used to transfer data automatically.

Learning Objectives

At the completion of this unit you should know

1. what data types are compatible with Microsoft Access,

2. the differences between attaching, importing, and exporting data files,

3. how to use the Windows Clipboard to copy objects between databases.

At the completion of this unit you should be able to

1. attach an external data file to Access,

2. import a data file into Access,

3. export an Access table to another data file,

4. copy files between different Access databases,

5. use a macro to transfer data between Access and other packages.

Important Commands

Edit | Copy

Edit | Paste

File | Attach Table

File | Export

File | Import

File | Imp/Exp Setup

Query | Make Table

Compatible Data Types

Access provides *data translators* for many popular data types. The data translators are able to convert the data from one format to another without much intervention on the part of the user. Each new version of Access has new or improved data translators. Microsoft has promised to make more translators available in the future, particularly for use with mainframe or minicomputer databases.

Database Programs

It is not uncommon for database users to need to transfer data from one program to another, typically as the organization switches to a new program. For example, the company may use DOS programs but wants to begin the conversion to Windows-based software. Access is able to translate tables from the most popular database programs. Compatible program files with their identifying extensions include Microsoft Access (.MDB), dBASE III and IV (.DBF), Paradox 3.x and 4.x (.DB), FoxPro 2.x (.DBF), Btrieve, and several network SQL databases such as Microsoft SQL Server, Oracle Server, and Sybase SQL Server. Access will make use of database index files if they are available.

The network SQL database server applications require use of Microsoft's *ODBC drivers*, special data translators written for these databases. ODBC stands for Open Data Base Connectivity, Microsoft's plan for linking different databases in a homogeneous fashion. The ODBC driver sits between the application and the SQL database server on the network. The driver translates the SQL statements into the specific commands required by the other application, in this case Access. The ODBC drivers and associated help files might not be installed on your computer if you are not using an SQL database.

Spreadsheet Programs

Although most spreadsheet programs have limited data storage capabilities, you might find the need to exchange data with one of these popular programs. Access includes translators for Lotus 1-2-3 (.WKS, .WK1, and .WK3) and Microsoft Excel (.XLS from versions 2.0 to 4.0 and 5.0) worksheet files. In some cases you might want to send data to the spreadsheet program; in other cases you might bring data into Access from the spreadsheet.

Text Files

A text file is composed of rows of text characters representing field values. Access is able to work with two kinds of text files: fixed-width and delimited. *Fixed-width text* means that the field values in consecutive rows have the same width in each row. Once you define how wide each field should be, each row (record) will align. *Delimited text* uses a character such as a comma or tab character to separate adjacent fields in the same record. Many word processors allow you to save a document (say, a customer list) as an unformatted text (or ASCII) file, which can then be imported into Access—saving a great deal of rekeying of data.

Microsoft Word for Windows Merge Print

Access is also able to send *merge print* data to Microsoft Word for Windows. Merge printing refers to the process of inserting data into a single word processing document, creating multiple customized copies of that document. Word for Windows can print those documents. Think of merge printing as preparing a customized form letter.

Attaching, Importing, and Exporting

Attaching and importing involve bringing data into an Access database from an external program. Once the data is accessible to Access, you can treat the data from the external file as though it were a regular Access table. Exporting takes data from an Access table and converts it to an external file that can be read by one of the applications listed in the previous section.

Attaching

When you *attach* an external file to Access, you are creating a link to that file in its native format. That is, the file stays in its original format and Access reads it directly, without importing it into an Access table. You can make changes to the data table and use it to create other Access objects. Use the Attach procedure when you plan to continue using the external application program. That way Access will have access to the most current version of the data whenever you activate the link to that data file. Use Attach also when you plan to make changes in the data from within Access but don't want to do a separate export step. The Attach method is usually less efficient at processing external data than the import procedure.

Importing

The process of converting data into an Access table is called *importing*. When you import a table, it becomes a permanent part of the current Access database. In most cases Access is able to read the external data file and convert the characteristics of that file into Access properties. Of course, once the file has been imported, it is not linked with the external program. If you were to make changes to the external data file in dBASE or Paradox, those changes would not be represented in the Access database. In that case you would want to import the data again to make the Access database current. With some data types, Access will process data faster if it is imported rather than attached.

Use Import when the data are being converted from one system to Access, or where there is little need to take the data back to the external software application. Use Import when the data in the original software package are not likely to change in the future.

Exporting

The process of converting data from an Access table to the data file format of the target application is called *exporting*. Use this technique when you must use a program other than Access to perform functions such as merge printing or data analysis. Some people are not familiar with a full-featured database program such as Access and might want to work with the data in their own package. You may want to transfer data to another site that does not use Access. The Export process will save most data values in the new data file type but may not transfer all of the properties if the new program does not support them. Some packages cannot support all of the Access data types. In fact, if you intend to use the Export feature frequently, you should study the Microsoft Access *User's Guide* and on-line Help to learn about special limitations with certain kinds of exports.

Attaching External Files

Access is able to read and write certain external data files directly. The File | Attach Table command lets you open a table file in its native format from another database application and treat it as if it were an Access object. You can open a datasheet containing the data file, then use it in a query, form, or report. Any changes you make to field values in the file are automatically made in the file itself, unlike the File | Import procedure in which changes are only made to the internal Access table, not the external file.

Although you cannot change an attached file's structure, you can assign values to its properties after it is attached. You can add descriptions to the fields, particularly if the field names were not very descriptive. You can change the Format, Decimal Places, Default Value, Validation Rule, and Validation Text properties for each field in the attached file.

FIGURE 16.1
*The Attach
dialog box for
selecting data
source*

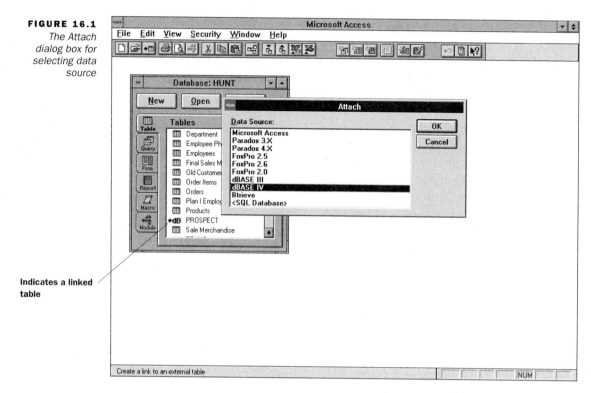

Indicates a linked
table

Attaching the File

To attach a table stored as an external file on your PC or a network, switch to
Table mode in the Database window. Issue the File | Attach Table command and
select the type of file you wish to attach, from the dialog box shown in Figure 16.1.
There are ten database types available in Access version 2.0, and more will probably
be available in the future. After you specify the type of file to attach, Access will display the Select File dialog box with a list of files including the designated file extension in the default drive and directory. If you will be the only person using the
attached file, click the *Exclusive* checkbox. That informs Access that you are using
the file and will prevent anyone else from opening the file while you are using it (if
you are on a network). Opening dBASE and Paradox files in exclusive mode will
speed up file access operations. Then select the desired file and click Attach.

Access will create a link to the external data file, then allow you to specify any
index files that are to be loaded. Specify the index files by name, then click the Close
button. Index files allow much faster access to the table's contents. Although Access
is able to build its own indexes to database files, any changes made to the linked
table while in Access would not be updated in the index files unless they are also
linked at this time. Access cannot build indexes for attached tables. Finally, if you do
not wish to attach any additional files at this time, close the Select File dialog box.

Using an Attached File

Access lists attached tables in the Table mode of the Database window with a
special symbol, an arrow pointing to an abbreviation of the file type. The arrow

signifies that this is a **linked table**, available to but not a part of the current database. You can use the table as long as the file remains linked. Access will automatically create the link whenever the database containing the attached table is opened. In fact, the link remains active until you highlight the linked table and press the [Del] key. If you delete the linked table, only the link is erased. The data in the table remain unaffected. You can later establish a link again if one is desired.

If another user makes a change to the linked file, that change is automatically made available to Access. Of course, if you opened the external file in exclusive mode, nobody else will be able to view the file so long as you have open the database that contains the link.

GUIDED ACTIVITY 16.1

Attaching an External Data File to Access

In this Guided Activity you will attach an external data file and use it in Access.

1. Start Windows and load Access. Open the HUNT database.

2. Choose the Attach Table command from the File menu.

3. In the Attach dialog box select the dBASE IV data source and click OK.

4. In the Select File dialog box highlight the PROSPECT.DBF file and click Attach. When Access displays a list of index files, click the Close button.

CHECKPOINT 16A How can you change the drive and directory in the Select File box if the PROSPECT.DBF file is not in the current Access directory?

5. Access will create the link to the external database file and display a message for you if the attach is successful. Click OK, then click Close to close the Select File box.

6. You should see the PROSPECT table listed among those in the HUNT Database window. Access uses a special table symbol (with an arrow) in front of the attached file to signify that it is an attached table rather than an internal table.

NOTE *If there were another table called Prospect already in this database, Access would have named the attached table as PROSPECT1.*

7. Double-click the PROSPECT table in the Database window and Access will open that table in Datasheet view, shown in Figure 16.2. Then close the open window.

Importing Other Files into Access

As mentioned earlier, you can import data from an external file directly into a table in an Access database. The process begins by opening the Access database into which you want to import the data. Choose the Import command from the File menu. Access will display the Import dialog box, asking you to select the type of data file (Data Source) to import. Version 2.0 of Access offers 16 choices in the option box, including separate choices for different versions of the same program. For

FIGURE 16.2
*Datasheet view
of attached
Prospect table*

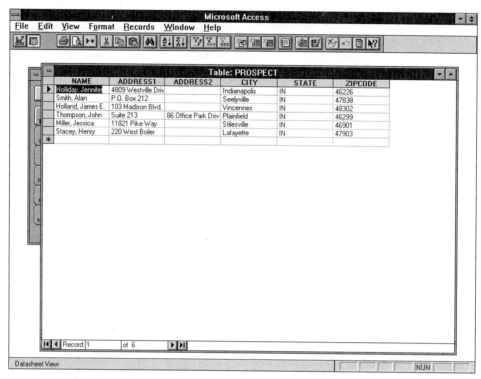

instance, Lotus 1-2-3 uses different file extensions for the 1.X, 2.X, and 3.X versions of the program.

After choosing the data source, Access will display the Select File dialog box in which you enter the drive, directory, and file name of the external data file. Access will use a wild card file name pattern that matches the type of file you chose in the previous step. After selecting the file, click the Import button. Next you may see an *Import Options dialog box* that is specific to the kind of file import being done. The following sections describe the import options when importing spreadsheet, database, and text files.

Importing a Lotus or Excel Spreadsheet

For spreadsheets, you will see the Import Spreadsheet Options dialog box shown in Figure 16.3. You can specify whether to create a new table or append the data to an existing table. You can select a range of cells to import or bring in the entire spreadsheet. If the first row of the worksheet's data range contains the field names, click the check box to indicate that the field names are available. Otherwise, when you create a new table Access will number the fields and you must go into the Design view of Table mode and give proper names to the fields.

If you append the records from the spreadsheet to an existing Access table, the spreadsheet fields must be in the same order as the table fields, as well as of the same data type as the table fields. If your spreadsheet's first row contains field names, they must match *exactly* the field names in the table to which the spreadsheet is appended.

FIGURE 16.3
*The Import
Spreadsheet
Options
dialog box*

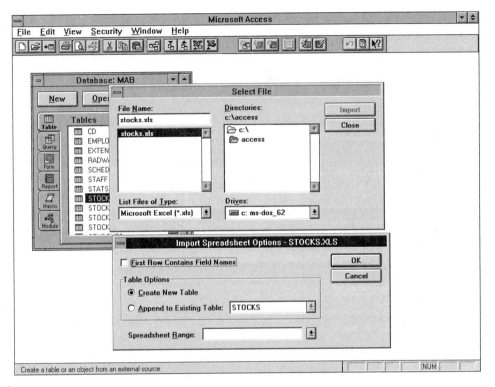

Importing a dBASE or Paradox Database Table

The database program data sources will usually translate completely without displaying an Import Options dialog box. Access is able to read the table definition information and create a new table automatically. You are not given the option of appending the external data to an existing Access table. To do this, first import the file into a new table, then copy records from the new Access table into the Windows Clipboard. Copy those records from the Clipboard into the existing Access table.

GUIDED ACTIVITY 16.2

Importing a dBASE File

In this Guided Activity you will import a dBASE IV database file into Access, creating a new table.

1. Close any open windows and return to the HUNT Database window. Switch to Table mode.

2. Choose the Import command from the File menu or click the Import button. Access will display the Import dialog box with the various data source types, shown in Figure 16.4. Locate the dBASE IV selection and click OK.

3. You will next see the Select File box shown at the top of Figure 16.5. Choose the drive and directory that contains the dBASE .DBF file, then choose the proper file, in this case PROSPECT.DBF. When you are finished, click the Import button to translate the dBASE IV file into the Access data format.

FIGURE 16.4
*The Access
File Import
dialog box*

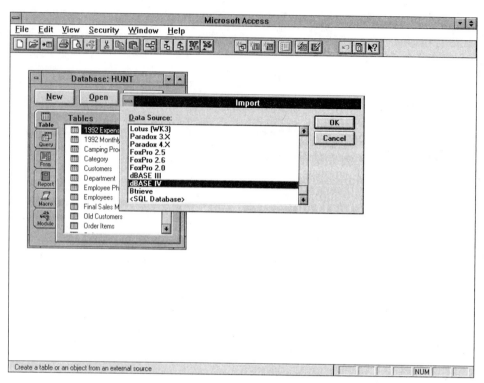

4. As shown in Figure 16.5, Access should display an information box stating that it has successfully imported the PROSPECT file. Access will automatically open a new table with that name to hold the data. If another table of the same name already exists within the current database, Access will place a "1" at the end of the table name so that it is unique.

5. To see what Access brought into the HUNT database, click OK to close the message box, then click Close to close the Select File box.

6. Return to the Database window. Scroll down until you see a table named PROSPECT in the list. Click the Open button to see the contents of this table. Figure 16.6 shows the Datasheet view for this table.

7. Widen the first two columns of the datasheet by dragging the border between the columns so that you can see the entire contents of each field.

 CHECKPOINT 16B What would happen to the PROSPECT.DBF file now if you make a change to one or more of the fields in the PROSPECT table of the HUNT database?

8. Close the open Datasheet window.

Importing Data from Another Access Database

The first choice for the Data Source in the Import dialog box is Microsoft Access. You will be asked to specify the name of the other Access database. Then you will see the Import Objects dialog box in which you can specify what type of database object

FIGURE 16.5
*The dBASE IV
Select File
dialog box*

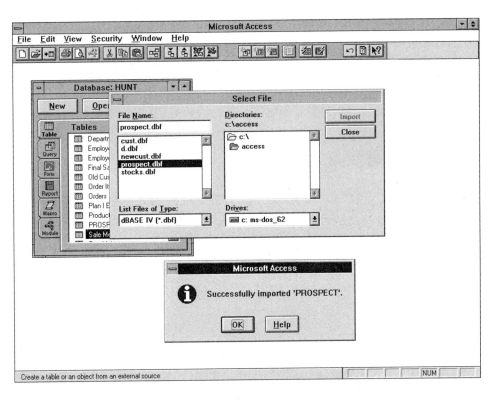

FIGURE 16.6
*Imported
dBASE IV file*

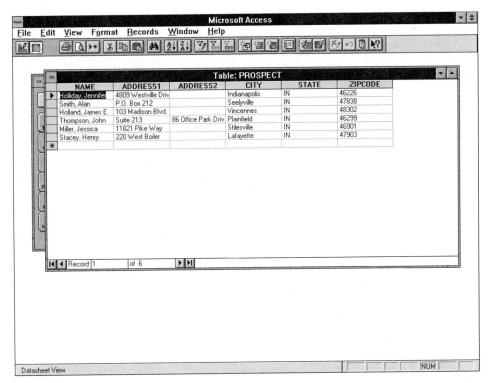

you want to import. You can pick from Tables, Queries, Forms, Reports, Macros, and Modules in this list. Access will display all objects of the selected type, similar to the Database window when you switch modes. You have the option of importing the *structure* alone, or the structure and the data. Importing the structure alone means that you bring in the design of a table, but none of the data in that table. The structure-and-data option appears only for tables. For other types, only the structure is imported.

Importing Text Files

When importing a text file, you will see the Import Text Options dialog box shown in Figure 16.7. In the top portion are the same options that appeared with the Import Spreadsheet dialog box. You can choose to create a new table or append the data to an existing Access table. Click the check box if field names are contained in the first row of the text file. If your text file does not have field names in its first row and you create a new table, Access will assign numbers as field names.

HINT *You can easily edit the text file, using the Windows Notepad to add the field names above the first record.*

The lower portion of the dialog box is available if you click the Options button, which we did to produce the figure. In this box you can make changes to the default setup for text files. You can attach a name to a custom specification and save it for later use when you import the same kind of text file, which will conserve time and ensure accuracy of file conversion.

FIGURE 16.7
The Import Text Options dialog box

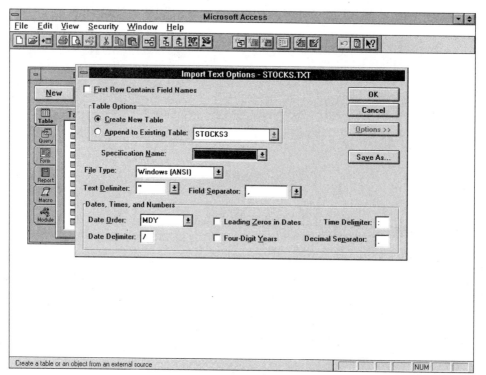

DELIMITED TEXT FILES

In the default specification for delimited files, text is *delimited* with the double quote character (") and fields are *separated* with the comma. That means that the text field values are enclosed in double quotes, with a comma between each two fields. The following line shows what a delimited record from a stock price table would look like:

```
6,"BOEING","NYSE",61.875,38.5,54.625,500
```

The two text fields are enclosed (delimited) with quotes, and all fields are separated by commas. The number fields at the end represent high price per share, low price per share, purchase price per share, and number of shares. With delimited text files, fields take only as many characters as needed; long fields use more space while short fields take less space.

The following activity shows how to import a delimited text file and append it to the end of an existing table.

GUIDED ACTIVITY 16.3

Importing a Delimited Text File

In this Guided Activity you will import into Access a delimited text file and append it to an existing Access table.

1. Close any open windows and return to the HUNT Database window.

2. Select the Import command from the File menu or click the Import button.

3. At the Import dialog box choose Text (Delimited) and click OK.

4. At the Select File box highlight the file called CAMP29.TXT. A copy of the delimited text file is shown in the Windows Notepad in Figure 16.8. Notice that all text fields (including field names in the first row) are enclosed in quotes and fields are separated with commas. This file contains new camping products to be added to the database.

5. Once the proper text file has been selected, click the Import button. Access will display the Import Text Options box shown in Figure 16.9. Click the "First Row Contains Field Names" check box in this dialog box. Also click the "Append to Existing Table" check box and select the Camping Products table.

CHECKPOINT 16C What do these two check boxes imply about the destination of the text file's data values? What if the first row did not contain field names?

6. When finished, click the OK button in the Import Text Options box and Access will perform the import, adding the new camping products to the end of the Camping Products table. Click OK on the import results box and close the Select File box. Then open the Camping Products table.

FIGURE 16.8
*Delimited text
file showing new
Camping records*

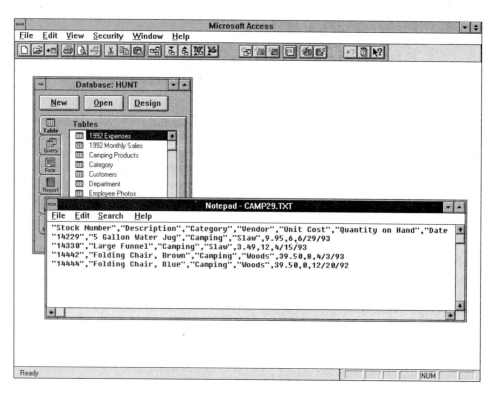

FIGURE 16.9
*The Import Text
Options dialog
box for new
Camping
Products*

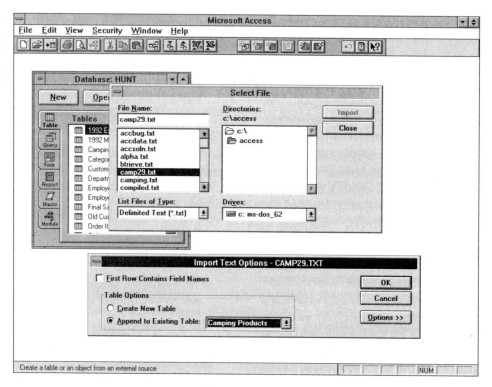

FIGURE 16.10

Camping Products table with four imported records

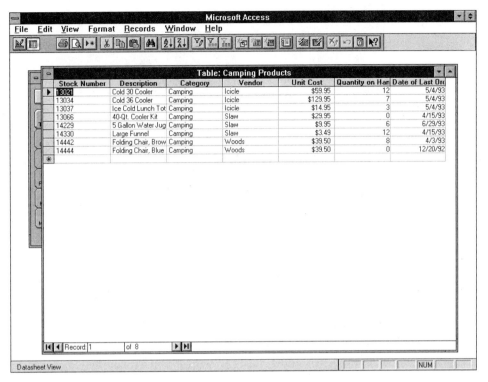

7. The Camping Products table is shown in Figure 16.10. The last four records with Stock Numbers beginning with 14 are the new ones brought in from the delimited text file. Close the active table window to return to the Database window.

Fixed-Width Text Files

A fixed-width text file uses specific starting and ending points for each field; the same field in different records uses the same number of characters. Two fixed-width records from the stock table might look like:

```
5 BOISE CASCAD    NYSE    48       39.25   41.5    2000
6 BOEING          NYSE    61.875  38.5    54.625  500
```

Notice that there are no delimiters or separators with this data format. You must provide the starting position and width for each field in the file for importing and exporting. Use the Imp/Exp Setup command from the File menu in the Database window to create the specification before you use the File | Import or File | Export commands with fixed-width text files. We will illustrate this dialog box in a later guided activity where we export fixed-width text records.

Handling Import Errors

If Access detects any errors in the import process, it creates a special table called *Import Errors* that contains the description of each error. Check the Database window in Table mode for this table. When an error is found in the Import process,

Access does not actually import the data. Correct the error and repeat the File | Import command.

Exporting Data Files from Access

Just as we are able to import data directly into Access from external data files, so can we use Access to create external data files from Access tables. The procedure is very similar to the File | Import command. Choose the Export command from the File menu, then select an external file type from the list of available types. Access will prompt you for the name of the Access table that you wish to export, then for a name to save it, using the default file extension of the destination package. All of the records from that table will be exported to the indicated file. We will illustrate two different export methods in this section.

Exporting Data to a Spreadsheet File

You can export data from Access to the common spreadsheet file formats Lotus 1-2-3 and Excel. The procedure is simple: choose the File | Export command, then select the type of file in the Export dialog box. Then give the file name for the export, and click OK. The entire table is saved in the appropriate file format, one field per column and one row per record. Access automatically places the field names in the first row of the spreadsheet file. Text fields are converted to spreadsheet labels. Numeric and yes/no fields are converted to spreadsheet values. For the latter, Yes is saved as a 1 and No as a 0. Where possible, field format properties are converted to corresponding cell formats. Date fields are converted to dates in the spreadsheet file and given a date format. When you examine the spreadsheet file, widen the spreadsheet columns to view the full data field.

GUIDED ACTIVITY 16.4

Exporting Data to a Spreadsheet

In this Guided Activity you will export a table to a Lotus 1-2-3 spreadsheet file.

1. Close any open windows and return to the HUNT Database window.

2. Switch to Table mode and give the File | Export command or click the Export button.

3. At the Export dialog box, choose the Lotus (.WK1) file type.

4. In the Select Microsoft Access Object box, locate the Final Sales Merchandise table, then click OK.

5. In the Export to File dialog box, select the directory and name for your spreadsheet file. In this case, Access will fill in FINAL_SA.WK1. Click OK to export to this file.

FIGURE 16.11

*Lotus 1-2-3
display of
exported
spreadsheet
data*

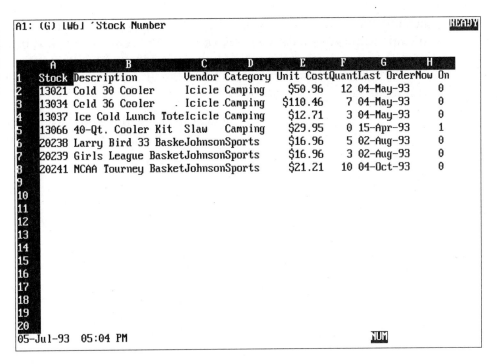

6. If you have Lotus 1-2-3 or another spreadsheet program that can read a .WK1 file, retrieve the exported file and view its contents. Figure 16.11 shows the spreadsheet displayed in Lotus 1-2-3.

Exporting Data to a Fixed-Width Text File

Unlike the method used to export the entire table to a spreadsheet file, with fixed-width text files you must create and use an *import/export specification*. This describes the fields that are to be included in the text file, the field type, the starting location, and the number of characters to use for each field. This specification can be saved with an appropriate name and reused later for import or export jobs. If you try to export without an import/export setup in place, Access will stop the process and display a warning message box.

GUIDED ACTIVITY 16.5

Exporting Data to a Fixed-Width Text File

In this Guided Activity you will create an Import/Export Setup specification, then export data from the Vendors table to a fixed-width text file.

1. Close any open windows and return to the HUNT Database window.

2. Switch to Table mode. Select the Vendors table but do not open the table at this time.

3. Choose the Imp/Exp Setup command from the File menu. Access will display a blank dialog box.

4. Each export field needs an entry in the table for name, data type, starting position, and number of characters. Click the Fill Specifications Grid from Table button in the lower part of the dialog box. Click OK in the Fill Specifications Grid from Table dialog box. Access will fill in the grid with names and field lengths from the table.

 CHECKPOINT 16D If we shorten the length of some of the text fields, will we lose any information in the export to the text file?

5. Modify the grid as shown in Figure 16.12. Delete the Address Line 2 and Telephone Number fields. Revise the start and width cells as necessary.

6. Click the Save As button to save this specification. Use the name Vendors Export for this specification. You can reuse this specification for export in the future. Click OK to go on to the next step. Click OK again in the Import/Export Setup dialog box.

7. Issue the File | Export command from the File menu bar or click the Export button. Select the Text (Fixed Width) option in the Export dialog box and click OK.

8. Select the Vendors table in the Select Microsoft Access Object dialog box and click OK.

9. Access will display the Export To dialog box, and suggest a file name called VENDORS.TXT in the C:\ACCESS2 directory (or the path where you store database files). If this directory path is acceptable, click the OK button.

FIGURE 16.12
The Import/Export Setup dialog box with Vendors Export specification

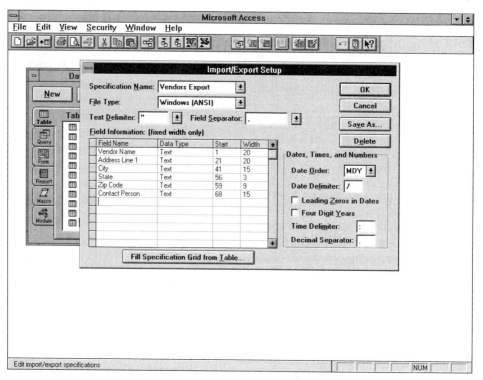

FIGURE 16.13
Fixed-width text file created by export

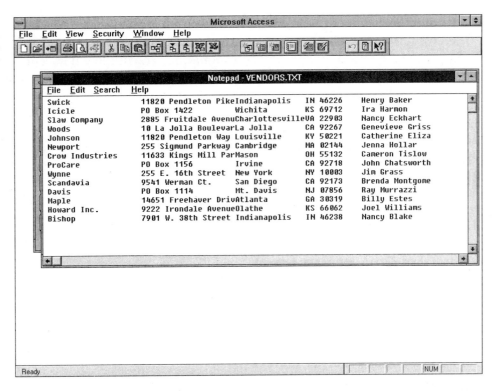

10. Finally, Access will display the Export Text Options box with the names of the Import/Export specifications saved on your computer. Choose the Vendors Export specification you created in step 6 above and click OK to complete the export.

11. Figure 16.13 shows the VENDORS.TXT file in the Windows Notepad window. Notice that some of the fields have been truncated on their right sides according to the import/export specification you prepared.

Exporting Data from a Query

In Access 1.X you could not export data directly from a query datasheet. Only Access tables could be exported. To solve this problem you would have made a Make Table query, converted the query into a table, and exported the newly-created table.

However, Access 2.0 allows you to export directly from a query. In the Select Microsoft Access Object dialog box, make sure that the Query or Both button is pushed, then select the query and continue with the export.

Using the Windows Clipboard to Exchange Files

Many Windows applications are able to swap data via the Windows Clipboard. The procedure is simple: mark text to be copied in the sending Windows application, then use the Edit | Copy command from that package. Whatever was selected is copied from that application into the Clipboard. Then switch to the receiving Windows application and use the Edit | Paste command to transfer the data from the Clipboard.

For instance, you can mark records in an Excel or Lotus 1-2-3 spreadsheet under Windows, then go through the Clipboard to copy those records into an Access table. The copy can be as new records, or you can replace existing records with the contents of the Clipboard. Some Windows applications cannot create data values that are compatible with Access tables—try the Clipboard method with a small sample.

This method is particularly useful when swapping data between two Access databases. Open the first database, copy the object to the Clipboard, then open the second Access database and paste the object into the second database. Access will permit you to copy any kind of database object with this method, not just tables. The disadvantage of using this method with two Access databases is that you can only copy a single object through the Clipboard at a time. Remember that you can only have one Access database open at a time. With the File | Export or File | Import methods, you can copy multiple objects in the same session.

Using a Macro to Transfer Data

You can use a macro to automate and make virtually foolproof the process of transferring data from one data file to another. Although macros were covered in the previous two units, it is appropriate to cover the specific transfer actions here, now that you are familiar with attaching, importing, and exporting in Access.

Transfer Macro Actions

Access offers three macro actions for transferring data between itself and external applications and files. You can specify transfers for databases, spreadsheets, and text files. These actions produce the same results that you could produce with the File | Import, File | Export, and File | Attach Table commands from the menu bar.

The *TransferDatabase* action is used to attach, import, or export data between the currently open Access database and a compatible external database file. There is an extensive set of arguments for this action, including settings for type of transfer, type of database, path where the database file is located, object type (if you are transferring from another Access database), name of source file, and object name in the destination database.

The *TransferSpreadsheet* action is used to import or export data between the currently open Access database and a compatible external spreadsheet file. Like the previous action, there are arguments for type of transfer, type of spreadsheet (Lotus or Excel), Access table name, spreadsheet file name (with full path), specifying whether the first row contains field names, and spreadsheet range to import. If you are appending spreadsheet rows to an existing Access table, you must have a compatible structure in terms of the type and sequence of data fields.

The *TransferText* action is used to import or export data between the currently open Access database and a delimited or fixed-width text file. Arguments include type of transfer (import delimited, import fixed-width, export delimited, export fixed-width, and export Word for Windows merge), text options specification name, Access table name, text file name, and whether the first row contains field names. The same data compatibility rules apply to spreadsheet and text files, particularly if you are appending data to an existing Access table.

A Data Transfer Macro

If you have not already studied macros in Units 14 and 15, you should do so at this time. The Data Transfer macro should use the general macro structure of other macros in this book. You can attach the data transfer macro either to a command button or to a property of a form. The transfer itself is straightforward, once the proper instructions are placed into the transfer action arguments.

The following simple macro will export Employee data to a dBASE IV file. All of the arguments are set as constants within the macro itself, but you can use a form to receive special instructions from the user when the macro runs, placing those instructions in the arguments of the macro. To place the contents of a form control in an argument, use the format `=Form!formname!controlname`. Fill in the appropriate names for the form and the control in the expression.

GUIDED ACTIVITY 16.6

Using a Macro to Transfer Data

In this Guided Activity you will create a simple macro to automatically export data from an Access table to a dBASE IV database file.

1. Close any open windows and return to the HUNT Database window.

2. Switch to Macro mode and click the New button to open the macro window.

3. Leave the first line's Action cell empty and enter the following comment in the first Comment cell: `Sample data transfer macro`.

4. In the second line's Action cell, choose the TransferDatabase action. The arguments for this action and the comment are shown in Figure 16.14. Enter each argument in the lower pane of the macro window. You may need to specify a different location for Database Name if your computer does not have a directory called C:\ACCESS2\. This argument specifies where the dBASE file will be created; if the path does not already exist, Access will display an error message and halt the macro.

5. Use the File | Save command to save the macro under the name `Transfer Employee Data`.

6. Run the macro by clicking the Run button in the toolbar (or use the Macro | Run command from the menu bar).

7. Access will create the dBASE IV database file named EMPL.DBF. If the file already exists, Access will replace it with the current contents of the Employees table *without warning you*.

FIGURE 16.14
Macro Transfer-Database action arguments

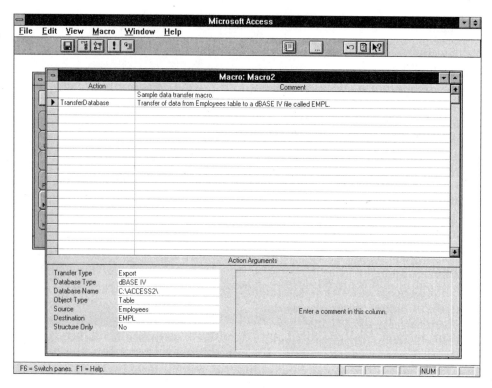

8. Figure 16.15 contains a dBASE IV screen that shows a portion of the contents of the EMPL.DBF file created by the macro.

CHECKPOINT 16E How would you use a macro to export only certain records from the Employees file?

9. Close the active macro window to return to the database window.

FIGURE 16.15
dBASE IV display of exported data from macro

EMPLOYEE_I	LAST_NAME	FIRST_NAME	MIDDLE_INI	DEPARTMENT	DATE_HIRED	SA
10002	Brendan	Harvey	S.	Shipping	03/01/86	
12722	Shirley	Anne	E.	Marketing	12/17/89	
19834	Johnson	Rebecca	J.	Accounting	03/16/88	
21022	Huffman	Donald	G.	Maintenanc	03/18/93	
22323	Howard	Jennifer	K.	Sales	12/15/91	
26114	Weber	Gary	L.	Accounting	02/01/91	
26331	Shaw	Christina	P.	Sales	07/15/91	
26332	Williams	Tom		Sales	07/15/91	
29623	Blessing	Andrew	D.	Shipping	09/01/92	
30119	Hamilton	Matt	J.	Sales	04/01/93	
31244	Pierce	William	S.	Sales	08/01/93	
31250	Harris	Elizabeth	L.	Accounting	08/02/93	

Records   Organize   Fields   Go To   Exit

Browse   C:\access\EMPL   Rec 1/12   File   Num

Command Review

Edit | Copy	Copy selected text into Windows Clipboard.
Edit | Paste	Copy contents of Windows Clipboard into current document.
File | Attach Table	Invoke attach table procedure.
File | Export	Invoke export file procedure.
File | Import	Invoke file import procedure.
File | Imp/Exp Setup	Create a specification for fixed-width text file import or export.
Query | Make Table	Convert the query's datasheet into an Access table.

Exercises

Use the Hunter River database contained within the HUNT.MDB file on the West Student Data Disk for these exercises.

1. Import the spreadsheet file called ADBUDGET.WK1 from the data disk to the HUNT database. Create a new table. Use the named range called ITEMS from the spreadsheet. The first row of this range contains the field names. Print a copy of the contents of the imported table within Access.

2. Export the query called Alphabetical Customers to a delimited text file called ALPHA.TXT. Print a copy of the text file.

3. Attach the Paradox 3.5 table called TEAMS from the data disk. Its password is team165. This table gives a partial list of the teams in several of the sports leagues that are administered by Hunter River. Print a copy of the contents of the table, then delete its link from the Database window.

NOTE *To do this exercise your computer may need to have SHARE.EXE /L:500 in its AUTOEXEC.BAT file. See your instructor for details.*

4. Modify the sample macro shown in Guided Activity 16.6 so that it is launched with a command button of a form. The form should have a control in which the user enters the names of the table and the external data file. Your macro should use those values in the arguments of the TransferDatabase action.

Review Questions

1. Explain reasons why one might want to use the Attach procedure with Access.

2. List the compatible data types that Access can import to or export from. Categorize those applications by type of program.

3. Give reasons for choosing the Import procedure rather than the Attach procedure for using data from an external data file.

4. What is exclusive mode, and why is it important when attaching to an external data file? Under what conditions might you not want to use exclusive mode?

5. Explain how you can append data to an existing table rather than create a new table when you import a file. Is the append option available with all types of data files?

6. If you choose to import from another Access database, what kinds of objects can be copied?

7. What is the purpose of the Import Errors table?

8. Explain the differences between delimited and fixed-width text files. Which is simpler for exports, and why?

9. Suppose you have a text file that you want to import into Access. How would you examine the contents of this file while in Windows?

10. Discuss use of the Windows Clipboard for importing and exporting objects. When is the Clipboard preferred to the usual File | Import and File | Export methods?

11. Describe reasons for using a macro to transfer data between Access and an external data file.

Key Terms

Attach	Import Errors table	ODBC driver
Data translator	Import/Export	Separator
Delimited text file	specification	Structure
Delimiter	Import Options dialog box	TransferDatabase action
Exclusive mode	Importing	TransferSpreadsheet
Exporting	Linked table	action
Fixed-width text file	Merge print	TransferText action

Documentation Research

Use the printed documentation and the on-line Help available with Microsoft Access to answer the following questions. If you use one of the manuals, provide the page number for your reference in the manual.

1. Use the Access Cue Cards help called Import Data.

2. List the steps in attaching to data from an SQL server. This material is covered in the "Cue Cards: Import Data" section and in regular on-line Help.

3. Discuss the steps in preparing export data for the Microsoft Word for Windows Merge Print option.

Building an Application with Access

17

This unit illustrates how to create a complete application using Microsoft Access. An application is a coordinated set of database objects—tables, forms, macros, queries, reports, modules—that enable a user to maintain the data for an organization's database. The unit begins with a discussion of the systems analysis and design process, then continues with a discussion about designing an Access application. The Northwind Traders application from Microsoft is examined. The unit includes the development of a working application for the Hunter River Sporting Goods store. The unit concludes with a discussion of advanced application techniques that are illustrated in the applications packaged with Access.

Learning Objectives

At the completion of this unit you should know

1. the purpose of systems analysis and design,

2. the definition of an Access application,

3. the main components of an Access application,

4. the steps in designing an Access application,

5. some advanced techniques used in Access applications.

At the completion of this unit you should be able to

1. run an existing Access application,

2. create a menu switchboard form,

3. add Paintbrush pictures to a switchboard form,

4. create macros that cause actions to occur when buttons are pushed,

5. start an application automatically.

Designing an Application with Access

An Access *application* is a coordinated set of database objects—tables, forms, macros, queries, reports, modules—that enable a user to maintain the data for a particular set of tasks, whether they be business forecasting, accounts receivable, inventory control, or hospital administration. The Access application is a customized *information system* for the organization. Instead of using the regular Access menus, the application presents a set of custom menus that are designed specifically to accomplish the data management tasks. Thus, individual users of the application do not need to know very much about Microsoft Access to operate your application.

The overall process of developing any information system begins with systems analysis and design, described next.

Information Systems Analysis and Design

The process of investigating an organization and evaluating its information needs is called *systems analysis*. The systems analyst will spend a great deal of time interviewing users, examining existing documents, and evaluating current procedures. Careful attention is paid to the flow of data and information through the organization. It is not possible to develop a usable information system without having arrived at a thorough understanding of the needs of the organization. The end result of the systems analysis is a set of general recommendations for what ought to be done to provide the necessary information.

The next phase, in which detailed specifications are generated, is called *systems design*. In this phase the analyst designs tables, forms, reports, and procedures that will solve the information problems. Users are given an opportunity to react to *prototype* forms and reports. These prototypes are working models that provide a realistic preview of how the system will perform. The design phase is usually performed in several iterations. That is, the analyst prepares some forms and reports, then modifies them in accordance with user feedback. The process is repeated until all the users—whatever their competence—are satisfied that the system is providing the proper kinds of information.

It has been our experience that users rarely "tell" the entire story to analysts the first time around. Some users don't have the time to get fully involved with the project until the last minute. Other users may not have a realistic view of what information they need. Frequently, a user tells the analyst one thing, then changes directions once the user has a chance to work with a prototype form or report. Perhaps it is just a normal part of human nature to solve problems in layers. Whatever the case, it is vital to allow ample time for systems design and modification. Needless to say, Access can accommodate the needs of a range of users, providing an effective tool for rapid development of sophisticated and visually attractive database objects. And those objects can be modified just as quickly to meet changing requirements.

Components of an Application

An application consists of the database objects we have been developing throughout this book. In fact, the Database window lists all of the objects associated with an application. But the glue that holds them together is a series of menu forms called *switchboards* that present choices for users. When the user presses a button on a switchboard form, a macro executes and brings another switchboard form, report, or query into play.

TYPICAL MAIN SWITCHBOARD

Although the specific tasks for each application are different, most follow a similar pattern. The main switchboard presents a menu with these choices:

View Forms
Print Reports
Perform Summary
Database Window
Exit from Microsoft Access

The View Forms selection lets the user view data, make changes, and add new data to tables in the database. The second choice provides a means of printing reports. Both of these options would have secondary menus to let the user select a particular form or report to work with. The Perform Summary option allows the user to cause something to happen after the data are entered, such as closing out the month's accounts and posting them to the journal. The Database Window choice lets the user work directly with the Access Database window. The third and fourth selections might not be present in all applications. The last button is used to terminate the application, close Access, and return to Windows.

OTHER SWITCHBOARDS

The first two choices in the previous menu hint that there will be further choices for what forms or reports are viewed. In fact, macros attached to the command buttons in the main switchboard can open other switchboard forms that let the user choose from available database objects like forms and reports. You might imagine an upside-down tree or pyramid shape in which the top of the pyramid is the main switchboard. As you go down the pyramid it gets wider, reflecting the fact that more lower-level forms become available. We will demonstrate this principle later in this unit.

Steps in Developing an Application

The first step in developing an Access application is to do the systems analysis and decide what information the organization needs. Database design follows, with the development of tables and fields for the database. For a review of database design see Units 1 and 8.

It is very important to complete the design of tables and fields, including properties, before going on to create forms and reports. If you establish properties for the fields in Table Design view, Access will copy those properties into forms that you create. However, any changes made to table and field properties after a form is created will not be copied to the form's properties. Particularly important are the Format, Caption, Default, Validation Rule, and Validation Text properties. Also important is the field's Description property, which becomes the StatusBarText property for a form control containing that field.

Once the tables have been defined, it is appropriate to develop the forms and reports that the organization needs. Typically, these are developed with the cooperation of the users so that changes can quickly be made where necessary. Access provides a flexible environment to modify objects and add new objects without affecting existing objects. But if you change a table, you may have to modify each form and report that uses the modified table. Microsoft may correct this deficiency in a future release of Access.

NOTE *If you change a validation rule for a field in a table, Access will offer to check all the existing data in the table. However, the validation rule is* not *copied into the same-named property in the form.*

At the same time, the analyst can begin developing a set of menus on paper in outline format. Remember that good menus don't offer the user too many choices on one screen. A rule of thumb suggests that no more than four to six menu choices should be given in one menu. If you have more choices than that, consider combining menu items or splitting the menu into two or more lower-level menus.

Your menus should use descriptive labels with action words on the command buttons so that the user understands clearly what that command button does. For instance, "View Forms" and "Print Reports" leave little to the imagination. Although the "Database Window" label is somewhat confusing, your switchboard form can provide an explanatory message for the user.

Once the menu structure is established, you can build the switchboard forms that display the menus. Most analysts will build the forms one at a time, not trying to tie them all together at once. In fact, you can build the form with its command buttons but not attach the macros until a later time.

Once the forms are well into development, it is time to create the macros that cause action. See Units 14 and 15 for a discussion of Access macros. Most applications will have an AutoExec macro to open the main switchboard form when the database is opened. You will have macros that are attached to the On Click property of the command buttons in the switchboard.

After testing the macros and forms separately to be sure that they are correct, it is time to put them together with the switchboards. The Northwind Traders database (NWIND.MDB) packaged with Access provides a useful example of an Access application. We will use this application to demonstrate how to use a custom application in the next section.

FIGURE 17.1
Northwind database diagram query in Design view

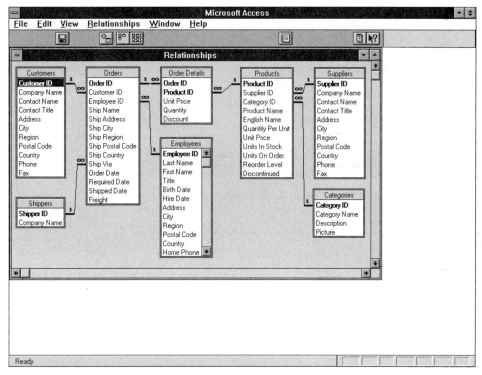

The Northwind Traders Application

NOTE *If your computer does not have the NWIND.MDB sample database available, check with your instructor or lab assistant.*

Northwind Traders is a small import/export business specializing in gourmet foods from around the world. The database is documented in Chapter 2 of the Microsoft Access *User's Guide.* The Edit Relationships diagram is reproduced in Figure 17.1. This query shows the eight main tables in the NWIND database and the relational links between tables.

You will note several similarities between the Hunter River database and the Northwind database. Both databases have tables for customers, employees, products, suppliers, orders, and order details. Northwind adds tables for product categories and shippers. This database comes with a large number of orders (more than 1,000) and otherwise is about the same size as the Hunter River database.

SWITCHBOARDS

The main menu is a form called Main Switchboard, shown in Figure 17.2. It features five large command buttons that lead to other switchboards for viewing forms and printing reports. The lighthouse at the left is a very dark Paintbrush picture; it reproduces better in color on the screen than in this textbook. The stylistic Northwind Traders logo at the top is another Paintbrush picture. The pattern background beneath the command buttons is yet another Paintbrush picture.

The Forms Switchboard form is shown in Figure 17.3. It contains six command buttons leading to specific forms, plus the larger command button at the right to

FIGURE 17.2
*Main
Switchboard for
Northwind
database*

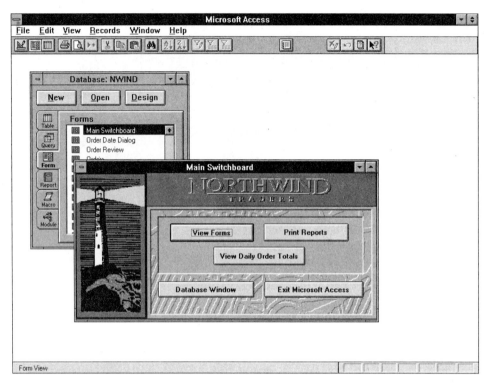

FIGURE 17.3
*Forms
Switchboard for
Northwind
database*

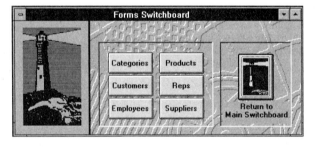

FIGURE 17.4
*Print Reports
Dialog box for
Northwind
database*

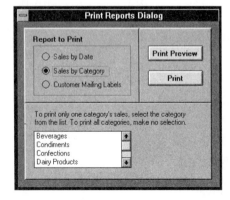

return to the Main Switchboard. The database designer chose to leave you in this menu until you specifically choose to return to the Main Switchboard. Thus, you can view several forms without having to reselect the View Forms from the main menu.

The Print Reports Dialog form is shown in Figure 17.4. It lists three types of reports with option buttons for each report type. The label control in the left center part of the form gives an explanation for the user. The Sales by Category report, highlighted in the figure, features a list box in the lower portion of the dialog box where the user can choose a particular category. After selecting the type of report, the user can push one of the two command buttons at right to choose Print Preview or Print macros. Notice that this form has no option to return to the main menu; after a report is viewed or printed, control automatically passes back to the Main Switchboard. You would have to select Print Reports again from the Main Switchboard to return to this menu.

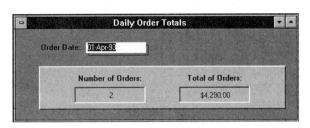

FIGURE 17.5
*Daily Order
Totals box in
Northwind
database*

The third choice in the Main Switchboard form provides for viewing the number and total amount of orders for a given date. This choice brings up a small dialog box that asks the user to enter a date between May 13, 1991, and April 1, 1994, then displays the Daily Order Totals box shown in Figure 17.5.

Although the various switchboards and forms are depicted individually in the last four figures, the Northwind database designer chose to open the dialog boxes on top of the Main Switchboard window. Thus, you would see the other boxes and sense the hierarchy of menus as the application operates. From the macro discussion in Units 14 and 15 you know that it is possible to hide a box, using the WindowMode argument of the OpenForm action.

OPERATING THE NORTHWIND TRADERS APPLICATION

There are two ways to start an application. As discussed in a previous unit, you can create a macro called AutoExec and save it in the database. When the database is opened, that macro will run automatically. The AutoExec macro would open the Main Switchboard form and allow the user to make further choices in that form, as described earlier.

Because the NWIND database is used to demonstrate all facets of Access in the Microsoft documentation, it is not set up to run automatically. To run the application the user must open the NWIND database, then manually switch the Database window to Form mode. The user next locates the Main Switchboard form and clicks the Open button to open the form.

The user sees the main Northwind Traders menu shown in Figure 17.2. Selecting any of the first four command buttons will cause something else to happen. The last button will close the database and exit from Access. We recommend that while developing an application you not actually exit from Access with this choice. Rather, have this choice close the Main Switchboard form and return to the Database window. Only when the application is fully tested should this choice actually close Access. That way you save time by not constantly restarting Access during the testing period.

The following activity will let you try out the Northwind Traders application. In it we will also describe some of the underlying Access objects that make the application work.

GUIDED ACTIVITY 17.1

Using the Northwind Traders Application

In this Guided Activity you will load the NWIND database and work through the menus and forms of the Northwind Traders application. See your instructor or lab assistant if the NWIND.MDB database is not available in your computer.

1. Start Windows and load Access as usual.

2. Open the NWIND database and switch to Form mode.

3. Select the Main Switchboard form and click Open. Access will display the main menu shown in Figure 17.2.

4. Click the View Forms button in the Main Switchboard. Access will display the Forms Switchboard shown in Figure 17.3.

5. Click the Products command button in the Forms Switchboard. Access will open the Products form and display the first record as shown in Figure 17.6. You can use the navigation buttons in the lower portion of the form to scroll through the various products carried by Northwind. There are 77 records in the Products table.

FIGURE 17.6
Products form of the Northwind database

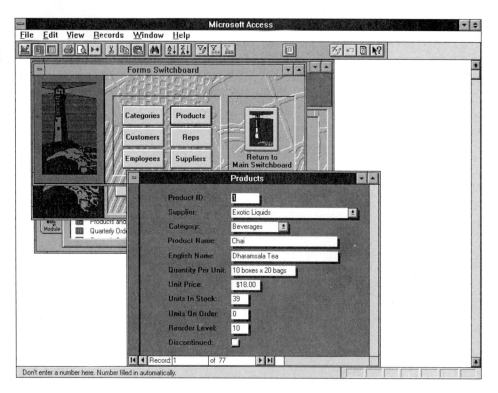

6. When finished with the Products form, close its window by double-clicking the Control-menu box. You will return to the Forms Switchboard.

7. Let's take a look at the design of the Forms Switchboard. Click on the Design View button in the toolbar (or give the View I Form Design command from the menu bar). To enlarge the display, click the maximize button in the upper-right corner of the Forms Switchboard window. Double-click on the Products command button to display its properties sheet. Your desktop should look like Figure 17.7. You may have to drag some of the boxes around to reveal parts of the design.

FIGURE 17.7
Design view for Forms Switchboard form

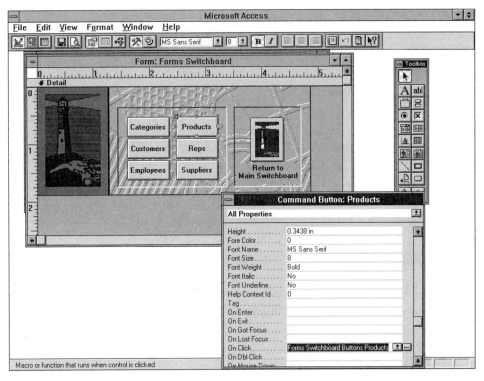

CHECKPOINT 17A Notice that the On Click property of this command button has been set to `Forms Switchboard Buttons.Products`. What does this phrase mean?

8. The macro described in the checkpoint is shown in Figure 17.8. You do not have to display this macro window. Whenever someone pushes the Products command button in the Forms Switchboard, this macro runs. The Products macro is simple: it uses the OpenForm action to open the Products form in Edit data mode, allowing changes. It then moves the Products form down 2 inches and over 2 inches with the MoveSize action.

FIGURE 17.8
Macro window for Forms Switchboard Buttons macro group

Macro Name	Action	Comment
		Attached to the buttons on the Forms Switchboard form.
Categories	OpenForm	Open the Categories form.
Customers	OpenForm	Open the Customers form.
Employees	OpenForm	Open the Employees form.
Products	OpenForm	Open the Products form.
	MoveSize	Move the Products form.
Reps	OpenForm	Open the Sales Reps form.
Suppliers	OpenForm	Open the Suppliers form.
Exit to Main	OpenForm	Exit to the Main Switchboard form.

Action Arguments

Form Name	Products
View	Form
Filter Name	
Where Condition	
Data Mode	Edit
Window Mode	Normal

Enter a macro name in this column.

9. You should still have the Design view of the Forms Switchboard on your screen. Click the Form view button in the toolbar to switch to that view. Click the Return to Main Switchboard button in that window. Access should close the Forms Switchboard and present the Main Switchboard again.

10. This time click the Print Reports button. Access will display the Print Reports Dialog box shown earlier in Figure 17.4. Click the Sales by Category option button, then select Beverages from the list box. When ready, click the Print Preview button. After a few moments to process the more than 1,000 order records, Access will display the print preview window shown in Figure 17.9. (Your window should not be maximized.) The window is shown maximized to display more of it. Not only does the report group data so that only the Beverages are shown, but an Access Graph is also prepared and displayed in the same window.

FIGURE 17.9
Sales by Category report for Northwind database

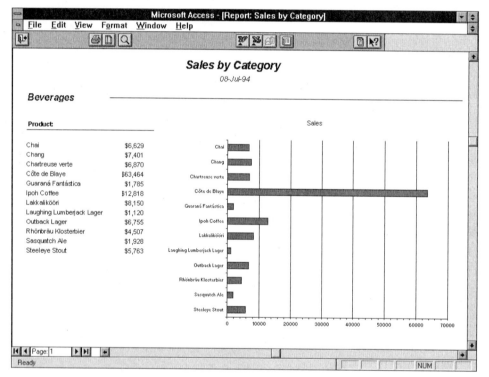

11. When you have finished viewing this preview, click the Close button. Access will close the Preview window and return to the Main Switchboard form.

12. From this form click the Database Window button. The macro attached to this button is shown in Figure 17.10. You do not have to display this macro. The SelectObject action in the Database Window macro will display the Database window if the Name of Object argument is left blank. Access will switch the Database window to the mode indicated by the Object Type argument.

13. Click anywhere on the Main Switchboard window to make it active. To leave the application, click on the Exit Microsoft Access button. As mentioned earlier, this

will close the NWIND database and close the Access window. Note in Figure 17.10 that the Quit action is used for the Exit macro in the Main Switchboard Buttons macro group. This is where you might substitute another action such as Close to close the Main Switchboard form rather than exit out of Access.

FIGURE 17.10
Main Switchboard Buttons macro group

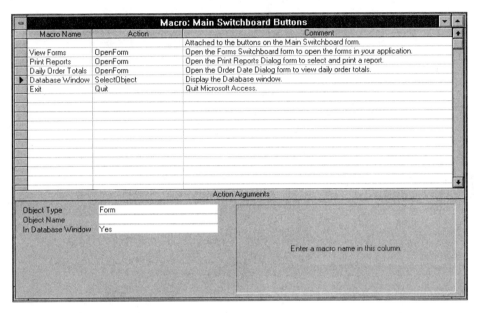

Building the Hunter River Application

The remainder of this unit will deal with creation of an application for the Hunter River Sporting Goods store. First we will deal with the systems analysis and design process, then look at menus. Because we have dealt with this organization throughout the textbook, many parts of the application have already been created.

Analyzing the Hunter River System

Recall that Hunter River is a medium-sized retail sporting goods store selling a wide variety of products in several product categories. From the discussion of relational database concepts in Unit 8 we developed the database design shown in Figure 17.11. The main tables are shown in this diagram, along with principal relational links between tables.

We have already developed forms and reports for most of the tables in this database. Now we need to provide forms for viewing customers, products, vendors, employees, and orders. We need reports for many of the same tables, plus a few other reports that deal with customers, employees, accounting data, and sales over time. Our application will parallel the Northwind Traders application in some respects.

FIGURE 17.11
*Hunter River
database design*

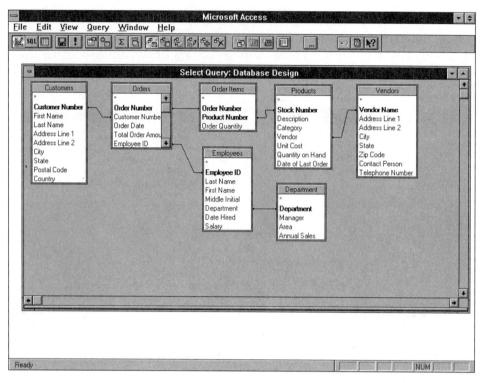

Developing Menus

We will have a Main Switchboard form to start the Hunter River application. It will have choices for:

View Forms
Print Reports
Show Summary Sales
Quit Application

These choices will be represented by a macro group with individual macros for each button.

The View Forms menu should present menu items for Customers, Employees, Products, Vendors, Department, and Orders. We also need a button to return to the Main Switchboard menu. The forms called by the command buttons should allow users to view and make changes to data as well as to add new data. All forms already exist within the HUNT Database window.

The Print Reports menu should have choices for Customer Labels, Salary, Inventory, and Product reports. All reports already exist within the HUNT Database window.

The sequence of our development of the application is shown below. We will do the first four items in Guided Activities, with the last three items left as exercises at the end of the unit.

■ Create the Main Switchboard form, including command buttons.

- Create the Main Switchboard Buttons macro group with individual macros for each command button. Attach these macros to the Main Switchboard buttons.

- Create the Forms Switchboard form, including its command buttons.

- Create the Forms Switchboard Buttons macro group with individual macros for each command button. Attach these macros to the Forms Switchboard buttons.

- Create the Reports Switchboard form, including its command buttons.

- Create the Reports Switchboard Buttons macro group with individual macros for each command button. Attach these macros to the Reports Switchboard buttons.

- Create the dialog box and form to show summary sales for a specified period of time.

GUIDED ACTIVITY 17.2

Building the Main Switchboard Form

In this Guided Activity you will create the Main Switchboard form with a textured background, the Hunter logo, and the four command buttons.

1. Close any open windows, then close the NWIND Database window with the File | Close command, if it is not already closed.

2. Open the HUNT database and switch to Form mode.

3. Click the New button to create a new form. At the New Form dialog box click the Blank Form button.

CHECKPOINT 17B Is it possible to create a new form without specifying a table or query as the data source?

4. Using the mouse, drag the form borders so that it is approximately 4 inches wide and 2.75 inches tall. If necessary, move the Toolbox and Properties boxes to the side.

5. Click the Object Frame tool in the Toolbox. Use the mouse to create an unbound object control that covers the entire surface of the form. If you need help with controls, refer to Units 9 and 10.

6. After you have created the unbound object frame control, Access will display the Insert Object box and prompt you for a file. Select Paintbrush Picture and click the Create from File button. Use the file named TEXTURE.BMP that is found on the data disk.

7. Access will place this background picture on the form. Adjust the size of the form to fit the picture.

8. Click the Rectangle tool in the Toolbox, the seventh box down in the right column. Use the mouse to create a large rectangle control in the center of the form, leaving about one-half inch on each side and one-quarter inch on top and bottom.

FIGURE 17.12
*Main
Switchboard
background
controls*

Unbound object
control

Rectangle control

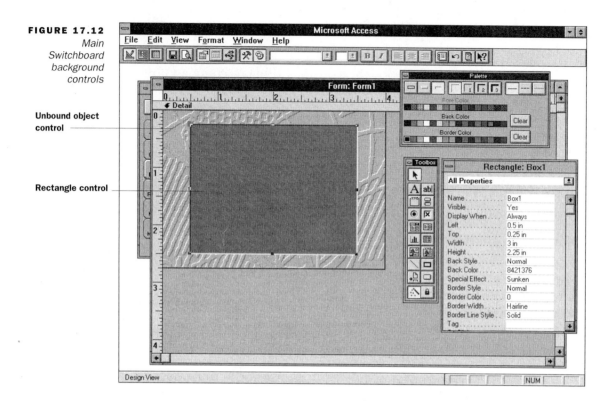

9. If the Palette dialog box is not already present, click the Palette tool in the toolbar
    or give the View | Palette command from the menu bar. With the rectangle control
    still selected, click the Sunken button (third from the left) in the Palette box. In
    the Back Color row of the Palette box, click the medium green shade, third from
    the right. Your form should look like Figure 17.12.

10. Click the Unbound Object tool in the Toolbox, then use the mouse to create a con-
    trol in the upper portion of the inset box in the form. This control should be
    nearly as wide as the box and about an inch tall. Refer to the next figure for
    precise placement. When prompted, select Paintbrush Picture and click the Cre-
    ate from File button. The file for this object is called HUNT2.BMP on the data
    disk. Access will place the Hunter River logo in the control. Adjust the size of the
    control to fit the logo.

11. Click on the Command Button tool in the Toolbox, the next to last button in the
    right column. Make sure the Control Wizard button is *not* pushed. Create a com-
    mand button underneath the logo, nearly as wide. Remember to leave room to
    place four buttons in the space available.

12. Repeat step 11 with three more command buttons. Use the mouse to move and
    resize the controls in the form as necessary. It takes some practice to get the but-
    tons to be the same size. See Figure 17.13 for placement and size of these controls.
    Notice that we pulled the bottom of the rectangle control down slightly to make
    room for the last button.

FIGURE 17.13
*Main
Switchboard
form with
command
buttons*

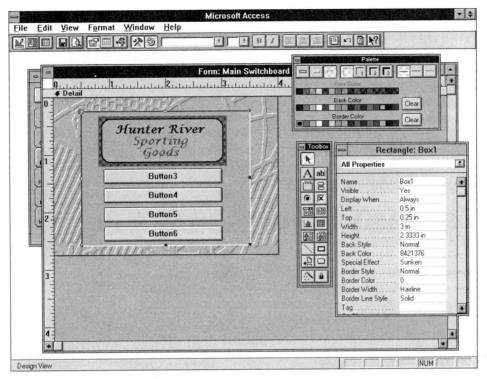

13. Now we need to place the labels in the command buttons. Click on the first button to select it, then use the mouse to highlight the Button 3 text. In its place type `View Forms`.

14. Repeat with the other three buttons. The labels are `Print Reports`, `Show Summary Sales`, `Quit Application`. Alternatively, you could fill the labels in the Caption property of each control.

15. Click in the gray area outside the form to select the Form. In the Form Properties box change the Scroll Bars property to Neither. (Menus do not need scroll bars.)

16. Use the File | Save As command. The name should be `Main Switchboard`.

17. Click the Form button to change to Form view. Your Main Switchboard should look like Figure 17.14. Close the form.

In the next activity we will build some of the macros in the Hunter River application.

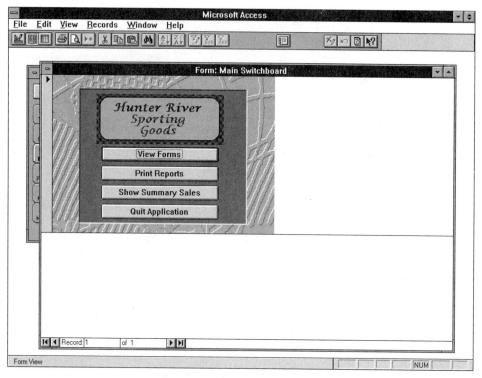

FIGURE 17.14
*Finished Main
Switchboard
form for Hunter
River application*

GUIDED ACTIVITY 17.3

Creating the Main Switchboard Buttons Macro Group

In this Guided Activity you will create the macros that operate the menu buttons in the Main Switchboard form.

1. Close any open windows and return to the HUNT Database window. In Macro mode click the New button to create a new macro.

2. With the Macro Window open, click the Macro Names button in the toolbar to display the macro name column. You could also use the View | Macro Names button from the menu bar.

3. In the first line fill in this Comment: `Attached to buttons on the Main Switchboard form.`

4. On the second line fill in the name `View Forms` in the first column. In the Action column select the OpenForm action. The Form Name argument is `Forms Switchboard`. The Comment is `Open the Forms Switchboard form to open the forms in your application.`

5. Repeat the previous step for the second button. The Macro Name is `Print Reports`. The action is OpenForm, and the Form Name argument is `Reports Switchboard`. The Comment is `Open the Reports Switchboard form to select and print a report.`

6. Repeat step 5 for the third button. The Macro Name is Show Summary. The action is OpenForm, and the Form Name argument is Show Summary Sales. The Comment is Open the Show Summary Sales dialog box.

7. For the fourth button use the Name Close Application. The Action is Close. The Object Type argument is Form and the Object Name argument is Main Switchboard. The Comment is Close the Main Switchboard form and return to the Database window.

8. Save the macro under the name Main Switchboard Buttons. The macro is shown in Figure 17.15.

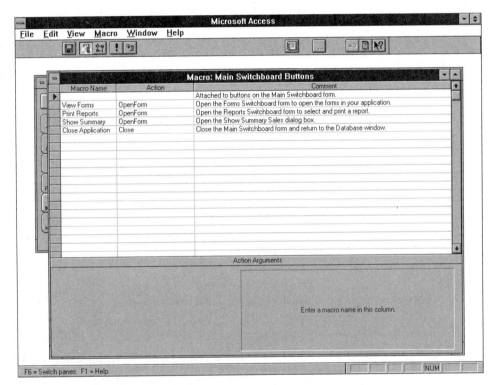

FIGURE 17.15
Main Switchboard Buttons macro group

9. Close the macro window.

10. Finally, we need to attach these macros to the command buttons in the Main Switchboard form. In the HUNT Database window, switch to Form mode. Select the Main Switchboard form and open the form in Design view.

11. Click twice on the View Forms command button to display its Properties sheet. In the On Click property, enter Main Switchboard Buttons.View Forms and press [Enter]. This notation means to run the View Forms macro within the Main Switchboard Buttons macro group.

12. Repeat the previous step with the other buttons, as shown below:

Button	On Click
Print Reports	Main Switchboard Buttons.Print Reports
Show Summary Sales	Main Switchboard Buttons.Show Summary
Quit Application	Main Switchboard Buttons.Close Application

CHECKPOINT 17C What will Access do if you misspell one of the macro names in the On Click property and then push that command button in the form?

13. Use the File | Save command to save the modified form. Close the Form window.

In the next activity we show how to create the Forms Switchboard form.

GUIDED ACTIVITY 17.4

Creating the Forms Switchboard Form

In this Guided Activity you will create the Forms Switchboard menu. If you need help with the details of this form, refer to Guided Activity 17.2 where similar procedures were done.

1. Close any open windows and return to the HUNT Database window.

2. Switch to Form mode and click the New button.

3. At the New Form dialog box click the Blank Form button.

4. Adjust the size of the form by dragging the borders so that it is 2 inches tall by 4 inches wide.

5. Place an unbound object control inside the form that occupies that entire form. Click the Create from File button. When prompted, select the Texture.bmp Paintbrush Picture for the background, just as we did in the Main Switchboard.

6. Place a large rectangle control in the left portion of the form, starting at the 0.25,0.25-inch coordinates and stretching to the 2.5,1.7-inch coordinates. Click the Back Color Clear and Sunken buttons in the Palette box for this control. You will see the texture pattern shown through this control.

TIP *If you have trouble selecting the proper control, select the texture object, then press the Tab key to cycle through all of the controls in the form.*

CHECKPOINT 17D What property of the rectangle control is changed when you click the Sunken button in the Palette box?

7. Place another rectangle control to the right of the first, centered in the remaining space within the form. This rectangle should also be Sunken and Clear, both set in the Palette box. Figure 17.16 shows the form so far.

8. Place six command buttons in the left rectangle and one button in the right rectangle. Figure 17.17 shows the way this form should appear after the command buttons are added. You may need to enlarge the buttons slightly to hold the

FIGURE 17.16
Preliminary design of Forms Switchboard

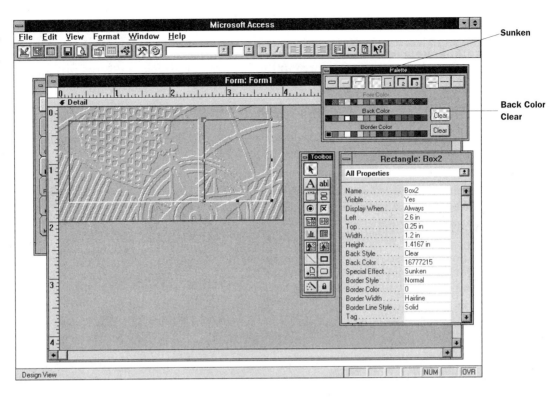

FIGURE 17.17
Forms Switchboard form for Hunter River application

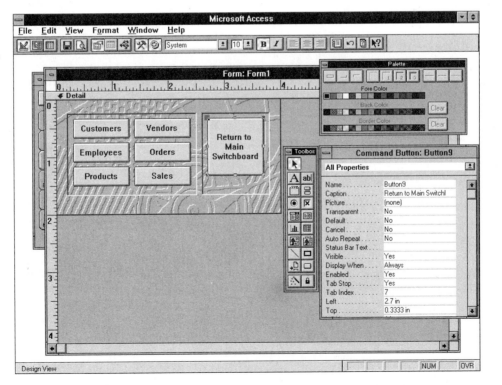

caption. It is also possible to reduce the font size slightly to make the caption fit. The command buttons in this activity use the default 10-point font size.

9. Click outside the form in the gray area to select the form property box. Set the Scroll Bars property to Neither.

10. Save the form as `Forms Switchboard` and close the Form window.

In the next activity we will create the macro group that will be attached to command buttons in the Forms Switchboard form.

GUIDED ACTIVITY 17.5

Creating the Forms Switchboard Buttons Macro Group

In this Guided Activity you will create the macros that operate the menu buttons in the Forms Switchboard form. If you need help with details, refer to Guided Activity 17.3 where similar procedures were done.

1. Close any open windows and return to the HUNT Database window. Switch to Macro mode and click the New button.

2. When the Macro window opens, click the Macro Names button in the toolbar.

3. In the Comment cell of the first line enter `Attached to buttons on the Forms Switchboard form.`

4. In the Macro Name cell of the second line enter `Customers`. The Action is OpenForm. Press [F6] to move to the lower pane. The Form Name argument is `Customers`. Press [F6] to move to the upper pane. The Comment is `Open the Customers form.`

5. Repeat step 4 with the following information for the remaining five command buttons. (*Hint:* Copy the first macro and make changes.)

Button	Action	Form Name	Comment
Employees	OpenForm	Employees	Open the Employees form.
Products	OpenForm	Products	Open the Products form.
Vendors	OpenForm	Vendors	Open the Vendors form.
Orders	OpenForm	Orders	Open the Orders form.
Sales	OpenForm	Sales	Open the Sales form.

CHECKPOINT 17E   We use the default values for the other arguments for each OpenForm action. What changes might you consider making to the other arguments?

6. The last macro in this group is named `Exit`. Its Action is OpenForm, and the Form Name argument is `Main Switchboard`. If the Main Switchboard is already open, Access will switch to that window without closing the Forms Switchboard window. The comment for this action is `Return to the Main Switchboard`. The final macro group is shown in Figure 17.18.

FIGURE 17.18
*Forms
Switchboard
Buttons macro
group*

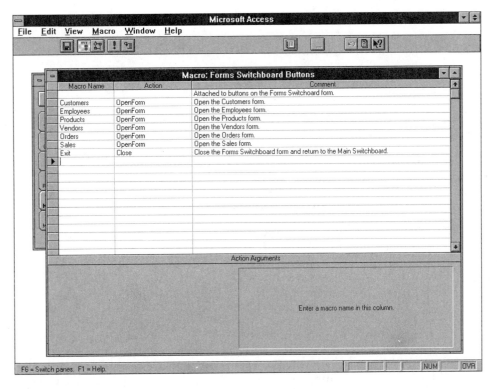

7. Save this macro as `Forms Switchboard Buttons` and close the Macro window.

8. Switch to Form mode in the HUNT Database window. Locate the Forms Switchboard form and click the Design button.

9. Click twice on the Customers command button to display its Properties sheet. In the On Click property enter `Forms Switchboard Buttons.Customers` and press Enter.

10. Repeat the procedure from step 9 for the remaining six command buttons:

Button	On Click
Employees	Forms Switchboard Buttons.Employees
Products	Forms Switchboard Buttons.Products
Vendors	Forms Switchboard Buttons.Vendors
Orders	Forms Switchboard Buttons.Orders
Sales	Forms Switchboard Buttons.Sales
Return to	Forms Switchboard Buttons.Exit

11. Save the form and close the Form window.

   In the next activity we show how the Hunter River application works.

GUIDED ACTIVITY 17.6

Running the Hunter River Application

In this Guided Activity you will work with the partially complete Hunter River application.

1. Close any open windows and return to the HUNT Database window. Switch to Form mode.

2. Select the Main Switchboard form and click Open. Access will open the Main Switchboard menu we created in a previous activity.

3. Click the View Forms button to open the Forms Switchboard.

4. At the Forms Switchboard click the Customers button. Access will display the first record of the Customers form.

CHECKPOINT 17F This form allows the user to make changes to the records in the Customers table. How can you prevent the user from making changes to this table?

5. Close the Customers form by double-clicking the Control-menu box. You should return to the Forms Switchboard menu, which is still open on the desktop.

6. Try out the other menu choices in the Forms Switchboard. When you are satisfied that all are working, click the Return to Main Switchboard button in the Forms Switchboard.

7. Click the Print Reports button in the Main Switchboard. What does Access do in this case? You will complete the application as an exercise.

8. Quit the application by clicking the Quit Application button in the Main Switchboard.

Other Application Techniques

Although we will not illustrate these techniques in this textbook, along with NWIND two other sample applications packaged with Access provide innovative ideas for applications. The ORDERS application is a sophisticated order entry and invoice printing system for the Northwind Traders company. The SOLUTION application offers structured assistance to those who want to build their own applications; highlight a component in this Access application and a special help system will show how to create that component.

The ORDERS Application

When you open the ORDERS database, an AutoExec macro automatically opens the Orders form and hides the Database window. This application displays a custom user interface in the main menu, shown in Figure 17.19. Access also displays a custom help system called Show Me that contains references to various parts of the

FIGURE 17.19
*Orders form
with custom
user interface
features*

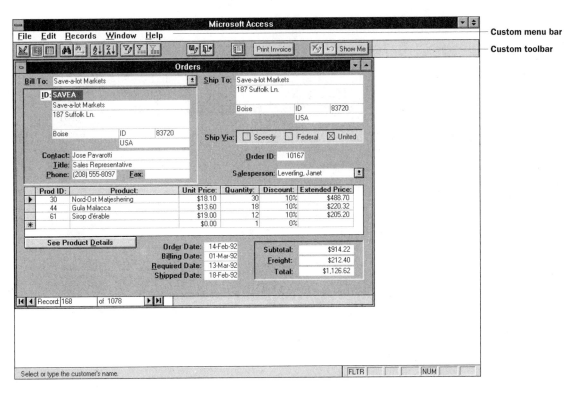

ORDERS application. You can select an item and learn how that portion of the
application was built. For example, Figure 17.20 illustrates the Show Me help
window and the custom File menu bar.

FIGURE 17.20
*Orders
application
showing custom
menu bar and
Show Me help
window*

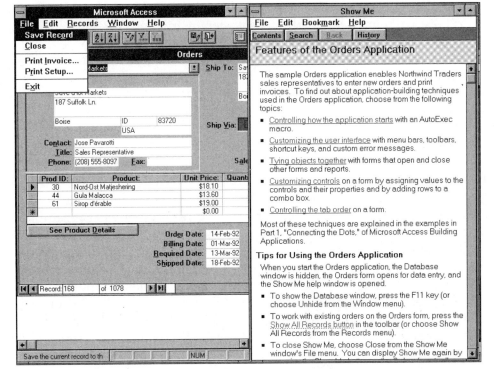

FIGURE 17.21
*Solutions form
with examples
of application
components*

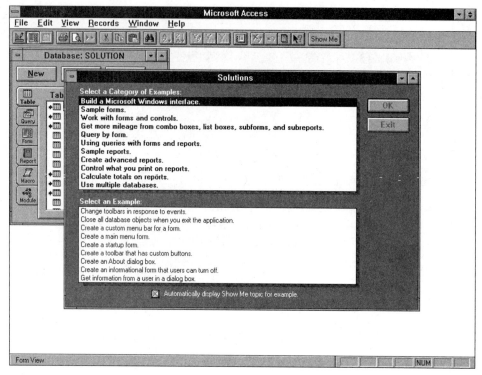

The SOLUTION Application

The SOLUTION database was designed to teach you how to create very sophisticated applications. Figure 17.21 shows the Solutions form, which contains examples for the "Build a Microsoft Windows interface" category. The SOLUTION database's Show Me help system gives step-by-step instructions for reproducing the example forms, reports, and interface elements commonly found in Access applications.

This database make extensive use of Access Basic modules; those techniques are beyond the scope of this textbook. You can learn more about modules by reading the Microsoft Access *Building Applications* manual and by studying the Show Me Help screens.

Other Applications Tools

Other Access 2.0 applications are available at extra cost as explained in the Access documentation. The Microsoft Access Solutions Pack has four ready-to-run business applications that can be used for your organization or used as samples to learn by. Included are Sales Manager, Asset Tracker, Registration Desk, and Service Desk applications.

The Microsoft Access Developer's Toolkit is a specialized version of Access 2.0 that enables the professional developer to create and distribute custom applications for clients. The Developer's Toolkit contains a run-time version of Access that enables the client to run the Access application without having to purchase a separate copy of Access. This version of Access also contains an *Advanced Topics* manual and the Microsoft Access *Language Reference* manual.

Exercises

Use the Hunter River database contained within the HUNT.MDB file on the West Student Data Disk for these exercises.

1. Create the Reports Switchboard form for the Hunter River application. The switchboard should allow for five reports (Customer Labels, Customers, Employee Salary, Inventory, and Product Report By Vendor) and have a Return to Main Switchboard button. You should add other features such as texture and background rectangles, similar to the Forms Switchboard developed in this unit.

2. Create the Reports Switchboard Buttons macro group, with individual macros for the buttons in the Reports Switchboard form. Attach these macros to the buttons in the Reports Switchboard form.

3. Create an AutoExec macro that opens the initial Main Switchboard form. Remember that you can defeat an AutoExec macro by holding down the [Shift] key when you open the database containing that macro.

4. Create a Show Summary Sales dialog box that can be used to show total sales for a particular period of time. Refer to the Northwind Traders database for an example of this form. Remember that the user must input data for a period that contains some orders, based upon the Orders table in the HUNT Database.

Review Questions

1. List the advantages of using an Access application to manage the database objects.

2. Define systems analysis and contrast it with systems design.

3. Why is prototyping useful when developing a new application?

4. Describe the steps in creating an Access application.

5. Why is it important to finalize database design, particularly table names and field properties, before creating Access forms and reports?

6. Explain what is meant by the following value for the On Click property in a form:
`Reports Switchboard Buttons.Mailing Labels`

7. How would you place a Paintbrush picture such as a logo or texture background into a switchboard form?

8. Why is it generally a good idea to avoid using the Quit action in a macro attached to the Main Switchboard?

9. Referring to Figure 17.2, the Main Switchboard for the Northwind database, list all of the controls that have been placed in the form.

10. Explain how to create the following effects in a control:

    a. Change the fill color.

    b. Make it a sunken control.

    c. Have the background control show through the foreground control.

    d. Make the control show only on the screen, not in printed reports.

11. Explain why it is helpful to use an AutoExec macro in an Access application.

Key Terms

Application	Prototype	Systems analysis
Information system	Switchboard	Systems design

Documentation Research

Use the printed documentation and the on-line Help available with Microsoft Access to answer the following questions. If you use one of the manuals, provide the page number for your reference in the manual.

1. Examine the other databases that are packaged with Microsoft Access. You may have to look in the *User's Guide* for startup instructions. Use the File | Open command to see whether these applications are installed in your computer.

2. For each of the databases in the previous question, open them in Access and work with the applications that start up automatically. Describe the purpose of each application. Explain the purpose of the AutoKeys macro found in the Orders database. (*Hint:* Look in the "Customize the User Interface" topic.)

3. What capabilities are possible with Access Basic modules? Explain why one might want to use modules in addition to macros.

Physicians' Medical Clinic (XII): Building an Application with Access

In this application you will design a custom application for the PMC organization, using the material covered in previous units. You will open the PMC database and create switchboard forms and macros to attach to command buttons. Read the directions carefully. Clearly identify which output goes with which part of the application.

At this time the clinic is primarily concerned with handling patient records and billing, so you have been asked by Dr. Greenway to focus on developing a design for this portion of the system. Your assignment has been structured in the parts below.

1. Design the menus that PMC could use for this Patient Records system. Consider the forms and reports that would be appropriate for this system.

2. Create Access switchboard forms for the main menu, forms menu, and print menu. Build macros that will handle moving between the switchboards and the appropriate forms and reports.

3. Create simple forms and reports that reflect the information displayed in the forms and reports switchboards. Make sure that your system actually produces the desired output.

Administering Database Management Systems

This unit presents an overview of some issues associated with administering a database management system and examines the role of the database administrator. The unit discusses Access features for a multiuser environment, including Access work groups and user members. Database security issues such as passwords, encryption, and use permissions are covered. Record and file locks are presented as alternatives to exclusive use in a shared environment. The unit presents issues of client/server computing, including use of Access as a front end for an SQL server.

Learning Objectives

At the completion of this unit you should know

1. the role of the database administrator,

2. the levels of security available with Access,

3. how to create a secure Access system,

4. the types of access permissions,

5. the importance of doing regular backups,

6. about using Access on a network,

7. the value of Access in client/server computing.

At the completion of this unit you should be able to

1. prepare a data dictionary,

2. change a user password,

3. add a new user account to Access,

4. change permissions for a work group or an individual account,

5. compact, encrypt, and decrypt a database file,

6. repair a damaged database file,

7. set the Default Record Locking option,

8. refresh the datasheet or form and set the Refresh Interval.

Important Commands

File | Add-ins | Database Documentor

File | Compact Database

File | Convert Database

File | Encrypt/Decrypt Database

File | Print Definition

File | Repair Database

Records | Refresh

Security | Change Password

Security | Groups

Security | Permissions

Security | Users

Role of the Database Administrator

The *database administrator* is responsible for managing the development and administration of databases within the organization's information systems. Depending on the size of the organization and sophistication of the information systems group, this role may be assigned to a single person or shared among several individuals. The database administrator may also be known as the *system administrator* in some organizations.

Specifically, the database administrator is responsible for the following:

- Providing documentation for the database, including a data dictionary about objects within the database

- Training users of the database, including development of user guides

- Developing security procedures including work groups, access permissions, passwords, and data encryption

- Generating compaction, backup, and recovery procedures

- Monitoring performance of the database and recommending changes as needed

- Working with users and technical personnel from the information systems department, arbitrating configuration changes in the database structure

- Participating in the development of new database systems, including establishing standards for the developers

Maintaining the Data Dictionary

Compared to most database management systems, Access provides a better environment for built-in definitions. Long field names provide an excellent way to explicitly name fields, and the Description property allows up to 255 additional definition characters. You can enter a field description in the table's Design view and a table description in the Table Property sheet. Thereafter, field description appears in the status bar text area whenever the field is dragged from the field list to a control in a form or report.

The *data dictionary* is a collection of the definitions of all objects within the database. It contains the names of tables, forms, fields, reports, queries, macros, and modules. Within each object the fields, indexes, and controls are carefully defined, with descriptions of possible values. Because many people ordinarily work with a single database, it is important to keep a central repository of information about the structure of the database. That way developers use the same naming conventions when creating new objects, and users can quickly identify the proper fields and their locations within the database objects. With a current data dictionary, it is much easier to prepare system and user documentation.

The data dictionary is typically maintained outside the database itself, although it can be maintained within Access by developing a special database just for this purpose. This documentation contains tables whose fields describe the kinds of objects found within the database. You can easily modify the data dictionary when it is maintained in this format. With Access's report capability, you can create reports to format the information in the desired fashion. Although we won't develop a data dictionary as a Guided Activity in this unit, a sample table is shown in Figure 18.1. Further development of this dictionary is left as an exercise.

New to Access 2.0 is the capability to produce documentation about the database or its objects. Use the File | Print Definition command to print the definition of a single database object such as a table, form, or macro. A more complete print capability is available through the File | Add-ins | Database Documentor command. With this command you can print definitions for a group of objects or all the objects in the database at one time. Use of these commands is left as an exercise.

Access Security Procedures

Many personal computer users in a business setting are not aware of the value of the data that they maintain or access through the database system. Every day, some are unpleasantly surprised to learn firsthand how the unauthorized knowledge of

FIGURE 18.1

*Design view
for a data
dictionary table*

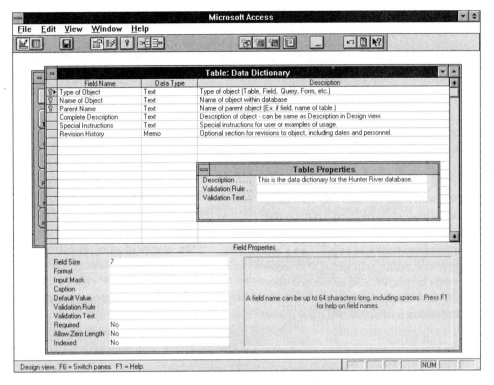

their company's plans may lead to significant financial loss. Disgruntled employees, even hackers not associated with the company, may sabotage data stored within the database. As a result, a company should ensure that only certain employees are authorized to access vital information. You as the database administrator may want to allow some employees to view data but not make changes to that data. For these reasons, most organizations activate a variety of the security methods provided by Access.

LEVELS OF SECURITY

Security is designed to provide timely access to authorized users yet keep unauthorized users out of the database. Security may be implemented in levels within the organization, described below:

- No security methods implemented

- Physical security measures such as door and keyboard or computer locks, preventing users from physical access to the computer

- System level (network level) security methods such as login passwords and other restrictions

- Access (application level) security methods, described in this unit—in this case the system is known as a *secure system*

You can set up an unsecured system with no access restrictions whatever. In this case, a user can read and make changes to all objects and data within the database.

All of the previous examples in this textbook assume this configuration. The user name in this case is "Admin" and has full rights within the database. If you do not activate any security measures, Access will create an unsecured system by default.

Access Work Groups

In a secure system each user will have both a *user name* and a *password* assigned. The user must log on to Access and provide the correct user name and password before being given access to the database. The user name may be up to 20 characters long and may contain spaces except at the beginning. Ordinarily, when you assign user names they are placed into one of several Access work groups.

An Access *work group* is a collection of users who share similar information needs and responsibilities. If you activate the groups feature, you can assign *access permissions* to an entire group at a time. All the members of that group inherit the access permissions for that group. Access permissions represent rights to perform operations (read, modify, and so on) on each type of database object (table, query, form, and the like) within the database. We will cover permissions in a later section of this unit.

Access creates three default work groups, although you can create more groups as needed. The *Admins group* represents users who have administrative responsibilities over the system—managers, financial officers, CEOs, and others. The Admin user is automatically placed in this group. Admins group members have full permissions for all objects in the database. The *Users group* holds new database users as they are added to the system—they could be managers, accounting personnel, inventory control staff, and others. The *Guests group* includes people who need to have occasional access to some information within the database but to whom you don't want to assign a user account.

CAUTION *The following discussion is made to illustrate the procedure of creating a secure Access system. It is not recommended that you make any changes to your Access security system without carefully studying the Microsoft Access documentation. If you forget the password you may lose access to both Access and your data!*

Creating a Secure System in Access

To create a secure system you must go through several steps, described in Chapter 14 of the Microsoft Access *Building Applications* manual and outlined below. Following the list is a discussion of each step.

- Activate the logon procedure.
- Log on and create a new system administrator account.
- Log on as the new system administrator and disable the Admin user account.
- Change the new system administrator password.
- Establish other user accounts and set permissions.

ACTIVATING THE LOGON PROCEDURE

Before you activate the logon procedure, Access automatically logs each user under the *Admin user* name, which has a blank password. If you change this password to some other value, the Logon dialog box is automatically displayed the next time you start Access. The Admin password can be up to 14 characters long and can include any character other than ASCII code 0. The password is *case-sensitive*, meaning that ABC and Abc are recognized as different. You will have to type in the password later exactly as you typed it here.

To change the password, choose Change Password from the Security menu with a database open. In the Change Password dialog box you first type in the old password to verify that you are the proper user, then type in the new password. The password displays as asterisks as you type it in so that no one else can see what you typed in. Then you must retype the new password to verify your entry. The next time you start Access, you will be asked to enter this user name and password.

CAUTION *If you forget the password you will not be able to recover it from the database, so protect the password.*

CREATING THE NEW SYSTEM ADMINISTRATOR ACCOUNT

You need to create a new system administrator account to replace the Admin account. It is prudent to change the system administrator account from Admin to some other user name. Otherwise someone else could log on as Admin and try to guess your password. If you change the user name as well, it would be much more difficult to guess both values.

LOGGING ON You must log on as the Admin user (or another member of the Admins group) to make these changes. When prompted in the Logon box, enter Admin as the user name. (Do not add the word "user" to the end of the user name as the author first did!) Press Tab to move to the Password line. In the password line enter the Admin account password established in the previous section. Click OK to complete the entry. Figure 18.2 shows the Logon dialog box.

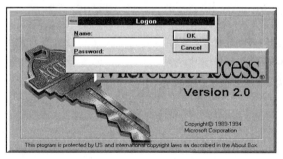

FIGURE 18.2
The Access Logon dialog box

If you have entered the correct password, Access will start up normally and you can open a database. If you did not enter the correct user name and password for that user name, Access will display a warning message and then return to the Logon dialog box. This process will continue until you enter the correct user name and password, or you click Cancel and return to the Program Manager without having started Access.

ADDING A NEW ACCOUNT To add a new user name, choose the Users command from the Security menu. The Security menu only appears when you have a database open and only in the Database window. In the Users dialog box you can add or delete

FIGURE 18.3
*The Users
dialog box for
adding/removing
users*

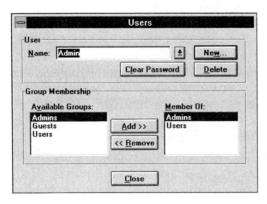

users and change their work group assignments. The Users dialog box is shown in Figure 18.3.

Suppose you were going to add a new system administrator account called "Master". Type `Master` in the Name box, then click the New button in the Users box. Access will display the New User/Group dialog box and ask you to enter a 4-20 character *personal identifier*, or **PID**, just like a bank's PIN for automated teller machine cards. In this box the PID will display as you type it in. The combination of user name and PID uniquely identifies this account to Access. Click OK to create the account.

When you return to the Users dialog box, you will see that the Master account is automatically assigned to the Users group. Select Admins in the Available Groups list, then click the Add button. Access will add the Master account to the Admins group. You can then log on as system administrator with this new user name. The initial password will be blank. You should change the password to a secret value.

CHANGING THE NEW SYSTEM ADMINISTRATOR PASSWORD You can exit from Access, then start Access again to log on with a new user name. In this case you would log on with the Master user name just created. Open the desired database, then use the Security I Change Password command to change the password. As before, you will be asked to enter the old password (now blank), then the new password and the new password again to verify its value. Now only you should know the new system administrator account's user name and password.

DISABLING THE ADMIN ACCOUNT To secure the system, after you have created the new system administrator account, you should disable the previous Admin account by changing its password and removing its permissions for the current database, discussed later. That way nobody else can log in as Admin and make unauthorized changes to the database. Unlike previous versions of Access, Access 2.0 will *not* allow you to delete the Admin account from the system.

NOTE *If you clear the password for the system administrator, the system becomes nonsecure and no logon process is required.*

ADDING OTHER USER ACCOUNTS

You can add other user accounts just as you did when creating the new Master account. To have access to the Security I Users and Security I Groups commands you must be logged on as a member of the Admins group. Create a user name and four-digit PID for each new user. They are automatically assigned to the Users group. After describing permissions in the next section, we will discuss alternate group assignments for new users.

It is up to each user to create a password when logging on in the future. Although the system administrator does not know that user's password and cannot find it out by querying Access, the administrator can clear the password in the Users dialog box. Issue the Security | Users command, select that user's name in the upper portion of the dialog box, then click the Clear Password button. That will reset the password back to blank, and the user can log on once more and make a change to a new value.

DELETING A USER ACCOUNT

To do this you must log on as a member of the Admins group. Then issue the Security | Users command and select the desired user name in the Users dialog box. Click the Delete button to remove this user. You will be asked to confirm the deletion, so think carefully before responding affirmatively. If you accidentally delete a user, you can add the user name again and re-create group assignments and permissions.

Access Permissions

Access permissions are attached to a specific database. That is, Access lets you grant permission to read or modify specific database objects to each user or group. There are eight different *permission types* as described below. They are listed in order of appearance in the Permissions dialog box.

TYPES OF PERMISSIONS

OPEN/RUN This permits you to open a database, form, or report, or run a macro.

READ DESIGN This permits you to view all objects in Design view. It does not allow reading the data contained within objects, however.

MODIFY DESIGN With this permission you can view, replace, and delete the design of objects, but cannot read data contained within objects.

ADMINISTER This permission gives you full access to objects and data, including the ability to assign permissions.

READ DATA This permission allows you to view data in tables, queries, and forms, or to run an action query.

UPDATE DATA This permits you to view and modify data in tables, queries, and forms, but not insert or delete data.

INSERT DATA With this permission you can view and insert but not modify or delete data.

DELETE DATA With this level of permission you can view and delete data but not modify or insert data.

ASSIGNING PERMISSIONS TO USERS

Users inherit the permissions of the groups to which they belong. You can also assign specific permissions to users. Use the Permissions command from the Security menu to activate the Permissions dialog box shown in Figure 18.4. The upper-left

FIGURE 18.4
*The
Permissions
dialog box for
Master account*

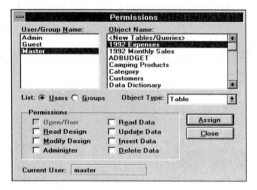

portion shows the particular user or group to whom you are assigning permissions. The upper-right portion of the box shows the specific object within the current database. The middle portion of the box shows the type of database object involved, and the lower part contains check boxes for the permission levels. Note that this box does not show permissions that a specific user has inherited from the group. To learn those permissions, change the List to Groups and select the group to which this user belongs.

While developing the application, the developers will need to have Administer permission to view and modify objects. However, once the application is completed, most users will not need permission to modify objects such as macros, forms, and reports. Careful consideration of usage patterns will guide you in determining which users need greater permission levels.

CHANGING PERMISSIONS FOR A WORK GROUP Because it is considerably easier to assign permissions to groups, do this first. Since all users belong to the Users group, that is the likely group you will work with first. However, it is easy to create a new work group and assign users to that group. You can then customize the permissions for that group.

CHANGING PERMISSIONS FOR A SINGLE USER Any user can change the permissions for objects that he or she created, but you must be an Admins user to change permissions for objects created by other users. Select the user name in the Permissions box, then the type of object that you wish to modify in the middle portion of the box. Click the check box to add or remove permission levels. Remember that the user has inherited permissions from the groups that each belongs to, so if you are removing a permission, it may still be granted through the group permissions.

Repeat the previous step with various types of objects until all permissions have been set, then choose the Assign button. When finished, Close the Permissions box. When you exit from Access, the permissions are stored both within the database and within the system files and become effective when the user logs in again.

Encrypting and Decrypting Database Files

Although the previous security measures prevent unauthorized users from starting Access and using portions of the database, they all rely on Access to deter unwanted users. In fact, if someone copies the database file (HUNT.MDB) to another computer that uses Access, that thief can have "full access" to your data! To remove this possibility, you can *encrypt* the database, causing Access to encode the data in such a way that only authorized user accounts can read the data.

ENCRYPTING A DATABASE FILE

Only Admins group users can encrypt a database file. Start Access but do not open a database file. To encrypt a database file, choose the Encrypt/Decrypt Database command from the File menu. The Encrypt/Decrypt dialog box appears, as shown in Figure 18.5. Choose the database file you want to encrypt, then click OK. If the file has not been encrypted, you will see the Encrypt Database As dialog box. Select a name and click OK. Access will encrypt the file and save it on the hard drive. You can use the encrypted file normally.

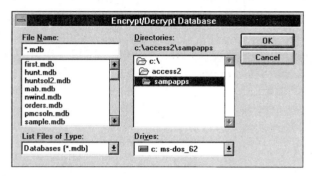

FIGURE 18.5
The Encrypt/ Decrypt Database dialog box

Once the database has been encrypted, it remains encoded while stored on the hard drive or network. With proper authority, Access users can still use the database, but Access will slow down somewhat while it temporarily *decrypts* the data, converting it from encoded form back to regular text as you access objects within the database.

DECRYPTING A DATABASE FILE

If the file already is encrypted, you can decrypt the file permanently. Choose the Encrypt/Decrypt Database command from the File menu. You will see the Decrypt Database As dialog box. Select the name for the decrypted file and click OK. You may use the same file name for both files. After a few moments, Access will produce a decrypted file.

WHEN TO ENCRYPT A FILE

Ordinarily, you do not encrypt a database file while developing the database. In fact, many database administrators will not apply any security to the database while it is under development. However, as you populate the database with confidential information, it is appropriate to initiate security features, including encryption. When multiple users share sensitive information in database files, encryption is recommended. We suggest that the database administrator monitor performance of Access when it decodes the encrypted data.

Compaction, Backup, and Recovery

Although we would like to think that hardware problems do not happen very often, in fact disk crashes and power failures do occur. We need to be able to restore the database in case a portion of it or the entire database is lost or damaged. Following a careful backup schedule is an important part of running a successful application.

Compacting the Database

Before you back up the database files, it is useful to *compact* the database. Over time, the database becomes fragmented (portions of it are stored in widely separated sectors on the hard disk) and grows larger in size with inefficient disk storage. By compacting the database, you defragment the file and recover the physical storage space of deleted objects within the database file. Compacting should be done on a regular basis, possibly weekly or monthly, depending on usage.

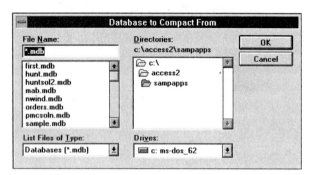

FIGURE 18.6

The Compact Database dialog box

You must close the database file before you compact it. Select the Compact Database command from the File menu. You will see the Database to Compact From dialog box shown in Figure 18.6. Select the name of the database file to compact, then click OK. Access will prompt you for the new file name. You may use the same name if you have enough space to temporarily store the file while it is being compacted. The process takes a short time. When it is finished, you can use the compacted database normally. You do *not* have to expand the database to use it.

Backing Up the Database File

The first step in backing up the database is to generate an appropriate backup schedule. Remember that in case of failure, you may lose everything created since the previous backup was made. For some systems this may mean that weekly backups are needed. Most systems use daily backups. For critical data, even more frequent backups are warranted. Remember that the cost of rekeying the lost data (if you have a copy of it) can be very high if you do not have a recent backup of the database.

The method for backing up the database files is usually external to Access. Although Access provides a File | Export command, this is not efficient for large file sizes. Most systems use magnetic tape or floppy disks for backups, running special disk backup programs that compress the data and check the media while copying data. The Backup program provided with MS-DOS 6.X is much more usable than previous versions.

In any event, the backup procedure involves copying the .MDB file containing your database, along with the SYSTEM.MDA file, which contains some of the security information. Most administrators will keep several backups and rotate between them, just in case there is a need to restore data from a past period. Don't forget to *test* the backup set to be sure that your backup is valid. In some backup packages this is called a Verify operation.

Restoring a Backup File

In case of database loss, you will usually want to copy (restore) the .MDB file and the SYSTEM.MDA file from the backup media to the Access directory, then try to open the database. Remember that this will re-create the database in existence at the time of the backup. Any database changes made after the backup was done will not be present in the database. For this reason it is a good idea to maintain a *paper trail* of documents that reflect transactions posted to the database. If there is a loss of data and the backup is restored, you can use the paper trail to rekey the transactions and bring the database up to current conditions.

Repairing a Damaged Database

If you quit Access without closing the database, if the power fails, or if your system reboots with an Access database still open, there may be damage to the database file. Either you may get a message from Access indicating that the database file is corrupted, or it may just behave erratically. In either case Access provides a facility to help you *repair* the database.

FIGURE 18.7
The Repair Database dialog box

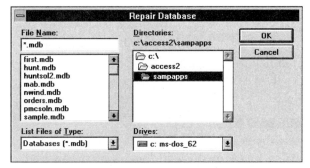

Start Access as usual, but do not open the database file. Choose the Repair Database command from the File menu to open the Repair Database dialog box shown in Figure 18.7. Select the damaged database and click OK. Access will attempt to rebuild the database file and repair the damage. When finished with the repair, Access will display a message box, indicating if the repair was successful.

Converting Older Access Databases

Access 2.0 is capable of reading versions 1.0 and 1.1 Access databases without conversion to the Access 2.0 format, but you will get a warning message that certain features are not available, and you will not be able to save changes made to the design of database objects.

To solve this problem, the File | Convert Database command is used to convert older Access databases to version 2.0 format. Once you have converted an older database, it *cannot* be converted back to the older format, nor can it be read by an earlier version of Access. If you intend to use an older Access version for some time, it is probably best to make any design changes in the older version of Access, and only read the data in Access 2.0. Figure 18.8 shows the Conversion dialog box.

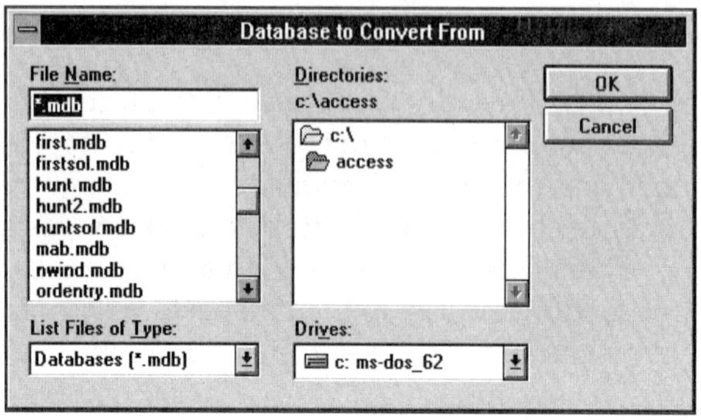

FIGURE 18.8
*Conversion
dialog box*

FIGURE 18.8
Conversion dialog box

Using Access in a Network Environment

Many organizations today have connected their personal computers in a *local area network (LAN)*. The LAN permits users to share information and resources such as hardware and applications software. In a LAN each personal computer is attached to a network cable, as is the *server* computer. The server holds application programs and data. When the personal computer, also known as the *workstation* or *client* computer, makes a request for data or a program, the server sends it to the client via the network cable at very high speeds.

You can share expensive hardware resources over a network so that each "client" computer can take advantage of those resources. Examples include high-speed laser printers, color printers, image scanners, CD-ROM drives, high-speed fax modems, tape drives for backup, and a large amount of hard disk space. The LAN also provides a gateway so that users can communicate with the outside world. Rather than connect these resources to each computer, they can be connected just once to the network and thereby be made available to all users.

Another advantage of using the network is that it provides simultaneous access to shared databases. This means that more than one user can be logged onto Access at the same time, using the information stored in the databases to perform his or her job. Some systems are even able to share data stored on the central server and on individual client computers.

The Client/Server Environment

Not only is a LAN less costly than a larger computer, but it can be significantly more powerful than larger computers. Remember that with a mainframe or minicomputer system, the central computer must divide its calculating power among all of the users. With a network, each personal computer can put its own calculating power to solving the problem for its user. As you add more users to a network, each brings another discrete amount of computing power, rather than bogging down a central shared processor.   (Set Record Locks to 10,000)

This approach, known as *client/server computing*, places the database in a central server computer along with the database management software. Each client computer runs the application programs as well as the user portion of the database management software. When the application program needs some data from the database, it places a request through the DBMS (database management system) to the network server. When the server retrieves the data, it sends it across the network to the client computer that requested it.

Installing Access on a Network

You can install Access on each client computer in the network, just as we did for a single computer. That way you can run Access whether the network is operating or not. Unfortunately, Access requires a great deal of storage space, up to 23MB for a complete installation. You must have a valid, legal copy of Access for each computer where it is installed.

The other way to install Access is to place it only on the network server. Client computers must run a copy of Access from the server that is transmitted over the network cable. It saves a great deal of hard disk space because only a single copy is actually installed. It runs slightly slower because the software must first be transferred from the server to the client. The network transfer rate depends on the kind of network and the amount of network traffic on the cable. You must have a valid Access license for each user who uses Access in this way.

If you install Access on the server, you must take care to place certain portions in areas of the server's hard drives that are write-enabled, and other portions that are read-only. The read-only portion cannot be changed by individual users, while the write-enabled portions permit users to make changes to the configuration and individual database files. For example, if you allow users to change security arrangements, they must have "write" permission for the directory where the security files are stored. Refer to the *User's Guide* for more details about installing Access on a network server.

Sharing Database Files

So far, nearly all that we have discussed in this textbook assumes that you are the only person using Access at the time. Even the secure system discussion earlier in this unit presumes that one person logs on at a time. But, with a network, many users can be logged on and using Access. This presents some interesting challenges, particularly when two or more persons want to read or make changes to the same data simultaneously.

OPEN FILES IN EXCLUSIVE MODE

You can open a file in *exclusive mode*, ensuring that you are the only user of that file for the entire time you are using it. Of course, other users who want to use the file will understandably be perplexed. No one else can open the file until you close it. Access uses exclusive mode by default in single-user mode. The Exclusive check box appears in the right portion of the Open Database dialog box.

OPEN FILES IN SHARED MODE WITH LOCKS

You can open the file in *shared mode*. Access will apply *record locks* when you want to make changes to the database. A lock is just that—it prevents other people from using the locked portion of the database until you remove the lock. Access temporarily stores locking information in an .LDB file with the same database name.

Access provides several kinds of locks, depending on what database operations you are performing. If you open a table that another user already has open (or if that user is viewing a query, form, or report based on that table), you will not be able to make changes to the table's design. If you make design changes to a database object

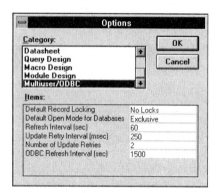

FIGURE 18.9
The Multiuser Options dialog box

that someone else has changed since you opened it, you will be given a warning message by Access. If you save the object, it will overwrite the other changes. You could save the object under a different name.

More problems occur when you want to make changes to the data in a table, form, or query datasheet. When you edit a record, Access automatically locks that record and prevents other users from changing it until you are finished. You can set the locking option with the View I Options command. The Multiuser/ODBC options are shown in Figure 18.9. You can select No Locks, All Records, or Edited Record for the Default Record Locking option.

CHOOSING THE METHOD OF LOCKING   The default value for this option is *No Locks*, in which case you edit the record without locks. If you save changes to a record that someone else has just changed, Access displays a message. You have an opportunity to cancel the save, save to the Clipboard, or save the record with changes, overwriting the other person's changes. The No Locks option is the most flexible because you (and others) can always edit the record.

If you select the *Edited Record* option, Access will temporarily lock the record you are editing and prevent other users from editing or locking it. It may also lock nearby records in the same table if they are stored within the 2,000-character locking window that Access uses. This option guarantees that the user can complete editing once it is begun, unlike the No Locks option. Access will not grant the lock to a particular record if another user already has it locked.

The *All Records* option locks all of the records in the underlying tables while you have them open. No one else can open them or lock them. This is the most restrictive type of lock and should only be used when you are the sole person likely to need to edit records at a given time.

EDITING DATA WITH MULTIPLE USERS   Because other users may be working with the same tables, you must be aware of the status of your data. For instance, if another user has a record locked, you will see a circle with a line through it—∅—in the record indicator section in Datasheet or Form view. This means you cannot make changes to that record until the lock disappears. If you are editing a record but your changes have not been saved, you will see a small pencil icon in the record indicator section.

If other users are changing the table, you may not be looking at the most recent version of data. Although Access automatically updates the records at certain intervals, you may want to update them manually. To do so, choose the Refresh command from the Records menu in Datasheet view.

From Figure 18.9 you can see that the *Refresh Interval* option has been set to 60 seconds. That means that Access will automatically refresh the records in the table one time per minute. You can change this option to a lower (more frequent refresh) value if you wish; it will cause Access to do slightly more work in keeping your table synchronized with others.

When the datasheet or form is refreshed, Access places new values in the fields but does not reorder the records, add new records, or remove records that no longer match a filter or query. To make these changes, you must manually rerun the query against the underlying data.

Working with SQL and ODBC Databases

Brief mention was made of attaching to these types of databases in Unit 16. Now that you have more background on networks and the use of Access in a multiuser environment, we can pursue them in more depth.

Both the Structured Query Language and the Open Data Base Connectivity database types are examples of client/server computing where the database resides on the network server but where Access and the application run on the client computer. When the application needs data, Access will place a network request to the SQL server. The server will make sure the user is authorized to access that data, then retrieve the data and make it available to Access. The user is completely uninvolved in this process. Access simply retrieves the data and makes it available to the application. In fact, the user may not even know that the data is coming from outside the client workstation.

We expect that this Access method will grow quickly in prominence. Client/server computing uses the best features of both sides. Because Access provides a very powerful *front end* for the user, it is easy to retrieve and manipulate the data within Access. You can build forms and reports very quickly within Access, using standard tables or queries as the data source. The server is able to maintain a very large database and make it available to simultaneous users. Because the bulk of the computing effort is being performed by the client workstation, adding more users does not tend to bog down the server. In fact, if an individual user has insufficient computing throughput (total amount of processing done in a given time), you can make a relatively inexpensive CPU upgrade to the client workstation and apply the performance increase exactly where it is needed.

Command Review

File | Add-ins | Database Documentor	Print a list of the design elements of database objects.
File | Compact Database	Defragment a database file, reducing it in size.
File | Convert Database	Convert a version 1.0 or 1.1 Access database to version 2.0.
File | Encrypt/Decrypt Database	Encode a file so that others cannot read it.
File | Print Definition	Print information about the definition of a single object.
File | Repair Database	Rebuild a damaged database file.
Records | Refresh	Do a manual refresh of records in a form or datasheet.
Security | Change Password	Change the password for a user account.
Security | Groups	Create or remove work groups.
Security | Permissions	Set permissions for a user or a group.
Security | Users	Add or remove users.

Exercises

Use the database called FIRST.MDB for these exercises. Do not use the HUNT Database unless otherwise told by your instructor.

1. Change the password of the Admin user to Admin so that Access presents the logon menu when you start it up. Add a new user account with your first initial and last name, without spaces, such as B.McLaren.

2. Exit from Access and restart Access. When prompted, try to log on with your new user name. Remember that the password is blank. Once in Access, change your password to something other than blanks. Be sure to write down your password so that you can use it the next time you log on. Exit from Access, then restart Access. Use your own user name and the new password.

3. Exit from Access once more, then restart Access. Log on with the Admin user name and add your personal user name to the Admins work group. Exit from Access and restart Access, logging in with your own user name. Verify that you can access the Security \| Users command, confirming that you are in the Admins group.

4. Develop a data dictionary for the Hunter River database.

5. Explore the new documentation features built into Access 2.0 by printing the definitions of the Employees table and the Open Customers macro.

Review Questions

1. Explain the need to have a data dictionary for a large Access database. How can Access assist in the preparation of such a dictionary?

2. List the duties of the database administrator.

3. Discuss what is meant by the term secure Access system. How can you make a system secure?

4. Why is it useful to have both a user name and a password for Access users?

5. Suppose you forgot your Access password. What can the system administrator do to resolve this problem?

6. Discuss the differences between the Admins, Users, and Guests group. Give an example of a user who might be assigned to each group.

7. How do you activate the Access logon procedure? Suppose you decide later that you do not want to use the logon procedure. How would you turn it off?

8. Why is it generally preferred to grant permissions to groups before granting permissions to individual accounts?

9. Explain why Access offers different permission types instead of granting everyone full access.

10. Discuss reasons for doing the following File operations in Access:

    a. Encrypt/Decrypt Database

    b. Compact Database

    c. Repair Database

    d. Convert Database

11. Why do we want to connect a client workstation to a network?

12. What is client/server computing, and why is Access such a valuable front-end tool?

13. Contrast the differences between opening a file in exclusive and shared modes. Which is preferred in a multiuser environment, and why?

14. Discuss the use of record locks in Access. Which method of record locks is preferred?

15. Suppose someone else is using the same underlying Access table as you and you notice the ∅ symbol in the record indicator area of your datasheet. What does this mean? A few moments later you notice that the table changes slightly on your screen, and you did not enter any commands. What does this mean?

16. List the options available when using the File | Print Definition command for a table and for a query.

Key Terms

Access permissions	Edited Record Locks	Record lock
Admin user	Encrypt database	Refresh Interval
Admins group	Exclusive mode	Repair database
All Records lock	Front end	Secure system
Case-sensitive	Guests group	Server
Client	Local area network (LAN)	Shared mode
Client/server computing	No Locks	System administrator
Compact database	Paper trail	User name
Data dictionary	Password	Users group
Database administrator	Permission type	Work group
Decrypt database	Personal identifier (PID)	Workstation

Documentation Research

Use the printed documentation and the on-line Help available with Microsoft Access to answer the following questions. If you use one of the manuals, provide the page number for your reference in the manual.

1. Search the Access on-line Help to learn about the Update Retry multiuser options.

2. Are Access user names case-sensitive? Are Access passwords case-sensitive?

3. What is the minimum amount of disk space required to install Access on a client workstation?

Glossary of Microsoft Access Database Terms

ACCESS BASIC The programming language used within Microsoft Access modules.

ACCESSORIES The collection of miniapplications included with Microsoft Windows. The accessories include Write, Paintbrush, Notepad, Calculator, Clock, Terminal, Cardfile, Recorder, and more.

ACTION A command or instruction contained within a macro. Actions usually have arguments to clarify the meaning of the command.

ACTION FAILED DIALOG BOX When a macro fails to run properly, Access displays this dialog box and gives a message about what part of the macro failed.

ACTION LIST The list of all actions possible for a macro, available by clicking the arrow in the action cell in the upper portion of the macro window.

ACTION QUERY A query that causes some sort of action to occur. Action queries can append data to other tables, delete data from tables, make a new table, or update values in an existing table.

ACTIVE The active object is the one that has the focus. You may have several windows open within Access and switch between these windows. The title bar of the active window is highlighted.

ARGUMENT Additional instructions or parameters given with a macro action. Arguments are entered in the lower portion of the macro window.

AUTO-EXECUTE MACRO A macro that executes as soon as the database containing it is opened. It is named AutoExec. You can defeat the auto-execute macro by holding down the `Shift` key when the database is opened. You can also specify a startup macro by using the /X command line option if you start Access from the File | Run command in the Program Manager.

AUTOFORM A type of Form Wizard that automatically creates a single-column form using all of the fields without requiring that the user answer any questions. You can change the default settings. This feature is new to Access 2.0.

AUTOREPORT A type of Report Wizard that automatically creates a single-column report using all of the fields without requiring that the user answer any questions. You can change the default settings. This feature is new to Access 2.0.

BACKUP The process of copying the contents of the hard drive to another medium such as floppy disks or magnetic tape. In case the hard drive is damaged, the backup contents can be restored.

BAR CHART A type of chart in Microsoft Graph in which the data values are displayed in horizontal bars.

BITMAP FILE Type of graphic file in which each pixel is represented by several bits in the file. Paintbrush bitmap files use the .BMP or .PCX file extension. You can embed a bitmap file such as a photograph or map within Access as an OLE object.

BLANK FORM BUTTON Use this button to create a custom form from scratch, without the Form Wizards.

BLANK REPORT BUTTON Use this button to create a custom report from scratch, without the Report Wizards.

.BMP EXTENSION The default file extension used with Windows Paintbrush bitmap files.

BOUND CONTROL A control that is bound (linked) to a field in a table or dynaset.

BOUND OBJECT FRAME CONTROL A type of control that uses an OLE object bound to a field in the table.

BUILDERS Access 2.0 contains a series of builders that help you create expressions or control objects. Press the right mouse button to select the Build command for an object.

BUILT-IN FORMATS Standard ways you can display text, number, and date/time fields. You can control the number of decimal places, display dollar signs, show certain date and time formats, and so on.

BUILT-IN FUNCTIONS Functions that can calculate values such as average, maximum, interest rate, and many other commonly used values. Access includes functions for mathematical, statistical, financial, date/time, text, and other kinds of calculations.

CALCULATED CONTROL A control whose value is calculated in an expression rather than being taken from a stored value in a table or dynaset.

CALCULATED FIELD A field in a query whose value is calculated in an expression rather than being taken from a stored value. Every time the underlying values change, the calculated field is recalculated.

CASE-SENSITIVE Indicates whether the text value depends on matching an uppercase or lowercase pattern. If an item is case-sensitive you must enter the value exactly as specified. Most Access items are *not* case-sensitive. However, certain user name/password combinations are case-sensitive in a secure system.

CELL The intersection of a row and column in a datasheet or grid. We place information into cells in query and macro grids, among other Access objects.

CHART TYPE Microsoft Graph offers eight basic chart types, with many options. Basic types include area charts, bar charts, column charts, line charts, pie charts, radar, doughnut, and XY charts.

CHECK BOX CONTROL A type of control that indicates whether an option has been selected or cleared. When selected, that control will have an X in the check box.

CHOOSE Choose an item by double-clicking its icon, or click once to select that item and then press Enter. Windows will execute the item you choose.

CLICK Click once with the left mouse button to select an item.

CLIENT/SERVER COMPUTING A cooperative computing scenario in which the client workstation runs a portion of the database system while the remaining part of the application runs on the server.

CLIP ART Predrawn artwork in a variety of objects that can be inserted into an object to represent a logo or other graphical image.

CLIPBOARD The Windows Clipboard is used to temporarily store information (text and graphics) while it is copied from one application window to another.

COLUMN Represents a field in a table, QBE grid, or filter grid. Columns are also used to hold information in other Access grids such as the macro window.

COLUMN CHART A type of chart in Microsoft Graph in which the data values are represented by vertical bars.

COLUMN DIVIDER The area between two columns in the datasheet or QBE grid. You can change the width of the column by dragging the column divider border between two columns.

COLUMN SELECTOR The area at the top of the column in a datasheet or grid. You can select a column by clicking on the column selector.

COMBINATION CHART   A type of chart in Microsoft Graph in which the data values are shown both by line and column elements.

COMBO BOX CONTROL   A type of control in which you can select an item from a prespecified list or can type the value in the combo box directly.

COMMAND BUTTON CONTROL   A type of control that can cause a macro to run. By clicking the command button you can cause a certain action to take place.

COMMAND LINE   The text characters used to start a program. For example, it is possible to start Access from the Run command in the File menu of the Program Manager by typing in the name of the program, plus any optional command line parameters, then pressing Enter.

COMMENT   Used to document an Access database object in Design view. You can provide comments for fields in tables, macro actions, and other Access objects.

COMMIT   After a change has been made to the values or structure of a table, Access will commit those values by making the changes permanent. The pencil icon in the record indicator area shows changes that have *not* yet been committed.

COMPACT DATABASE   An operation done periodically to eliminate deleted records and make the storage of a database more efficient. You can compact the database to a new database or use the same name.

COMPOUND CONDITION   A set of two or more conditions within the same expression. An *AND* compound condition requires that both conditions be true in order for the overall condition to be true; an *OR* condition allows either or both conditions to be true.

COMPOUND CONTROL   A control consisting of two or more controls. For example, when you drag a field from the field list to a form or report, Access creates a text control to hold that field's value and a label control containing the name of the field. Compound controls can be manipulated together or separately.

CONCATENATION   Provides for combining two text strings, forming a single text string. We frequently concatenate a first name with last name to form a full name. Access allows the "+" and the "&" operators for concatenation. The latter is a SQL standard.

CONTINUOUS FORM   A form that displays more than one record on the same form on the same page in Form view. You can create a continuous form by setting the Default View property to Continuous Forms.

CONTROL   A graphical object placed in a form or report to display data, lines, or text; to show a graphical object; or to decorate the form. There are 16 types of controls contained in the Toolbox.

CONTROL MENU   The Control-menu box, designated by a short horizontal line, appears in the upper-left corner of most windows. It contains commands to move, resize, or close the window.

CONTROL PANEL   Used to make adjustments to Windows settings such as colors, mouse, fonts, ports, printers, and more. The Control Panel appears in the Main program group.

CONTROL PROPERTIES   Attributes that affect the appearance or behavior of a control in a form or report. The property sheet can be displayed by double-clicking a control or clicking the Properties button.

CONTROL TOOLBOX   The set of tools used to place controls in the form or report. The Toolbox usually appears at the lower-left portion of the desktop but can be moved to the side as necessary.

CONTROL WIZARDS   Built-in tools that automatically create customized controls in forms and reports by asking you a series of questions. Control Wizards are particularly useful for option groups, command buttons, combo boxes, and list boxes. This feature is new to Access 2.0.

COPY TO CLIPBOARD   This operation will copy the selected text or object to the Windows Clipboard, also leaving the text or object in its original location. You can paste information from the Clipboard into a different location or a document.

COUNTER DATA TYPE   Used to store numbers sequentially. You can use a counter field to number the records in a table automatically. Counter fields are frequently used as the primary key in a table.

CRITERIA   The condition in a select query or filter for retrieval of records. Records that meet the criteria condition are displayed.

CROSSTAB QUERY   A type of query in which summary totals for groups are prepared by row and column.

CUE CARDS The companion help system in Access that leads you through many types of database operations. Cue Cards are available through the Access Help menu.

CURRENCY DATA TYPE A number data type that automatically formats values with dollar signs, inserts commas in large numbers, and controls the number of decimal places. It maintains a large number of significant digits.

CURRENT DATABASE The database opened with the Open command from the File menu.

CURRENT RECORD INDICATOR The triangular icon in the record indicator area of the Datasheet view that indicates the current record pointer.

CURSOR The pointer used in Windows and Access to select commands, select database objects, and work in Design view. The cursor changes its shape, depending on its location on the desktop. There are over 20 different shapes for the cursor.

CUT TO CLIPBOARD This operation will copy the selected text or object to the Windows Clipboard, removing the text or object from its original location. You can paste information from the Clipboard into a different location or a document.

DATA The information stored in a database in tables. Data refers to values and the structure of the values.

DATA DICTIONARY A collection of the definitions of all objects maintained in the database. The data dictionary provides important system documentation, and is maintained by the database administrator.

DATA SHARING The method by which several users share the same database simultaneously. Care must be taken to avoid overwriting changes made by another user. Multiuser access generally implies having a secure system with user accounts and passwords.

DATA SOURCE The source of the data values for a form or report. The data source can be a table or a query dynaset.

DATA TRANSLATOR The programs packaged with Access that enable it to convert data from one database format to another. Access can translate tables from several database types, several spreadsheets, and text files.

DATA TYPE The characteristics of a field in a table that describe the kind of data that field can hold. Access data types include Text, Memo, Number, Date/Time, Currency, Counter, Yes/No, and OLE Object.

DATABASE A collection of related data in tables, queries, reports, forms, macros, and modules. In Access the database is stored in a large file with an .MDB file extension.

DATABASE ADMINISTRATOR The person responsible for managing the development and administration of databases within the organization's information systems. This role may be assigned to one person or shared across several individuals.

DATABASE CAPACITY Describes the capacity of the database in terms of number of tables, number of records, and size of objects created in the database. Access 1.1 and 2.0 databases can be up to 1GB in size (128MB in version 1.0). A database can have up to 32,768 tables, 255 of which can be open at a time. Unit 1 describes the database capacity of Access.

DATABASE DOCUMENTOR Will print definitions or design of one or more database objects for use in a data dictionary.

DATABASE MANAGEMENT SYSTEM (DBMS) A set of computer programs (such as Microsoft Access) for managing and displaying data from a database.

DATABASE OBJECTS The tables, queries, forms, reports, macros, and modules that compose the database.

DATABASE SYSTEM The set of computer programs (Microsoft Access) to manage the objects and the data that compose the database. This is another term for Database Management System (DBMS).

DATABASE WINDOW The window that appears when you open a database in Access. The object buttons in the Database window let you choose which database mode you work in.

DATASHEET A window that displays data from a table or a query in row and column format.

DATASHEET VIEW A window that displays data from a table or query dynaset in row and column format.

DATE/TIME DATA TYPE A field type for storing dates and times. You can choose from a wide variety of formats for displaying date/time fields.

DEBUGGING The process of testing and removing errors ("bugs") from an Access macro or module.

DEFAULT CONTROL PROPERTIES The properties established when you create a control for a form or report. If you create the control from a field, the control will inherit some of the field's properties. You can make changes to the default properties in the control's property sheet.

DELETE QUERY An action query in which records that match the condition in the query are permanently deleted.

DELIMITED TEXT FILE A text file containing data that is separated (delimited) by a certain character, usually a comma. Text fields in delimited files are ordinarily enclosed in quotes. You can import data from a text file or export data to a text file.

DESCENDING SORT ORDER In this order records appear in decreasing order, from highest to lowest value.

DESIGN VIEW A window in which you create and edit tables, queries, forms, and reports.

DETAIL SECTION A section in a form or report that displays field values. The detail section appears between the header and footer for that object.

DIALOG BOX A window that allows you to make choices before a command is executed in Windows or Access.

DOCUMENT WINDOW A type of window that contains a document or other object within an application. We can contrast this with an application window that contains the entire application. Within Access the Database window is an example of a document window.

DOUBLE-CLICK Click two times in rapid succession with the left mouse button on an item on the desktop. This is equivalent to choosing that object. The time between clicks may be adjusted with the Mouse icon in the Windows Control Panel.

DRAG-AND-DROP METHOD Method of moving an object with a mouse. Highlight the object, then press the left mouse button and hold it down while you move the object to a new location. Release the mouse button to drop the object in the new location. In Access this is also used to select fields from a field list or to create links between tables in a query.

DROP-DOWN MENU A standard menu in Windows that drops down from the menu bar and stays open until you choose a command from that menu.

DYNASET The set of records that results from running a select query. A dynaset appears like an Access table.

ELLIPSIS (...) Transfers the macro condition immediately above the current line to apply also to the action on the current line.

EMBEDDED OBJECT An OLE object that has been inserted into the current document (table in Access) using the Insert Object command from the Edit menu.

ENCRYPT DATABASE Coding the data in such a way that someone else cannot read the contents of the database. You must provide the correct password to decode (decrypt) the database.

EQUI-JOIN Type of join between two tables in a query in which a joined record is created whenever there is a matching value between the two tables. This is the default type of join in Access.

EVENT A user action that occurs when using a form or other database object. You can instruct Access to run a macro whenever a certain event occurs such as opening a form, changing a value, clicking the mouse, and so forth.

EXCLUSIVE MODE Opening the database by a single person at a time. Other users cannot open a database that has been previously opened in exclusive mode. This is the default mode when using Access in single-user mode.

EXPORT Copies a portion of the database to another Access database or translates an Access table to another application format. In the latter case you produce one or more external files containing the data.

EXPRESSION An algebraic combination of identifiers, constants, operators, fields, and controls that evaluate to a single value. Expressions can have numeric, logical (yes/no), or string results. Some expressions result in date/time values.

EXTERNAL TABLE A table stored as an external file, outside Access. You produce an external table when you export data from an Access database, and can import or attach to an external table from Access.

F1 FUNCTION KEY Pressing the F1 function key will cause the Access Help system to load, providing context-specific help for the current window or dialog box.

FIELD A measurement or attribute about an object that is stored in a table. In Access we usually associate a field with a column in a datasheet or a control in a form or report.

FIELD BOX A list box that appears in Form view and in the toolbar of a datasheet. You can select a field by choosing it from the field box or by clicking on the field if it is present on the desktop.

FIELD DATA TYPES Access provides several data types for fields, depending on the type of information to be stored in the field. Standard data types include text, memo, number, date/time, currency, counter, yes/no, and OLE object.

FIELD LIST A small window containing the fields in the data source for an object that can be opened while in Design view. You can drag fields from the field list to place on a form, report, or query.

FIELD PROPERTIES Attributes of a field that affect its appearance or behavior. Each data type has its own set of field properties that appear in table Design view. Commonly used field properties include Field Size, Format, Decimal Places, Caption, Default Value, Validation Rule, and Validation Text.

FIELD SELECTOR A small box at the top of a column in a datasheet that allows you to select the entire column.

FIELD SIZE Property used to set the size of a field in a table. Data values too large to fit within the field size are not saved in the database. For text fields, the field size is the number of characters; for number fields, you can choose a number subtype (byte, integer, single, double) that describes the amount of precision needed for the field.

FILE A collection of records about an entity in a database system. In Access a file corresponds to a table. The term also refers to a computer file that exists separately on the disk drive.

FILE MANAGER A Windows application from the Main program group that provides a means of working with files on the computer. With File Manager you can view directories and file names, copy files, move files, delete files, rename files, and start an application by double-clicking the name of a file created by that application. We do not need to use File Manager while working in Access.

FILE MENU The left-most menu in the menu bar of most Windows applications. This menu is used for creating a new object, opening an existing object, saving an object, printing an object, and exiting from Access. The File menu changes for each Access mode.

FILTER A set of conditions or criteria used with a form that limits the records viewed in that form.

FILTER WINDOW The window used to create and edit form filters.

FINANCIAL FUNCTIONS The set of functions used for time value of money and depreciation calculations.

FIND COMMAND Used to search for records that match certain conditions. Similar to a query but used temporarily.

FIRST NORMAL FORM The first step in normalizing a database in which the database is represented by two-dimensional tables in which there are no repeating groups. That is, repeating groups of data are placed in separate tables.

FIXED-WIDTH TEXT FILE A type of external data file in which data appear without separators, in the exact width for each field in the table. Fixed-width files can be read by Access after you specify the names, data types, and width of each field in the file.

FOCUS The active object (window, section, control) on the desktop. The active object has the focus, and commands will operate on the object that has the focus. Any mouse commands or text typed at the keyboard will apply to the object that has the focus.

FONT BOX A small dialog box on the menu bar that lets you select the font name for the selected object.

FONT SIZE You can choose the font size in points from this box. The font size is also stored in the property sheet for a control.

FONT STYLE You can choose bold, underline, and italic style for text in a control.

FOOTER Refers to the text or graphics displayed after a set of records. You can place subtotals, page numbers, current date or time, and other information in the footer. Access uses page footers that appear on each page, form or report footers that appear at the end of the form or report, and group footers that appear after a group of records.

FOREIGN KEY A field in a table that is used as the primary key in another table. Frequently, you will use this field to link or join two tables, matching common values between the foreign key and its matching primary key in the other table.

FORM   A database object for entering, editing, and displaying data values. You can also print a form, but forms are primarily designed for use on the screen.

FORM DESIGN VIEW   The window in Form mode for creating or editing a form's design. In this view you see the controls placed in the form but not the data values displayed by those controls.

FORM PROPERTIES   Characteristics or attributes of the form that affect its appearance or behavior.

FORM VIEW   The window in Form mode for displaying or entering the data values according to the form design.

FORM WINDOW   The window in which you work with forms. You can select Form view, Design view, or Datasheet view while in the Form window.

FORMAT MENU   The menu in Microsoft Graph in which you can choose cell formats, column width, font, size, and style. Other Windows applications use a Format menu for similar purposes. Access itself does not use the Format menu from the menu bar.

FORM WIZARDS   Built-in tools that automatically create customized forms by asking you a series of questions. Form Wizards are very easy to use but have some limitations.

FUNCTION   Access provides two kinds of functions. Built-in functions are preprogrammed calculations for a wide variety of mathematical, financial, date/time, text, and other situations. You can also create user-defined functions in modules for situations in which there is no built-in function.

GRAPH CONTROL   An Access control type that causes Microsoft Graph to load as an OLE server and display the graph stored in the control. A graph control can be placed in a form or report.

GRAPH WINDOW   The window in Microsoft Graph for creating and editing graphs.

GRAPHIC   Any nontext image that can be displayed in a table, form, or report. Graphics include bitmaps, pictures, lines, and rectangles.

GRAPHICAL USER INTERFACE (GUI)   Refers to a program's use of icons and visual menus instead of its asking users to type commands. Windows is a GUI.

GRAPH WIZARD   Built-in tool that automatically creates customized graphs and charts by asking you a series of questions. Graph Wizard works through Microsoft Graph, another application packaged with (but not a formal part of) Microsoft Access.

GRID   The rectangular array of dots in Design view that help you align controls in forms and reports. You can cause controls to snap to the grid so that they expand to fit the closest grid dot in each direction. You can change the spacing in the grid as needed.

GRID DOTS   The dots that appear on the screen when the grid is activated in Design view. With some grid configurations, you do not see the individual dots but they still function.

GROUP   A set of records that share a common characteristic. You can display the group and have introductory and summary information about the group in a report. In a secure system, the work group is a group of user accounts that share common permissions.

GROUP FOOTER   The text and graphics that appear after a group of records. You might have a count or sum of a field for each record in the group.

GROUP HEADER   The text and graphics that appear just before a group of records. You might have the group name in the group header, along with column headings for the fields that appear in the detail section just after the group.

GROUP WINDOW   A window that lets you determine grouping and sorting choices. *See* Sorting and Grouping Box.

GROUPS/TOTALS REPORT WIZARD   The kind of report in which records are combined into groups that share common characteristics and are displayed in a tabular fashion. You can calculate a subtotal for number fields in each group and a grand total for all of the groups.

HANDLE   The handles of a control allow you to move and resize the control. The upper-left handle is the move handle; the remaining handles allow you to resize the control. The corner resize handles let you resize the control in two directions at the same time.

HEADER   The text and graphics that appear before a set of records. Access uses three kinds of headers: page header, form or report header, and group header.

HELP The hierarchical Help system built into Windows and included with most Windows applications. In Access you can activate help in a number of ways: click the Help icon in the menu bar, press F1, use the Help command from the menu bar, and use the Shift F1 help system that gives you context-specific help on any object that you click on after pressing Shift F1. Access also has Cue Cards, a built-in coaching system to lead you through the creation of database objects. *See* Cue Cards.

HELP BUTTON The question mark icon that appears in the Access menu bar.

HELP MENU The Access Help menu has three main choices: Contents, Search, and Cue Cards. Contents provides a list of major help topics; Search lets you specify a topic for help; Cue Cards leads you through the creation of database objects.

HORIZONTAL SCROLL BAR The scroll bar appearing at the bottom of the desktop within a window. You can use the horizontal scroll bar to scroll the screen sideways on the display if it is wider than the display.

I-BEAM INSERTION POINT The nickname for the insertion point cursor is I-beam, which refers to the shape of the cursor when it points to the location where text will be inserted into a control or box.

ICON A graphical representation of a command or program. Icons are designed to resemble the operation they identify, making it easier for the user to choose the appropriate action.

IDENTIFIER The name of a database object or a control or field within that object.

IMPORT Converting an external database object or table into a form that is compatible with Access, and making that external object a permanent part of the current database.

INDEX A technique to speed retrieval of records in Access by ordering the records by the values in a field or combination of fields.

INDICATOR Portion of the Database window next to a record that is used to show the current record, locked records, a new record, and a record that has been edited but not yet saved.

INFORMATION SYSTEM The combination of data, applications (programs), people, procedures, and environment that allow an organization to conduct its affairs efficiently.

INPUT AREA A box in which you can type values. Access uses many kinds of input areas to accept responses from the user.

INPUT MASK A field property that lets you place a pattern or template around certain data values. For example, a phone number input mask might be (999)-000-0000. There is an Input Mask Wizard to help you build input masks. This feature is new to Access 2.0.

INSERT MODE The default mode in which new characters typed in an input area are inserted into the text already there. That is, the new text "pushes" the existing text over. Press the Ins key to switch between Insert and Overtype modes.

INTEGER DATA TYPE A number subtype that permits integer (whole number) values only.

JOIN A database operation that combines records from two tables by matching common values in both tables. Access supports three types of joins: equi-join, outer join, and self-join.

JOIN LINE The line in the query Design view that connects two tables that have been joined. The line connects the fields that are matched.

KEY The field or combination of fields that identify a record in a table. The primary key is a unique identifier. Access tables are required to have a primary key. Secondary keys are used to break ties within the primary key. A table may have one or more secondary keys.

LABEL CONTROL A control containing text that describes or identifies a portion of the form or report. We use label controls for form or report titles, column headings, and labels for individual fields. A text control contains a field value and is not the same as a label control, which contains only a constant text phrase.

LANDSCAPE ORIENTATION Print orientation in which the printer prints the output in a sideways fashion, with the long side of the page across the top. Laser and inkjet printers are capable of landscape printing. The default is portrait orientation in which the long side of the page is down the side.

LINE CHART A type of chart in Microsoft Graph in which the data values are displayed as points connected with a line.

LINE CONTROL A straight line that can be placed in a form or report. The thickness and color of the line control are set in the Palette dialog box.

LINKED OBJECT   An object in Access that is linked to a separate Windows application. Any changes made to the object in the external application are automatically made to the copy within Access.

LIST BOX CONTROL   A type of form or report control in which choices for the form are shown in a drop-down list. You can access this list by clicking on the down arrow at the right of the list box.

LOCAL AREA NETWORK (LAN)   A communications configuration in which the individual workstations are connected to a network server. The server provides software and hardware resources for the LAN. Each workstation in the LAN can also have its own hardware and software resources. In Access a LAN can be used to allow several users to simultaneously access a database that is stored on the network server.

LOCK TOOL   The bottom portion of the Toolbox that locks the next selected tool. Thus, you can add several controls of the same kind without having to reselect the specific tool. The default is not to lock the Toolbox; after each use, the pointer reverts to the pointer tool at the top of the Toolbox.

LOCKED RECORD   When a database is opened for shared use, Access locks a record when someone is editing that record. Other users are prevented from changing the locked record until the first person has finished the editing operation.

LOGICAL OPERATOR   An operator that compares two expressions or values and results in the answer of true or false. This is another name for Comparison Operator.

MACRO   A set of actions executed together that you can use to automate a task. Macros are frequently attached to command buttons in a form so that clicking on the command button causes the macro to run.

MACRO GROUP   A single macro containing several related macros that can be executed individually.

MACRO WINDOW   The Access window that is used for creating, editing, and running macros. The top portion of the macro window contains the macro actions; the bottom portion contains the arguments for each action.

MAILING LABELS REPORT   A report format resembling that used for mailing labels. Rather than displaying separate records on successive lines, the mailing labels report can show several records on the same line.

MAILING LABELS REPORT WIZARD   The Report Wizard that is able to create a mailing label report.

MAIN PROGRAM GROUP   In Windows the program group containing icons for the Control Panel, File Manager, Print Manager, MS-DOS Prompt, Clipboard Viewer, and Windows Setup.

MAIN/SUBFORM FORM WIZARD   The Form Wizard used to create a form consisting of a main portion and a subform portion. Records in the subform portion are usually related to the main portion by common field values.

MAKE-TABLE QUERY   An action query that results in creation of a new table with records that meet the selection criteria.

MATHEMATICAL FUNCTIONS   A set of built-in functions that perform mathematical, statistical, and engineering calculations.

MAXIMIZE BUTTON   Clicking this button will cause Windows to display the window in full size on the desktop.

.MDB FILE   Access stores all of the database objects in a single file ending with the .MDB file extension. Although you can choose a different extension, we recommend that you only use this default extension.

MEMO DATA TYPE   A data type for textual fields that may be very long. Memo fields are variable in length, expanding to just fit the data in each record. Conversely, text fields are fixed in length; the text field in each record uses the same amount of storage whether it is needed or not.

MENU   A pull-down menu offers commands that can be chosen. Most Windows applications use a common menu structure so that it is possible to move from program to program with minimal interruption.

MENU BAR   A horizontal bar beneath the title bar that contains the names of the menus for that window. In Access the menu bar changes for the view chosen for each database mode.

MENU MACRO   Displays a menu and is associated with a switchboard form. You can also create a custom menu bar for use in an Access application.

MERGE PRINT   A procedure in which data from a database is merged into a document, creating customized copies of that document. Access supports merge printing through both exporting a file to Microsoft Word and creating a file that can be merged into other word processing packages.

MESSAGE BOX   A dialog box that displays information to the user. You can create a custom message box with the MsgBox action in an Access macro.

MICROSOFT ACCESS WINDOW   The window that appears when Access is started. You can open a database document window within the Access application window.

MINIMIZE BUTTON   Clicking this button will cause its window to shrink to an icon at the bottom of the desktop. You can restore the window to its former size.

MODULE   A set of programs written in Access Basic that perform customized functions. It is possible to create libraries of such programs that can be shared across more than one database.

MOUSE   A pointing device that is essential to work with Windows. A mouse is used to select menu items, position the insertion pointer, select items, and resize controls.

MOVE HANDLE   The upper-left corner handle of a control that permits it to be moved to another location on the form or report.

MS-DOS PROMPT   An icon in the Main program group that brings up a DOS session within Windows.

MULTI-COLUMN REPORT   A report that "snakes" in several columns like a newspaper. That is, the report proceeds to the bottom of the first column, then continues at the top of the second column, and so forth.

MULTIPLE LEVEL GROUP REPORT   A group report in which there is more than one group level. For example, you might have a student report in which students are grouped first by school, then by department within the school.

MULTIUSER (SHARED) DATABASE   A shared database can be used by more than one person at a time in a secure system. Care must be taken, however, to prevent one user's changes from being overwritten by another user. Record locks are used to prevent this accidental overwriting.

NATURAL ORDER   The original order of the records in a table, before any indexes are applied.

NAVIGATION BUTTONS   The buttons that appear at the bottom of the datasheet and form windows that allow the user to move from one record to another. There are buttons for next and previous record, first and last record, and a specific record number.

NETWORK   *See* Local Area Network.

NORMALIZATION   The process of designing a relational database that is easy to work with and that reduces the possibility of database anomalies.

NULL FIELD   A field that has no entry in it. A null field is different from a field that contains blanks.

NUMBER DATA TYPE   A field type that is used to hold numeric values such as salary, quantity on hand, and the like. It is usually not appropriate to use a number data type to hold such text data as a phone number or zip code, even if those items contain digits. We usually reserve number types for fields on which we could perform arithmetic operations.

NUMERIC EXPRESSION   An Access expression that results in a numeric value.

OBJECT   Can refer to a database component such as a table, query, form, report, macro, or module. Can also refer to an OLE object.

OBJECT BUTTONS   Used in the Database window to switch to the desired mode. Modes include table, query, form, report, macro, and module.

OBJECT LINKING AND EMBEDDING (OLE)   A protocol by which an object such as a graph or image can be linked or embedded in another Windows application. OLE is a follow-on protocol to DDE.

OLE OBJECT DATA TYPE   A data type that includes graphic images, sounds, and other documents such as a spreadsheet that can be embedded in an Access table.

OLE SERVER   The source application that provides the OLE object to Access. In this book we demonstrated two OLE servers: Windows Paintbrush and Microsoft Graph.

OPEN DATA BASE CONNECTIVITY (ODBC)   A set of database standards that allow packages to exchange data freely. Access includes ODBC drivers that allow other ODBC-compliant database systems to use its data.

OPERATOR   An operator is a symbol or word that describes some kind of operation to be performed on two or more elements in an expression. Access includes arithmetic, logical, comparison, and concatenation operators.

OPTION BUTTON CONTROL The control that can be selected or cleared; a selected option button is a small circle that is filled in, sometimes called a radio button.

OPTION GROUP CONTROL A group of binary (on/off) controls, treated as a single control, that represent a set of alternatives to choose from. Binary controls include check boxes, toggle buttons, and option buttons.

OPTIONS DIALOG BOX A dialog box to fill in options for importing, attaching, and exporting data.

OR CONDITION A compound condition that is true if either (or both) parts are true.

OUTER JOIN A join that consists of all records from one table and only those records from the other table that match records from the first table.

OVERTYPE MODE The mode in which new text that is typed into the input area replaces existing text in that box. You can toggle between Insert and Overtype modes by pressing the [Ins] key.

PAGE BREAK CONTROL A control that inserts a page break into a report or form.

PAINTBRUSH A Windows accessory application used for drawing images. Paintbrush can be used to create and embed OLE objects into Access.

PALETTE The dialog box or toolbox for setting the line width, special effects, and color of controls in a form or report.

PAPER TRAIL A set of paper documents that reflect the nature of the transactions made with the database system. In case of loss of data from the database, you might be able to reconstruct the entries made by studying the paper trail. Accountants will audit the database by comparing the results in the database with the paper trail of documents.

PARAMETER QUERY A query in which you can specify the criteria at the time the query is run rather than at the time the query was designed and saved. To convert a select query to a parameter query, enclose the field name from the criteria row in square brackets. At run time Access will ask the user to input the value in square brackets, then execute the query.

PARENT Refers to a linked record in another table that has a field value that matches a field in the child table.

PASSWORD The private identification of a user to accompany the user name in a secure system. The password should be kept secret. An unauthorized person trying to gain access to a database must know both the user name and the password for that account, greatly reducing the likelihood of a break-in.

PASTE FROM CLIPBOARD You can insert into a Windows document material that has been copied or cut to the Clipboard. Only one item (text or graphics) can be placed in the Clipboard at a time. A new item placed there replaces the previous Clipboard contents.

.PCX EXTENSION The file extension of a PC-Paintbrush bitmap file that can be read by Windows Paintbrush. A .PCX file can be created by a scanner and embedded into Access tables.

PENCIL ICON The record indicator that implies that the record has been edited and not yet saved (committed) in the database.

PERMISSIONS The set of attributes that determine whether a particular user can have access to a database object. Users inherit permissions from their work group and can be given additional permissions individually.

PERSONAL IDENTIFIER (PID) The 4- to 20-character ID used with a user name when creating a new user account in a secure system. This ID is used by the system administrator when creating or changing a user account. The PID is not the same as the password used by the individual user when logging on to Access.

PIE CHART A type of chart in Microsoft Graph that is helpful when displaying values that are part of a whole.

POINT SIZE The size of a font used in a control. There are 72 points to an inch, so a 12-point font is about ⅙-inch tall.

POINTER The tool at the top of the Toolbox that looks like an arrow. The pointer is used to select a control from the Toolbox.

POINTING DEVICE A device such as a mouse or trackball used to select commands or items from the desktop.

PORTRAIT ORIENTATION The printing orientation in which the short side of the page runs across the top. This is the default for virtually all printers. Some laser and inkjet printers are also capable of printing sideways in landscape orientation.

PRIMARY KEY A unique key that identifies each record in a table. Access tables must have a primary key. If you do not specify one, Access will offer to create a counter field as the primary key. The field(s) designated as the primary key will have a small key icon in the field selector area in table Design view.

PRINT MANAGER The Windows application that manages printing for Windows. It is not necessary to use the Windows Print Manager with Access. Print Manager is found in the Main program group.

PRINT PREVIEW The command to view forms, reports, and datasheets as they would appear when printed. You can zoom in on a portion of the output and scan more than one page at a time. When finished with preview, you can send the output to the printer or cancel the Print Preview command.

PROGRAM MANAGER The portion of Windows that you use to manage and run application programs. The Program Manager contains the program groups and is also used to exit from Windows.

PROPERTIES BUTTON The button in the toolbar that displays the property sheet for an object or control. Use the same button to remove the property sheet.

PROPERTY An attribute of an object, field, or control that affects its appearance or behavior.

PROPERTY SHEET The window that contains the properties for an object, section, or control.

PROTOTYPE A model that can be built quickly and used for experimental purposes. In database systems, it is useful to build a prototype of the information system components and let the users work with the prototype. With their feedback you can make changes in the system design and produce a more effective system.

PULL-DOWN MENU A menu that, once activated, remains open until you have made a choice from the menu. In Access you can activate a menu from the menu bar by clicking on its name with the mouse, holding down Alt and pressing the

underlined letter of the menu name, or pressing F10 and using the arrow keys to choose the desired menu name.

QBE GRID The grid that appears in the lower portion of the query window. In the QBE grid you can select fields to be displayed, give sorting and total instructions, and provide criteria expressions.

QUERY A means of selecting certain records from a table or dynaset. Select queries merely select certain records. Action queries cause some sort of action to occur for selected records. Action queries include delete, make-table, append, and update queries.

QUERY WINDOW The window in which you create or edit a query design. In the upper portion you choose tables and fields and provide links between tables. The lower portion of the window contains the QBE grid where you select specific fields to be displayed and give criteria for including records.

QUERY WIZARDS Built-in tools for creating crosstab, find duplicates, find unmatched, and archive queries. This feature is new to Access 2.0.

QUICKSORT The capability to sort records in a table or form in ascending or descending order without having to create a query or filter. This feature is new to Access 2.0.

RANDOM ACCESS MEMORY (RAM) The portion of volatile memory used to hold the operating system, programs, and data while the program executes. Access 2.0 requires a minimum of 6MB of RAM. If you run several Windows applications at the same time, 8+MB are recommended.

READ-ONLY If a database object is read-only, it can be examined but not changed or deleted.

REBOOT Causing the computer to restart, loading the configuration files. Anything not saved before the reboot is lost. Warm boots are accomplished with the Ctrl Alt Del command; cold boots can be done by pushing the reset button or turning the computer off then on.

RECORD A collection of fields representing a set of measurements or attributes about an entity. In Access the record is represented by a row in Datasheet view.

RECORD LOCK A method of preventing other users from accessing a record until the current edit transaction is completed and written to the disk drive.

RECORD SELECTOR The area at the left edge of a datasheet window that is used to indicate the current record or records that are locked. You can select one or more records by clicking in this area.

RECTANGLE CONTROL A control shaped like a square or rectangle that can be placed in a form or report.

REFERENTIAL INTEGRITY The principle that if a field in one table refers to a field in another table, there is at least one parent record in the other table that matches. If you enforce referential integrity, Access will prevent you from deleting the parent record from the other table that would create an orphan record in the current table.

REFRESH Access will periodically redisplay the field values in a table that has been opened in shared mode and changed elsewhere.

REFRESH INTERVAL The period of time between refresh operations. This defaults to 60 seconds.

REGISTRATION DATABASE A part of Windows that assigns a file extension to a particular Windows application program. Thus, if you choose a file whose extension appears in the registration database, Windows will automatically start its application and open the file in that application.

RELATIONAL DATABASE The database model that places data in separate two-dimensional tables that can be joined by matching common data values. The relational database model is simple to understand and offers a significant amount of flexibility to accommodate changes in the database. This model is somewhat less efficient at data retrievals than other more-structured data models.

RELATIONSHIP A relationship represents two tables that have been joined in a query. The relationship can be one-to-one, one-to-many, or many-to-many.

REPAIR DATABASE Access can fix damage in a database that occurs when the computer is rebooted without first closing the database.

REPEATING GROUP Represents a set of one or more fields that occur more than one time for a given parent record. For instance, one student takes more than one class in a given semester. The group of records pertaining to a class is considered a repeating group. In a normalized database, you place repeating groups in a different table from the master record.

REPLACE COMMAND The process of finding data that meets a certain condition and automatically replacing that data with a new value.

REPORT A database object that displays data in a customized fashion, primarily intended for printed output. Whereas a form usually displays a single record at a time, a report typically displays multiple records.

REPORT PROPERTIES Characteristics of reports that affect the way they appear or behave.

REPORT WINDOW The window in which you create or edit Access reports.

REPORT WIZARDS Access tools that create customized reports in response to your answers to questions posed.

RESIZE HANDLE Corner and edge handles of a control that let you change its size. The upper-left handle is for moving the control.

RESTORE BUTTON Causes a window to return to its former size and location on the desktop.

ROW The horizontal component of a datasheet. A row corresponds to a record in a datasheet or an action in a macro window.

ROW SELECTOR The area just to the left of each row that allows you to select a row or group of rows in a datasheet or a grid window.

RULERS Horizontal and vertical scale marks that appear in Form and report Design view. The rulers help you place controls in the form or report.

SCALABLE FONT A font that can be increased or decreased to the desired size. Scalable fonts differ from fixed fonts that exist only in a specific size.

SCANNER An optical device that shines a bright light at an image and converts the image into a digitized computer file. Hand scanners are moved by hand and scan a narrow portion of the document, up to 4 inches wide. A flatbed scanner scans an entire page at a time.

SCROLL BARS Horizontal and vertical bars at the right and bottom sides of a window, respectively. The scroll bars let you bring a portion of the display onto the screen if the display is larger than the viewing area on the screen. Scroll bars are optional in Access.

SEARCH BUTTON The button in the Help system that allows you to specify a certain topic for help. You can also access the Search command from the Help menu bar.

SEARCH DIRECTION The direction (forward or backward) that you want Access to search when looking for particular values in a table. Access defaults to a forward search.

SECOND NORMAL FORM The second step in normalization in which data are in first normal form and there are no partial dependencies. That is, each field in the table depends on the whole primary key, not just a portion of the key.

SECTION A portion of a form or report. Sections include page header, detail, page footer, group header, group footer, and more.

SECURE SYSTEM An Access system in which users must log in and provide a user name and password. A secure system is needed when multiple users access a database at the same time. You can create a secure system by assigning the Admin user a password.

SELECT QUERY The default type of query in which conditions or criteria are provided for selection of certain records.

SELF-JOIN A type of join in which records in a table are joined to other records in the same table. Example: in an employee table one of the employees may be the manager of other employees in the same table. To do a self-join you must use two copies of the same table.

SEPARATOR A character used to separate two fields in a list or a delimited text file. The usual separator is a comma.

SERVER A file server is a computer in a local area network that provides software and hardware resources to other computers in the network. An OLE server is a Windows application that provides an OLE object such as a graph, image file, or sound to another Windows application.

SETTING The value of a property that affects how a control acts or behaves. You can change a property setting in the properties sheet or with a special dialog box such as the Palette box.

SHARED DATABASE MODE The mode in which the database is opened for more than one user at a time. You need to consider locking mechanisms to prevent one user from overwriting another user's changes to the shared database. When a user opens the database in exclusive mode, no

other user can access the database until the first user closes the database.

Shift F1 HELP COMMAND This special help feature allows you to click on any part of the desktop, whereupon Access (or Windows) will provide context-specific help about the object that was selected. For example, if there is an icon that you don't understand, press Shift F1, then click on the icon to receive help.

SHORTCUT KEY A function key or Shift or Ctrl key command that can be entered quickly to save time. For instance, the F11 key will bring the Database window to the front of the desktop. Shortcut keys perform the same action as the corresponding menu bar command.

SHOW BOX The check box in the QBE grid that indicates that a field is to be displayed in the query.

SIMPLE CONDITION Criteria or condition containing only a single conditional expression.

SINGLE-COLUMN FORM WIZARD This Form Wizard prepares a form in which each field appears vertically in a single column.

SINGLE-COLUMN REPORT WIZARD This Report Wizard prepares a report in which each field appears vertically in a single column.

SINGLE-STEP MODE A debugging mode for macros. When you run a macro in single-step mode it executes one action at a time, giving the user a dialog box to determine the next step. This mode helps you pinpoint the cause of errors.

SIZE TO FIT When this command in the Layout menu is checked, Access will enlarge or shrink a control to fit the text it contains.

SNAP TO GRID When this command in the Layout menu is checked, Access will only size a control so that it aligns with the nearest grid dot in the form or report.

SORT ORDER You can select ascending (increasing) or descending (decreasing) order when sorting in Access.

SORTING AND GROUPING BOX The dialog box in which you define the sort order and grouping characteristics for a group report.

SOURCE The application or document to be inserted in a Windows DDE or OLE operation.

SPECIAL EFFECT PROPERTY Provides for normal, raised, or sunken characteristics for sections and controls in forms and reports. The default is normal.

STARTUP MACRO Called AutoExec, this macro is automatically executed each time the database is opened. This macro can display special menus, make changes to the environment, and perform other tasks automatically. You can defeat the execution of this macro by holding down the `Shift` key when the database is opened. You can specify a startup macro by using the /X command line option if you start Access from the File | Run command in the Program Manager.

STARTUP WINDOW The initial window when you first start Access. Only the File and Help menus are visible in the startup window.

STATUS BAR The lower portion of the desktop that provides status information while using Access. Access displays the status of the lock keys, help phrases, and description of the object that has the focus.

STRING A group of one or more characters of text that can include digits.

STRING EXPRESSION An expression containing one or more text strings.

STRUCTURE The design of a database object. The structure of a table includes the name of the table and its fields. The structure contains the fields, their data types, and properties of the fields.

STRUCTURED QUERY LANGUAGE (SQL) The standard data manipulation language used by Access and other database management packages when working with a relational database. SQL was designed for IBM's DB2 relational database system.

STYLE The format or appearance of controls in a form or report. Style can also refer to text features such as bold, underline, and italic.

SUBFORM A type of form that is contained within another form.

SUBFORM/SUBREPORT CONTROL A type of control that allows an existing subform or subreport to be placed within another form or report. This control displays the subform or subreport.

SUBREPORT A type of report that is contained within another report.

SUBTOTAL A total of a numeric field calculated across a group of records. A subtotal may be placed in a group footer or within a form or report.

SWITCHBOARD FORM A type of form that displays a menu and allows the user to select the desired option. In a switchboard form each command button is tied to a macro that executes when that command button is pushed.

SYSTEM ADMINISTRATOR The individual responsible for the administration and efficient operation of the database system.

TAB ORDER The order of controls in a form as the user proceeds from one to the next. Unless overridden, the tab order will be the same order as the controls are placed in the form.

TABLE The basic structure in a relational database. Data are stored in a table, with columns representing fields and rows representing records.

TABLE PROPERTIES Characteristics that affect the behavior or appearance of a table. The most common are the table description and the table's primary key.

TABLE WINDOW The window in which tables are created, edited, or displayed. Design view is used for editing the structure of the table, and Datasheet view shows the values stored in the table.

TABLE WIZARDS A set of several dozen business and personal table designs that can be used or modified for your own tables. There are hundreds of fields in these tables. This feature is new to Access 2.0.

TABULAR FORM WIZARD A type of Form Wizard in which fields are displayed left to right across the form, with field labels shown at the top of the form.

TASK LIST A window containing the names of all of the open windows. You can switch the active window to one in the task list or close one of the open windows. Activate the task list box by pressing `Ctrl` `Esc`.

TEXT Data consisting of ASCII characters (letters, digits, punctuation) that compose words and some number-like attributes such as phone numbers and zip codes.

TEXT BOX CONTROL A control used to display text, memo, number, yes/no, and date/time field values in forms and reports. A text box is *not* limited to displaying text data only.

TEXT DATA TYPE   A field type that is used to store text data. The maximum size of a text field is 255 characters.

TEXT MANIPULATION FUNCTIONS   The set of built-in functions that allow you to perform operations such as extracting characters from a text string, truncating extra blank characters, and returning the length of a string.

THIRD NORMAL FORM   Data in third normal form is already in second normal form and contains no transitive dependencies.

3-D CHART   A type of chart that gives a three-dimensional effect to the data presented.

TITLE BAR   The upper-most bar in a window that contains the name of the window. The active title bar appears in a highlighted color on the desktop.

TOGGLE   To reverse the value of a binary setting. If the setting is on, toggling the setting reverses it (off). Many Access menu settings are toggles. Display the menu to see whether the setting appears with a check mark in front of it, indicating that the setting is on.

TOGGLE BUTTON CONTROL   An on/off control that is used to indicate the state of something in a form. When "on," the toggle button appears to be "pushed in" on the desktop. Click the toggle button to turn it off; the button appears normally.

TOOL LOCK   The button at the bottom of the Control Toolbox. The tool lock is used to fix the tool selected so that you can add several controls of the same kind. The default value is unlocked.

TOOLBAR   The button bar at the top of the window, just below the menu bar, that contains icons or buttons representing commonly used commands. Each database object mode has a different set of toolbar buttons in Access.

TOOLBOX   The window that appears in form and report Design view, containing buttons that represent controls to be added to the form or report.

TOOLTIPS   The name of the tool that appears when the mouse pointer is placed on a tool icon. This feature is new to Access 2.0.

TOTALS QUERY   By activating the Totals button, you can calculate and display totals in a select query.

TRANSACTION   A database operation in which a record is added, edited, deleted, printed, or displayed. In general, we can refer to a request for data from a database as a transaction. We can measure the performance of a database in terms of transactions processed per second. We also must maintain paper trails of transactions for auditing purposes and in case there is a system failure and data is lost from the database.

UNBOUND CONTROL   A class of control that is not taken from any control or field. We use unbound controls to represent text instructions, lines, rectangles, logos, and other graphic images that decorate the form or report and make it easier to view.

UNBOUND OBJECT FRAME CONTROL   A control used to hold an unbound OLE object in a form or report.

UNDO BUTTON   A button in the toolbar that will cancel the effects of the most recent command.

UPDATE GRAPH   A Microsoft Graph command that updates the graph within Access, making it consistent with the changes just made in Microsoft Graph. Unless you update the Access graph, the changes are only temporary.

UPDATE QUERY   A type of action query in which changes are made to specified fields only in the records that match the criteria expressions.

USER ACCOUNT   An account for a single user in a secure database system. Users must enter the correct user name and password to gain access to that user account.

VALIDATION RULE   An expression that describes valid values for a particular field. Data values that do not fit the validation rule are not accepted for the table.

VALIDATION TEXT   The customizable message that is displayed to the user when a data value fails a validation rule. The validation text should explain why the data is invalid.

VALUE   The contents of a field or control.

VALUE AXIS   The vertical axis in a chart prepared by Microsoft Graph. The category axis is the horizontal axis in the chart.

VERTICAL SCROLL BAR   The scroll bar appearing at the right edge of a window that allows the user to view a portion of the display that is too large to fit on the screen.

VIEW   The window that allows you to work with a database object in a certain way. There are four types of views for a form: Design, Form, Datasheet, and Print Preview.

WELCOME SCREEN The initial screen that appears when Access first opens. The screen clears automatically to display the startup window.

WHERE BOX A box used to give a condition for selecting a record.

WILD CARD CHARACTERS Characters used for matching a character position in an expression. The * wild card will match any number of characters in that position or later; ? will match any single character in that position; # will match any number in that position; [X-Z] will allow any character between X and Z to fill that position.

WINDOW The basic rectangular display used in Windows to hold applications, documents, and dialog boxes. Certain portions of the window are used for resizing, moving, and identifying the window.

WINDOWS The name of the graphical environment within which Access runs. Microsoft Windows 3.1 is demonstrated in this textbook.

WORK GROUP The set of users in a multiuser secure system who share the same characteristics and access permissions. You can create any number of work groups. Access provides three built-in groups: Admins, Users, and Guests.

WORKSTATION A single-client computer, typically connected to a local area network.

XY CHART A type of chart in Microsoft Graph that plots points according to their X and Y coordinates.

YES/NO DATA TYPE A type of data field holding data that can take on the values of Yes (True) and No (False.) Yes/No data fields make it easier to express conditions in a query.

ZOOM BOX A text box that contains an enlarged view of a particular value. Press [Shift][F2] to activate the zoom box. When an entry is too long to display in the given input area, it is useful to work with the value in a zoom box.

APPENDIX B
Answers

Answers to Checkpoints

0A. Use [Alt] followed by the underlined letter of the menu you want to open. You can also click on the desired menu with the mouse.

0B. The mouse pointer will turn into a two-headed arrow pointing left and right. If you press the left mouse button and drag the border to the left, the window will get wider.

0C. In most cases the window will slide off the desktop until only a small portion still appears. You can drag the window's title bar to reposition the window on the desktop.

0D. You could Search for help on the Headers in the Help menu bar, or look for an underlined reference to that topic in the current help screen. Clicking on that reference will bring up the screen on Headers. Some Windows applications have a section of the Help display called "See Also" where related topics are listed.

0E. The highlighted command button has a dotted box around the caption. Pressing the [Enter] key is equivalent to clicking this button. In this case, pressing [Enter] will cause the changes to be saved in the current document before the Write window is closed.

3A. The database name is a regular DOS file name, so it can have up to eight characters plus an optional three-letter extension. Access uses .MDB for the file extension by default.

3B. In this combo box you can type the data type directly or choose it from the drop-down list. In fact, you can abbreviate the data type by typing its first letter or two so long as that phrase uniquely identifies the type. For example, both Currency and Counter begin with "C" so you must use two letters. When you press [Enter], Access will complete the entry for you.

3C. Because you established a validation rule for the product's category and typed in a category that was not in the allowable list, Access rejects the entry and displays the validation text in a message box. You must enter a valid entry before Access will accept it.

3D. The table will appear as a table icon in the lower portion of the desktop with the caption "Table:Final Sales Merchandise" beneath it. You can restore it to its previous size with the next activity step.

3E. Clicking the > key will add a single field at a time to the table; clicking >> will add all of the fields from the sample to the new table. It might be easier to add all of the fields at one time, then remove a field you don't want by selecting it and clicking the < button.

4A. No records match "Camp" as a category; therefore, none will appear in the dynaset.

4B. If you leave the "Camping" criteria and add >15, no records appear in the dynaset. If you remove the Category criteria and just use >15 in the Quantity on Hand column, two records will appear in the dynaset.

4C. Add the >10 expression to the QBE grid in the same row as "Other" and run the query.

4D. You could use criteria such as >= #1-Jan-93# And <= #3/31/93#. You can also use Month([Date of Last Order]) In(1,2,3) And Year([Date of Last Order])=1993 as the criteria. Even simpler, use Between #1/1/93# and #3/31/93#.

4E. Because Access uses the left-most field as the primary sort key, this sort is not quite correct. If you reverse the order of the two columns in the QBE grid, Access will sort first by Category and then alphabetically within each category.

4F. In this Totals query Access has summed all of the Quantity on Hand data values to get the total of 310. If you remove the Sum phrase from the Total row you will see a line for each record.

4G. In this dynaset Access displays the sum of the Quantity on Hand field for each of four categories.

4H. Because there were 14 vendors, you will see a record in the totals query for each vendor. The counts represent the number of products represented by each vendor.

5A. By double-clicking on the data source table you select it and also automatically select the highlighted command button for Blank Form instead of Form Wizards.

5B. You can reverse the wrongly added field by highlighting the field to remove and clicking

the < button. You can remove all fields by clicking the << button.

5C. Access will add vertical and/or horizontal scroll bars to the form's borders so that you can scroll to view all the fields of the form. It is better to size the form so that all of the fields appear, if possible.

5D. The pencil icon means that the changes just made to the current record have not yet been saved (committed) to the database.

6A. You can reverse the wrongly added field by highlighting the field to remove and clicking the < button. You can remove all fields by clicking the << button.

6B. It is not appropriate to add together unit costs and quantities. Those subtotals should be removed. However, it would be appropriate to add together the value of the inventory on hand: the product of each unit cost and the quantity on hand.

6C. The upper-left handle is the move handle. The other three corners represent resize handles that work in two directions at once. The top and bottom handles let you change the height of the box.

6D. Access uses Expr1 for the first calculated control, Expr2 for the second, and so on. You can change this name to something like Invy Value. You cannot use either name to refer to this calculated control in other expressions, however.

7A. Access will take much less time if it only has to search the start of each field instead of the whole field, particularly for long fields.

7B. A total of 34 out of the 51 records are either Sports or Hunting category items.

7C. The Month( ) function extracts the month number (1–12) from the Date of Last Order field. That field name is enclosed in brackets because it contains spaces. The In( ) operator looks to see whether the month is one of 3, 6, 9, or 12. You could place Month([Date of Last Order]) in the Field cell of the filter grid, then write 3 in the first criteria row, 6 in the second, and so forth. This will produce the same result.

7D. The rows will first appear by category, then be listed chronologically within each category. As with Access sorts, the left-most field is considered the primary key. You can select the Date of Last Order field by clicking its column border, then drag it to come before the Category field.

7E. Access substitutes `Like "[A-M]*"`. The criteria expression means that the Last Name field must begin with one of the letters between A and M. Anything that follows that initial character will match. These strings would not match: Nicewander, Xircom, and Palmer.

8A. Only those items with positive Quantity on Hand values qualify for this action query.

8B. The numbers in the cells represent the count of the products that fall into each combination of Category and Vendor. For instance, the 3 in the first row means there are 3 Bishop products in the Hunting category. Notice that none of the vendors in this screen has products in more than one category.

9A. The grid dots allow you to align controls horizontally and/or vertically. The Layout | Snap to Grid command will place controls only at grid points.

9B. You can select the control, then drag the top move handle up with the mouse. This will make the box taller. For some controls, if you use the Layout | Size to Fit command, Access will enlarge the box to fit its contents.

9C. Access will automatically increase the width of the box to accommodate a longer text phrase.

9D. The Format | Size | to Fit command is easier to use but it might produce a box that is not quite the correct size, requiring that you still adjust it manually.

10A. A list box only offers the drop-down list; if your item is not on the list, there is no way to type it in the box as you could with a combo box control. The combo box may be simpler to use if the value is not too long to type in—you don't have to take your hands off the keyboard to work with the mouse.

10B. Access typically assigns the option values to a control that may be tied to a field in a table. If you were to click on the middle button in this example, Access assigns the value of 2 to the Method of Payment field.

10C. This query has linked the order items with the product information based on matching the Product Number fields in both tables.

10D. The next time you open the main form with the embedded changes, Access will use the most recent version of the subform. Thus, changes are picked up automatically.

11A. You can select a single control by clicking on it. You can select a group of controls by holding down the [Shift] key and clicking on each control in that group.

11B. This report will use column headings in the Page Header section to identify field values. We do not need to display labels for each field in the Detail section.

11C. This space will display above and below each group of records. By closing up the space you will tighten the display somewhat. It does not affect the values that are displayed, just the appearance of the final output.

11D. You can double-click on an object in Design view to display the properties sheet. You can also use this command (or View | Properties or click the Properties button in the toolbar) to remove the properties sheet if it is already displayed.

11E. You remove both the Report Header and Report Footer at the same time with the Report Hdr/Ftr command; you can't remove just one. So by resizing it to no height, the footer effectively disappears.

12A. A bound object is associated with a particular record in a table like any other field in that table. As you move to a new record, you can view a different object for that record. An unbound object is not associated with a table. Rather, it is a picture or some other OLE object placed in a form or report.

12B. [Ctrl][Esc] brings up the Windows Task List dialog box. In this box you see all the application windows that are currently open. You can highlight a window and click on Switch To, or double-click a window to switch directly to that window.

12C. You can change the path by typing it in directly in the File text box, or you can click the Browse button to open the Browse dialog box. In the Browse box you can use the mouse to select the drive in the lower-right corner, then choose the directory in the upper-right portion, similar to the Open dialog box used elsewhere in Access.

13A. Graph will use one of the fields as a label for the X-axis and the other field as a numeric value to be plotted on the Y-axis. Previous Graph versions required that you enter the number field first, but Graph 5.0 allows entry in either order.

13B. We have one graph for the entire report, so we place it in the Page Footer section. Putting the graph in the Detail section would associate a copy of the graph with each record, not the whole report.

13C. In the format $#,##0_);($#,##0) the dollar sign means to insert a dollar sign in front of the left-most digit. The comma means to insert commas between hundreds and thousands if the number is that large. The pound signs represents locations for digits. The zero means to display the digit, even if it equals zero. The underscore leaves a space after non-negative numbers. Negative numbers are enclosed with parentheses.

13D. Although the changes have been made to the *design* of the Access form or report, you do not have to save those changes in the database. If you close the form or report window without saving that object, the changes are not made permanent.

14A. If you drag the macro from the Database window to a form, Access will automatically create a command button control with the name of the macro as its caption; it will put the name of the macro in the button's On Push property.

14B. The message Type argument can be (nothing), Information, Warning?, Warning!, and Critical. The message type determines which icon

(nothing, information "i", question mark, exclamation mark, stop sign) appears within the message box.

14C. The IsLoaded( ) function checks to see whether the indicated object is open on the desktop. Therefore, the Not IsLoaded("Customers") expression returns true if the Customers form is not now open, and false if the Customers form is currently open.

14D. Because the Products form is not open, Access will not display a message for the last line of this macro.

14E. The Single Step dialog box shows the name of the macro, the condition value (true or false), the name of the action currently ready to execute, and a brief summary of the arguments for that action. You can choose to take the next Step in the macro, to Halt (stop) the macro, or to return to full execution speed (cancel the step mode) with the Continue button.

15A. The Read Only setting means that the user can view data but cannot make any changes or add any new records to the database.

15B. You can select the command button control, then use the Format I Size I to Fit command to increase the size of the control to fit its caption. You can also use the manual resize handles to increase the size of this control.

15C. The Vendor for this product is Slaw. Because there is no vendor named Slaw in the Vendors table, Access displays blank fields in the Vendors form. To solve this problem, add the information about the Slaw vendor to the Vendors table. In the future, you can add a validation rule that specifies that the vendor must exist before you can add a product from a new vendor. This is often a major problem in real-world databases. We use the term referential integrity to mean that there is always a matching record in the linked table.

15D. Having a separate macro for each letter means there will be fewer records retrieved for each command button. With a very large number of records this could be important.

15E. This name refers to the macro group, Report Switchboard, and the individual macro within that group called Labels.

15F. Because you renamed the macro, it is no longer called AutoExec. Only a macro with the latter name will execute automatically when the database is opened. To reactivate, rename it AutoExec. (Capitalization makes no difference.)

16A. You can directly enter the drive and directory path followed by the file name, such as `C:\ACCESS\PROSPECT.DBF`. Or you can use the middle panel of the Select File dialog box: the drive letter is at the bottom of the box and the directory tree for that drive is in the upper box. Select the appropriate drive and directory, then select the file in the first box on the left.

16B. An imported table is "cut off" from the original file: any changes made within Access are only made to the internal Access table. However, if you attach a file, changes made in Access are evident to other users of the external version of that file.

16C. If the first box is checked, Access will use the first row of the text file to learn the field names used in the text file. If these are existing field names in an Access table, Access knows where to place the data values. The second box suggests that the records should be appended to the end of an existing table rather than be placed in a new table. If there are no field names, Access will import the records into a new table and name the fields with generic names. You would have to edit those field names to something meaningful.

16D. If we shorten some of the fields, any information coming after the last position in the field is permanently lost when we export the data.

16E. Use an Access query as the Source for the TransferDatabase macro action. In that query you can specify the criteria for the appropriate records. When the macro executes, only those records will be exported to the dBASE file.

17A. The phrase means to run the macro named Products in the Forms Switchboard Buttons macro group.

17B. You can create a blank form or blank report without specifying a data source. If you activate the field list in Design view, it will be empty. You can still add a table or query to the form by placing its name in the Record Source property of the Form or Report property sheet.

17C. If Access cannot find the object named in the On Click property of the command button, it will display an information box with the message `Macro 'xyz' not found`. When you click OK, you will return to the switchboard form and can select another button.

17D. The Special Effect property becomes Sunken if you click that button in the Palette dialog box.

17E. You might select a different View for some of the forms; for example, the Customers form might be displayed in Datasheet view so that more records appear on the screen at one time. If you want users to be able to view forms but not make changes, change the Data Mode to Read Only. With the MoveSize action, you can change the size and move the forms to different parts of the screen.

17F. To prevent users from changing a particular table, in the Data Mode argument of the OpenForm action use Read Only instead of Edit.

Answers to Odd-Numbered Review Questions

0-1. A GUI describes the display and the way in which the user instructs the computer what to do. The user sees pictures (icons) and uses a pointing device (typically a mouse) to select applications and to make selections from pull-down menus.

0-3. The cursor is called the pointer in Windows. In some applications the cursor also is called the insertion point. Access uses over 20 different shapes for the pointer depending on where it is located on the desktop and what command or tool the user has selected.

0-5. A minimized application is one whose window has been reduced to an icon, typically found at the bottom of the screen. It makes room for other windows on the desktop. However, a minimized application continues to run and use Windows resources.

0-7. Applications are gathered together into program groups according to function. It is easier for the user to find applications that way. Windows features Main, Accessories, Applications, StartUp, and Games program groups at setup. You can create new program groups from the Program Manager's File | New command.

0-9. Selecting an object means highlighting it by clicking its name with the mouse. Choosing it means to select the object first, then click the OK button. You can double-click an object to choose it.

0-11. The left mouse button is typically used to select an object. Some Windows applications make use of the right (and middle) buttons. Left-handed users can use the Control Panel to change the role of the left and right mouse buttons.

0-13. The simplest way to obtain help about a menu choice is to select that choice, then press the F1 key. Some dialog boxes offer a separate Help button that you can click. Some Windows 3.1 applications offer context-specific help: press Shift F1, then click on the menu choice you would like help about.

0-15. Nearly all Windows applications have a File menu. Press Alt F, then choose the Exit command by pressing X. You can also tap the Alt key to highlight the Control-menu box; press Enter and you can use ↓ to highlight the Close command. Finally, most applications permit you to close them by pressing Alt F4 to close the applications window.

1-1a. A database management system is a package of computer programs and documentation that lets you establish and use a database. Access is an example of a database management system.

  b. A database is a collection of related data in tables, queries, reports, forms, macro programs, and modules. The database is organized for easy user access.

  c. A field is a single measurement or attribute of some object or event. In Access you declare a field's name, its data type, and its width, and can give a description of the field before storing a data value in the field. The field corresponds to a column in a table.

  d. A key is a field (or combination of fields) that is used to identify a record. The primary key must be unique for that record.

  e. A record is a group of related fields of information about one object or event in the database. The record corresponds to a row in a table.

  f. A table is the part of the database that holds the data, consisting of rows (records) and columns (fields.) In Access the table is also known as the datasheet.

  g. A form is used to input and present data in a customized fashion. Forms can be on paper or in electronic form on the computer screen.

1-3. A field represents a single measurement about the object or event stored in the table. A record contains one or more related fields about a single object or event.

1-5a. The minimum width for Stock Number is 5 characters.

b. The minimum width for Description is 38 characters, considering the longest value in the field. Other products might have a longer description that requires more space.

c. The minimum width for Unit Cost is 6 characters, but numbers are stored in a different manner in Access. We will describe number field types in a later unit.

d. The minimum width for Quantity on Hand is 2 to 4 characters, depending on the largest possible value for this field.

e. The minimum width for Date of Last Order is 6 characters if the slashes are not stored as part of the field, or 8 characters with the slashes. Access uses a special data type for dates.

2-1. To run Microsoft Access you must have a 386SX or better microprocessor with at least 6MB of RAM (8+MB strongly preferred), at least 5.5MB of free disk space (23MB required for full installation), a pointing device, and an EGA or VGA graphics display.

2-3. The Access Database Window contains the six kinds of database objects by name—Tables, Queries, Forms, Reports, Macros, and Modules. Click the mode button and the Database window will display all of the objects of that type.

2-5. You can press [F1] (or click the Help icon in the toolbar) to activate the on-line Help system in Access. You will receive context-specific help about the current menu or dialog box. You can also use the [Shift][F1] Help system by clicking on an object that you want help about. You can use the Search command to look for help about a specific topic. Access also provides Cue Cards, an on-line coach that leads the user through the steps in creating a database object. Cue Cards remain on the screen while you work with Access menus, a major advantage. The Access Wizards, introduced in Unit 5, also provide assistance in creating forms and reports. All types of Help are useful in Access.

2-7. A form is designed to display records on the screen, while reports are primarily intended to be printed. However, forms can be printed

and reports can be viewed on the screen in Print Preview mode. You can also use a form to add data to a table, whereas a report can only be used to display data values.

2-9. There are three manuals packaged with Access. The *Getting Started* manual provides a tutorial for new users and demonstrates many Access features. The Access *User's Guide* is a comprehensive reference manual with numerous examples but would not be as useful for new users. *Building Applications* provides an introduction to programming modules.

3-1. Access stores all of the database in a single database file with the .MDB file extension. It also uses a few other files such as SYSTEM.MDA to hold security information about your system.

3-3. The toolbar buttons are shortcut keys for frequently used commands. The toolbar changes to meet the needs of the specific Access window that is open. There is a menu bar equivalent to all of the toolbar buttons. Conversely, there are some menu bar commands that are not available in the toolbar.

3-5a. The Double size is for floating-point number fields where you must store a large number of decimal places, up to 15, and/or a large or small magnitude. Example: a scientific measurement.

b. The Long Integer size does not allow decimals (whole numbers only) but provides for large integer numbers up to 2.1 million. Example: the number of units sold in a year.

c. The Integer size permits only whole numbers up to 32,767. Example: the quantity on hand for a smaller business such as Hunter River.

d. The Byte size requires the smallest amount of storage and provides for whole numbers from 0 to 255. You could use this to refer to a truck dock number in a warehouse provided that there were no more than 255 docks.

e. The Single size allows floating-point numbers to have up to 7 decimal places and a magnitude up to 1,038. These can also refer to scientific measurements but could be used to calculate statistics such as average weight per batch.

3-7a. The Format property is used to specify the way in which the field value should be displayed. There are standard formats available for number and date/time fields, but you can also create a custom format.

b. The Caption will appear in the status bar whenever the field is selected. If there is no Caption, Access will display the full Description property, which is generally longer.

c. The Validation Rule is applied whenever a value is stored in the field. If the field does not meet the validation rule, the Validation Text is shown in a message box and Access will prevent the invalid data from being stored in the field.

d. The Validation Text is displayed in a message box whenever a field value does not meet the validation rule.

e. The Index property is used to specify whether this field is to be indexed. If it is indexed, you can specify whether duplicates are allowed in the index. The primary key cannot have duplicates, however.

3-9. You can change the width of the column by dragging its border sideways to widen or narrow it. You can also change the order of columns so that a field appears earlier in the list.

4-1. The *select query* displays certain records that meet the criteria given in the query. You can also sort the rows of a select query (and all other queries). Example: display customers from a particular state. The *update query* changes field values in certain records that meet criteria. Example: change the cost per credit hour in a set of student records. An *append query* will add new records to the end of another table. Example: append to another table customer order records sold in July. The *make-table query* creates a new table with records that meet the criteria. Example: create a new table for customers who have purchased firearms. The *delete query* will remove records from a table that match criteria. Example: remove customers who have not made a purchase in the last two years. The

crosstab query will categorize data into groups, showing the count or sum of a field in each group. Example: group sales by product category by vendor. The *parameter query* lets the user specify the query criteria (as a parameter) when the query is run, rather than when the query was created.

4-3a. A dynaset is the result of a select query. It holds the records that meet the criteria and is displayed like a datasheet. The dynaset is automatically updated whenever the query is run.

b. Compound criteria means that you have conditions for two or more fields in the query's criteria. An AND compound condition means that both conditions must be true for the record to qualify. An OR compound condition means that either condition can be true in order for a record to qualify.

c. A logical operator is a comparison operator: <, <=, =, >=, >, and <>. Access also provides the Like, In, and Between operators. The answer to a logical expression is true or false.

d. The Group By expression explains how records should be grouped in a query that provides totals or other calculations for the group.

e. Concatenation means to join two text strings together, such as First&Last or City&State. Access uses the + or & operators to refer to concatentation. If you intend to do SQL queries, use the & operator.

4-5. A simple criteria expression might be `State="IN"`. A compound criteria expression might refer to `State="IN"` and `Total Sales>100`. In an Access query you would enter the expressions in the QBE grid without the field names as part of the expression.

4-7. To remove the unwanted field from the dynaset, click the Show check box to remove the check. You can drag fields to a new position in the QBE grid to change the order in which they appear.

5-1. Form Wizards lead you through the preparation of several types of forms automatically by asking questions and creating the form for you. You do not need to know how to use the Form Design menus if you use the Form Wizards.

5-3. The field list screen has four keys: the > key adds the selected field to the form and the < key removes the selected field from the form; the >> key adds all fields to the form while the << key removes all fields from the form. When you are finished placing fields in the form, you can go to the next screen. The sequence in which fields are added to the form becomes the Tab Order when you use the [Tab] or [Enter] keys to move through the form.

5-5. A form can use a table or a query as its data source. If a query is used, the underlying tables in the query become the actual data source. In most cases, any changes made to form fields tied to a query are also made to the underlying tables.

5-7a. The vertical scroll bar is used to move to a new record or to display the contents of a memo or long text field.

b. The Next Record button will advance the record pointer to the following record.

c. The record selector is used to choose a record and also gives status information about a selected record. A triangle appears in the current record. If a pencil icon appears, the record has been changed but not yet saved. For multiuser database systems, the record selector also indicates if the record is locked.

d. The Control Toolbox is used to select different types of controls to be placed in forms and reports.

6-1. A form is designed to display records on the screen, while reports are primarily intended to be printed. However, forms can be printed and reports can be viewed on the screen in Print Preview mode. You can also use a form to add data to a table, whereas a report can only be used to display data values. Forms are also used to communicate with the user via menus called switchboards, covered in Unit 17.

6-3. The first step is to select the data source for the report, then choose the type of Report Wizard. Next, select the fields to place in the report in the desired order. For group reports, select the field to group on and the fields to sort on. Select the presentation style, then give a title for the top of the report.

6-5. The "group by" phrase means that Access should group all records having the same value for the group by field or expression; those records will appear together in the report. You can print summaries for the records in each group. The "sort by" phrase means that the records should be sorted by the indicated field or expression. The report will appear in that order, but alike records will not appear in a group.

6-7. To print this report, first create a query that uses the two conditions as criteria. The second condition can be expressed as the date of hire > two years before the current date, or a similar expression. The two conditions should appear on the same line of the QBE grid to imply the AND condition. Then create a Report Wizard report, using that query as the data source.

7-1. The Find command enables you to locate the next record in a table that matches the text condition for the specified field in the table. You can apply the Find command repeatedly to find successive records that match the criteria. The Replace command also allows you to locate the next record in a table that matches the text condition, but Access will replace the value with the new value specified in the dialog box. This is particularly helpful when you want to replace several instances of a field with the same value.

7-3. The Search Fields as Formatted check box allows you to enter a formatted search string in the Find What box, whereupon Access will check the formatted value of each field against the search string. Because some kinds of fields (numbers, date/time, currency, and yes/no) are stored differently internally, this option makes it easier to enter a search string. Example: specify the month of a date in the Find What box as the search string, and Access will look for dates falling in that month.

7-5. The Where box allows you to search through any part of the field, to search only the start of the field, or to search for strings that must match the whole field exactly as entered. For large files you can speed up searching by choosing the start of field option; if the search string is not present at the start of the field, Access will go directly to the next record without searching through the rest of the field. Of course, to use this option your field values must be entered properly so that the value does begin at the start of the field.

7-7. A filter restricts which records appear in a form. The filter is preferred to a query when you expect to make frequent changes to the criteria and don't want to go through the process of changing the query in Design view and rerunning the query. Because filters work only with forms, queries are somewhat more flexible since they work with tables or forms. You can save a filter as a query to use again in the future, and can convert a query into a filter.

7-9. The filter dialog box provides a Sort row to specify whether that field is to be used as a sort key. With more than one key in a filter, the left-most field will be the primary key and fields to the right are secondary keys. If the fields are not in the proper left-to-right sort order in the filter box, drag them to the correct sequence.

8-1. A relational database is composed of two-dimensional tables that can be linked (related) by matching common field values. This offers much more flexibility than working with a single large table that contains the data. We create a relational database design through the process of normalization. Normalized databases are easier to work with, eliminating redundancy and reducing data anomalies.

8-3a. A repeating group describes one or more fields that occur more than once for an owner object and are best placed in a different table than the owner object's table. For a student database, the owner is the student; the repeating groups refer to classes that a student takes.

b. We don't like to store redundant data in every record of a table. Rather, we can place it in a separate table where it can be referenced when needed. This item can be changed in just one place rather than in every record. Example: the current cable TV installation fee.

c. Partial dependency refers to a field that depends on one of the key fields in a table but not on the whole key. We move that field to a separate table and refer to it there. This is a special case of redundant data. Example: the cost of taking a trip to a certain destination on a certain date; if the trip cost depends only on the location and not on the date, put the destination and trip cost in a separate table and refer to them from there.

d. A calculated field takes up extra space in the database. Calculated values can get out of sync with the fields that are used to calculate them; a player's batting average is calculated as of a certain time and should be recalculated if the hits or at-bats change. If the field can be quickly recalculated, don't store it in the database.

8-5. A join occurs when Access matches common field values in two tables. The default type is an equi-join where Access will display all combinations of records that match between the two tables. Example: match customer number between the cable TV customer file and the customer number in the service requested file. An outer join will include all records from both tables whether there is a match or not. Example: same as previous example, but the result will show where there are customers without a service request or a service request without a matching customer record. A self-join matches field values within two copies of the same table. Example: a bill of materials file in which the vendor of a component product is also the consumer of a component product.

8-7. The update query changes field values in certain records that meet criteria. Example: change the cost of a certain clinic service. An append query will add new records to the end of another table. Example: append patient records from July to another table.

The make-table query creates a new table with records that meet the criteria. Example: create a new table for patients who have had a particular procedure such as a mammogram. The delete query will remove records from a table that match criteria. Example: remove patients who have not made a visit in the last three years.

8-9. A parameter query is one in which the criteria are enclosed in [brackets]. Access will ask the user to enter the criteria value when the query executes, allowing much more flexibility without requiring that the user get into the Query Design view and make a permanent change there. Although not covered in the unit, a parameter query can also be used by an Access program module in a custom application.

8-11a. This means to retrieve the Description field from the Products table.

b. This is a criteria expression specifying the Date of Last Order before 1/1/93 and Quantity on Hand times Unit Cost is at least 250.

c. This indicates that we are to sort by the Category field from the Products table.

9-1. Controls represent objects placed in forms and reports. Controls can be text labels, lines or boxes, data values from fields, calculated values, command buttons, check boxes, OLE graphical objects, and other shapes. Controls have properties that can be customized to fit a wide variety of situations. Some control properties can be inherited from field properties.

9-3. A label control is pure text—it merely identifies a portion of the form or report. We use label controls for titles, column headings, to identify other types of controls, and for messages. Text controls hold field values or calculations and can be used to display or input values for those fields.

9-5. First select the control by clicking once on it. Then slowly move the mouse over the upper-left move handle until the pointer changes shape into a hand. Then you can drag the control to a new location. If the hand has a single extended index finger, you will move that one control. If the hand has all fingers out-

stretched, you will move the text box and its associated label at the same time.

9-7. To resize a control, first select the control by clicking once on it. Then slowly move the mouse over one of the seven resize handles until the pointer changes into a two-headed arrow. Then drag the handle in the desired direction. The three corner handles allow the control to be moved in two dimensions at once.

9-9a. The Row Source Type property specifies the type of data source for that control. It can be a table or query, a list of values, or a list of field names.

b. The Visible property is used to determine whether the control is displayed or hidden. Some controls can be initially hidden, then upon some event's occurrence the Visible property can be changed and the control will be displayed.

c. Font Alignment is used to determine whether text is flush left, centered, or flush right in the control box. General alignment implies that numbers and dates are right-aligned and text characters are left-aligned.

d. The Locked property determines whether the value in the control is locked or can be changed in the form.

e. Can Grow is used to determine if the control box can expand to display a longer value.

f. The Help Context ID property is used with custom help systems to identify a particular control. The custom help system can display a special help screen for that particular ID.

10-1. Although the Form Wizards can quickly produce a sophisticated form, there are some options that are only available in Form Design view. You might want to make minor changes to the Form Wizard design, or wish to create a form from scratch. You might want to combine the styles available from the Form Wizards. Experienced users will probably use the Blank Form approach more often, but not necessarily exclusively.

10-3a. The Detail section holds the field values from each record that appears in the form.

b. The Form Header displays on the top of the first page of the form and has the form's title, column headings, and possibly the date or some instructions for the form. The form header may contain command buttons that cause other action to occur, such as displaying a second form.

c. The Page Header only appears when the form is printed but prints at the top of each page of the form.

d. The Form Footer appears at the bottom of the form. It can contain information similar to that in the Form Header section. It can contain headings, dates, and page numbers.

e. The Default View property gives the opening view of the form—Form View, Datasheet View, or Design View.

10-5. An option group control is a group of on/off controls (radio buttons, check boxes) that represent choices for a single value. The user clicks the item in the group that represents the selection for that control. The option group control is only practical when there are a small number of predefined choices. Example: in an appliance service organization, using an option group to indicate what kind of service contract the customer has purchased for the particular appliance.

10-7. The page break control will cause the remaining controls to appear on a different screen than the previous controls. It is useful to divide controls into groups of related controls. You can move between the pages or screens with the record navigation keys.

11-1. Although the Report Wizards can quickly produce a sophisticated report, there are some options that are only available in Report Design view. You might want to make minor changes to the Report Wizard design, or to create a report from scratch. You might want to combine the styles available from the Report Wizards. Experienced users will probably use the Blank Report approach more often, but not necessarily exclusively. Sometimes it is simpler to let the Report Wizard create the basic report, then make manual changes to the design.

11-3a. To select a single control, click once on it.

b. To select two adjacent controls, move the pointer to an area outside the two controls; then drag the mouse to create a rectangle that includes a portion of the controls to be selected. Also see 11-3c.

c. To select nonadjacent controls, hold down the ⇧Shift key and click once on the first control. While holding down the ⇧Shift key, click on the second control. The move/resize handles of all selected controls will be visible.

d. To line up the left edges of selected controls, use the Format | Align | Left command.

e. Click once on the text box and you will select both it and the attached label control. Move the pointer to a location within the control and drag the selected controls to a new location. The pointer will change its shape into a hand with all fingers outstretched.

11-5. To create a calculated field control, first create a text box control in the desired location. Modify its label caption as needed. Then in the Control Source property of the text control type an equal sign, followed by the Access expression. In the Format property select Currency.

11-7a. The Font Name property lets you choose the Windows font type for the control or group of controls. The default font in most systems is MS Sans Serif. You can set this and the remaining font properties by using the toolbar.

b. The Font Size refers to the point size. The default size in most systems is 8 points.

c. The Style is represented by three properties: Font Weight, Font Italic, and Font Underline. For Font Weight you can choose from eight different levels from Extra Light through Normal to Extra Bold and Heavy. Font weight of bold or normal can be set with the toolbar. The remaining font weights must be set in the Properties box. Italic and Underline are Yes/No properties.

d. Alignment refers to left-, center-, or right-aligned within the control box.

11-9. You must create the subreport and save it. Then create the main report, and insert the subreport into the main report by dragging it from the Database window. You can link the reports by setting the Link Child Fields and Link Master Fields properties to matching field values. Save the main report design, then use Print Preview mode to view the results.

12-1. OLE fields enable you to insert graphical objects into an Access database. You can insert photographs, drawings, maps, artwork, and logos. Other OLE objects include sounds and OLE-compliant objects such as spreadsheets. A real estate office could use photographs of the home and a floor plan for the multiple listing service. The real estate broker could insert a plat map or drawing of the lot the house sits on. The real estate office could include a photograph of the broker as part of the database.

12-3. The registration database associates a file extension with a particular Windows application program that created the file type. Thus, if you choose a file with that extension, Windows will automatically start the host application and load the file.

12-5. In Datasheet view you can double-click the field containing the OLE object. Access will automatically start the OLE server application and display the OLE object. Use the File | Exit and Return to Microsoft Access commands to return to Access.

12-7. Clip art refers to predrawn artwork stored as bitmapped files. You can open a clip art file in Paintbrush (or another OLE-server application) and insert it into Access. Thus, a non-artist is able to make use of attractive graphics that represent the object being modeled.

13-1a. Use a pie chart to show each category as a percentage of Total Expenses.

  b. For monthly data over the past 48 months, use a line chart.

  c. Use the High/Low/Open/Close format for a column chart or a line chart.

  d. Use an area chart to show the sales from the top ten vendors.

  e. Use a bar chart or area chart to show product sales by category for the last eight quarters.

13-3. The Graph Wizards are very comprehensive and provide an easy way to link Access data to Microsoft Graph. Most of the Graph features are available through the Graph Wizards, and changes are more difficult to make by hand in Graph.

13-5. The Graph Format menu is used to set cell formats such as dollar signs, commas, and percent signs; to show negative numbers in parentheses; and to set colors. These show in the scale tick marks and in the way cell values are presented in the chart. You can change the column width in the Graph datasheet. You can also use the Format menu to change the font name, style (bold, italic, underline), and font size for text in the chart.

13-7. If the OLE object is linked to the database, any changes made in the underlying data values will automatically be made to the OLE object. Thus, a graph will automatically reflect any changes in the underlying table the next time you open the form or report containing the graph.

14-1a. An Action is a macro command that causes something to take place, such as opening a form, displaying a message box, or printing a report.

  b. An Argument is a parameter to an action, providing details about that action such as what form to open, what message to display, and what report to print.

  c. The Comment is a way of documenting the steps of a macro. The Comment is optional and has no effect on the execution of a macro.

  d. A Condition lets you specify whether a particular action will execute, based on conditions in the database. For example, if a form is already open, you could have the macro close that form.

14-3. Before you can enter a macro's actions, you must have a good idea about what it should do. That means starting on paper, to list the steps the macro must follow. Then list the actions that are needed to accomplish those steps. Finally, you can enter the actions and arguments in the macro window. Be sure to use comments. You should test the macro as it is developed.

14-5. It is customary to gather related macros together in a single macro group, rather than have them saved as individual macros. It is much easier to keep track of them that way, and it reduces the complexity of the database. In some cases you can keep all of the macros that are attached to the command buttons on a single form in a macro group. Because you must prefix the macro name with the macro group name and a period, it takes longer to specify the name of the macro in a macro group.

14-7. You use different levels of information in a message box to convey the seriousness of the message. Access will place a suitable icon in the message box to help convey the message. The Type argument conveys the type of message. An Information message can give additional instructions to the user. The Warning? and Warning! types convey additional caution; the only difference is the use of a question mark or exclamation point icon in the box. Use those to indicate to the user that an entry is invalid. The Critical type implies a very serious problem and displays a stop sign icon. Use the last type only when there is a serious problem in the database. For example, you could use a Critical message when a user is attempting to delete a customer record when there are unpaid orders for that customer in another table.

14-9a. This condition is true if the Category field of the Products form is equal to Camping.

b. The IsLoaded( ) function is part of the module supplied with the NWIND database and can be copied to your database via the Windows Clipboard. This condition is true if the Employee Salaries object is not open on the desktop.

c. This condition is true if the Category is Sports and the Date of Last Order was before 1993.

d. This condition is true if the value of the state field from the Customer form is IN, IL, or MI.

e. This condition is true if there has been no entry in the Customer Number field.

15-1. You can open a form in the Edit, Add, or Read Only data modes. Edit means that the user is permitted to make changes to existing records; Add means that the user can edit existing records and add new records; Read Only means that the user can view data values but make no changes. Edit is the default.

15-3. You can drag a macro from the Database window to a form. When you release the mouse button, Access will create a command button whose caption is the name of the macro and whose On Push property is the name of the macro.

15-5. You can cause action to occur when a macro is attached to a form property. Events such as opening a form, making changes to a record, deleting a record, and closing a form are represented by form properties. For instance, when a form is opened you might display an information message. When data in a form is changed you could do a validation check with a macro. You can also tie macros to changes made in a single control or to pushing a command button.

15-7. If you want to apply a condition to (or sort) the records that are displayed when you open a form, you can use either the Filter Name or the Where Condition arguments. Neither is mandatory, but they ordinarily are not used at the same time.

15-9. This condition is true if the company name field begins with L, M, or N. Any characters can follow the first character.

15-11. A switchboard is a menu form. When the user selects a particular option, the switchboard form will "switch" control to the object that the user selected. Typically, a switchboard contains command buttons that are attached to macros, which in turn open the object or cause the action described by the command button.

16-1. If you must share data with other applications, it is useful to be able to attach a table from another database package. That way you can read the data and make changes to the table in its native format. When other users want to read the data, they will see the changes that you have made. If you need to transfer data into Access from another source such as a database, text file, or spreadsheet, you can import the table. After the data import is done, the data becomes a permanent part of Access.

16-3. See question 16-1. Although you can view data and make changes to values of an attached table, you cannot change its structure. Access is more efficient at retrieving data from an imported table than from an attached table. Unless you export a table that has been imported and modified, other users must use Access to view those changes.

16-5. You can append data to an existing table by clicking on a check box in the Import Options dialog box. Append is available when you import a spreadsheet or text file to Access. When you import a database table, the entire table is brought in and you are not given the opportunity to append at that time.

16-7. The Import Errors table informs you about any irregularities that occurred during the import procedure. It generally means that the import process has failed and explains the reasons for the problem.

16-9. You can examine and edit the contents of any text file with the Windows Notepad accessory, located in the Accessories program group of the Program Manager.

16-11. If you regularly transfer data between Access and other applications, it will be simpler and more foolproof to use a transfer macro to do the work. That way the user does not have to be trained to use the Import, Attach, and Export menus.

17-1. By using an application to control the database, you present the user with a consistent set of menus that are customized to the particular situation. The users do not need to know very much about Access, and the application can protect against inadvertent data manipulations by inexperienced users. The application automates certain operations and makes

it easier to use the system with fewer mouse clicks and keystrokes.

17-3. Prototyping means rapid development of a working database system so that users can work with the system and make suggestions for improvements. Changes can be made quickly and the cycle repeats.

17-5. Controls in forms and reports inherit some of the properties of fields when they are placed in the form or report. If you make changes to fields after the form or report has been created, those changes are not automatically transferred to form and report properties.

17-7. You can create an unbound control in the background area of the switchboard form, then insert the Paintbrush picture into that control box. To improve the look, place a slightly larger rectangle of the same color in the form first, using the Sunken and Clear special effects in the Palette dialog box.

17-9. There are five command button controls for the menu items. The buttons are sitting inside a rectangle control, which in turn is sitting inside the textured Paintbrush picture unbound object control. The Northwind logo picture is an unbound object control sitting inside another rectangle control. The lighthouse logo is an unbound object control. There are a total of ten controls in this form.

17-11. An AutoExec macro will execute as soon as the database containing it is opened. Thus, you can display a Main Switchboard form and control the access to database items. You can override the auto execution by holding down the Shift key when you open the database.

18-1. A data dictionary lets all the developers and users refer to system documentation, including the names and definitions of all objects stored within the database. It helps avoid duplication and suggests standard ways of naming data objects. You can place the data dictionary within the database by using one or more tables for this purpose. Then use the Access report capabilities to print copies of the data dictionary in the desired format.

18-3. A secure Access system requires that each user log on to Access. The user must provide a user name and a password to start Access. Presumably, the system administrator has granted appropriate access permissions to authorized users of the databases in the system. To activate the secure system feature, the system administrator must use the Security menu to create a password for the system administrator Admin account. Then all users must go through the logon process. If the password for the system administrator is changed back to blank (null), the system becomes nonsecure and no logon process is required, even if accounts with user names have been created.

18-5. The system administrator can clear the password for a given user account. The next time that user logs on, the user can change the password from blank to a new value. The administrator cannot look up a password in the database, however.

18-7. To activate the logon procedure, the system administrator must provide a password for the system administrator himself or herself. Thereafter, all users must have a valid user name and password to use Access. To turn off the secure system feature, the system administrator must remove the password for the Admin user name account.

18-9. Access allows the system administrator to grant access only to those people who must have access to particular data fields. That per-

mission might be just to read the data values, or to make changes or even delete records. Each user can have different permissions for different parts of each database.

18-11. When several users must share access to the same database, the network provides an ideal way to connect those users. The individual stations can share expensive hardware resources that are attached to the network. In the network the server contains the database, and each client makes requests for data as needed.

18-13. When a file is opened in exclusive mode, only that user may have access to it. In effect, other people who want to use the database will have to wait until the first user closes the database. In shared mode, several users can access the database at the same time. However, if the users want to make changes to the database in shared mode, there must be some system that prevents one user from overwriting the changes just made by another user. See question 18-14.

18-15. This symbol means that another user has this record (or a nearby record) locked. You will not be able to make any changes to this record until the lock is removed. In multiuser mode, Access will refresh (update) an open datasheet frequently as other users make changes to that table. The refresh is done automatically according to a preset frequency, usually every 60 seconds.

Microsoft Access Commands

This appendix contains a list of the commands in Microsoft Access version 2.0. The commands are listed in the order they appear on the Access menus. For more information, consult the body of this manual and the Access *User's Guide*.

NOTE *Commands within certain menus will change, depending on the database mode and view currently in use.*

General Windows Menus

Control Menu

RESTORE is used to restore the active window to its previous size and location.

MOVE is used to reposition the active window.

SIZE is used to change the size of the active window.

MINIMIZE is used to reduce the application window to an icon at the bottom of the desktop.

MAXIMIZE is used to enlarge the application window to fill the entire screen.

CLOSE is used to close the active window.

SWITCH TO is used to list all currently open application windows and activate the one you select.

NEXT is used to switch to the next open window. Windows appear in the order they were opened.

Window Menu (appears in all modes and views)

TILE is used to redisplay the open windows in a tile fashion so that they all are visible on the desktop.

CASCADE is used to display the open windows in a cascade fashion so that only their title bars are showing on the desktop.

ARRANGE ICONS will rearrange the icons in the active window so that they align with one another and use the default icon spacing.

HIDE will hide the active window.

UNHIDE will redisplay a hidden window.

1, 2, 3,...9 will switch to the numbered window.

Startup Window

File Menu

NEW DATABASE is used to create a new database.

OPEN DATABASE is used to open an existing database.

COMPACT DATABASE is used to rewrite the database file, removing deleted records and making the file storage more efficient.

CONVERT DATABASE will convert an Access 1.0 or 1.1 database to version 2.0 format.

ENCRYPT/DECRYPT DATABASE is used to encrypt or code a copy of the database file so that users must provide a special password before the database can be accessed. This command is also used to reverse the process of encryption.

REPAIR DATABASE is used for making repairs to a damaged database file. The database file can be damaged if the computer is rebooted without saving the database file.

TOOLBARS is used to show, hide, or customize toolbars.

UNHIDE is used to display hidden windows in Access.

RUN MACRO will run an Access macro.

1, 2, 3, 4 are the four most recent databases used in Access. You can open one of these databases by clicking its name, without going through the File | Open Database command.

EXIT is used to close the Access application and return to the Windows Program Manager.

Help Menu (appears in all modes and views)

CONTENTS will display a list of the main help topics, by subject.

SEARCH lets you bring up help screens about a specific topic that you select.

CUE CARDS activates the Access Cue Cards system.

TECHNICAL SUPPORT will show help about product support from Microsoft.

ABOUT MICROSOFT ACCESS gives a brief description of the version of Access you are using, license information, and a statement of Windows memory resources remaining.

Database Window

File Menu

NEW DATABASE is used to create a new database. The current database is closed first.

OPEN DATABASE is used to open an existing database. The current database is closed first.

CLOSE DATABASE is used to close the current database.

NEW is used to create a new database object. You will see a menu from which you can specify the type of object: table, query, form, report, macro, or module.

RENAME is used to give a new name to the selected database object.

OUTPUT TO will copy the current object to a text or Excel file.

IMPORT is used to copy an external file of a specified file type into the current database.

EXPORT copies the selected database object to an external file of the specified file type.

ATTACH TABLE is used to link an external table file to the current database.

IMP/EXP SETUP is used to create the specification for importing or exporting a text file.

PRINT SETUP is used to make changes to the printer configuration.

PRINT PREVIEW is used to open the Print Preview window, which is used to display on the screen how a database object would appear if it were printed.

PRINT will print the highlighted database object on the current Windows printer.

PRINT DEFINITION is used to print information about the design of selected objects.

SEND will send the output of the current object by MS Mail.

RUN MACRO will execute the specified macro.

ADD-INS will activate the Add-in Manager and Database Documentor.

EXIT will close Access and return to the Program Manager.

Edit Menu

UNDO will cancel the most recent command.

CUT will remove the selected text or graphic from the active window and place it in the Clipboard.

COPY will copy the selected text or graphic from the active window to the Clipboard.

PASTE will place the contents of the Clipboard at the insertion point of the active window.

DELETE will delete the selected object without placing it in the Clipboard.

RELATIONSHIPS is used to describe relationships between tables. These include join fields, type of relationship, primary key fields, and whether to enforce referential integrity.

View Menu

TABLES will display the tables of the current database.

QUERIES will display the queries in the current database.

FORMS will display the forms in the current database.

REPORTS will display the reports in the current database.

MACROS will display the macros in the current database.

MODULES will display the modules in the current database.

CODE will open the Module window.

TOOLBARS will show, hide, or customize toolbars.

OPTIONS will display the Options dialog box for making changes to the configuration.

Security Menu

PERMISSIONS is used for defining access permissions for users and work groups.

USERS is used to add new users to or delete existing users from a secure system.

GROUPS is used to add new groups to or delete existing groups from a secure system.

CHANGE PASSWORD is used to change the password of a user account.

CHANGE OWNER is used to change the owner of a specified object

PRINT SECURITY will print a report about user and group information.

Form and Report Design View

File Menu

NEW will create a new form or report.

CLOSE will close the current form or report.

SAVE will save the current form or report under its existing name. If there is no name yet, Access will display a dialog box and ask you to enter a name.

SAVE AS will save the current form or report under a different name that you supply.

SAVE AS REPORT will save the current form as a report.

OUTPUT TO will output the current object to a file.

PRINT SETUP is used to set the printer configuration.

PRINT PREVIEW will execute the Print Preview command for the current form or report.

PRINT will print the current form or report.

PRINT DEFINITION will print information about the design of the selected object.

SEND will send the definition of the current object by mail.

RUN MACRO will execute a macro.

ADD-INS will invoke the Add-in manager.

EXIT will close Access and return to the Program Manager.

Edit Menu

UNDO will undo the previous command.

CUT will remove the highlighted text or graphics from the active window and place it in the Clipboard.

COPY will copy the highlighted text or graphics from the active window to the Clipboard.

PASTE will place the contents of the Clipboard at the insertion point of the active window.

PASTE SPECIAL will allow you to link or embed an OLE object from a source application to the current form, report, or datasheet.

DELETE will delete the highlight object without placing it in the Clipboard.

DUPLICATE will create a duplicate and aligned copy of the current control.

SELECT ALL will select all controls in all sections of the form or report design.

SELECT FORM will select an entire form in Design view prior to setting a form property.

INSERT OBJECT will allow you to embed an object from an OLE server into the current form, report, or datasheet.

LINKS will update, modify, or delete OLE and DDE links in selected object.

(OBJECT) reflects the name of the OLE object selected in a form or report. Use this command to make changes to that object.

TAB ORDER is used to view or make changes to the tab order in a form.

View Menu

TABLE DESIGN, **FORM DESIGN**, and **REPORT DESIGN** indicate that you are in Design view for the designated object type.

FORM will switch to Form view for the current form.

DATASHEET will switch to Datasheet view for the current form.

SORTING AND GROUPING is used to display the Sorting and Grouping dialog box for reports.

FIELD LIST will display (or hide) the Field List dialog box.

PROPERTIES will display (or hide) the Property sheet dialog box.

CODE will open Module window.

RULER will display (or hide) the design rulers.

GRID will display (or hide) the design grid.

TOOLBOX will display (or hide) the Control Toolbox.

PALETTE will display (or hide) the Palette dialog box.

CONTROL WIZARDS will turn Control Wizards on or off.

TOOLBARS will show, hide, or customize toolbars.

OPTIONS will display the Options dialog box for making changes to the configuration.

Format Menu

APPLY DEFAULT is used to apply the default property settings to selected controls.

CHANGE DEFAULT is used to change the default property settings of new controls of the same type added to the form or report.

BRING TO FRONT will bring the selected control to the top of other controls that it overlaps.

SEND TO BACK will push the selected control to the bottom of other controls that it overlaps.

SNAP TO GRID will place the upper-left corner of a control in alignment with the grid dots in a form or report.

ALIGN will align the selected controls on the selected side (left, right, top, or bottom), or to the nearest gridlines.

SIZE will let you choose from size options such as expanding the control to fit its contents, or aligning with the tallest, shortest, widest, or narrowest object in a group.

HORIZONTAL SPACING will let you adjust the horizontal spacing between controls.

VERTICAL SPACING will let you adjust the vertical spacing between controls.

PAGE HEADER/FOOTER will display (or hide) the page header and footer sections in a form or report.

FORM HEADER/FOOTER will display (or hide) the form header and footer sections in a form.

REPORT HEADER/FOOTER will display (or hide) the report header and footer sections in a report.

Form View; Table, Query, and Form Datasheet Views

File Menu

NEW is used to create a new table, query, or form.

CLOSE is used to close the current table, query, or form.

SAVE TABLE/QUERY/FORM is used to save the current database object.

SAVE QUERY/FORM AS is used to save the current database object under a different name.

SAVE RECORD is used to save changes to the current record.

PRINT SETUP is used for making changes to the printer configuration.

PRINT PREVIEW is used to activate the Print Preview window for the selected table, query, or form.

PRINT will print the current document.

SEND will send the output of the current object by mail.

RUN MACRO will execute a macro.

ADD-INS will invoke the Add-in Manager.

EXIT will close Access and return to the Program Manager.

Edit Menu

UNDO will undo the previous command.

UNDO CURRENT RECORD/CURRENT FIELD is used to reverse all changes made to the current record or field since Access last saved the record.

CUT will remove the highlighted text or graphics from the active window and place it in the Clipboard.

COPY will copy the highlighted text or graphics from the active window to the Clipboard.

PASTE will place the contents of the Clipboard at the insertion point of the active window.

PASTE SPECIAL will allow you to link or embed an OLE object from a source application to the current form, report, or datasheet.

PASTE APPEND is used to append one or more records from the Clipboard to the end of the current table's datasheet or form.

DELETE will delete the highlighted object without placing it in the Clipboard.

SELECT RECORD is used to select the current record, letting you work with the record as a whole.

SELECT ALL RECORDS will select all records of the form or datasheet.

FIND is used to find records that match certain conditions.

REPLACE is used to replace values that match certain conditions with another value.

INSERT OBJECT will allow you to embed an object from an OLE server into the current form, report, or datasheet.

LINKS will update, modify, or delete OLE and DDE links in selected objects or fields.

(OBJECT) reflects the name of the OLE object selected in a form or report. Use this command to make changes to that object.

View Menu

TABLE DESIGN, **FORM DESIGN**, **QUERY DESIGN**, and **REPORT DESIGN** are used to switch to design view for the designated object type.

SQL will display the query in SQL view.

FORM will switch to Form view for the current form.

DATASHEET will switch to Datasheet view for the current form.

TOOLBARS will show, hide, or customize toolbars.

OPTIONS will display the Options dialog box so that you can make changes to the setup configuration.

Format Menu (not in Form View)

FONT is used to select the typeface used for field name and data values in a datasheet.

ROW HEIGHT is used to adjust the height of all rows in the datasheet. Access automatically adjusts the row height when you change the font size.

COLUMN WIDTH is used to adjust the width of a particular column in the datasheet.

HIDE COLUMNS is used to hide particular columns so that the field values do not display in the datasheet.

SHOW COLUMNS is used to display or hide specified columns in the datasheet.

FREEZE COLUMNS is used to freeze specified columns on the left side of the window, keeping them from scrolling off the display as you move to additional columns on the right side of the datasheet.

UNFREEZE ALL COLUMNS is used to unfreeze all columns, allowing normal scrolling movement in the datasheet.

GRIDLINES is used to display (or hide) gridlines on the datasheet between rows and columns.

Records Menu

DATA ENTRY will display a new, blank record at the end of the table or form, hiding other records.

GO TO is used to reposition the record pointer in the current datasheet or form.

REFRESH will display new values for the current datasheet or form, particularly useful if you are using Access in multiuser mode and other users are making changes to your database.

QUICK SORT will sort data on the selected field in ascending or descending order.

EDIT FILTER/SORT is used to create or make changes to a filter used with a form.

APPLY FILTER/SORT activates the filter with a form, displaying only those records that meet the filter conditions.

SHOW ALL RECORDS will remove any filter and reapplies any query to the database, showing the most current records in Datasheet view or Form view.

ALLOW EDITING will open the datasheet or form and permit (or not permit) changes to be made to the field values.

Query Design View

File Menu

NEW will create a new query.

CLOSE will close the current query.

SAVE will save the current query under its existing name.

SAVE AS will save the current query under a new name that you provide.

OUTPUT TO will send output of the selected object to a file.

RUN MACRO will execute a macro.

ADD-INS will invoke the Add-in Manager.

EXIT will close Access and return to the Program Manager.

Edit Menu

UNDO will undo the effects of the most recent command (if possible).

CUT will remove the highlighted text or graphics from the current query and place it in the Clipboard.

COPY will copy the highlighted text or graphics from the current query and place it in the Clipboard.

PASTE will place the contents of the Clipboard at the insertion point of the current query.

DELETE will remove the selected object without placing it in the Clipboard.

CLEAR GRID will remove all fields from the lower section of the QBE grid.

INSERT ROW will insert a new criteria row in the QBE grid.

DELETE ROW will delete the selected criteria row from the QBE grid.

INSERT COLUMN will insert a column in the QBE grid.

DELETE COLUMN will delete the selected column from the QBE grid.

View Menu

QUERY DESIGN will display the query in Design view.

SQL will display the SQL commands created for a query.

DATASHEET will display the result of the query in Datasheet view.

TOTALS is used to display (or hide) the Totals row in a query when you want to perform calculations across all the records in the dynaset.

TABLE NAMES will control the display of table names in the QBE grid.

PROPERTIES will display (or hide) the Query Properties dialog box.

JOIN PROPERTIES is used to control the type of join in the query.

TOOLBARS will show, hide, or customize toolbars.

OPTIONS is used to change the setup configuration.

Query Menu

RUN will run the query and display the datasheet.

ADD TABLE is used to add another table to the query design.

REMOVE TABLE is used to remove a table from the query design.

SELECT is used to display the Select Query window in Design view.

CROSSTAB is used to prepare a crosstab query.

MAKE TABLE is used to prepare a make table action query.

UPDATE is used to prepare an update action query.

APPEND is used to prepare an append action query.

DELETE is used to prepare a delete action query.

SQL SPECIFIC is used to prepare specific SQL options such as a pass-through query or data definition query.

JOIN TABLES displays a message that explains how to join tables.

PARAMETERS is used to prepare a parameter query.

Macro Window

File Menu

NEW will create a new macro.

CLOSE will close the macro window.

SAVE will save the macro under its existing name.

SAVE AS will save the macro under a different name that you supply.

PRINT DEFINITION will print information about the selected object.

RUN MACRO will execute a macro.

ADD-INS will invoke the Add-in Manager.

EXIT will close Access and return to the Program Manager.

Edit Menu

UNDO will reverse the effects of the most recent command.

CUT will remove highlighted text from the current window and place it in the Clipboard.

COPY will copy highlighted text to the Clipboard.

PASTE will place the contents of the Clipboard into the current macro.

DELETE will remove the selected object without copying it to the Clipboard.

SELECT ALL is used to select all rows of the macro in Design view.

INSERT ROW is used to insert an action row above the highlighted row in the macro window.

DELETE ROW is used to delete the selected action row from the macro window.

View Menu

MACRO NAMES will display (or hide) the Names column in the macro window.

CONDITIONS will display (or hide) the Conditions column in the macro window.

TOOLBARS will hide, display, or customize toolbars.

OPTIONS is used to make changes to the setup configuration.

Macro Menu

RUN will execute the macro.

SINGLE STEP is used to select (or cancel) the single-step mode used to debug a macro.

Index

Commands

[Alt], 11
[Alt][F4], 22, 27
[Alt][H], 18
[Alt][-] (hyphen), 12
[Alt][Spacebar], 12, 27
[Ctrl], 216
[Ctrl][Break], 341
[Ctrl][Enter], 265
[Ctrl][Esc], 14, 20, 27, 295, 455
[Ctrl][F4], 22, 27
[Del], 72, 131, 151, 228, 331
[Enter], 203
[Esc], 11, 321
[F1], 19, 54, 227, 448
[F11], 249, 349
[F6], 68, 328, 335
[PgUp], [PgDn], 132
[Shift], 219, 261, 331, 367
[Shift][F1], 55
[Shift][F2], 74
[Shift][Tab], 76, 246
[Tab], 68, 76–77, 246

A

Access Basic, 51, 441
Access (Office) Program Group, 43
Accessories, 5, 441
Access overview, 41–59
Action
    argument, 328, 329–330, 441
    list, 329, 330, 333, 441

    macro, 327, 329–330, 335, 441
    query, 93, 193–198, 441
Action Failed dialog box, 342–343, 367, 441
Active object, 227, 441
Add
    new account, 427–428
    new database, 61–62
    new field, 72
    table, 95
Adding data, 75, 76, 132, 253
Admins group, 426, 428
Aggregate function. *See* Calculations, summary
Align controls, 216, 217–219, 267
Alignment buttons, 245, 261
Allow Zero Length property, 71
And condition, 96
Anomalies, 184–185
Appearance of table, 79
Append query, 93, 194, 195–196
Application
    Access, 395–420
    program, 4
    Program Group, 5
    window, 5
Apply Filter/Sort button, 171–173, 357
Area chart, 308
Arrow keys, 11, 15, 16, 246
Ascending sort order, 108, 174
Attach file, 374–377
Auto-execute macro, 367–368, 398, 441
AutoForm, 125–126, 441
AutoReport, 145, 441
Avery labels, 157

Quick Reference

Microsoft Access Toolbars

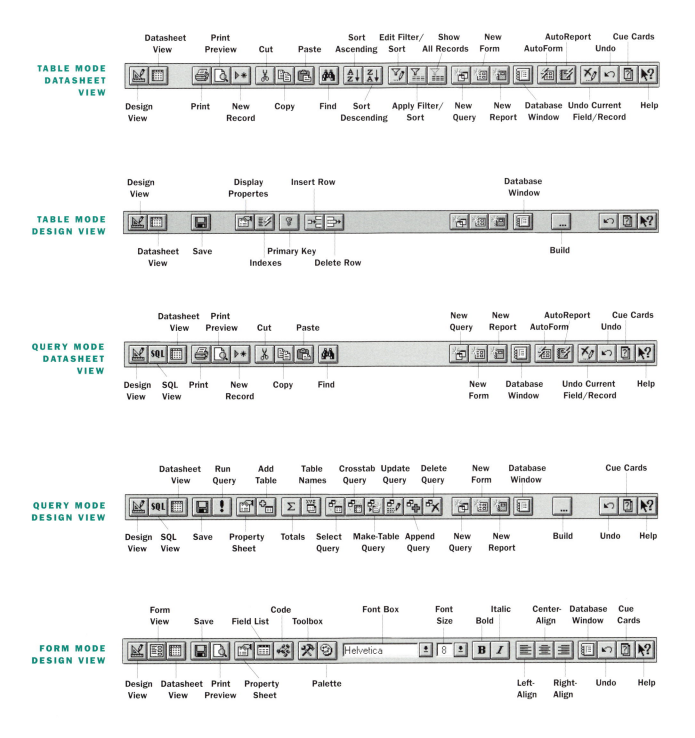

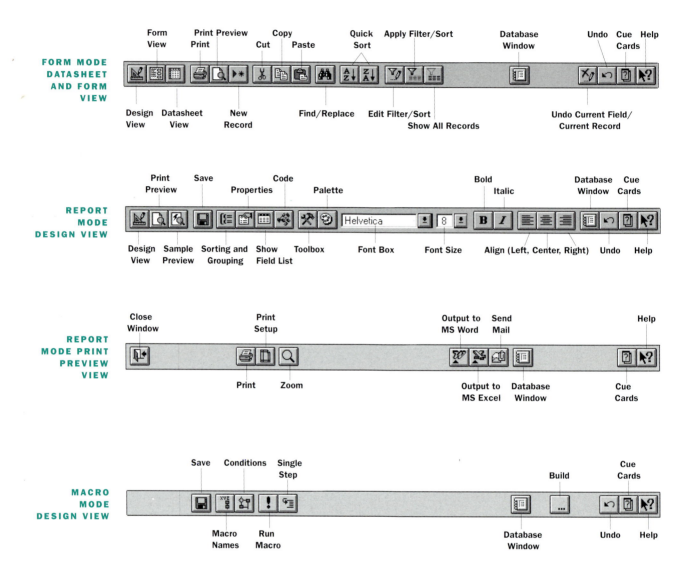

FORM MODE DATASHEET AND FORM VIEW

Form View · Print Preview · Print · Cut · Copy · Paste · Quick Sort · Apply Filter/Sort · Database Window · Undo · Cue Cards · Help

Design View · Datasheet View · New Record · Find/Replace · Edit Filter/Sort · Show All Records · Undo Current Field/Current Record

REPORT MODE DESIGN VIEW

Print Preview · Save · Properties · Code · Palette · Bold · Italic · Database Window · Cue Cards

Design View · Sample Preview · Sorting and Grouping · Show Field List · Toolbox · Font Box · Font Size · Align (Left, Center, Right) · Undo · Help

Helvetica · 8

REPORT MODE PRINT PREVIEW VIEW

Close Window · Print Setup · Output to MS Word · Send Mail · Help

Print · Zoom · Output to MS Excel · Database Window · Cue Cards

MACRO MODE DESIGN VIEW

Save · Conditions · Single Step · Build · Cue Cards

Macro Names · Run Macro · Database Window · Undo · Help

CONTROL TOOLBOX

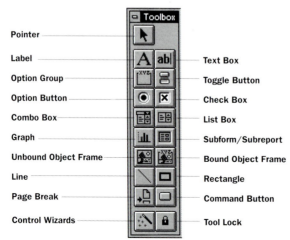

Pointer

Label — Text Box

Option Group — Toggle Button

Option Button — Check Box

Combo Box — List Box

Graph — Subform/Subreport

Unbound Object Frame — Bound Object Frame

Line — Rectangle

Page Break — Command Button

Control Wizards — Tool Lock